Advance Praise for PGP: Pretty Good Privacy

"I even learned a few things about PGP from Simson's informative book!"

> — Phil Zimmermann
> *Author of PGP*

"This book contains an excellent, accurate history of public key cryptography, from its invention to the present."

> — Jim Bidzos
> *President, RSA Data Security, Inc.*

"Simson Garfinkel tells well one of the most fascinating stories in the history of computing . . . a clear and engaging introduction to the most revolutionary computer program ever written."

> — Marc Rotenberg
> *Director, Electronic Privacy Information Center (EPIC)*

"A great introduction to cryptology and PGP. Useful for anyone interested in using modern crypto tools for ensuring liberty in our modern age. Every cypherpunk needs a copy!"

> — Tim May
> *Co-founder of Cypherpunks*

"I thought I knew everything about PGP, but I didn't! There are some things in here I'd never heard of. Authoritative."

> — Eric Hughes
> *Co-founder of Cypherpunks*

"Since the release of PGP 2.0 from Europe in the fall of 1992, PGP's popularity and usage has grown to make it the de-facto standard for email encryption. Simson's book is an excellent overview of PGP and the history of cryptography in general. It should prove a useful addition to the resource library for any computer user, from the UNIX wizard to the PC novice."

> —Derek Atkins
> *PGP Development Team, MIT*

PGP: Pretty Good Privacy

Simson Garfinkel

O'Reilly & Associates, Inc.
103 Morris Street, Suite A
Sebastopol, CA 95472

PGP: Pretty Good Privacy
Simson Garfinkel

Copyright © 1995 O'Reilly & Associates, Inc. All rights reserved.
Printed in the United States of America.

Editor: Deborah Russell

Production Editor: Nancy Crumpton

Printing History:

January 1995:	First Edition.
March 1995:	Minor corrections.

ISBN: 1-56592-098-8

On the afternoon of October 16, 1994, in the courtyard of the Harvard University Hillel Foundation, I was wed to Elisabeth C. Rosenberg. Although the preparation of this book did interfere with the planning of our nuptials, I have promised Beth that it will not interfere with our honeymoon in Israel. After we return from the Promised Land, I hope that my new wife will look at this dedication to her—and smile.

S.L.G. to E.C.R., October 16, 1994

Table of Contents

List of Figures

List of Tables

Foreword

1994 was not a good year for privacy in the United States. In the spring, the White House announced its support for the Clipper proposal. The National Security Agency's encryption scheme was designed to make it easy for the government to decode private messages. The least popular technical proposal ever to come out of Washington is now the official standard for voice, fax, and low-speed data communication for the federal government.

Later in the year, Congress passed the FBI wiretap legislation. The Communications Assistance for Law Enforcement Act requires equipment manufacturers and telecommunications carriers to develop network technologies that are readily wiretapped. In other words, desktop surveillance. Over the next several years, the United States government will spend more money making it easy to wiretap the Information Highway than it will connecting schools, libraries, and hospitals.

Meanwhile legislative proposals in Washington, DC for privacy protection have fallen by the wayside. Privacy laws to safeguard medical records did not pass the last session of Congress. Proposals for a privacy agency, to extend safeguards to the communications infrastructure and the high-tech workplace, did not become law.

Even our foreign policy disfavors privacy. Export controls developed by the National Security Agency in the midst of the Cold War remain in place as people around the globe now seek access to the communications web. U.S. officials lobby overseas against privacy initiatives while pushing for the adoption of Clipper-like standards.

That all this should occur in the same year when opinion polls show public concern about privacy at an all-time high underscores how little government understands about the importance of privacy in the information age.

Or perhaps government understands too well. Viewed differently, 1994 might easily be seen as the year in which the United States set out to develop a national infrastructure for communications surveillance. Join together the technical design of Clipper with the legislative requirements of the wiretap law, and the foundation is in place.

Senator Frank Church predicted this day. A generation ago, he held hearings on the monitoring capabilities of the intelligence agencies in the United States. "If the surveillance capabilities were ever turned on the American people," he warned, "there would be no place to hide."

Fortunately, not everyone is prepared to let this story run its course. Every generation brings forward people who simply by virtue of their determination are unwilling to let fate have the final say.

Phil Zimmermann is one such person. With the development of Pretty Good Privacy, Phil reminds us that the future is still in our hands. While PGP is no guarantee of world peace or social harmony, it is an important contribution to the protection of privacy in the information age. It is one tangible way to safeguard that freedom which has been described as the most comprehensive of all rights.

PGP is privacy for the people. And that is what makes the government so uneasy. It is also why you should read this book and become a PGP user. *PGP: Pretty Good Privacy* gives you both an easy-to-follow introduction to the mechanics of PGP and a behind-the-scenes report on the controversy surrounding one of the most revolutionary pieces of software ever created.

Although 1994 marks the year that the government endorsed Clipper, it is also the year that the people endorsed PGP. The program can now be found on Internet sites around the globe. Along with RSA and other good cryptographic systems, the tools for privacy protection are now in the hands of the users.

Supporters of Clipper take note: The battle has just begun.

Marc Rotenberg
Director, Electronic Privacy Information Center (EPIC)
Washington, DC
November 1994

Preface

*A man has a right to pass through this world, if he wills, without having his
pictures published, his business enterprises discussed, his successful experiments
written up for the benefit of others, or his eccentricities commented upon, whether
in handbills, circulars, catalogues, newspapers or periodicals.*

—Chief Justice Alton B. Parker (New York Court of Appeals),
decision in *Roberson v. Rochater Folding Box Co.*, 1901

This book is about an encryption program called PGP, which stands for Pretty Good
Privacy.

You can use PGP to encrypt the files on your computer with a password so that no
one else can read them. You can also use PGP to encrypt your electronic mail so that
no one other than the intended recipients can read it. Finally, you can use PGP to
"sign" documents with a tamper-proof digital signature to prevent someone from
forging a document and then claiming that you are the author of it, or from modifying
a document after you've signed it and then claiming that the modified document is
really the original that you signed.

Best of all, you can now use PGP without worrying about the patent and U.S. export
problems that you would have faced in the past. I describe these problems in detail
later in the book.

Encryption is for Everyone!

It used to be that only spies and the military could use data encryption to protect their
privacy. That's because effective encryption could be performed only with bulky and
expensive equipment that required special training to use.

Is PGP Legal?

PGP has had problems with both patent violations and U.S. export restrictions in the past. Now that new versions of the program exist, how can you be sure that you are using PGP legally?

- Early versions of PGP could not be used in the United States without violating patents on public key cryptography. It is now possible to use PGP Version 2.6 and later versions for noncommercial purposes in the United States, thanks to a license agreement I describe later in this preface.

- If you wish to use PGP for commercial purposes within the United States, you must purchase a license for the program from ViaCrypt. (Appendix A describes how.)

- Any version of PGP can be used outside the United States without infringing on public key cryptography patents. However, PGP cannot be exported without violating U.S. export restrictions.

- Outside the United States, use PGP Version 2.6ui. This so-called "unofficial international" version was developed in Europe from an earlier version of PGP. It is readily available there, interoperates with Version 2.6, and does not have the restrictions on commercial use that the domestic versions of PGP have.

- Outside the United States, do not use Version 2.6 (or later versions). Inside the United States, do not use Version 2.6ui. But those inside the United States (using Version 2.6 and later versions) and those outside the United States (using Version 2.6ui) can communicate freely with each other without violating export restrictions.

- Outside the United States, be sure to check with your own country's authorities about the legalities of using encryption programs. Some countries prohibit private citizens from using such programs.

After World War II, many governments came to recognize the value of encryption for protecting routine diplomatic communications. In the United States, President Harry Truman created the National Security Agency and charged it with protecting presidential, diplomatic, and military communications while, at the same time, developing ways of "cracking" the secret codes used by other countries. Other governments launched similar initiatives. This heavy government involvement had the side effect of keeping effective encryption out of the hands of ordinary people as well as businesses that were not directly involved in military work. Nearly everything that was known about effective encryption was classified.

The scenario has changed dramatically. Governments, diplomatic missions, and military commanders are no longer the only targets of electronic eavesdroppers; everyone is. Today many businesses engage in espionage, having unfortunately discovered that it's often cheaper to steal ideas, strategies, and plans from their competitors than it is to develop them on their own. Despite laws against it, the wiretapping of private citizens has likewise become a growth industry—the resulting information is used in lawsuits, divorce proceedings, and, sometimes, just for kicks.

The increasing reliance on electronic mail and other forms of computer-mediated communication over the Internet only increases the need for cryptographic protection of information. Just a few years ago, the Internet was mostly unknown outside academia and a handful of research organizations. These days, the Internet increasingly plays a pivotal role in personal and corporate communications. Unfortunately, without encryption, information sent over the Internet is open to anyone's prying eyes. And those eyes can be highly sophisticated computer programs, scanning through gigabytes of information for specific names, places, or key words. Indeed, the Information Superhighway may be the most efficient system ever imagined for monitoring the flow of ideas and information within a country or around the world.

Some people have been willing to accept the risk of wiretapped electronic mail. Others simply haven't known that the risk existed. But for businesses considering commerce over the Internet, the lack of encryption has been a major stumbling block: sending a credit card number over the Internet without encryption simply invites fraud and abuse.

Fortunately, the days are past when effective cryptography was available only to major governments and the largest corporations. With sophisticated programs like PGP, encryption is now available to everyone! This book shows you how you can use encryption for your own business and personal purposes.

The Need to Know

Unfortunately, simply using encryption is not enough; you need to know how to use your encryption system properly, because improperly used encryption offers little more protection—and sometimes even less protection—than using no encryption at all.

You also need to know what kind of encryption system you are using. Different systems have different strengths, and cryptography that *seems* secure to you might not, in fact, be secure enough to protect against a person who is determined to monitor your communications. You should also know the fundamentals of how your cryptography software works, so you know what information is truly protected, what isn't, and what you need to protect in order to ensure your privacy. Hence this book.

In the pages that follow, I'll teach you, step by step, everything there is to know about using PGP to protect your privacy. I won't show you cryptic operating system commands and then expect you to figure them out; instead, I'll take you by the hand and show you example after example. If you have a computer with a copy of PGP, you can follow along with these examples as I explain them. (If you don't have a copy of PGP, you can find instructions in Part IV of this book on how to get PGP for free and how to set it up on different platforms.)

This book will also teach you the *hows and whys* of encryption: I'll show you a little of how the math works (it's not very complicated), discuss the lengths you should take to protect information, and show you the ways that people can get around your cryptographic protection if you are not careful. I believe that you are more likely to use encryption properly (and thus securely) if you have an understanding of what is going on inside your computer and why a particular encryption program does what it does.

Finally, I'll share with you the interesting history of the PGP program itself, and the personalities behind it. It's a fascinating and much-discussed story, but one that most people know only in bits and pieces. Now, once and for all, this book brings all of those parts together.

Enjoy!

Scope of This Book

This book is divided into four parts:

Part I, *An Introduction to PGP*, introduces you to cryptography and to PGP. It contains the following chapters:

Chapter 1, *Introduction to PGP*, introduces PGP, gives you the basic vocabulary you need before you use the program, and shows you how to perform simple functions in PGP.

Chapter 2, *Cryptography Basics*, gives you a brief introduction to cryptography, provides basic examples of private and public key cryptography, and outlines the U.S. export and patent policies relevant to cryptography.

Part II, *Cryptography History and Policy,* tells the human story of the development of cryptography and PGP. It contains the following chapters:

Chapter 3, *Cryptography Before PGP*, is an abbreviated historical account of the science of cryptography before PGP came onto the scene.

Chapter 4, *A Pretty Good History of PGP*, covers the history of PGP and the legal and political battles that have beset it.

Chapter 5, *Privacy and Public Policy*, discusses government policies and the politics surrounding electronic privacy in the United States.

Chapter 6, *Cryptography Patents and Export*, describes how cryptographic patents affect and are affected by U.S. government policies, outlines late-breaking legal challenges to the patents, and briefly describes the current U.S. export policy on cryptography.

Part III, *Using PGP*, explains everything you need to know about using PGP. It contains the following chapters:

Chapter 7, *Protecting Your Files*, shows you the simplest way to use PGP: as a program to encrypt and decrypt files with the same key, using private key cryptography.

Chapter 8, *Creating PGP Keys*, explains how to create your PGP public and secret keys.

Chapter 9, *Managing PGP Keys*, explains how to give others a copy of your public key, how to obtain others' public keys (a must before you can send them encrypted mail), and how to perform other key management functions.

Chapter 10, *Encrypting Email*, explains how to encrypt a message with PGP and send it. It also explains how to read the encrypted mail that you receive.

Chapter 11, *Using Digital Signatures*, describes digital signatures and explains how to electronically sign a document and how to verify a digital signature attached to a document.

Chapter 12, *Certifying and Distributing Keys*, explains how you can sign a PGP key with its own digital signature so that when you send it to someone, the recipient knows it is an authentic key.

Chapter 13, *Revoking, Disabling, and Escrowing Keys*, explains how you can revoke your key, disable someone else's key, and set up a manual key escrow system.

Chapter 14, *PGP Configuration File*, explains how you can customize PGP.

Chapter 15, *PGP Internet Key Servers*, explains how you can register your PGP key with the PGP Internet key servers and how you can get someone else's key.

Part IV, *Appendices*, contains system-specific and summary material. It contains the following appendices:

Appendix A, *Getting PGP,* explains how you can obtain your own copy of PGP.

Appendix B, *Installing PGP on a PC*, explains how you can install and run PGP on a computer running DOS.

Appendix C, *Installing PGP on a UNIX System*, explains how you can get PGP up and running on most computers running the UNIX operating system.

Appendix D, *Installing PGP on a Macintosh*, explains how you can install and run PGP on a Macintosh computer.

Appendix E, *Versions of PGP*, describes the different versions of PGP.

Appendix F, *The Mathematics of Cryptography*, describes the underlying mathematics of the Diffie-Hellman algorithm that first defined public key cryptography, the mathematics of the RSA algorithm in PGP, and the mathematics of PGP itself.

The *Glossary* defines the special terms used in this book.

The *Bibliography* lists books and publications for further reading.

And finally, bound into the back of the book, you will find a handy reference card that summarizes the PGP commands, environment variables, and configuration variables.

Using PGP on PC, UNIX, Macintosh, and Other Platforms

Although PGP was originally developed for the DOS operating system, today the program runs on dozens of different kinds of computers and operating systems. This is because PGP was originally distributed as free software, complete with source code: it doesn't take a lot of work to grab the source code for PGP (which is widely available and written in C) and recompile it for a new platform. Many people have recompiled PGP, and the changes that have been necessary were folded back into the master distribution.

Today, PGP Version 2.6.x[†] runs on the following platforms:

PC operating systems:

> DOS
> Windows
> OS/2

UNIX systems:

> Berkeley UNIX
> AT&T 3B1
> AUX

[†] As this book is being written, PGP Version 3.0 is under development.

HP UX (68K and PA-RISC)
IRIX
Linux
Mach (386)
Ultrix (VAX and MIPS)
NetBSD
NeXTSTEP (Motorol, HP, and Intel versions)
SCO (Xenix 286 and 386, and UNIX)
RS/6000
RT
SGI
Sun-3, Sun-4, SunPC, and Solaris
System V/386

Other microcomputers:

Macintosh
Amiga
Archimedes

Portability comes at a price, however. The most obvious is PGP's command line interface, which, for those accustomed to graphical user interfaces, may seem clumsy and archaic. There is a pragmatic reason that PGP does not have a graphical user interface. Although there are some development environments for creating a single program that runs on Microsoft Windows, UNIX/X, and on the Macintosh, none of these development environments are free. Furthermore, none of these cross-platform systems support as many different platforms as PGP.

Fortunately, since the release of PGP, a number of people around the world have written "shells" that put a friendly face on PGP; each comes with its own documentation. Nevertheless, in this book I focus on the command line version of PGP because it is the same on every computer and it is the one that is the mostly widely available. However, I also describe the Macintosh version of PGP because if you are using a Macintosh computer, you can't use PGP's command line interface.

It may be obvious, but it's worth stating: although PGP provides a wonderful way to encrypt the electronic mail you send, it does not itself send email, however. Furthermore, all of the friendly shells are still only shells; they don't send mail either. Over time, you're likely to see email systems that seamlessly incorporate PGP into their shells, and you'll simply be able to select encryption as another option. For now, you'll have to use PGP as a separate tool.

Is It DOS or is It UNIX?

The examples in this book were mostly created on PCs (running DOS) and UNIX systems. Fortunately, the DOS and UNIX versions—indeed, all the versions of PGP—are nearly identical. For the purposes of PGP, there are just three differences between the DOS and UNIX operating systems:

- DOS uses backslashes (\) to separate filenames from directories, whereas UNIX uses forward slashes (/).

- With DOS, a filename may contain a drive letter (such as *C:\pgp\crypto.asc*) to denote a physical hard disk. With UNIX, most files are specified with absolute pathnames (such as */home/simsong/pgp/crypto.asc*) or pathnames that are based on the user's home directory (such as *~/pgp/crypto.asc*).

- Most DOS computers are used by a single person, whereas most UNIX systems are used by many different people, often at the same time.

This last point is probably the most important when dealing with PGP. When you are the only user of a single computer, you can be reasonably sure that no one else is reading your files while you are creating them. It is much harder for you to have this assurance on a computer that is being used by several people at the same time. (And it may be downright impossible to guarantee privacy if you are using certain kinds of networked UNIX workstations.)

Thus, even people who are primarily UNIX users may prefer to use a low-cost DOS- or Windows-based computer to encrypt and decrypt their private files. On the other hand, if your interest in using PGP is to protect your email messages from interception *en route*, it is probably safe to rely on the limited security offered by most UNIX systems.

Understanding the Examples

The DOS and UNIX versions of PGP are so similar that examples from both operating systems are freely intermixed within the text of this book; I don't attempt to show you the two versions of every command because the two versions of PGP use the same commands, take the same user input, and produce the same output. In fact, just about the only way for you to tell the difference is to look at the prompt of the command line used to invoke PGP. If you see the familiar `C:\>` prompt, you know that the example is from a computer running DOS. If, on the other hand, you see a `unix%` prompt, you know that the example is from a computer running the UNIX operating system.

For example, if you run PGP on a DOS computer by typing **pgp** on the command line, PGP displays the following basic information:

```
C:\> pgp
Pretty Good Privacy(tm) 2.6 - Public-key encryption for the masses.
 (c) 1990-1994 Philip Zimmermann, Phil's Pretty Good Software. 23 May 94
Distributed by the Massachusetts Institute of Technology.  Uses RSAREF.
Export of this software may be restricted by the U.S. government.
Current time: 1994/07/19 15:34 GMT

For details on licensing and distribution, see the PGP User's Guide.
For other cryptography products and custom development services, contact:
Philip Zimmermann, 3021 11th St, Boulder CO 80304 USA, phone +1 303 541-0140

For a usage summary, type:  pgp -h
C:\>
```

PGP displays the exact same information when you run it without any options on a UNIX computer:

```
unix% pgp
Pretty Good Privacy(tm) 2.6 - Public-key encryption for the masses.
 (c) 1990-1994 Philip Zimmermann, Phil's Pretty Good Software. 23 May 94
Distributed by the Massachusetts Institute of Technology.  Uses RSAREF.
Export of this software may be restricted by the U.S. government.
Current time: 1994/07/19 15:34 GMT

For details on licensing and distribution, see the PGP User's Guide.
For other cryptography products and custom development services, contact:
Philip Zimmermann, 3021 11th St, Boulder CO 80304 USA, phone +1 303 541-0140

For a usage summary, type:  pgp -h
unix%
```

The main differences between using PGP under DOS and UNIX have to do with installing and setting up the program. For this reason, Appendix B and Appendix C describe the installations for PC and UNIX systems, respectively; Appendix D describes Macintosh installation and operation.

Which Version of PGP?

This book describes PGP Versions 2.6, 2.6.1, 2.6.2, 2.7, and 2.6ui. Version 2.6 is the first version of PGP that can be used inside the United States without potentially infringing on the RSA public key algorithm. (I describe this situation briefly in Part I.) PGP Version 2.6 also fixes many bugs in previous versions of PGP and is a very desirable version of PGP. PGP Version 2.6 and later versions may be freely used and redistributed for noncommercial purposes. Versions 2.6.1 and 2.6.2 fix minor bugs in Version 2.6.

As a condition for allowing noncommercial use of PGP, Phil Zimmermann, the author of PGP, was required to insert code in the program that makes PGP Version 2.6 incompatible with previous versions. If you have a version of PGP that is earlier than Version 2.6, you will probably want to upgrade to Version 2.6 or later so that you can read messages encrypted by people who are using the current version (Version 2.6.2 at the time of this writing).

If you would like to use PGP outside the United States, you can use PGP Version 2.6ui. This version, based on PGP Version 2.3, does not have the commercial use restriction of PGP 2.6. You should be aware, however, that using PGP Version 2.6ui within the United States places you at risk of a patent infringement lawsuit.

Most of the examples in this book were created in Version 2.6, probably the most commonly used version today. Version 2.6.1 behaves identically to Version 2.6 but has a slightly different installation procedure, which is described in Appendix B and Appendix C.

If you wish to use PGP within the United States for commercial purposes, you can purchase a version from ViaCrypt. The current ViaCrypt version is 2.7.

Appendix A explains how you can get free and commercial versions of PGP.

At the present time, Phil Zimmermann, the author of PGP, is working on a new version of PGP, which is Version 3.0. This new version of PGP is a complete rewrite of previous PGP versions. For this reason, I do not expect it to be generally available until the fall of 1995. At that time, I expect to revise this book. Purchasers of this book will be able to buy the Version 3.0 edition directly from the publisher at a 25 percent discount.

Comments and Questions

Please address comments and questions concerning this book to the publisher:

O'Reilly & Associates, Inc.
103 Morris Street, Suite A
Sebastopol, CA 95472

1-800-998-9938 (in the U.S. or Canada)
1-707-829-0515 (international or local)
1-707-829-0104 (FAX)

You can also send us messages electronically. To request a catalog, send email to:

nuts@ora.com (via the Internet)

To ask technical questions or comment on the book, send email to:

bookquestions@ora.com (via the Internet)

Conventions Used in This Book

The following conventions arc used in this book:

Italic	Is used for introducing new terms. It is also used for the names of files, directories, programs, and commands, and for email and FTP addresses.
`Courier Constant Width`	Is used to show output from PGP
`Courier Bold`	Is used to show text that is typed verbatim by the user
`%unix`	Is the standard prompt in UNIX (the C shell). Although this prompt varies according to the shell you are using, I use this prompt consistently throughout the book to indicate UNIX examples.
`C:\>`	Is the standard prompt from DOS. Although this prompt changes to reflect the current drive and directory, I use it consistently to indicate DOS examples.
~~Strikeout~~	Is used to show text that you type but which PGP does not echo. This is used mostly for PGP pass phrases.

Acknowledgments

This book, like PGP itself, came about because of Phil Zimmermann. Phil came to me at the 1994 Computers, Freedom and Privacy Conference and asked if I could put him in touch with a publisher who would be interested in publishing the *PGP User's Manual* and the complete source code for PGP. A few feet away from me at the conference was Robert Prior of MIT Press, who had just asked me if I knew of anyone who was itching to write a book. Since I thought that MIT might agree to Zimmermann's terms, it seemed like a natural match.

Over the months that followed, negotiations between Zimmermann and MIT Press dragged on. At one point, I suggested to Phil that he try O'Reilly & Associates, the publishing house that published my first book, *Practical UNIX Security* (O'Reilly & Associates, 1991). Debby Russell at O'Reilly was intrigued by the idea of publishing a book on PGP, but she thought that Phil's user's manual would need work to make it as easy to understand as an O'Reilly Nutshell Handbook. I agreed to co-author the book with Phil, and Debby and Phil began to talk.

In the meantime, MIT and Phil reached an agreement, and Phil decided to have MIT Press publish the *PGP User's Manual* after all. That left me and Debby with a great idea, but no one to do it. At her suggestion, I decided to write this book by myself. Although Phil and I are, in a sense, writing competing books, we remain friends.

Special thanks to Jim Bidzos, president of RSA Data Security, who took the time to talk with me on numerous occasions, answered a multitude of questions, and reviewed large parts of this manuscript. Jim and Phil have had their battles, but they both helped me tremendously in writing this book.

I am extremely grateful to the giants of cryptography, Whitfield Diffie, Ronald Rivest, Ralph Merkle, and Len Adleman, who took the time to talk to me about their work, past and present. Ron Rivest also took the time to work with me on revising an article on factoring, which he and RSA Data Security, Inc., allowed us to include in Appendix F.

Thanks as well to others who allowed me to interview them for this book: Robert B. Fougner of Cylink, Eric Hughes and Hugh Daniels of the Cypherpunks, Marc Rotenberg and David Sobel of the Electronic Privacy Information Center (EPIC), and Charlie Merritt. Special thanks to Marc Rotenberg for writing the foreword to the book.

A very big thank you to those who reviewed drafts of this book: Hal Abelson, Derek Atkins, Jim Bidzos, Michael Grant, Peter Gutmann, Tim May, Charlie Merritt, Jon Orwant, Bradley Ross, Marc Rotenberg, Jeff Schiller, and Phil Zimmermann. Bruce Schneier graciously reviewed the mathematics portions of this book and answered numerous questions. Carl Ellison of Trusted Information Systems also answered my questions.

Special thanks to Brock N. Meeks, a reporter from Washington D.C. who has covered the privacy beat for many years and who wrote large parts of Chapter 5, *Privacy and Public Policy*. And thanks to Jerry Cleveland of the *Denver Post* for sending us, under deadline pressure, a photograph of Phil Zimmermann.

Gary B. Edstrom has written a marvelous list of Frequently Asked Questions about PGP, which appears regularly in the Usenet group *alt.security.pgp*. It is a wonderful reference; reading it has been an inspiration for this project. An anonymous cyberspace person who goes by the name Xenon has also produced some valuable texts that I found very useful. Check out the Bibliography for information on how to get your own copies of these works.

The MIT libraries have proved invaluable to me on this project, as on others. I am eternally grateful that MIT opens its libraries to the community at large, and I encourage other universities to follow the MIT example.

Thanks to everyone at O'Reilly & Associates who prepared this book for publication. I am especially indebted to Debby Russell for her help, support, and perseverance on this project. Nancy Crumpton copyedited and indexed the book and did final production. Edie Freedman designed the cover, and Jennifer Niederst the interior design. Chris Reilley created the illustrations.

A very big thank you to my agent, Matt Wagner, from Waterside Productions.

And finally, special thanks to my wife, Beth Rosenberg, for coming up with the name Pretty Good Pizza and for her constant love and support.

PGP Overview

This part of the book discusses the need for encryption and introduces PGP. It contains the following chapters:

- Chapter 1, *Introduction to PGP*, introduces PGP, gives you the basic vocabulary you need before you use the program, and shows you how to perform simple functions in PGP.

- Chapter 2, *Cryptography Basics*, gives you a brief introduction to cryptography, provides basic examples of private and public key cryptography, and outlines the U.S. export and patent policies relevant to cryptography.

1

Introduction to PGP

The right to be let alone—the most comprehensive of rights, and the right most valued by civilized men.

—Justice Louis D. Brandeis,
dissenting opinion in Olmstead v. United States, 1928

PGP is a program that uses encryption to protect the privacy of your electronic mail and the files that you store on your computer. You can also use PGP as a tamper-proof digital signature system, allowing you to prove that files or electronic mail messages have not been modified.

Here's what PGP can do:

- Encrypt files. You can use PGP to encrypt your files with IDEA, a powerful private key encryption algorithm. Once encrypted, a file can be decrypted only by someone who knows the file's encryption pass phrase. (File encryption is described in Chapter 7, *Protecting Your Files.*)

- Create your secret and public keys. You need these keys to encrypt and sign the messages you send and to decrypt the messages sent to you. (Key creation is described in Chapter 8, *Creating PGP Keys.*)

- Manage keys. You can use PGP to create and maintain a database containing the public keys of the people you correspond with; think of the database as a kind of address book. (Key management is described in Chapter 9, *Managing PGP Keys.*)

- Send and receive encrypted email. You can use PGP to encrypt email you send and to decrypt email you receive. (Email encryption and decryption are described in Chapter 10, *Encrypting Email.*)

- Use digital signatures. You can use PGP to electronically sign documents. You can also use PGP to verify people's signatures. (Digital signatures are described in Chapter 11, *Using Digital Signatures.*)

- Certify keys. You can use PGP to electronically sign people's public keys. (Key certification and distribution are described in Chapter 12, *Certifying and Distributing Keys.*)

- Revoke, disable, and escrow keys. If your keys or those of others are compromised, you can revoke or disable them. You can put keys in safekeeping via a manual escrow facility. (These features are described in Chapter 13, *Revoking, Disabling, and Escrowing Keys.*)

- Customize PGP. You can change the settings in the PGP configuration file to suit your own site and encryption needs. (The configuration file is introduced in the "PGP Configuration Variables" section later in this chapter and is described in detail in Chapter 14, *PGP Configuration File.*)

- Use the PGP Internet key servers. You can add your public key to a key database, and you can obtain other people's keys from the servers. (The key servers are described in Chapter 15, *PGP Internet Key Servers.*)

I explain the terminology used in this book in the "Basic PGP Terminology" section later in this chapter. But first, let's look briefly at why you need PGP—and encryption—in the first place.

Why PGP? The Case for Encryption

More than a hundred million electronic messages traverse the world's computer networks every day. People use electronic mail for the same purposes for which they have historically used paper mail, the telephone, and fax machines. Most electronic mail is routine; lots of it speeds business transactions; some of it is just chitchat; and some of it matters—it really matters a lot. Unfortunately, most of this electronic mail is vulnerable.

The Internet is doubling in size every year. Electronic mail is one of the main reasons for this fantastic growth. Electronic mail is lightning-fast and nearly free, and, unlike faxes, is used to send documents that people can edit with computers at the other end. Today, contracts, business plans, proposals, and even book manuscripts are routinely sent by email.

Cryptography is Just the Beginning

If you are considering using encryption, you probably are concerned about the information that is stored on your computer or transmitted by your telecommunications system. But, if you are going to take the time to use encryption, you should also make sure that you adopt an overall strategy of computer security so the extra effort you spend encrypting your data isn't undone by some other problem.

Computer security means many different things to many different people. In general, though, computer security is concerned with several fundamental goals:

- **Privacy**—One goal of computer security is to keep your private documents private. While this goal is sometimes addressed with encryption, it is also handled with passwords and other access-control systems.

- **Integrity**—Another goal of computer security is to make sure that your data and applications are not modified without your consent.

- **Authentication**—Another goal is to ensure that the people using a computer system are actually the people that they claim to be; the system, likewise, should prove its identity to its users. Authentication of users helps ensure privacy and integrity by preventing unauthorized people from using your computer system. Techniques that authenticate programs and the system in general are designed to thwart problems like computer viruses and malicious programs.

- **Availability**—The previously described goals are designed to ensure another goal: that the computer and the data that it contains are available to you when you need them.

An effective computer security plan includes many other components. Physical security, for example, ensures that people don't steal your computers. Good management practices are designed to prevent you from hiring someone who might smash your computer with a sledgehammer when he gets frustrated. And data integrity and audit techniques ensure that people won't modify your data without your knowledge. These goals work together to keep your system running smoothly and securely.

Although email is similar to paper mail and telephone conversations, there is one important distinction: email may be far more easily intercepted and copied without the knowledge of either the sender or the recipient. Indeed, *the very act of sending an email message from one person to another involves making a copy of that message.* Consider what happens as a message makes its way from sender to recipient (as shown in Figure 1-1).

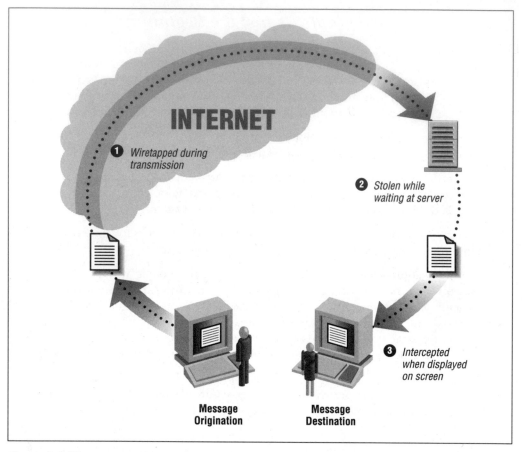

Figure 1-1. Threats to your message

- If the message travels over a network, such as the Internet, the message passes through many computers. Each computer along the way can make a copy of the message.

- When the message arrives at its destination, it waits until the intended recipient picks it up. During this time, the message is vulnerable to being read or copied by the computer's operator.

- Depending on how the recipient reads his mail, the message may be susceptible to electronic eavesdropping; both telephone lines and local area networks can easily be wiretapped. When the message moves from the destination computer's hard disk to the screen, it can be invisibly intercepted.

If you are using electronic mail today, people you have never seen—people whose names you don't even know—can intercept and read your most personal communications. In many cases, these people are busy system administrators, who may simply glance at your messages and forget about them. In other cases, more sinister forces may put your messages—and perhaps your business—at risk.

If you are the target of a really nefarious scheme, your opponent may not stop at merely reading your mail: she might alter it. It takes only a few keystrokes to change a love note into a "Dear John" letter or to change a message that welcomes a new customer to your organization into a suggestion that the customer look elsewhere.

Your Mail Can Go Astray

Electronic mail is sometimes delivered to the wrong party. Ask anybody who uses email, and you'll learn that it happens *a lot*.[†] It's happened to me. It's probably happened to you. It's certainly happened to other people:

- In June 1994, Jeffrey Austen, an assistant professor at the Tennessee Technological University in Cookeville, discovered the following electronic mail message in his mailbox:

```
Date: Wed, 15 Jun 1994 16:18:31 -0500
From: mailcoll@austin.ibm.com
Subject: Misdirected IBM Mail
To: info-dce@transarc.com
Message-id: <9406152118.AA156234@netmail.austin.ibm.com>
Content-transfer-encoding: 7BIT

One of IBM's electronic mail distribution nodes experienced a
problem routing mail from Wednesday June 8, 1994, through
approximately 7:00pm Thursday June 9, 1994. This may have
resulted in your having received proprietary information that
was not intended for you. If you have received such
information, please return it to the Internet address:
                    mailcoll@austin.ibm.com
without retaining any copies of it. If you have already
destroyed or discarded the information, please confirm this by
sending a note to this address stating that the information
you received has been destroyed.

If you are not sure whether you should have received certain
information or if you have any other questions, please call
Marc Flaherty at (512) 555-7920.

Dana Janssen
IBM Corporation
```

---

† Paper mail is often delivered to the wrong party as well. The big difference, though, is that paper mail is sent in envelopes that are usually returned, unopened, to the post office.

Austen forwarded a copy of IBM's plea (with the personal information removed) to the Internet *comp.risks* mailing list with the wry comment: "Quite amusing. I wonder if the CIA would send out a similar message if one of their secrets got out?"[†]

- In 1989, the United States Secret Service seized several computer systems from Steve Jackson Games, a game publishing company in Austin, Texas. One of the confiscated computers contained a bulletin board system that was used by hundreds of people around the country to exchange electronic mail. Although the seizure was eventually ruled illegal by a federal court, the ruling came years too late for the BBS users, whose electronic mail had been scanned and analyzed by Secret Service agents in search of illegal activities.

- A few years ago, I sent a personal letter to Len Tower of the Free Software Foundation, telling him how I admired what he had done with his life and how he had become a role model for me. An error in my computer's *sendmail* program caused the letter to be delivered not to Len Tower but instead to an private, social electronic mailing list called *suspects*, which is received by hundreds of people all over the country.

As electronic mail becomes more pervasive in our society, incidents in which email is accidentally misdirected or intentionally intercepted are going to become more common.

Protecting Your Privacy

Paper mail has an effective yet simple technology for protecting your privacy: envelopes. Most of us learn how to protect our privacy with envelopes in early childhood. Here's what we learned to do:

1. Write the message on a piece of paper.
2. Seal that piece of paper in an envelope.
3. Write the name of the intended recipient on the outside of the envelope.
4. Mail the message.

Most people have never enjoyed this level of privacy with electronic mail. Instead of mimicking sealed, first-class letters, most of today's email systems are built on little more than electronic postcards, with the names of the sender and the recipient written on one side, and the message written on the other. Anyone who comes across an electronic postcard can read it.

---

† The names and telephone numbers of the IBM employees have been changed in this example.

Figure 1-2. Paper mail, with envelopes, provides privacy

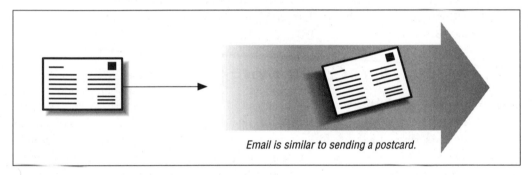

Figure 1-3. Email, like postcards, offers little privacy

The privacy of most people's email is protected by good manners and the law. It's simply rude to read other people's mail. It's also illegal. Under the 1986 Electronic Communications Privacy Act, intercepting and reading other people's electronic mail is a felony.†

The insecurity of electronic mail has been a problem since email was first exchanged; the stories I've mentioned are merely the tip of the iceberg. An astonishingly large number of people who use email have had their messages perused by people for whom the messages weren't intended.

---

† There are several important exceptions to the Electronic Communications Privacy Act. The ECPA does not apply to system operators who read their users' mail in the course of their system administration activities. It also doesn't cover companies that spy on their own employees. Recently, in the case of Steve Jackson Games, a federal appeals court further ruled that the ECPA did not apply to mail files on a seized computer, because the mail was not seized while it was being transmitted.

Use Encryption Well

Anyone can use encryption. Unfortunately, it's also true that anyone can use encryption badly. Using encryption badly is worse than not using encryption at all. If you know that you are not using encryption, you will probably be careful with the files and email messages that contain information that you would like to keep secret. You might think twice before creating documents that contain damaging information. But if you are using bad encryption or if you are using good encryption badly, you might be lulled into a false sense of security while your confidential information remains available to others.

Encryption is a way of putting an end to this problem once and for all.

Chapter 2, *Cryptography Basics*, describes how encryption works. It introduces the basics of cryptography: codes, ciphers, keys, and private and public key cryptography. It also introduces some U.S. government policy and patent issues I explain in Part II of this book. The rest of Chapter 1 introduces PGP itself. Part II describes in detail how PGP works.

Where Did PGP Come from?

Phil Zimmermann started writing PGP in the mid 1980s and finished the first version in 1991. He gave the program to a friend who made it available on the Internet. At the time, PGP was distributed as free software—that is, it was made freely available without charge. But PGP contained something that wasn't Zimmermann's to give away: the rights to the public key cryptography patents. Zimmermann had no license for the RSA or Merkle-Hellman patents. Instead of being freeware, PGP was actually banditware. Anyone using it in the United States was liable under the patent code for patent infringement damages. (I talk more about patent issues in Chapter 6, *Cryptography Patents and Export.*)

Because of PGP's legal status, many people were unwilling to publicly endorse it or even say that they were using it. Public Key Partners pressured online services such as CompuServe and America Online not to make the program available to their customers. Schools were told not to make it available to their students. Nevertheless, PGP attracted a large underground following in the United States.

Overseas, interest in PGP mushroomed. Even though it is a violation of United States arms trafficking laws to export cryptographic software without the permission of the State Department, versions of PGP soon appeared in Europe, Japan, and Australia. There, unencumbered by patent problems, PGP was posted on bulletin boards and made widely available.

In late 1993, ViaCrypt, a company that had a valid license for the Public Key Partners' patents, negotiated with Phil Zimmermann to distribute a commercial version of PGP.

In May 1994, a new version of PGP was released based on the RSAREF toolkit developed by RSA Data Security, Inc. The toolkit included a license from RSA Data Security for the patents on the condition that any program built from the toolkit be used only for noncommercial purposes.

And so it came to pass that, after years in legal limbo, PGP was finally available for people to use without the threat of legal repercussions.

Chapter 4, *A Pretty Good History of PGP*, describes in some detail the development of PGP, its legal battles, and its current status. Appendix A, *Getting PGP*, explains how you can get the free and commercial versions of the program.

At the time this book went to print, versions of PGP were available for DOS-, Windows-, and OS/2-based personal computers, for the Apple Macintosh, Commodore Amiga, Atari ST, and Archimedes platforms, and for VMS and many UNIX workstations. Since PGP is written in the C programming language, it is easily ported to new platforms.

Basic PGP Terminology

Before you learn how PGP works, it's helpful to understand the terminology I use to describe it.

Keys: Public, Secret, and Session

The security for all encryption systems is based on a cryptographic key: the key is literally the key to cryptography's electronic lock.

Private key encryption systems, which PGP calls *conventional cryptography*, use a single key, a *private key*, for both encryption and decryption. You and the person you're communicating with must both use the same key—you to encrypt and your friend to decrypt.

With public key systems, on the other hand, a mathematical process generates *two* mathematically related keys. A message encrypted with one key can be decrypted only with the other.

The *public key*

> You use another person's public key to encrypt a message for that person; only that person can decrypt and read it. That person uses your public key to encrypt messages that only you can decrypt and read. The key is called the "public" key because you can make it public without compromising the security of your system (for example, you can publish it in the phone book).

The *secret key*

> You use your secret key to decrypt messages that have been encrypted with your public key. The key is called the "secret" key or the "private" key because you must keep it secret. If someone else gets your secret key, they can read your encrypted messages.

With public key cryptography, public and secret keys serve another purpose as well; they can be used to make and verify digital signatures, which I describe in "Digital Signatures" later in this chapter.

Unfortunately, every public key system ever devised has one problem: such systems are computationally intensive and thus are extremely slow to use. Software implementations of public key algorithms, such as the RSA algorithm, are actually a thousand times or more slower than the equivalent software implementations of private key systems like the Data Encryption Standard (DES) or IDEA. (I describe all of these algorithms in Chapters 2 and 3.) One of the reasons for this disparity is that public key systems routinely perform multiplication and exponentiation on numbers that are hundreds of digits long, unlike private key systems, which do most of their math on smaller quantities that computers are optimized to handle.

For this reason, practical public key systems (such as PGP) use a third kind of key as well:

The *session key*

> The session key is randomly generated for every message encrypted with PGP's public key encryption system. PGP's session key is a 128-bit IDEA key.

When you use PGP to encrypt a mail message and send it to a friend, the following occurs:

1. PGP creates a random session key for the message.
2. PGP uses the IDEA algorithm to encrypt the message with the session key.
3. PGP uses the RSA algorithm to encrypt the session key with the recipient's public key.
4. PGP bundles the encrypted message and the encrypted session key together and prepares the message for mailing.

PGP handles session keys automatically, without any intervention on your part. The handling of session keys is so automatic, in fact, that PGP doesn't even bother to tell you what they are.

Key Certificates

PGP keeps each public key in a *key certificate*. Each key certificate contains:

- The public key itself

- One or more user IDs for the key's creator (usually that person's name and email address)

- The date that the key was created

- Optionally, a list of digital signatures on the key, provided by people who attest to the key's veracity

You can think of the public key as the notches on a conventional house key, and the user ID, creation date, and optional digital signatures as words that are stamped on the base of the key, as shown in Figure 1-4.

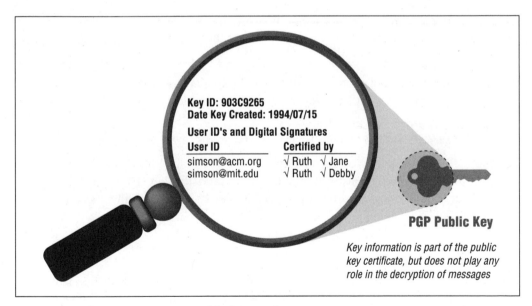

Figure 1-4. Information on a PGP public key certificate

My Public Key

I said that public keys are called "public" because they can be made public. Here is my own public key:

```
-----BEGIN PGP PUBLIC KEY BLOCK-----
Version: 2.6

mQCNAi4mq/gAAAEEAPcbmtIyFTyqdpwU3HFP7XEIBGu1CXKZpzxDgDY21gKwy5uJ
nxsSbTaz//AxrHE6R1LXZXnZgEFJWp/AIrlPdwjKciRJFIvqdqooyZHSPFQ9r8oS
3Fq+0xPpOCEyPDb9+Ghv9HYcIepLwJJrcORinor5ZdzfWRyW13D7CbCQPJJ1AAUR
tDJTaW1zb24gTC4gR2FyZmlua2VsIDxzaW1zb25QG51eHQuY2FtYnJpZGdlLm1h
LnVzPg==
=oQEX
-----END PGP PUBLIC KEY BLOCK-----
```

Using my public key and a copy of PGP, you can send me secret messages that no one else can read!

Even though I've always been a rather trusting person, I'm not going to publish my secret key—not here, not anywhere. If I published my secret key, then anyone who intercepted an encrypted message that was intended for me could read that message! By keeping my secret key secret, I ensure the privacy of those messages, protecting not just myself, but the people who sent them as well.

PGP's –kv (key view) option prints certificates in an easy-to-read format. PGP prints a particular key certificate that I use for many of the examples in this book:

```
Type bits/keyID    Date       User ID
pub   512/43744F09 1994/07/07 Phil's Pretty Good Pizza <phil@pgp.com>
```

This key is a public key, created on July 7, 1994, for Phil's Pretty Good Pizza (email address *phil@pgp.com*). The key is 512 bits long, and the key ID is 43744F09. (The key ID is actually the lower 64 bits of the public key itself.) Practically speaking, every PGP public key has a unique key ID.

Key Rings

PGP keeps all of the public keys for the people you communicate with in a single file called the *key ring*. Using one file for everyone's public keys is more efficient than keeping each key in its own file. Storing keys in a key ring shortens the time it takes to search for someone's public key. It is faster to search for a public key in a single file than to open and read the contents of dozens or hundreds of files.

Most PGP users have at least two PGP key ring files:

secring.pgp
> This file is your secret key ring. PGP uses your secret key ring to hold all of your secret keys.

pubring.pgp
> This file is your public key ring. PGP uses this file to hold the public keys of every person with whom you communicate.

You can create as many key rings as you like, although you typically have several public key rings and only one secret key ring, as shown in Figure 1-5.

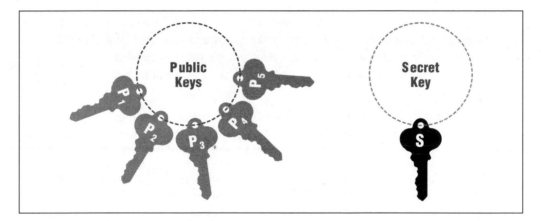

Figure 1-5. PGP key rings

NOTE

> If you communicate with a lot of people, you might find it faster to keep only the keys for the people who you correspond with frequently in your *pubring.pgp* file and to keep the public keys for everyone else in another, less frequently used file. This arrangement dramatically shortens the time it takes PGP to look up public keys.

Pass Phrases

Each time you create a public key/secret key pair, PGP asks you to create and enter a *pass phrase*. A PGP pass phrase has several functions; the most important is that it decrypts the secret key that is stored on your secret key ring. This pass phrase provides yet another layer of security for messages encrypted with PGP; if someone does not know your pass phrase, he cannot use your secret key.

You can have a separate pass phrase for each secret key, or all your secret keys can use the same pass phrase; it's up to you.

PGP pass phrases are used under several circumstances:

- When you start to decrypt a message that has been sent to you, PGP asks you for your pass phrase. The pass phrase decrypts the secret key corresponding to the public key used to encrypt the message so you can use the secret key to decrypt the message.

- When you start to sign a message with your secret key, PGP again asks you for your pass phrase, which it uses to decrypt your secret key so that you can sign the message.

- When you start to encrypt a file using private key cryptography (which PGP calls *conventional encryption*), PGP again asks you for a pass phrase for the file. This pass phrase can be the same as the pass phrase used to protect your secret key, or it can be different. (Chapter 7, *Protecting Your Files*, describes how to encrypt files.)

Your pass phrase is similar to the passwords used by many computer systems because it controls access to some functions of the PGP application. However, there are important differences:

- PGP does not compare the pass phrase that you type with a pass phrase that is stored on your hard disk to determine if you should be allowed to use the PGP program. Instead, PGP uses the phrase to encrypt or decrypt a file; if you type the wrong pass phrase, the decryption fails.

- Whereas most computers limit passwords to eight characters, PGP pass phrases can be as long as you wish. Naturally, the longer your pass phrase, the harder it is for someone to guess it.

Why bother encrypting your secret key with a pass phrase? Well, suppose someone steals your computer. If your secret key is not encrypted, the thief who steals your computer will be able to read your encrypted electronic mail and to impersonate you by sending out "signed" messages. Or suppose you share your computer with a friend, an officemate, or a spouse. If you each have your own pass phrases, you won't (rightfully) be able to read each other's encrypted mail or sign one another's signatures (unless you know each other's pass phrases).

Chapter 7 contains a complete discussion of how to select good pass phrases.

Digital Signatures

PGP has a powerful system for signing electronic documents called *digital signatures*. This section describes digital signatures and why you should use them.

Sometimes you don't particularly need to encrypt documents; you simply want to keep them from being changed. You want a way to prevent other people from distributing fraudulent messages in your name or the name of your organization. You want a way to prevent people from changing your words without your permission and claiming that you were the original author. You want a way of proving that you wrote a document, without having to give your phone number to thousands of people so they can call you for verification. Digital signatures can be used for all of these functions.

Why bother with digital signatures?

- In the fall of 1993, a student at Dartmouth University sent forged electronic mail saying that the midterm exam in Professor David Becker's course on Latin American politics was canceled because Professor Becker had a family emergency. The mail message was sent at 11:00 p.m. the night before the test. Only half of the class showed up for the exam the next morning.

- In January 1994, an out-of-work janitor pleaded guilty to giving false radio commands to pilots at the Roanoke Regional Airport in Virginia. The janitor told pilots to abort landings, change altitude, and alter their courses. Some pilots followed the janitor's directions.

Without digital signatures, there is no way to tell whether an electronic message is authentic. Using desktop publishing and electronic mail, anyone can forge names and letterheads. Society needs digital signatures to prevent the types of fraud that are becoming increasingly easy to perpetrate.

Digital signatures have many possible uses:

- You can use digital signatures to prevent someone from changing critical information in electronic mail that you send and then claiming that you are the author of the changed mail.

- You can use digital signatures to prevent the forgery of email or news postings.

- Companies can use digital signatures to distribute price lists and catalogs containing verified prices.

- Organizations and government agencies can use digital signatures to sign official announcements, press releases, rules, regulations, and other official documents.

- Colleges and universities can use digital signatures as seals on official academic documents. You can verify these seals without having to contact the academic institution (provided you have a copy of that institution's public key).

- Digital signatures provide the basis for an electronic "notary public," who can sign documents with a timestamp that cannot be contested.

Indeed, digital signatures are so swift and nifty that they should be stamped on every document you create and every email message you send as a matter of course. The only reason that this isn't done today, in fact, is that the programs that create them have traditionally been unwieldy, and the algorithms used to create them are patented, as I describe later in this book.

How do digital signatures work with PGP? To make a digital signature, PGP processes your message with a *message digest function*, producing a 128-bit number. A message digest (described in detail in Chapter 11) is a mathematical function that distills all of the information in a file into one large number. This number is then signed with your private key, producing a PGP signature block, which is placed at the end of your message. The digital signature is a promise by you that the document is a true and corrrect copy of the original (see Figure 1-6).

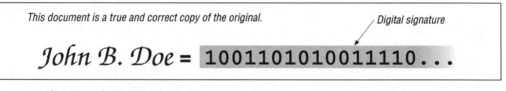

Figure 1-6. A digital signature

A digital signature is a seal at the end of an electronic document. Like a seal, a digital signature at the end of a document gives you the impression that the document is important and official. (Of course, it might simply mean that the person who is sending it just got a new toy!)

Nevertheless, the mere presence of a digital signature at the end of a document doesn't really tell you anything. Digital signatures, like conventional ones, can be forged. The difference between digital signatures and conventional ones is that digital signatures can be mathematically verified. Authentic signatures verify; forged ones don't.

PGP signatures look like this:

```
-----BEGIN PGP SIGNED MESSAGE-----
```

message —
```
Really Good Electronics - Chip Prices

1MB 2 CHIP 80 NS         $20.25
1MB 2 CHIP 70 NS         $20.75
1MB 8 CHIPP 80 NS        $18.70
1MB 8 CHIP 70 NS         $19.60
1MB FX (ANY SPEED)       $16.80

For information, call 800-RAM-GOLD
```

```
-----BEGIN PGP SIGNATURE-----
Version: 2.6
```

signature —
```
iQCVAgUBL1qEEHD7CbCQPJJlAQEMXgQAueUPPrpYeb13RZMPD4f8QmW+pQs/ay2P
vrtD+kL0zz3LczxoK3XDdvRj1eRYviXYaJhvSt13cK7+D7lnolmFHWv3DS7tBJzp
G3hJRUr6guRoekcYwXFR7OZhW9VIUHNoIG/OpK23HCatd9f+81TafeUc160k9/CM
Kj034kZlhz8=
=jRLh
-----END PGP SIGNATURE-----
```

When you receive a signed message, PGP verifies the signature by taking the portion of the message between the "-----BEGIN PGP SIGNED MESSAGE---" and the "----BEGIN PGP SIGNATURE----" and running the same message digest function that it ran on the original message. PGP then decrypts the signature block using your public key. Finally, PGP checks the two message digests to see if they match. If they match, PGP determines that the file was not modified after the signature was made. If the two message digests do not match, PGP recognizes that the file was modified and warns you.

When the key and the signature match, you receive a straightforward message like the following:

```
Good signature from user "Really Good Electronics <chips@rge.com>".
Signature made 1994/08/23 23:25 GMT
```

On the other hand, if someone has maliciously changed the price of one of the chips or made a surreptitious change to RGE's phone number, you receive the following message:

```
WARNING: Bad signature, doesn't match file contents!

Bad signature from user "Really Good Electronics <chips@rge.com>".
Signature made 1994/08/23 23:25 GMT
```

Digital signatures can detect a change in a message that is as insignificant as an inserted space after a period or as substantial as an inserted paragraph, a deleted page, or a changed dollar amount. Unfortunately, a digital signature can tell you only that a document has been changed; it can't tell you *what* has been changed or *how much* has been changed in the document.

In practice, it is effectively impossible to "forge" a PGP digital signature—either by putting a signature from one document at the end of another or by changing the contents of a signed document while the signature still verifies.

The "Encrypting and Signing Email (–e and –s Options)" section later in this chapter explains how to use PGP to make a digital signature.

Signatures on Key Certificates

One difficulty with public key cryptography is the mechanics of distributing the public keys themselves. In order to send Jane an encrypted message, you must have Jane's public key. Likewise, she must have your public key to verify your signature.

Ideally, everyone's public keys could simply be listed—such as in a phone book. You could look up a person's public key before you sent her email. In fact, the Internet has PGP key servers that fulfill this function; I describe them in Chapter 15, *PGP Internet Key Servers*.

Unfortunately, there is really no effective way to verify that the public key published in a phone book actually belongs to the person it is supposed to belong to. For example, suppose that Jane's evil brother Bill has surreptitiously replaced her public key in the public key phone book with his own. Bill could then intercept Jane's mail, decrypt it with his key, read it, and re-encrypt it with Jane's real public key. Neither the sender of the message nor Jane is the wiser—until Bill uses the intercepted mail to embarrass Jane at the next family reunion.

PGP doesn't solve this key distribution problem, but it does make it less problematic by allowing people to *sign* each other's key certificates. The signature is a promise of truthfulness; it is a statement by the signer that the signed key is authentic and truly belongs to the person it claims to belong to.

Suppose the phone book contains two keys from people claiming to be Jane. One of these keys might have no signature on it, but the other is signed by Stacy, who just happens to be your best friend from high school. Clearly, you believe that the key signed by Stacy is the correct key to trust.

But, is Stacy's signature valid? Fortunately, you have been exchanging electronic mail with Stacy for years, so you already have a copy of her key. You verify Stacy's signature and, by doing so, convince yourself that Jane's public key is, in fact, hers. Now you can send Jane that private message, saying that you've loved her from afar for all these years and suggesting that you meet at the top of the Empire State Building on February 14.

This technique that PGP uses for building a library of validated public keys is called the *web of trust*. It is not as convenient as a single, centralized registry of public keys (such as those required by other types of encryption systems). On the other hand, since verification of the keys is distributed among many users, it is more difficult to subvert.

How to Run PGP

This section explains how you run PGP and use it to perform some common functions. Part III explains these and other functions in detail.

In these examples, I don't attempt to explain the cryptography behind the PGP functions. Chapter 2 provides an introduction to those concepts.

The Command Line Interface

PGP is designed to be run from the command line. This design accommodates the program's implementation on many different platforms. (Note that the Macintosh version of PGP, described in Appendix D, is merely a PGP "shell." When you run MacPGP, you actually see a window in which the MacPGP shell types commands to the real PGP program. The Windows version works the same way. Appendix A, *Getting PGP*, provides a list of FTP sites where you can obtain these shells and other PGP-related products.)

To run PGP, you simply type the command **pgp**. Each time PGP runs, it displays a basic copyright message and the time, as follows:

```
unix% pgp
Pretty Good Privacy(tm) 2.6 - Public-key encryption for the masses.
(c) 1990-1994 Philip Zimmermann, Phil's Pretty Good Software. 23 May 94
Distributed by the Massachusetts Institute of Technology.  Uses RSAREF.
Export of this software may be restricted by the U.S. government.
Current time: 1994/08/13 17:13 GMT

For details on licensing and distribution, see the PGP User's Guide.
For other cryptography products and custom development services, contact:
Philip Zimmermann, 3021 11th St, Boulder CO 80304 USA, phone +1 303 541-0140
```

```
For a usage summary, type:  pgp -h
unix%
```

You tell PGP what you want it to do by typing an option after the *pgp* command. PGP options begin with a dash (–). The following sections contain a few examples of some simple PGP functions.

Getting Help (–h Option)

You can get help very simply by specifying the –h option:

```
unix% pgp -h
Pretty Good Privacy(tm) 2.6 - Public-key encryption for the masses.
 (c) 1990-1994 Philip Zimmermann, Phil's Pretty Good Software. 23 May 94
Distributed by the Massachusetts Institute of Technology.  Uses RSAREF.
Export of this software may be restricted by the U.S. government.
Current time: 1994/08/24 03:45 GMT


Usage summary:
To encrypt a plaintext file with recipent's public key, type:
   pgp -e textfile her_userid [other userids] (produces textfile.pgp)
To sign a plaintext file with your secret key:
   pgp -s textfile [-u your_userid]         (produces textfile.pgp)
To sign a plaintext file with your secret key, and then encrypt it
   with recipent's public key, producing a .pgp file:
   pgp -es textfile her_userid [other userids] [-u your_userid]
To encrypt with conventional encryption only:
   pgp -c textfile
To decrypt or check a signature for a ciphertext (.pgp) file:
   pgp ciphertextfile [plaintextfile]
To produce output in ASCII for email, add the -a option to other options.
To generate your own unique public/secret key pair:  pgp -kg
For help on other key management functions, type:   pgp -k
unix%
```

Specifying Command Line Arguments

As you've already seen with –h (help), to execute the simplest PGP commands you simply type **pgp** followed by the particular option you want to run. Here's another example. To view the contents of your public key ring, you can use PGP's –kv (key view) option:

```
unix% pgp -kv
Pretty Good Privacy(tm) 2.6 - Public-key encryption for the masses.
 (c) 1990-1994 Philip Zimmermann, Phil's Pretty Good Software. 23 May 94
Distributed by the Massachusetts Institute of Technology.  Uses RSAREF.
Export of this software may be restricted by the U.S. government.
Current time: 1994/08/13 17:14 GMT
```

```
Key ring: '/Net/next/Users/simsong/Library/pgp/pubring.pgp'
Type bits/keyID     Date         User ID
pub  1024/E8E75081 1993/09/24 Michael A. Grant <Michael.Grant@East.Sun.COM>
                              Michael A. Grant <mgrant@digex.net>
                              Michael A. Grant <mgrant@fedeast.east.sun.com>
pub  1024/903C9265 1994/07/15 Simson L. Garfinkel <simsong@acm.org>
2 matching keys found.
unix%
```

In this example, you see a very simple public key ring that has two keys on it: one for me and one for Michael A. Grant.

Michael's key has three user IDs associated with it: *Michael.Grant@East.Sun.COM*, *mgrant@digex.net*, and *mgrant@fedeast.east.sun.com*. Despite the fact that there are three user IDs, there is only a single public key. (Chapter 8, *Creating PGP Keys*, describes how to create a key ring, and Chapter 9, *Managing PGP Keys*, describes how to add more user IDs.)

Some PGP options require that you to specify a particular file or key, which you can do by placing the filename or a part of the key's key ID or user ID on the command line following the option. For example, to encrypt a file *dynamite* with conventional private key cryptography, I'd type the following:

    unix% **pgp -c dynamite**

I explain how this works in Chapter 7, *Protecting Your Files*.

Some commands require that you specify several arguments. For example, the following command extracts a key ("simsong" is the user ID) from my key ring and puts it in a file (*simsong.asc*):

    unix% **pgp -kxa simsong simsong.asc**

Chapter 9, *Managing PGP Keys*, describes how this command works.

Using ASCII Armor (-a Option)

Modern computers store letters, characters, and symbols in 8-bit words called *bytes* using the ASCII encoding system. An 8-bit byte can represent any number between 0 and 255. ASCII assigns printable codes to the numbers between 32 (space) and 126 (the ~ character).

Unfortunately, a fundamental quality of a good encryption algorithm is that encrypted data may take on *any value*. For example, suppose you were to encrypt the phrase "Pretty Good", which has the following ASCII representation:

```
Phrase: P   r   e   t   t   y       G   o   o   d
ASCII:  80 114 101 116 116 121  32  71 111 111 100
```

The resulting encrypted data isn't ASCII—it's binary data that is spread all over the character map. For example, the previous phrase might encrypt as follows:

```
Encrypted:208 223 150  82 160 118 231 160  33  48 160
BINARY:    -  ë  Ö  R  ©  v  ñ  ©  !  0  ©
```

There's no problem with putting binary data in files, but unfortunately, binary data can't be sent by electronic mail. (It also can't be easily printed in books.)

PGP has a system to get around this limitation called *ASCII armor*. Whenever you use PGP to encrypt or sign a file or to create a key, you have the option of protecting the file with ASCII armor by specifying the PGP –a (ASCII armor) option. The PGP ASCII armor version of the encrypted file shown previously looks like the following:

```
-----BEGIN PGP MESSAGE-----
Version: 2.6

rBdiBXN0ZGluAAAAANDfllKgduegITCgCg==
=E6T8
-----END PGP MESSAGE-----
```

The "armor" is actually a file encoding (called Radix 64) that uses four ASCII characters to represent three binary characters. ASCII armor thus requires 33 percent more space than unarmored binary files.

The last line of the ASCII armor (=E6T8 in the example) is a checksum. PGP uses this value to determine whether the contents of the ASCII armor have been modified. This isn't the same kind of check as the message digest in PGP's signature. It's easy to intentionally modify a checksumed file in such a way that the checksum still matches; it's also possible to simply put a different checksum at the bottom of a file that's been modified. But that's okay; the purpose of the checksum at the bottom of the PGP message isn't to detect malicious tampering but to catch transmission errors. PGP's signature function protects against tampering.

If you are encrypting a very long message, PGP can split the message into smaller chunks that are more easily handled by some electronic mail systems.

Encrypting and Signing Email (-e and -s Options)

Let's look at a typical use for PGP. Suppose I want to order a really special pizza from Phil's Pretty Good Pizza. I want to be sure that my message is kept secret; I also want to be sure that my message is not modified.

I create a file containing my order and use PGP to do the following:

- I encrypt the message with Phil's public key.

- I sign the message with my secret key.

Phil and I are assured of the following:

- Since the message is encrypted (with Phil's public key), I am assured that no one except Phil can read it.

- Since the message is signed (with my secret key), Phil is assured that I am the sender of the message.

- Since the message is signed, Phil is further assured that the message sent by me has not been modified on its journey.

Since Phil and I use PGP, Alice, an obnoxious and technically adept high school hacker Phil knows, can't play tricks on us. Alice can intercept my messages and send them to Yoshi's Sushi Parlor, but Yoshi won't be able to read the messages because he doesn't have Phil's secret key. Alice can't order $200 worth of sushi from Yoshi's or a dozen pies from Phil's and send them to me, because Alice can't sign my digital signature. Finally, since my email is encrypted with Phil's public key, Alice can't read my credit card and charge a new stereo system at The Wiz to my VISA account.

To encrypt and sign my email, I'd typically run PGP with the –seat (sign, encrypt, ASCII armor, text) option. The –s option puts a digital signature on the message; –e encrypts it; –a puts ASCII armor on it; and –t makes sure that the text of the message is readable on Phil's computer (if it's running on a different operating system from my own). The –u option in the example tells PGP to use Simson's public key when it signs the message. These options are all explained in detail in subsequent chapters; for now, let's just take a look at what PGP does.

This particular example uses the UNIX operating system, but you'll see the same output from any other system you use.

Assume that my pizza order is in a file called *order*:

```
unix% pgp -seat order phil -u simson
Pretty Good Privacy(tm) 2.6.1 - Public-key encryption for the masses.
(c) 1990-1994 Philip Zimmermann, Phil's Pretty Good Software. 29 Aug 94
Distributed by the Massachusetts Institute of Technology.  Uses RSAREF.
Export of this software may be restricted by the U.S. government.
Current time: 1994/09/20 18:34 GMT

A secret key is required to make a signature.
You need a pass phrase to unlock your RSA secret key.
Key for user ID "Simson L. Garfinkel <simsong@acm.org>"

Enter pass phrase: Nobody knows my namePass phrase is good.
Key for user ID: Simson L. Garfinkel <simsong@acm.org>
1024-bit key, Key ID 903C9265, created 1994/07/15
Just a moment....
```

```
Recipients' public key(s) will be used to encrypt.
Key for user ID: Phil's Pretty Good Pizza <phil@pgp.com>
512-bit key, Key ID 43744F09, created 1994/07/07
   .
Transport armor file: order.asc
unix%
```

PGP creates a file called *order.asc*. The contents of the file look like the following:

```
unix% cat order.asc
-----BEGIN PGP MESSAGE-----
Version: 2.6.1

hEwDJ19DTkN0TwkBAf98FZTHXuI1SKAcp4VpKzolWbPQne+Dp/kvXDzJ3KvKjsfc
6UFPZ6AvRGLyKSSQivXBH/Jd++h/ivdLaWMe1Rx9pgAAATy7Dqx+btxXn7rUzds4
SFb3W61ZBcf4MJI/TFIqiISbKq/FFFHfiym5zXc8405IPav/nsxoIqddBLLly35v
35+fXZfW21/k+YuKVaPah918mUuoM5oihmEC3c2m8uVTOMewAtZT0rZ6d3TATRak
rSmmPYsuLAj7bpk3wPLSEReilAfSD46J9KZDk0TDkt2KEvfO+e2fONKd06D+TmOr
PNT1wy/y/8b2tpX0mfng7waAIM0NFS5Z/IMA1J6QkDd7Vu6ELU9AZHO+8xBCoSb1
X9EahcVDJO8249WdC/y3hpj+FxwlS4/pOdcCbEr37FG5295MhP0hEL4s+wA//05P
5eXTe3jtY2pPzm810sR8RMneYvFyVtsrWTEsRgcH/n1CLG8glCdOzzprjMPkZHx2
paN7OVc+SkOKagZKbO4v
=v5KD
-----END PGP MESSAGE-----
unix%
```

I can send this file to Phil using any email system; in this case, I'm using the UNIX *mail* command:

```
unix% mail phil@pgp.com < order.asc
unix%
```

When Phil receives this email, he first needs to save it in a file that he decrypts with PGP. Phil doesn't need to supply any options to PGP. The program examines the input file and automatically decrypts anything that is encrypted (if it has the suitable secret key) and verifies the signature of anything signed (if it has the suitable public key). Phil sees the following:

```
phil@pgp.com--> pgp order.asc
Pretty Good Privacy(tm) 2.6.1 - Public-key encryption for the masses.
(c) 1990-1994 Philip Zimmermann, Phil's Pretty Good Software. 29 Aug 94
Distributed by the Massachusetts Institute of Technology.  Uses RSAREF.
Export of this software may be restricted by the U.S. government.
Current time: 1994/09/20 18:46 GMT

File is encrypted.  Secret key is required to read it.
Key for user ID: Phil <Pretty Good Pizza>
512-bit key, Key ID 43744F09, created 1994/07/07

You need a pass phrase to unlock your RSA secret key.
```

```
Enter pass phrase: Eye,Eye,PizzaPiePass phrase is good.  Just a moment......
File has signature.  Public key is required to check signature. .
Good signature from user "Simson L. Garfinkel <simsong@acm.org>".
Signature made 1994/09/20 18:34 GMT

Plaintext filename: order
phil@pgp.com-->
```

Phil can now read the message with any display program (quickly, Phil, I'm starving!):

```
unix% cat order
Phil,
        Please send me a large pizza with triple cheese, triple
onion, double garlic, and pimientos on top. Spare no expense!

-Simson
unix%
```

PGP File Extensions

PGP uses the following standard file extensions to indicate the type of file it is dealing with:

.txt

A text file you create with a text editor or a word processor has the *.txt* extension before it is encrypted. This is plaintext.

.pgp

This is a binary PGP file. Once you encrypt a file, it has a *.pgp* extension. This extension is also used for key rings.

.asc

This is an ASCII-armored file. If you use the –a option to create an encrypted file, it will have an *.asc* extension.

.bin

Used for the *randseed.bin* file, which stores the seed for PGP's random number generator. This file is created when you use PGP's –kg (key generate) option.

Unlike many UNIX programs, PGP will add a file extension if you do not type it yourself. For example, if you want to refer to a PGP-encrypted message called *message.pgp*, you can refer to it either as *message.pgp* or simply as *message*.

PGP also examines the filenames you provide as arguments and tries to make intelligent decisions based on the file's contents. Usually, PGP ends up doing exactly what you want it to. You'll see how this works in the examples throughout this book.

PGP Environment Variables

The DOS and UNIX versions of PGP use certain environment variables that tell PGP where to find the files it needs to run.

The following variables are supported by the current version of PGP. For more information about using them with your particular operating system, see the appendices.

PGPPASS

Holds your pass phrase. If you store your pass phrase in PGPPASS, PGP won't need to ask for the pass phrase each time it starts up. However, there is a danger in using this environment variable: storing your pass phrase in memory makes it entirely too easy for someone to access your secret key. For example, under UNIX, you can easily read another person's environment with the *ps* command.

I strongly recommend that you do not use the PGPPASS environment variable.

PGPPASSFD

Specifies a file descriptor from which your pass phrase should be read. This is an advanced PGP feature that you might want to use if you are building graphical shells that use PGP.

PGPPATH

Specifies the directory used to store PGP's standard files.

TMP

Specifies directories in which PGP stores its temporary files (if the TMP environment variable is not set in the configuration file). If you are using PGP on a multi-user computer system, this should be a directory that no one else can access.

TZ

This variable indicates the time zone you are in; it is used mostly by DOS computers.

With a DOS-based computer, you can set the environment variables with the *set* command:

```
C:> SET PGPPATH=C:\PGP
C:>
```

With a computer running UNIX, the way you set an environment variable depends on which shell you are using. If you are using the Bourne, Korn, or bash shells, you set an environment variable as follows:

```
$ PGPPATH=/usr/simsong/.pgp;export PGPPATH
$
```

If you are using the C shell, you set your PGPPATH path environment variable as follows:

```
% setenv PGPPATH ~simsong/.pgp
%
```

Normally, environment variables are set in startup files rather than being typed at the keyboard. Appendices B and C describe how to modify your startup files on DOS and UNIX operating systems, respectively.

PGP Configuration Variables

PGP's configuration file allows you to change the behavior of PGP when it runs. You can change the standard *config.txt* file that comes with the program if you want to customize your copy of PGP.

PGP has nearly 30 configuration variables. They determine where PGP puts its files, how verbose its output is, how secure its key certification is, and more. For example, the configuration file that is distributed with PGP specifies that a maximum of 720 lines can be put into a single ASCII-armored file with the following statement:

```
Armorlines = 720
```

To change this configuration variable (for example, if you are using Fidonet, you must limit your files to 450 lines), you can edit the PGP configuration file with a text editor.

You can also override a value that is specified in the configuration file by specifying a different value on the command line when you run PGP. To encrypt and sign a file with the configuration value ARMORLINES set to 450, you might run PGP as follows:

```
% pgp -seat message +Armorlines=450
%
```

For more information on PGP's configuration file and a complete summary of the configuration variables, see Chapter 14, *PGP Configuration File*.

The PGP Language File

PGP is truly an international program. Volunteers from around the world have contributed to its development and ongoing improvement. One important contribution of these international volunteers is the translation of PGP prompts and messages into different languages.

PGP gets its multi-lingual support through a special file called *language.txt*. Inside the file *language.txt* is a collection of all the messages that PGP can print. For each

message, the file also contains translations of that message in other languages that
PGP supports. Here are a few lines from the file:

```
"\nPress ENTER to continue..."
fr: "\nAppuyez sur la touche Retour ou Entr\351e pour continuer..."
es: "\nPulse ENTER (retorno) para continuar..."

"\nGood signature from user \"%s\".\n"
fr: "\nBonne signature de l'utilisateur \"%s\".\n"
es: "\nFirma correcta de \"%s\".\n"
```

Lines in the first group contain a simple message. Lines in the second group contain
both a message and a space for a parameter—in this case, a string parameter. When
PGP prepares to display a message, it first checks to see what the current language is.
If the language is English, PGP simply displays the message. But if the language is not
English, PGP searches the file for the message and displays a suitable translation, if
possible.

Some alternative language files are available with the standard distribution of PGP.
Others may be obtained separately. See Appendix A, *Getting PGP*, for information
about how you can get these files.

PGP and Its Competitors

PGP is not the only system for exchanging encrypted electronic mail: it isn't even
necessarily the most popular—yet!

One of the first systems for sending encrypted electronic mail with public key cryptography was a program developed by Charlie Merritt, which he called SECURE/32 and
which was used by a limited number of large customers. (Chapter 4 describes Merritt
and his role in the development of PGP in some detail.) A few years later, RSA Data
Security developed a more extensive program called MailSafe. The program, which
runs under DOS, encrypts and decrypts files, signs files with digital signatures, and
manages cryptography keys. The program was released in 1986 and has tens of thousands of users around the world—mostly in the commercial and government sectors.
In many ways, PGP was inspired by MailSafe. (The president of RSA Data Security,
Jim Bidzos, goes further, saying that PGP appropriated MailSafe's features without attri-
bution; it is possible that both products were inspired by SECURE/32.)

In the late 1980s, the Internet Engineering Task Force (IETF) began work on a mail
encryption standard for Internet-based electronic mail. The standard is called PEM,
short for Privacy Enhanced Mail.

PEM differs from PGP in the following significant ways:

- Unlike PGP, PEM is a standard, not an application program. In order to use PEM, you need to have an application program that "speaks" the PEM standard. Several programs that do just that are available today for UNIX workstations, PCs, and Macintosh computers.

- PEM does not allow anonymous messages. With PEM, messages may be signed and encrypted, but the signature is "outside" the encryption envelope. Anybody can verify the signature on a PEM-encrypted email message—even people who can't decrypt the message.

- With PEM, public key certificates must be "signed" by a signing authority. For example, every student at a university might have a key that is signed by the university. The university, in turn, would have its own key and certificate that might be signed by the central Internet key signing authority. (The requirement for centralized key certification was dropped from the PEM Version 2.0 standard.)

  PGP's model of key certification is not centralized but distributed; anyone can make his own PGP key and publish it. You can have your keys signed by anyone you wish, and you choose whose signatures you trust, and whose you do not.

Nearly all of the differences between PEM and PGP are consequences of the fact that PEM was designed by a committee over several years, while PGP was designed by a person and then by a user community that was actively using the program. PEM was designed to address theoretical issues and, to some extent, to satisfy partisan politics; PGP was designed from real-world trial and error.

Key Certification with PGP

The third difference between PGP and PEM listed in the previous section is so important that it deserves amplification.

One of the main criticisms of PGP is that you can't get a person's public PGP key from the Internet or a published phone book and be sure who really owns that key. PEM relies on a hierarchy of authorities to convey trust, whereas PGP uses an informal web of trust. (I explore this concept in detail in Chapter 12, *Certifying and Distributing Keys.*)

But how important is this difference, really?

When I printed my PGP key earlier in this chapter, you had to trust me, my publisher, and the printer of this book that the key printed on the book's pages is actually the key for Simson L. Garfinkel; someone determined to keep my readers from sending me encrypted mail could, in theory, bribe someone at the printing plant to print a different key. If this happened, not only would I be unable to read any email sent to me with the public key, but the person who bribed the printer would then be able to intercept and read my encrypted mail with impunity.

PEM could avoid this problem. Instead of printing just the public key, we would have printed a certificate signed by O'Reilly & Associates (ORA). We would also have printed ORA's key certificate, perhaps signed by the Internet PCA Registration Authority. If you were interested, you could then type that certificate into your computer and verify the signature. You could be sure.

Sound like a lot of work? It is. Although the high security offered by PEM might possibly be important when you are encrypting such things as troop movements, cash transactions, and offers to purchase stock at a certain price, it's not needed in most cases.

If you are corresponding over the Internet with someone who you have never met in person, you may not really care if his actual name is "Jim Nosmis" or "James P. Nosmis, III" or even "Alexander Zelig." Indeed, all you probably care about is that each time you get a message from Jim Nosmis, it is the *same* Jim Nosmis, and that, when you send your replies, they go to the same person. If you are corresponding with Jim Nosmis and a person with the same name posts a message to the Usenet, you probably want a way of verifying whether they are the same person.

Indeed, later versions of PEM have removed the requirement for a centralized trust authority. Unfortunately, as of this writing, few implementations of PEM actually implement the new standard. These programs will probably be a few years in the works. When they are released, the world will once again have two competing standards for encrypted electronic mail: PGP and PEM. Observers say that the two standards may well merge with the Internet standard for multimedia electronic mail (called MIME).

Since PGP is widely distributed in source code form, PGP will almost certainly be modified to cope with the new standard when it is finally written.

2

Cryptography Basics

> *At the outbreak of the Second World War, possibly no shortage was more acute—or less publicized—than that of qualified cryptographers. Our military and naval forces are now spread over the two hemispheres. The secrecy of communications is vital. A cipher message speedily broken by the enemy may mean a major disaster for our forces.*
>
> —Laurence Dwight Smith in *Cryptography: The Science of Secret Writing*, 1941

This chapter explains the basic cryptography on which PGP is based and introduces some of the broader patent and export issues surrounding cryptography. Part II of this book discusses in greater detail how cryptography—and PGP itself—developed, and it further explores these policy issues.

How Does Simple Cryptography Work?

Instead of depending on good manners, common decency, and the force of law, encryption relies on a branch of mathematics called *cryptography* to protect the privacy of your messages.

Although the mathematics that make cryptography work are somewhat complicated, the principles behind cryptography are quite simple. Every practical encryption system consists of four fundamental parts:

- The message that you wish to encrypt (called the *plaintext*)

- The message after it is encrypted (called the *ciphertext*)

- The encryption algorithm, which is the mathematical function used to encrypt your message

- The key (or keys), which can be a number, a word, or a phrase that is used by the encryption algorithm

The goal of cryptography is to make it impossible to take a ciphertext and reproduce the original plaintext without the corresponding key.

Figure 2-1 illustrates in the simplest terms how these four fundamental parts fit together.

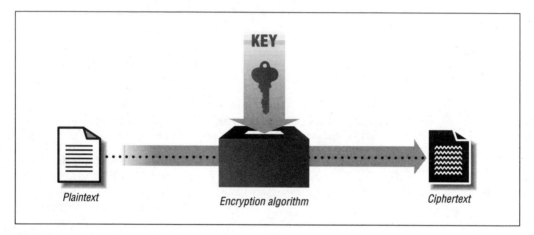

Figure 2-1. A simple example of encryption

Codes

The simplest way to send a secret message to someone is to use a prearranged secret code known only to the two of you.

For example, suppose the King of Plutonia has recently come upon a fleet of nuclear missiles. Being the ruler of a small country, the king does not want to invest in buying the computers and hiring the mathematicians necessary to make modern, twentieth-century codes that he can use to communicate with his army. To make matters worse, the king doesn't even have a copy of PGP! Fortunately, he needs to communicate only one of two messages to his army: "Launch the missiles" or "Don't launch the missiles." The king solves his problem by creating a simple codebook, which is depicted in the following table:

Code Word	Meaning
Mobius	Launch the missiles.
Zebra	Don't launch the missiles.

The king creates two copies of this codebook: he keeps one and gives the other to the head of his army, who is stationed inside a bunker at the missile silo. When the king calls the general, he speaks a single code word, and the general knows what to do. If the general hears "Mobius," he launches; if he hears "Zebra," he doesn't. (If he hears a third word, he knows that someone is trying to impersonate the king. In this circumstance, the general might want to launch the missiles at the palace!)

Codes like Plutonia's are unbreakable the first time they are used. There is no way that an eavesdropper could know beforehand each word and its meaning.

The problem with codes is that they lose security with each use. If an American foreign agent is intercepting the king's communications, it won't take long for the agent to realize the difference between the codes "Mobius" and "Zebra." With this in mind, the king might want to create a new codebook that has hundreds of codes for not firing the missiles: each day, he could use a different code. Such a code would remain unbreakable as long as each word was used only once.

Ciphers

Another problem with the codebook approach is that the king can send only a small set of prearranged messages. What if the king wants to send other messages, such as "Launch half the missiles" or "Attack our allies" or even "Disarm the missiles"? He can't.

The king doesn't need a code—he needs a cipher. A *cipher* is a technique for scrambling the letters of a message so they can be unscrambled by the intended recipient but remain indecipherable to eavesdroppers.

Substitution ciphers

The simplest ciphers are *substitution ciphers*, in which each letter of a message is substituted with a different letter. One well-known substitution cipher is the Caesar Cipher, which Julius Caesar allegedly used to communicate secretly from Gaul to Rome. To encode a message with the Caesar Cipher, simply shift the alphabet three places to the right. In the following example, the King of Plutonia uses a modified version of the Caesear cipher, shifting the alphabet ten places to the right:

```
A B C D E F G H I J K L M N O P Q R S T U V W X Y Z 0 1 2 3 4 5 6 7 8 9
0 1 2 3 4 5 6 7 8 9 A B C D E F G H I J K L M N O P Q R S T U V W X Y Z
```

The king could then code the message "LAUNCH THE MISSILES" as "B0KD27QJ74QC8II8B4I" (using the letter *Q* to denote spaces between words).

Ciphers like these have been used for a long time. During the Rennaissance and the Enlightenment, the Freemasons used a secret cipher (which they called a code). Figure 2-2 shows how this cipher is applied.

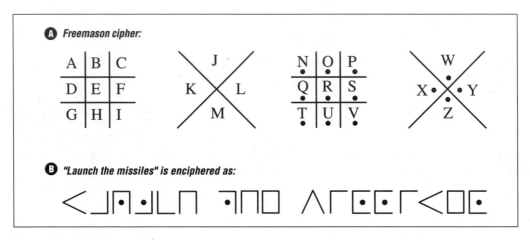

Figure 2-2. Freemason cipher

George Washington used a more sophisticated cipher in which each word was assigned a number. Figure 2-3 shows the first few words from Washington's codebook.

The problem with all of these ciphers is that they are much easier to crack than the king's original codebook. A codebreaker merely needs to collect several encrypted messages and then look for regularities. For an experienced cryptanalyst, just a few words may be enough to reveal all of the secrets.

One-Time Pads

The way to get the flexibiliy of a cipher and the security of a code that is used only once is to use a special kind of cipher called a *one-time pad* or a *Vernam cipher*.

One-time pads get their name from the pads of paper used by spies. Each page of the pad has a different codebook, as shown in Figure 2-4.

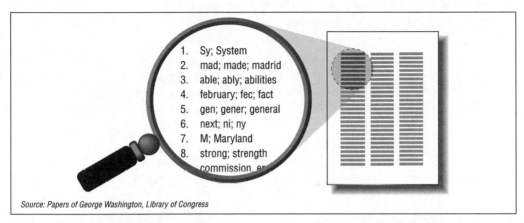

Source: Papers of George Washington, Library of Congress

Figure 2-3. George Washington's codebook

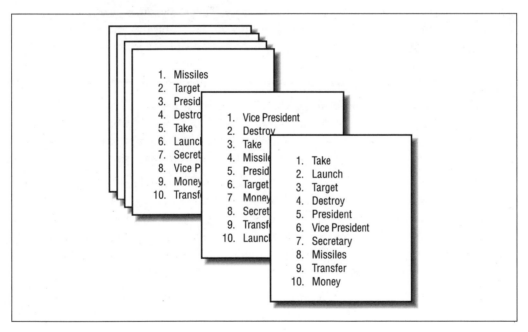

Figure 2-4. One-time pad

The spy would encrypt a few words with one page, rip the page from the pad, burn it, and then move to the next page. Eventually the entire message would be encrypted. The only way to decrypt the message would be with an identical one-time pad back at Spy Central.

Modern one-time pads don't use pads of paper; they use streams of numbers. For example, the king can turn his relatively insecure substitution cipher into an unbreakable one-time pad by giving his general the following book of numbers:

```
06 00 14 20 01 00 32 21 02 17 22 24 20 26 18 05 08 07 23 07 21 33 04 24 17 13
14 18 12 25 21 18 25 00 19 27 16 15 28 34 32 14 22 32 20 20 18 09 07 05 16 28
18 01 32 35 14 11 34 26 16 35 09 22 15 28 13 11 23 21 10 00 16 12 12 00 13 30
25 00 35 06 29 18 07 05 33 21 16 11 28 13 27 01 35 22 09 28 34 32 13 24 32 29
00 25 10 29 19 35 30 35 21 03 33 28 08 30 ...
```

Each number corresponds to one letter of an encrypted message: it tells the general how many places to shift each character of the encrypted message in order to decrypt it. Using the above one-time pad, the message "LAUNCH THE MISSILES" would encrypt as the following:

```
R A 8 7 D H W E J V M A 2 I A N T L F
```

As long the king uses a truly random number generator to create his one-time pad, the cipher it produces is theoretically secure. That's because the one-time pad produces a different substitution cipher for every letter of the message, and each substitution cipher is used exactly once. There is none of the redundancy necessary for breaking code.

Another way to think of it is like this: you need both the encrypted message and the matching one-time pad in order to produce the plaintext message. There exists a one-time pad that can convert the encrypted message into any conceivable plaintext of the same length. Only the original one-time pad used to encrypt the message and produce the ciphertext can reconstruct the original text from that same ciphertext.

In practice, one-time pads are used only in rare circumstances. It is rumored that the "hotline" between the White House and the Kremlin was encrypted with a one-time pad, as were the cable lines between the State Department and the U.S. Embassy in Moscow. In most circumstances, however, one-time pads are too unwieldy. It is expensive to transport the pads from Washington to Moscow and expensive to ensure that no one else obtains a copy in the process. So people make compromises.

One simple compromise that the King of Plutonia could make is to use only five numbers of his one-time pad for each message. The first number could be used to encrypt the first letter of his message, the second number could encrypt the second letter, and so on. When he reached the sixth letter, he would use the first number again, and so on. In this manner, the first five numbers of the king's one-time pad, 06 00 14 20 01, would become the *key* to his message. Naturally, such a system would be less secure.

Keys and Key Length

From the user's point of view, cryptographic keys are very similar to the passwords you use to operate automatic teller machines and to control access to computer systems. Simply type the correct key or password, and you can access your data. Enter the wrong key or password, and you can't.

Just as different computer systems allow passwords of different lengths, different encryption systems also use different length keys. And, as with passwords, the longer your key, the more security an encryption system generally provides.

Whereas the length of a password is usually measured in digits or letters, the length of a cryptographic key is almost always measured in bits (binary digits). A bit can be a 1 or a 0. A key that is two bits long can have one of four possible values: 00, 01, 10, or 11. The more bits that a particular cryptographic algorithm allows in its key, the more keys are possible, and the more secure the algorithm becomes. (However, this statement does not imply that an algorithm that has a 112-bit key is necessarily more secure than an algorithm that has a 56-bit key: there can be other mitigating factors, as we shall soon see.)

The following table shows the lengths of the keys for two systems you may be familiar with and, for each, the number of possible keys and the equivalent binary lengths.

System	Key Length	Number of Possible Keys	Equivalent Length
Automatic teller machine secret code	4 digits	10,000	~14 bits
UNIX passwords	8 characters	$126^8 = 6.3 \times 10^{16}$	~56 bits

Breaking the Code

There are several different ways that an adversary might try to decrypt a message that was encrypted with a cryptographic cipher ("breaking the code," in the vernacular).

Brute force (key search) attack

The simplest way to crack a code is by trying every possible key, one after another (assuming that the codebreaker has the means of recognizing the results of the correct key). Most attempts will fail, but eventually, one of the tries will succeed and either allow the cracker into the system or permit the ciphertext to be decrypted. These attacks, illustrated in Figure 2-5, are called *brute force attacks*.

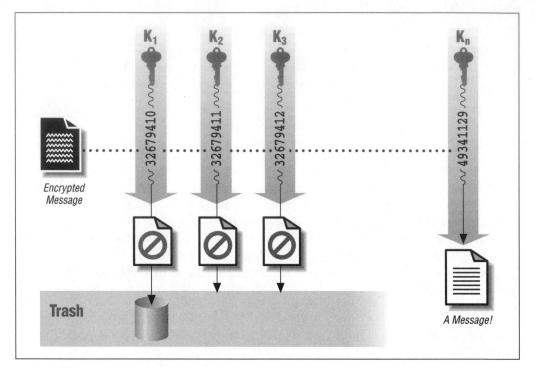

Figure 2-5. Brute force attack

Brute force attacks are also called *key search attacks* because they involve searching every possible key for the correct one.

Brute force attacks are not very efficient. Sometimes they are not even possible: often there are simply too many keys to try and not enough time to try them all. For example, one of the two encryption algorithms used by PGP is the IDEA algorithm, which has a 128-bit key for 2^{128} (3.4×10^{38}) possible keys. If a computer existed that could try a billion different keys in a second, and you had a billion of these computers, it would still take 10^{13} years to try every possible IDEA key. (This timespan is approximately a thousand times longer than the age of the universe, currently estimated at 1.2×10^{10} years.)

Cryptanalysis

If key length were the only factor determining how secure a cipher was, everyone interested in exchanging secret messages would simply use codes with 100-bit keys, and all cryptanalysts (people who break codes) would have to find new jobs. Cryptography would be a solved branch of mathematics, like simple addition.

What keeps cryptography interesting is the fact that most encryption algorithms do not live up to our expectations. Brute force attacks are seldom required to pummel a cipher into submission. Most algorithms can be defeated by using a combination of sophisticated mathematics and computer power. The result is that someone can decipher encrypted messages without knowing the key. A skillful cryptanalyst can sometimes decipher encrypted text without even knowing the encryption algorithm. Thus, keeping a bad encryption algorithm secret rarely improves the security of encrypted messages.

A cryptanalytic attack has two possible goals. The cryptanalyst might have ciphertext and want to discover the plaintext, or the cryptanalyst might have ciphertext and want to discover the encryption key that was used to encrypt it. (These goals are similar but not quite the same.) The following attacks are commonly used:

- *Known plaintext attack*

  In this type of attack, the cryptanalyst has a block of plaintext and a corresponding block of ciphertext. Although this may seem an unlikely occurrence, it is actually quite common when cryptography is used to protect electronic mail (with standard headers at the beginning of each message) or hard disks (with known structures at predetermined locations on the disk). The goal of a known plaintext attack is to determine the cryptographic key, which can then be used to decrypt other messages.

- *Chosen plaintext attack*

  In this type of attack, the cryptanalyst can have the subject of the attack unknowingly encrypt blocks of data, creating a result that the cryptanalyst can then analyze. Chosen plaintext attacks are simpler to carry out than they might appear. (For example, the subject of the attack might be a radio link that encrypts and retransmits messages received by telephone.) The goal of a chosen plaintext attack is to determine the cryptographic key, which can then be used to decrypt other messages.

- *Differential cryptanalysis*

  This attack, which is a kind of chosen plaintext attack, involves encrypting many texts that are only slightly different from one another and comparing the results.

Different encryption algorithms have different susceptibilities to these attacks. Algorithms that are difficult to crack are called *strong*; algorithms that are easily subverted are called *weak*.

It is very difficult to develop a new cryptographic algorithm. Not much is known about designing strong algorithms, and most of what is known is classified. There are many cases in which algorithms were proposed, implemented, and then discovered to have weaknesses. (One of the most spectacular cases was the VC-I video encryption algorithm used for early satellite TV broadcasts. For years video pirates sold decoder boxes that could intercept the transmissions of keys and used them to decrypt the broadcasts. This demonstrates that, when a lot of money is at stake, people *will* find the flaws in a weak encryption system and those flaws *will* be exploited.)

The only reliable way to determine if an algorithm is strong or weak is to publish the algorithm and wait for someone to find a weakness. This peer review process isn't perfect, but it's better than the alternative: no review at all. Do not trust people who say they've developed a new encryption algorithm, but they can't tell you how it works because the strength of the algorithm would be compromised. If the algorithm is being used to store information that is valuable, an attacker will purchase a copy of a program that implements the algorithm, disassemble the program, and figure out how it works. True cryptographic security lies in openness and peer review.

Private Key Cryptography

The type of cryptography that has been used for centuries, and the one used by the King of Plutonia in our examples, is known as *private key cryptography* or *secret key cryptography*. This name comes from the fact that both the sender and the recipient of a communication share a key, which must be kept private. If you want to communicate secretly with someone, you first have to tell that person the cryptographic key you are using for the communication. This process is called *key distribution* and is difficult to do properly. Because the key is literally the key to your security, you have to find a way of getting the key to the recipient of your secret message without having the key fall into the wrong hands. And if you have a secure means of sending the key, why not just send the message in the first place?

For years, the United States used couriers to distribute its cryptographic keys. A courier was given a locked briefcase filled with keys to encrypt diplomatic messages for the following month. The briefcase was handcuffed to the courier's wrist, and the courier would board an aircraft for some hostile land. At the destination, an embassy official greeted the courier, took him to the embassy, and unlocked the handcuffs (usually the courier did not have the ability to unlock the cuffs himself). If the courier was intercepted by enemy agents, officials in Washington soon found out and would know not to use the keys in the briefcase.

Private key cryptography is also known as *symmetric cryptography* because the same key is used on both sides of a communication. Symmetric cryptography is a handy phrase to know if you want to sound like a cryptography expert.

Private Key Algorithms

There are many private key algorithms. Some of the more popular are described briefly in the following list and in greater detail in later chapters:

DES

The Data Encryption Standard was adopted as a U.S. government standard in 1977 and as an ANSI standard in 1981. The DES uses a 56-bit key. The DES is a strong algorithm, but it is conjectured that a machine capable of breaking a DES-encrypted message in a few hours can be built for $1 million. Such machines probably exist, although no government or corporation admits to having one.

Triple-DES

Triple-DES is a way to make the DES twice as secure by using the DES encryption algorithm three times with two different keys. (Simply using the DES twice with two different keys does not improve its security because of what's called a "meet-in-the-middle" attack.) Triple-DES is currently being used by financial institutions to extend the life of the DES.

RC2, RC4[†]

Rivest's Code #2 and #4 are named after MIT Professor Ronald Rivest, the co-inventor of the RSA public key encryption algorithm. These algorithms are proprietary encryption algorithms distributed by RSA Data Security. They can be used with keys from 1 to 1024 bits in length. With a small key (fewer than 48 bits), these codes can be relatively easily broken. Since they are proprietary, no one knows how secure they are with longer keys. RC2 is a block cipher, similar to the DES. RC4 is a stream cipher; the algorithm produces a stream of pseudo-random numbers that are XORed with the message data.

An algorithm claiming to implement RC4 was anonymously posted to the Internet in September 1994; many experts were surprised by how simple the algorithm seemed.

IDEA

The International Data Encryption Algorithm is a block encryption algorithm developed in Zurich, Switzerland, by James L. Massey and Xuejia Lai and published in 1990. IDEA uses a 128-bit key. Since IDEA has not been around for long, no one knows if IDEA is secure. So far, the algorithm appears to be strong. (Massey is widely regarded as a world-class cryptographer.) IDEA's 128-bit key effectively eliminates the possibility of someone using computers as we understand them to implement a brute force attack.

---

† RC2 and RC4 are both registered trademarks of RSA Data Security, Inc., as are the trademarks RC1, RC3, RC5, RC6, RC7, RC8, and RC9. As of this writing, Ron Rivest has not yet created ciphers corresponding to each of the trademarked cipher names.

Skipjack

A secret algorithm developed by the National Security Agency for civilian use, the Skipjack algorithm is at the heart of the NSA's Clipper chip, described in Chapter 5. Skipjack uses an 80-bit key, making a brute force attack impossible for the next ten years. Skipjack may be secure, but Clipper is not; the Clipper chip is actually designed to allow law enforcement officials with court-ordered wiretaps to easily decrypt messages that are encrypted with the system.

A Private Key Example

Let's look at a simple example of private key cryptography. Suppose I have a message that I would like to send to a coworker:

Plaintext #1:

```
Congress shall make no law respecting an establishment of religion, or
prohibiting the free exercise thereof; or abridging the freedom of speech, or
of the press; or the right of the people peaceably to assemble, and to
petition the government for a redress of grievances.
```

Now I'll encrypt this message. In this case, I'll encrypt it with the key "nosmis" using the DES. The recipient of the message and I both know what this key is; in theory, no one else knows.

In printable characters, the resulting ciphertext looks like this:

Ciphertext #1 (encrypted with "nosmis"):

```
…0"!>GÜêSdÁF»…ìaj\5Æ…bX~˙        ,%vý»wi/ó4NüBü+Nàä)ZÈ
˙·ûyhäe+Ö,sêÎ+ø¸Å«ÛŒ¬H?˘Ëº
P@»ÚZ)ÿ
                                  =e=0Ä –Ù»ÙÀ§Y*~6lkC2àì®^M]oÿãó?`$%:-
v?Ù?EççaÚc!{mÒœ$^h3ERŒ'cT&p0öC;%Ú†•ß";…?z?¸Êä¤?„˘åë»ÚT?Ê"4†?ËYÚóÍíäu?ApL'4î¨m"-
Sà*{9Îm*¿ë?Òø2`Ï  Õª
Hæ®"s4,êMè?Ä
```

Now I'll encrypt the same message with the same encryption algorithm, but this time I'll use the word "asimov" as my encryption key. The encrypted text is still unreadable, but now it looks completely different.

Ciphertext #2 (encrypted with "asimov"):

```
êuîŒ„?«H            Èiou3JÍ œ^ño?Ó`^tà>kNLÑîJÑw?S(`´?gÔH<ô+˚
Yk4l,ÊÿÚºöc.?ØFenà?<Ñ&'·X??=Û"UhÃ9Wd©>=x'ón-
z?y;K?{ÍiP‰"êY,RWò>î´6ôxü\M˘PøÒ?4>`Î?¢é·¤aù˜zF?ú´?\m^JRt>Y"Ë@N^seùsã?g·?<
Él~6…˚fi âÆ
          »¿úcòH?[‡á`^F~Ù$ÕJåâêÜY
                                     ·[Ü".é~Sv(b0?0)f¬?FF?ÿ:x^kªpáJ'"¿
```

If I decrypt the first ciphertext with the key "nosmis", I get my original message:

Decrypted Text #1 (encrypted with "nosmis", decrypted with "nosmis"):

> Congress shall make no law respecting an establishment of religion, or
> prohibiting the free exercise thereof; or abridging the freedom of speech, or
> of the press; or the right of the people peaceably to assemble, and to
> petition the government for a redress of grievances.

On the other hand, if I decrypt the first ciphertext with the key "asimov", I'll just get garbage:

Decrypted Text #1 (encrypted with "nosmis", decrypted with "asimov"):

```
^?é5Ñnéi^`\?†v<è
*Ùx˙Éÿ˙%8TVK?ìço0̂1Ö, 92•RÂI< ?ß&C`??¢Á ʼVTʼ\ʼÃ?À=¿øìùân?ètLqÍi»ÖÂÇùxà95?‡å^Ç5%üp
zçk}¨,A~í3U2~Tì„Å?«n1?òJuÃŒt2?)ÛKŒfi(˝6fiÚbì

?fi`˙Sk2ËIA#Uq[? ʼW…?54ʼGÀÊÏ+åö˜Ë?
        ˙ÖhrBÙæ§ÓœDÉ[iª"?»#<„s+gM?Û]?Ûü=¯?˜Ú>àq̈j,^L˙øÅ      ˜®*œ
                                                        ?»?nÖñùû?ò·Ù
```

Incidentally, this example demonstrates how to stage a key search attack. Decrypt the ciphertext with every possible key until you get printable text. Then you've probably found the correct key.

Problems with Private Key Cryptography

Private key cryptography has been used extensively for military, intelligence, and financial and other business applications, but it has always had some clear problems. Most of the problems with private key cryptography have to do with the distribution of the keys.

Suppose that three people—Alice, Bob, and Chris—want to communicate securely using a private key system. They need only three keys: one shared by Alice and Bob, one shared by Bob and Chris, and one shared by Alice and Chris. Figure 2-6 illustrates a secure communication system for three people using private key cryptography.

The situation gets more complicated when Dawn and Eric join the system; now they need ten keys, as shown in Figure 2-7.

In general, if n people want to communicate securely using this system, they'll need $\frac{(n)(n-1)}{2}$ keys. For a city with 60,000 people, that's 1,799,970,000 keys. Think of the expense of distributing all of those keys—and most of them will never be used!

A second problem with private key is that it is impossible to send someone a secret message unless you already have the ability to send her a secret message—that is, you can't communicate with someone without prior arrangement.

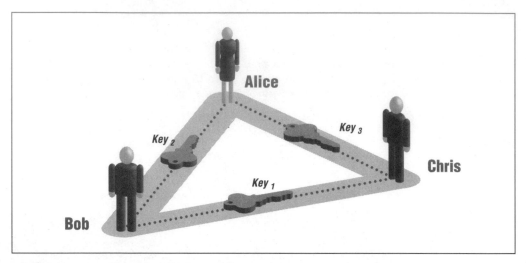

Figure 2-6. Private key cryptography with three people

The Key Distribution Center

One way around both of these problems is to use a key distribution center (KDC), which manufactures keys and distributes them to any pair of individuals who wish to communicate, as shown in Figure 2-8.

When Chris wants to talk to Dawn, he calls the KDC. The KDC rolls a few dice and hands out a *session key* to both Chris and Dawn, who can then have a private conversation. (To make this system work properly, both Chris and Dawn need their own private keys that are on file at the KDC. When the KDC sends the session key to Chris, the key is actually encrypted with Chris' secret key. Similarly, the session key that the KDC sends to Dawn is encrypted with Dawn's secret key.) Figure 2-9 shows how this system works.

This system is the one that the U.S. government has used for years to distribute the keys employed by the military and intelligence agencies; the National Security Agency makes the keys and distributes them. The main problem with a key distribution center is that it is relatively easy to subvert: you could simply bribe the people who hand out the keys, and neither Alice nor Dawn would be the wiser.

This scenario isn't just conjecture: a recent spy case involved an NSA agent named Ronald W. Pelton. The spy's crime, which went undetected for years, was not selling secrets, but selling cryptographic keys, to the enemy.

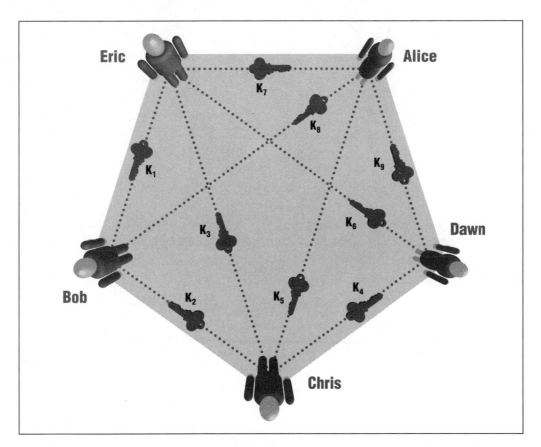

Figure 2 7. Private key cryptography with five people

The Outlook for Private Key

The net result of the vulnerabilities I've discussed is that private key cryptography is simply impractical for ordinary people to use in daily operation. If private key cryptography were the only form of cryptography available, cryptography would remain forever the tool of governments and large corporations, and private citizens would be condemned to insecure communications.

Fortunately, it's not, and neither are we.

Public Key Cryptography

In the 1970s, a mathematical breakthrough astounded cryptographers and the world of defense intelligence agencies. That breakthrough has since come to be known as *public key cryptography.*

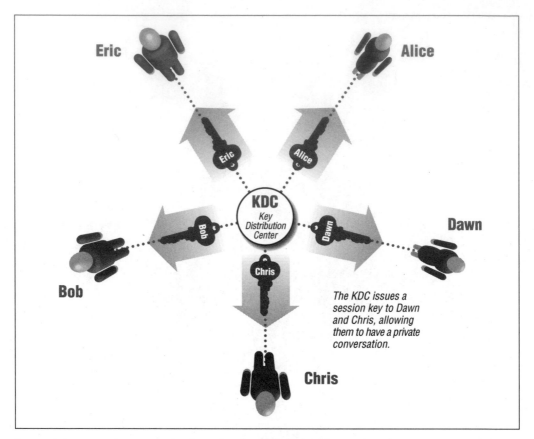

Figure 2-8. Private key cryptography with a key distribution center (KDC)

Public key cryptography turns traditional cryptography on its head. With private key systems, a single cryptography key is shared by two individuals. Both use the same key to encrypt and decrypt their messages for each other. With public key systems, a mathematical process generates two mathematically related keys for each individual. A message encrypted with one key can be decrypted only with the other key. The first key is the *public key*, and the other is the *secret key*. The public key can be known to anyone, but the secret key must be kept secret. When you encrypt a message for Alice to read, you encrypt it with her public key. When Alice receives the message, she decrypts it with her secret key. Although there are additional complexities that I'll describe, that's basically how public key cryptography works.

Public key cryptography is also called *asymmetric cryptography.*

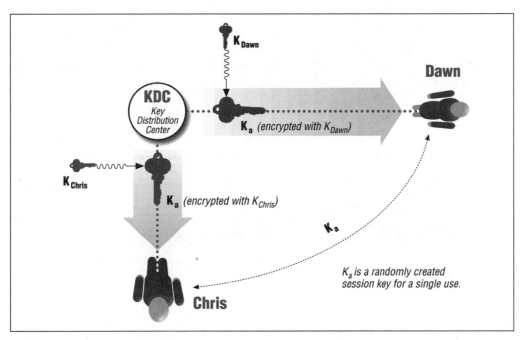

Figure 2-9. A session key from the KDC allows secure communication

Public Key Systems

The first public key system was described in 1976 by Whitfield Diffie and Martin Hellman. A short time later, two different systems were proposed: one by Diffie and Hellman, the other by Ronald Rivest, Adi Shamir, and Len Adleman. Another system was developed by Ralph Merkle and Martin Hellman. The main public key algorithms are described briefly in the following list and in greater detail in later chapters.

Diffie-Hellman

The Diffie-Hellman system was designed to be used by two active participants in a conversation. Each participant starts with her own secret key. Then, by exchanging information based on their secret keys, the participants can derive a third key called the *session key*, which they use to encrypt all of their future messages. Since an eavesdropper does not participate in the exchange, he can't determine the session key.

RSA

The RSA algorithm encrypts information with a readily available public key; the information can be decrypted only by someone who possesses the matching private key. RSA can also be used as a digital signature system. RSA is one of the most powerful forms of public key cryptography yet seen. RSA is the public key system used by PGP.

Merkle-Hellman

The Merkle-Hellman knapsack system was based on a mathematical game called the "knapsack" problem: given a collection of items, each with a different weight, can you pack a knapsack so it has a particular weight? Knapsack was explored for a number of years; eventually, a fatal flaw was discovered in the algorithm, which renders it useless for practical purposes.

Figure 2-10 shows a simple example of public key cryptography.

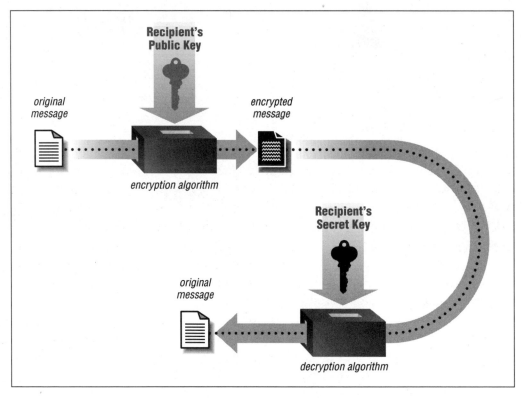

Figure 2-10. Public key cryptography

Advantages of Public Key Systems

Public key systems have a major advantage over private key systems. As the name suggests, with public key systems you can make your encryption key *public*. You can give it to your friends; you can shout it from the rooftops. With a public key system, anyone can use your key to encrypt a message and send it to you. No one who intercepts that message can do anything with it because you alone possess your secret key.

One of the implications of this aspect of public key cryptography is that you can publish your public key. In contrast to private key cryptography, which requires that you and your friend or colleague exchange a key ahead of time, public key cryptography makes it possible for people you have never met to send you encrypted electronic mail. For example, you might publish your public key in an electronic phone book that lists thousands of public keys for people all over the world. Or you might put it on your stationery or your business card. You might even publish it in a book that you write. That's what I did in Chapter 1.

Digital Signatures

Public key cryptography provides more than conventional private key cryptography. It gives you the ability to sign your messages with a digital signature. "Digital Signatures" in Chapter 1 explains what digital signatures are good for and shows briefly how you create them with PGP.

Using Private and Public Key Cryptography Together

I've finessed one important fact about PGP in this discussion. PGP actually uses both public key cryptography *and* private key cryptography. As Chapter 1 briefly explained, PGP creates a random session key for each message, uses the private key IDEA algorithm to encrypt the message with the session key, then uses the public key RSA algorithm to encrypt the session key with the recipient's public key. Finally, PGP bundles the encrypted message and the session key together for mailing. In later chapters, I explain in greater detail how PGP works.

How Good is Cryptography?

How can you tell what type of cryptography is effective and appropriate for you or your organization? What are the limits of cryptography? This section briefly discusses these issues.

The Strong and the Weak

There are two kinds of cryptography: good and bogus.

Good cryptography is strong cryptography. With good cryptography, your messages are encrypted in such a way that brute force attacks against the algorithm or the key are all but impossible. Good cryptography gets its security by using incredibly long keys (so long that it would take millions of years to try them all) and by using encryption algorithms that are resistant to other (cryptanalytic) forms of attack.

Bogus cryptography is the kind of cryptography you get from using the secret decoder rings that used to come free in cereal boxes. Unfortunately, it's also the kind of cryptography used by the majority of shrink-wrapped application programs on the market today. Bogus cryptography might use a very short key, making it possible to search all possible keys in just a few seconds. Or the program might not even use a key; it might simply put a password on the disk or in a file and refuse to open the file unless the user types a password that matches. Alternatively, bogus cryptography might use a very long key but have an easy-to-crack algorithm. (Such is the case with *crypt*, a popular UNIX encryption utility.)

How can you tell the difference between the good and the bogus systems? You probably can't. Many cryptographic systems that look secure can actually be broken by a trained expert in a reasonable amount of time. A commercially available cracking program can break the cryptography used by many commercially available programs. There are even cases of crypto systems that appeared strong to experts but nevertheless contained hidden flaws that allowed people to exploit them and decrypt encrypted transmissions. (Such was the case with the German Enigma cipher during World War II.)

A few years ago, cryptography was regarded by many people as a black art, required only by governments and major corporations. Times have changed. The widespread use of personal computers, the tendency of these computers to be stolen, and the increasing prevalence of electronic mail have led many people to demand cryptography for both their business and their personal lives.

The market has been quick to respond. In recent years, dozens of crypto systems for personal computers, workstations, and mainframes have become readily available. Standalone crypto products, such as secure telephones and fax machines, can also be readily purchased in the United States and abroad.

But "readily available" doesn't necessarily translate into quality and security. Most cryptography experts can find readily apparent flaws in a new cryptography system, but just because a flaw can't be found doesn't mean that the flaw doesn't exist. That has caused problems because cryptography isn't free, and good cryptography algorithms are difficult to write. Good algorithms also require time to encrypt and decrypt the user's data; bogus crypto systems are usually faster than good ones. Many of the best crypto systems are patented, adding to the expense of using them. As a result, many of the products that perform encryption use cryptographic algorithms that are weak or marginal at best.

Generally, the safest way to tell if your program's encryption system is strong or bogus is to rely on brand names—not brand names of software companies but brand names of encryption systems. Strong cryptography systems are usually the systems that have been published, discussed extensively, and analyzed by experts. Two private key systems in this category are the DES and IDEA. These systems rely on the secrecy of the cryptographic key for their security. As a result, when a company says that its product uses the DES, you know theoretically how much security the program can offer. (Of course, the company may have goofed on its implementation of the DES algorithm, or it may have a protocol that accidentally or intentionally reveals the key used to encrypt messages. You never know.)

Many companies claim that their programs use proprietary encryption algorithms. These companies assure you that their algorithms are secure but nevertheless won't reveal the algorithms that their products use. Ask them for details, and you're likely to be told, "If we told you, then the program would be less secure." You should avoid these programs; usually, the companies don't reveal their encryption systems because they are embarrassed by how easily the systems are broken. Remember, if the security of the encryption system really depended on the secrecy of the algorithm, a determined attacker would merely have to buy a copy of the product and disassemble the program in order to learn how it worked. He'd then be able to decrypt personal communications.

The first version of PGP used a symmetric cipher developed by Phil Zimmermann called Bass-O-Matic (named for the blender on the "Saturday Night Live" TV show that produced bass puree from a whole bass!). It was not very secure, as I discuss in Chapter 4. Version 2.0 of PGP uses the IDEA cipher. While IDEA has not been subject to the same extensive analysis as the DES, many cryptographers believe that it offers a high level of security. Certainly many graduate students in mathematics have explored the algorithm looking for holes, because fame and recognition (and possibly a Ph.D. thesis) awaits anyone who finds a serious flaw in the algorithm.

How secure are the messages you encrypt with PGP? It appears that they are *very secure*. For all practical purposes, PGP-encrypted messages are unbreakable. As you will see, the security of the programs described in this book is so good that all of the computers in the world working together for a hundred years could not break a message encrypted with these algorithms. At least, that is what most mathematicians familiar with cryptography believe today.

Indeed, if you are using encryption, then *you* are probably the weakest link in the entire system. To ensure the absolute security of your messages, you must keep your secret key secret. You must refuse to divulge it to anyone who asks for it. If you are kidnapped and threatened, you might have to die to keep your message secure!

The Case for Weakness

Is there anything wrong with using weak cryptography? The answer to this question depends on why you are using cryptography in the first place. If your reason for using cryptography is to prevent your children or a colleague from casually reading the contents of a file, you might not need much in the way of sophisticated crypto-graphic protection (depending on the sophistication of your children and colleagues, of course).

Certainly there are applications for weak cryptography; weak cryptosystems are perhaps sufficient for businesses that don't really care about the privacy of their communications but want to claim in their advertisements that they use encryption. Weak cryptography is usually faster than strong cryptography; it is also usually cheaper, because most companies that use weak encryption are using algorithms that they developed themselves. If you want to give people the *impression* that you are using cryptography, but you are really not interested in protecting information, then by all means, use weak cryptography.

However, if you are trying to defend your information against someone who might possess even a small amount of technical skill or might have the financial incentive to read your messages, then weak cryptography is worthless. It is easier to break codes than make them. Even if your adversary isn't a cryptography genius, many people are, and some of these people have written programs that are readily available on public bulletin board systems. For any reasonably determined adversary, weak cryptography presents little more challenge than a cheap lock on a file cabinet.

What Encryption Can't Do

Cryptography is a powerful system for protecting your privacy, but it isn't a panacea. You can use the best cryptography that's theoretically possible, but if you're not careful, you'll still be vulnerable to having your confidential documents and messages published on the front page of the *New York Times*. Likewise, cryptography isn't an appropriate solution for many problems, including the following:

*   *Cryptography can't protect your unencrypted documents.*

Even after you encrypt files, the unencrypted versions of the files remain on your computer. Unless you delete those files (taking precautions so that the files cannot be "unerased" with a suitable utility), your original files and messages are vulnerable to attackers who have physical access to your machine.

- *Cryptography can't protect against stolen encryption keys.*

  The whole point of using encryption is to make it possible for people who have your encryption keys to decrypt your files or messages. Thus, any attacker who can steal or purchase your keys can decrypt your files and messages.

- *Cryptography can't protect against destructive attacks.*

  Sometimes, an attacker doesn't want to read your files—she just wants to keep you from reading them. Even if an attacker can't get access to your crypto keys, she can cause you a lot of pain and suffering by erasing your documents or putting a screwdriver through your hard drive.

- *Cryptography can't protect against a booby-trapped encryption program.*

  Someone can modify your encryption program to make it worse than worthless. For example, an attacker could modify your encryption program to hide at the beginning of every encrypted file the secret key necessary to decrypt that file. Or he might modify your encryption program so that every file it encrypts is also sent by electronic mail to a computer in Finland. Or the encryption program might spawn network "daemons" that listen on a hidden network port and then, when they get a connection, allow someone to gain control of your machine.

  Fundamentally, unless you write all of the programs that run on your computer, there is no way to completely eliminate these possibilities. They exist whether you are using encryption or not.

- *Cryptography can't protect you against a traitor.*

  Human beings are the weakest link in your system. Your cryptography system can't protect you if your correspondent is taking your messages and sending them to the newspapers after legitimately decrypting them.

- *Cryptography can't protect you against the record of a message or the fact that a message was sent.* (In cryptanalysis, the study of such information is called *traffic analysis.*)

  Suppose that you send an encrypted message to Blake Johnson, and Blake murders your lover's spouse, and then you send another encrypted message to Blake. A reasonable person might suspect that you have some involvement in the murder, even if that person can't read the contents of your messages.

U.S. Restrictions on Cryptography

There are two important restrictions on the use of cryptography in the United States that have limited its availability. These restrictions concern patents and export controls.

Cryptography and the U.S. Patent System

Patents applied to computer programs, frequently called *software patents*, are the subject of ongoing controversy in the computer industry and in parts of Congress. As the number of software patents issued has steadily grown each year, the U.S. Patent and Trademark Office has come under increasing attack for granting too many patents for products that are apparently neither new nor novel.

Some of the earliest and most important software patents granted in the United States were in the field of public key cryptography. (I describe these patents in Chapter 3, *Cryptography Before PGP*, and in Chapter 6, *Cryptography Patents and Export*.) As a result, patents have played a role in public key cryptography from the very beginning.

The public key cryptography patents are now all exclusively licensed to Public Key Partners (PKP), a small company based in Redwood City, California.[†] Under U.S. patent law, a patent holder (or an exclusive licensee) can forbid anyone else from making, using, selling, or importing any device that contains a patented invention. However, patent infringement is not illegal: the penalties and damages are the jurisdiction of the civil courts, not the criminal courts.

Within the United States, practically every program that uses public key encryption comes with a license for the RSA and Stanford public key encryption patents. This is the case with programs such as Lotus Notes, Apple Macintosh System 7.5, and many products for Microsoft Windows. Nevertheless, encryption is still a novelty in many U.S. programs. Some people think that the added transaction costs, license fees, and difficulty in obtaining a license from PKP has kept encryption from attaining its full potential. Still, millions of copies of programs now use some form of encryption licensed either from PKP or from RSA Data Security.

The situation is very different overseas. Few countries outside the United States have granted patents on RSA or public key encryption because the RSA algorithm was described in print before its inventors filed for a patent. As a result, most firms in Europe and Japan can use most kinds of encryption without the trouble of negotiating a patent license and without the fear of costly patent infringement suits.

Chapter 6 of this book discusses the public key cryptography patents and the situation with Public Key Partners in detail.

---

† But a series of lawsuits filed in 1994 may jeopardize the PKP alliance; see Chapter 6 for details.

Cryptography and Export Controls

If you have fallen in love with PGP and are thinking of sending a copy of it to your grandmother in China (so you can exchange email with her without having it be read by the authorities), better think twice. Sending a copy of PGP out of the United States might subject you to a $1 million fine, ten years in jail, or both.

Under current U.S. law, cryptography is a munition, and the exportation of crypto-graphic machines (such as computer programs that implement cryptography) is covered by the Defense Trade Regulations (formerly known as the International Traffic in Arms Regulation—ITAR). In order to export a program that implements cryptography, you need a license from the office of Defense Trade Controls (DTC) in the State Department.

To get a license to export a program, you first must obtain an evaluation of the program from DTC. In practice, these decisions are actually made by the National Security Agency. Historically, programs that implement weak cryptography are allowed to be exported; those with strong cryptography, such as the DES, are denied export licenses.

A 1993 survey by the Software Publishers Association (SPA), a United States–based industry advocacy group, found that encryption is widely available in overseas computer products and its use is growing. The association noted the existence of more than 250 products distributed overseas containing cryptography. A lot of these products use technologies that are patented in the United States. (You can buy high-quality programs that implement RSA encryption literally on the streets of Moscow.)

Most European countries used to have similar regulations regarding software. Many were discarded in the early 1990s in favor of more liberal policies that allow mass market software to be freely traded.

In 1992, SPA and the State Department reached an agreement that allows the exporta-tion of programs containing RSA Data Security's RC2 and RC4 algorithms but only when the key size is set to 40 bits or less. These key sizes are not very secure.

Canada is an interesting case in the field of export control. Under current U.S. policy, any cryptographic software can be directly exported to Canada without an export license. Canada has also liberalized its export policy, allowing any Canadian-made cryptographic software to be exported abroad. But software that is exported to Canada cannot then be exported to a third country, thanks to Canada's Rule #5100, which honors U.S. export prohibitions on "all goods originating in the United States" unless they have been "further processed or manufactured outside the United States so as to result in a substantial change in value, form, or use of the goods or in the production of new goods."

Several companies are now avoiding the hassle of export controls by developing their software overseas and then importing the products back *into* the United States.

What about your grandmother in China? If you are using PGP, there is a simple way around export control: use PGP Version 2.6 (or above) inside the United States to communicate with people using PGP Version 2.6ui outside the United States. Since PGP Version 2.6 is readily available in the United States and PGP Version 2.6ui is readily available outside the United States, and since both versions readily interoperate, the U.S. laws restricting the export of cryptography won't hamper your efforts to communicate privately worldwide.

Cryptography History and Policy

This part of the book tells the human story of the development of cryptography and PGP. It contains the following chapters:

- Chapter 3, *Cryptography Before PGP*, is an abbreviated historical account of the science of cryptography before PGP came onto the scene.

- Chapter 4, *A Pretty Good History of PGP*, covers the history of PGP and the legal and political battles that have beset it.

- Chapter 5, *Privacy and Public Policy*, discusses government policies and the politics surrounding electronic privacy in the United States.

- Chapter 6, *Cryptography Patents and Export*, describes how cryptographic patents affect and are affected by U.S. government policies, outlines recent legal challenges to the patents, and briefly describes the current U.S. export policy on cryptography.

3

Cryptography Before PGP

> *Intelligence agencies have access to good cryptographic technology. So do the big arms and drug traffickers. So do defense contractors, oil companies, and other corporate giants. But ordinary people and grass roots political organizations mostly have not had access to affordable 'military grade' public-key cryptographic technology. . . . Until now.*
>
> —Phil Zimmermann in the *PGP User's Guide*, 1994

Many users of PGP know that Phil Zimmermann, a computer cryptography consultant in Boulder, Colorado, wrote PGP and released it in 1991, at the time that the U.S. Senate was considering a bill that would have effectively outlawed the use of strong cryptography in the United States. While these are the bare facts of how PGP came into being, the complete history of PGP is more complex and interesting.

This chapter describes the basic history of private key and public key cryptography. Chapter 4 focuses on the history of PGP itself.

Cryptography Through the Ages

Encryption is a method of information protection that dates back four thousand years; it's an ancient art that's taken on new significance in today's information society.

Through the ages, encryption has protected communications while they were being transmitted through hostile environments—usually involving war or diplomacy. The earliest ciphers date back to early Egyptian days, around 2000 B.C., when hieroglyphic funeral messages were carved in stone. In his monumental work, *The Codebreakers*, David Kahn traces the history of cryptography from ancient Egypt to India, Mesopotamia, Babylon, Greece, and to Western civilization and eventually modern times.

Although cryptography has always been of interest to some private citizens, it has been a central part of war and politics. Consider the case of Mary, Queen of Scots, who lost her life in the sixteenth century because an encrypted message she sent from prison was intercepted and deciphered. (Mary didn't use strong cryptography!) During the American Revolution, Benedict Arnold used a codebook cipher to communicate with the British.

In modern times, the invention of the telegraph and the discovery of radio waves increased the need for cryptography. Telegraph and radio allow virtually instantaneous communications among the different branches of an army or between an army and its command. But without cryptography, all of these communications can easily be monitored by spies with only a basic knowledge of wiretapping (in the case of telegraph communications) or directly by the enemy (in the case of radio). Without cryptography to keep messages indecipherable, military communications by telegraph and radio are worse than useless. Codebooks, and eventually cryptography itself, made electronic communications workable for the world's armies.

Cryptography owes its biggest boom to the scientific mobilization of World War II. The world's first digital computers were built to crack codes. Under the direction of Alan Turing in Britain, the Allies embarked on a monumental effort to break the Enigma code used by the Germans. Many people credit this effort with shortening the war. (For a complete discussion of the Enigma, see David Kahn's *Seizing the Enigma* or the biography of Turing by Andrew Hodges, *Alan Turing: The Enigma*.)

National Security and the NSA

After the war, the center of cryptographic activity in the world moved to the National Security Agency (NSA), a branch of the Department of Defense located at Fort Meade, Maryland, a half-hour's drive from Washington D.C. The NSA is among the most secret of agencies within the federal government. Until recently, its existence was publicly denied. (People who worked there joked that the initials actually stood for "No Such Agency" or "Never Say Anything.") The agency is so secret that its budget is classified.

What is known about the NSA is that it employs more mathematicians than any other organization in the world. The NSA is also the largest purchaser of computer equipment in the world. The NSA is also rumored to eavesdrop on more telephone conversations than anyone else in the world.

The NSA was created in 1952, by order of President Harry Truman, as the successor to the Armed Forces Security Agency. (Prior to Pearl Harbor, the U.S. military lacked a unified intelligence agency. A Congressional investigation after the surprise attack

National Security Agency
*(photo courtesy of Public Affairs
Office, National Security
Agency)*

concluded that the lack of a centralized intelligence agency was one of the factors that allowed the Japanese to catch the U.S. armed forces unaware.)

Although the NSA's charter is classified, it is widely believed that the agency has two missions: protecting U.S. executive and military communications from interception and intercepting and decoding communications belonging to other governments. To aid in these missions, the NSA operates a global intelligence network to supply agency analysts with information. The agency receives information from human intelligence sources, electronic interception, spy satellites, and other means. One of the most in-depth descriptions of the NSA and its activities is James Bamford's 1982 best-seller, *The Puzzle Palace.*

To read Bamford's book is to realize the extent to which the NSA has shaped the U.S. computer industry and, by extension, the world. "NSA certainly hastened the start of the computer age," Bamford quotes an agency official. In 1957 the agency initiated Project Lightning, a five-year, $25 million effort to increase the speed of electronic circuitry by a factor of 100. The project, one of the agency's few experiments in an open research initiative, resulted in more than 160 technical articles, 320 patent applications, and 71 university theses. For example, in the years that followed, the NSA became an eager customer for the fastest computer that the industry could offer. According to Bamford, IBM's early Stretch computer was so fast and so expensive that IBM thought there would only be two customers for it: the NSA to break codes and the Atomic Energy Commission to design nuclear weapons.

As recently as 1984, the NSA measured its total computer capacity not in MIPS, not in MFLOPS, but in *acres*. Indeed, for years the NSA was able to use the promise of the world's fastest computers as a lure for the nation's brightest college graduates.

The NSA continues to have a profound effect on the development and use of cryptography in this country and, as you'll see in Chapter 5, *Privacy and Public Policy*, on public policy as well.

Lucifer and the DES

For years the interest in codes and ciphers at the NSA was echoed outside the government as well. Cryptograms—simple word substitution ciphers—have been printed in newspapers and puzzle books for nearly a hundred years. The lay press has also published a steady stream of books on cryptography, each claiming to teach the basics: transposition ciphers, substitution ciphers, codes, and basic cryptanalysis.

Despite the keen civilian interest in cryptography, not much was known about strong, practical cryptosystems because not much needed to be known; most civilian communications took place on paper, for which envelopes and sealing wax provided adequate security.

The revolution in computers and electronic communications fueled the need for civilian research on cryptography. As wired and wireless communications grew financially in reach of companies and individuals, they discovered the same need for encryption that the government had long recognized.

In the late 1960s, IBM's chairman Thomas Watson, Jr., set up a cryptography research group at his company's Yorktown Heights research laboratory in New York. The group, led by Horst Feistel, developed a private key encryption system called "Lucifer." According to Bamford, IBM's first customer for Lucifer was Lloyd's of London, which bought the code in 1971 to protect a cash-dispensing system that IBM had developed for the insurance conglomerate.

Pleased by the initial sale, IBM created a group to turn the cipher into a commercial product. The team was headed by Dr. Walter Tuchman, a 38-year-old engineer with a doctorate in information theory, and Dr. Carl Meyer, a 42-year-old electrical engineer. The two set out to put Lucifer on a silicon chip. In the process, they submitted the algorithm to numerous tests, discovered some flaws, and strengthened the cipher against cryptanalytic attacks. They also received several U.S. patents (numbers 3,798,359, 3,798,360, 3,798,605, and 3,796,830). By 1974 the cipher algorithm and chip were ready for market.

IBM's experience with Lucifer was not unique in private industry. According to Bruce Schneier, author of the landmark work, *Applied Cryptography*, other companies sold codes and ciphers at the time, mostly to overseas governments. "They were all different; none of the devices could communicate with each other. And no one really knew if they were secure or not; there was no independent body to certify their security."

The National Bureau of Standards

Things were about to change. In 1968 the National Bureau of Standards (NBS—since renamed the National Institute of Standards and Technology, or NIST) began a series of studies aimed at determining the U.S. civilian and government needs for computer security. One of the results of those studies was the realization that the nation needed a single, interoperable standard for data encryption that could be used for both the storage and the transmission of unclassified data. (Classified data was still the province of the NSA.)

On May 15, 1973, the NBS published a request for proposals in the *Federal Register*. The bureau listed several requirements for the algorithm, including the following:

- The algorithm had to provide a high level of security.

- The algorithm had to be public, completely specified, and easy to understand.

- The security of the algorithm had to reside completely in the key, and not in the algorithm itself.

- The algorithm had to be available to all users.

- The algorithm had to be flexible, so it could be adapted to many different kinds of applications.

- The implementation of the algorithm in electronic devices had to be cost-effective.

- The algorithm had to be efficient.

- It had to be possible to validate the algorithm.

- The algorithm and devices containing the algorithm had to be exportable.

Schneier writes, "Public response indicated that there was considerable interest in a cryptographic standard, but that there was little public expertise in the field. Some mathematicians sent in crude outlines of algorithms. None of the submissions came close to meeting the requirement."

The NBS issued a second request in the August 27, 1974, *Federal Register*. This time they received one promising candidate: a version of the Lucifer algorithm that had been weakened in some ways and strengthened in other ways by the NSA. It was this algorithm that became the U.S. Data Encryption Standard (DES).

The NSA had known about Lucifer from the start of the project. According to Alan Konheim, a senior employee at IBM's Yorktown Heights laboratory (as reported by Bamford), "IBM was involved with the NSA on an ongoing basis. . . . [NSA employees] came up every couple of months to find out what IBM was doing."

There has been a lot of debate about whether the NSA involvement with Lucifer resulted in a weaker overall algorithm.[†] What is known is that IBM's original Lucifer algorithm used a key that was 128 bits in length, but after a number of closed-door negotiations with officials at NSA, IBM reduced the size of the key to 56 bits and changed the contents of some of the algorithm's eight substitution boxes (S-boxes). IBM also allowed NSA to classify the details of how the S-boxes used by the algorithm were designed. The resulting algorithm was accepted by NBS, published on March 17, 1975, in the *Federal Register*, and formally adopted on November 23, 1976, for use in all unclassified government communications. The actual document was published as a Federal Information Processing Standard (FIPS PUB 46).

The Security of the DES

How secure is the DES?

On the surface, the Data Encryption Standard appears to be a weaker cipher than the Lucifer cipher on which it was based. According to Bamford, cryptography historian David Kahn theorized that the DES had caused a secret debate within the NSA. "The codebreaking side wanted to make sure that the cipher was weak enough for the NSA to solve it when used by foreign nations and companies. . . . The codemaking side wanted any cipher it was certifying for use by Americans to be truly good. The upshot was a bureaucratic compromise. Part of the cipher—the 'S-boxes' that performed a substitution—was strengthened. Another part—the key that varied from one pair of users to another—was weakened."

Certainly, a 56-bit key is substantially weaker than a key that is 128 bits in length when other factors are held constant. Using a brute force or key search attack to crack a Lucifer-encrypted message with a key size of 128 bits was clearly impossible with 1976 technology, whereas a brute force attack against a 56-bit key was just barely possible. Less than two decades later, with all other factors held constant, building a machine that can crack a DES-encrypted message using a key search attack is merely an exercise in engineering, whereas a 128-bit key remains in the realm of science fiction.

But all other factors were *not* held constant. Other potential weaknesses in Lucifer have been uncovered over time, and it is not known whether the NSA might have been aware of these weaknesses at the time the algorithm was first proposed. In 1992 Eli Biham and Adi Shamir (both at the Weizmann Institute in Israel) published a paper showing that a weakened version of Lucifer (using 32-bit blocks instead of 128-bit blocks and 8 rounds instead of 16) could be broken with 40 chosen plaintexts and 2^{29} (536,870,912) steps using differential cryptanalysis. Since the NSA claims to have

---

[†] A U.S. Senate panel investigated the charges and upheld the integrity of the DES.

known about differential cryptanalysis for many years before the publication of the technique in the academic press, it is possible that the NSA discovered these flaws in Lucifer early on and did, in fact, strengthen the S-boxes against such attacks.

In May 1994, Don Coppersmith published an article in the *IBM Journal of Research and Development*, which describes the DES design criteria and the mechanisms of attacking the cipher. The article is recommended reading for anyone who wants to know the inside story on the DES.

DES Cracking

At the 1993 Crypto Conference (held annually at the University of California at Santa Barbara), Michael Wiener of Bell Northern Research presented a paper that described how to build a special-purpose machine to crack the DES. The machine is based on a special DES-cracking chip that tries 50 million DES keys every second. Wiener says the chip can be manufactured for $10.50 (based on a bid from an outside chip manufacturer). Thus, for $1 million a machine can be built that tries every DES key in seven hours. The machine might get lucky and find the solution to one code in just a few minutes; on average, it takes just 3.5 hours to crack any DES-encrypted message. Even better, the machine scales. For $10 million, a machine can be built that can crack any DES message in just 21 minutes. For $100 million, DES messages can be cracked in just two minutes.

These prices are considerably less than the amount of money that the NSA allegedly spends on computers each year. Given this fact, and the additional fact that part of the NSA's charter is rumored to be cracking codes, it is unreasonable to think that the NSA has not built such a machine. The NSA may have several of them. (Indeed, the NSA would not be fulfilling its taxpayer-funded mission if it has *not* built such a machine.) It's even possible that major corporations may have built them. (Wiener's own company has stated publicly that it hasn't.)

But you don't need a special-purpose multimillion-dollar machine to crack the DES. DES-encrypted messages can be cracked with conventional computers: you just have to wait longer. Table 3-1 gives estimates on the maximum time it would take to break a DES-encrypted message using brute force on a conventional computer. (Remember, these are brute force attacks; attacks based on differential cryptanalysis or other kinds of mathematics might be considerably faster.)

At the Crypto '94 conference, M. Matsui presented a new DES-breaking technique called "linear cryptanalysis." Using 2^{43} (8,796,093,022,208) known ciphertexts, he was able to break a DES key in 50 days with a desktop workstation.

Table 3-1. Time required to break a DES-encrypted message

Hardware	Number of Encryptions per Second	Years Required to Crack Message
Macintosh Quadra	23,200	98,488
1000 Macintosh Quadras	23,200,000	98.5
Power Macintosh 8100	100,000	22,652
1000 Power Macintoshes	100,000,000	22.7
"Typical" desktop computer in the year 2000	1,600,000	1,415
A university-sized network of computers in the year 2000	3,200,000,000	Less than a year

Alternatives to the DES

Problems with the DES have been widely acknowledged since the standard was first proposed. During public debates in the mid-1970s, Stanford University professors Martin Hellman and Whitfield Diffie led the charge against the DES, although the two researchers' complaints were largely discounted because of their involvement in public key cryptography (described in the next section), which was seen at the time as a competing technology.

Despite the debate about its strength, the DES was adopted as a standard, first by the U.S. government and later by the American Banking Association and the American National Standards Institute. Today the DES remains in wide use, despite the fact that it is routinely employed to encrypt information that is worth more than a million dollars—the cost of constructing a DES-breaking machine. Over the years, suggestions for strengthening the DES have included the use of longer keys, larger block sizes, and more encryption rounds. Variations such as Triple-DES are now commonly used. After nearly 20 years of DES use, the U.S. government is finally acknowledging that the algorithm is showing its age and is proposing an alternative. But many people think that the cure, which the government calls "Clipper," is worse than the sickness. (I talk more about Clipper in Chapter 5.)

Public Key Cryptography

In the early 1970s, a growing awareness of the need for data encryption in the computer community combined with the imminent deployment of the DES (an algorithm many computer scientists deplored), led to some serious thinking about alternatives—not only alternatives to the DES, but alternatives to the whole notion of private key cryptography.†

Private key cryptography has a fundamental problem: in order for one person to send an encrypted message to another, the two people must first agree on an encryption key. If an eavesdropper manages to intercept this encryption key, future communications between these two people are compromised.

As we saw in Chapter 2, the U.S. government solved this key distribution problem with a simple if crude technique: cryptographic keys were placed in locked briefcases that were handcuffed to couriers who physically transported them from Washington to embassies and consulates around the world.

As a first step on the road to public key cryptography, cryptographers asked this question: is there some way for two parties to communicate privately without prearrangement and over a link that might be monitored by a hostile third party? Ideally, the two parties should be able to work with each other in some way to agree on a key that they could then use to encrypt their future communications. With such a system, a sophisticated eavesdropper would be able to hear both sides of the conversation, but, since the eavesdropper would be only *monitoring*, rather than *participating*, he would not be able to figure out the key that the two active parties had agreed on.

Ralph Merkle's Puzzles

One bright person who spent time thinking about this problem was Ralph Merkle, who in the fall of 1974 was taking a course at the University of California at Berkeley taught by Lance Hoffman (now a professor of computer science specializing in computer security at George Washington University in Washington D.C.). Early in the term, Hoffman asked students to submit proposals for their term projects. Merkle decided to solve the problem of key exchange between two parties in his term project, which he named "Secure Communication over Insecure Channels." Hoffman didn't understand Merkle's proposal and asked him to pick a different project. Frustrated, Merkle dropped the course and wrote the project for submission to *Communications of the ACM*, the premier computer science journal.

---

† For much of the information in this section, I am indebted to Whitfield Diffie and to his paper, "The First Ten Years of Public-Key Cryptography."

Bidzos on the DES

Jim Bidzos of RSA Data Security theorizes that the publication of the DES was largely responsible for the interest in and early development of public key cryptography and that the NSA was furious with the result. Before the discovery of public key cryptography, two parties communicating over an encrypted link would repeatedly use the same DES encryption key. The NSA could easily break such a key, allowing the "encrypted" communication to be easily monitored. With the coming of public key cryptography, those same parties could use a different DES key for every conversation, dramatically increasing the cost of eavesdropping on the encrypted link. Bidzos says, "Since DES was published in March 1975, NSA could not possibly have anticipated the work of Diffie, Hellmann, Rivest, Shamir, and Adleman. All of a sudden, the strong DES could have key changes with every message! This would explain why [NSA] never published a new [encryption] algorithm again."

At the heart of Merkle's system is a set of cryptographic jigsaw puzzles. Each such puzzle can hold a few numbers or a message (such as a cryptography key) and takes approximately two minutes to solve.

Merkle's system works like this: in order for Alice and Bob to have a secure communication, Alice must first create a list of one million encryption keys for the conversation. Alice hides each key in a puzzle. She then sends all one million puzzles to Bob.

Bob receives the puzzles and picks one (it doesn't matter which). He unscrambles the puzzle (taking about two minutes), which reveals the encryption key inside. Bob then takes a message that he and Alice have previously agreed on (such as a block of zeros), encrypts the message with the encryption key, and sends it back to Alice.

Alice doesn't know which key Bob has picked, but she can refer to her list of the one million keys that she originally hid in her puzzles. Starting at the top of the list, she tries to decrypt the message that Bob has sent her with every key. One of them works. Now she and Bob can use this key for all further communications.

How secure are Merkle's puzzles? An eavesdropper who taps the line between Alice and Bob hears all one million puzzles go across and sees Bob's encrypted message go back. However, the eavesdropper doesn't know which puzzle Bob picked. The eavesdropper's only recourse is to try to unscramble *every puzzle*. Eventually the eavesdropper will find the right one. On average, however, he'll have to unscramble 500,000 puzzles first, which should take a little more than nine months. By that time, Alice and Bob have married and gone to live in Haifa.

What are the actual puzzles? In Merkle's proposal, the puzzles themselves are crypto-grams, scrambled blocks of numbers that are encrypted with a 20-bit key, yielding a little more than a million possible solutions. To hide a message in a puzzle, Alice encrypts it with a random 20-bit number. To "solve" the puzzle, Bob must try every key in order until he finds the correct one. If Bob is using a computer that can try 10,000 different keys every second (typical of most workstations), it takes Bob 100 seconds to try every one.

Merkle's system relies on the fact that the puzzles are small enough that a million of them can be sent over the telephone line in a reasonable amount of time. That's a reasonable assumption—if the puzzles are each 96 bits, it takes only 62 seconds to send them down a primary rate ISDN interface or a T1 leased line. (Both connections run at 1.544 megabits per second.) It also relies on the fact that Alice has a lot of CPU time on her hands (both to generate the million puzzles and to try a million different crypto keys in order to figure out the one Bob chose).

The puzzles were a neat idea, but Merkle didn't have much better luck with *Communications of the ACM* than he had had at Berkeley. One of his reviewers said that Merkle's puzzles were too far out of the mainstream of cryptography. Another said that the paper was bad science: everybody knows, wrote the reviewer, that it is impor-tant to keep cryptography keys secret. Eventually, CACM published the article in April 1978, after public key cryptography had become a household word—at least in most computer science departments. The paper was published with a special editor's note, stating the date that the paper had been received.

In his paper, "The First Ten Years of Public-Key Cryptography," Whitfield Diffie writes of Merkle's puzzles that the computation advantage that "the legitimate communica-tors have over the intruder is small by cryptographic standards, but sufficient to make the system plausible in some circumstances."

Merkle never put his system into actual practice, however. Within less than a year, two mathematical approaches had been discovered that gave legitimate communica-tors advantages that were considerably stronger—strong enough not just for transient communications, but for the long-term protection of secrets.

Diffie-Hellman Multi-User Techniques

In the fall of 1975, two researchers at the Stanford University Electrical Engineering Department, Whitfield Diffie and Martin Hellman, wrote a paper called "Multi-User Cryptographic Techniques," which outlined the newly developing field of public key cryptography.

The premise of the Diffie-Hellman paper was that it should be possible to create a multi-user cryptography system in which a message could be encrypted with one key and decrypted with another. The Diffie-Hellman paper didn't propose a workable public key system; it simply discussed what kind of applications would be possible if such a public key system existed. The paper was written for the National Computer Conference in 1976, but they finished it in December 1975 and sent preprints to others working in the same field.

One of the preprints went to a graduate student at Berkeley named Peter Blatman. I suspect that Ralph Merkle got a copy from Blatman, and recognizing a pair of kindred spirits, Merkle sent a copy of his own paper on secure communication to Diffie and Hellman. Another copy of the "Multi-User Cryptographic Techniques" paper ended up at MIT, where a graduate student handed it to his professor, Dr. Ronald Rivest.

Diffie-Hellman Exponential Key Exchange

The idea of multi-user cryptography is an intriguing one. Just how would you do it? Diffie tried to develop a system of digital signatures based on tables of exponentials but couldn't get it to work. Donald Knuth, a colleague of Diffie's and Hellman's at the Stanford Computer Science Department, observed that it is easy to multiply a pair of prime numbersr but that it can be very difficult to factor the result. (This approach was not used by Diffie but found use later, on the other side of the country, at MIT.) John Gill, another Stanford colleague, suggested that Diffie explore discrete exponentiation (calculating exponents of numbers in a modular arithmetic field), because the inverse problem (taking discrete logarithms) was very difficult. This turned out to be the solution that Diffie pursued in conjunction with Martin Hellman.

One morning in May 1976, while Diffie was working in his office, Martin Hellman called and explained the idea of exponential key exchange, which has since come to be known as Diffie-Hellman key exchange. (Their definitive paper, "New Directions in Cryptography," was published in *IEEE Transactions on Information Theory.*)

The Diffie-Hellman algorithm is a devilishly simple technique that allows two parties to exchange an encryption key with one another in such a way that a third party monitoring the exchange is unable to deduce the key's value. The participants each start with a secret key; by exchanging information based on those keys, they derive a session key that they use to encrypt future communications. Diffie-Hellman is based, in part, on the suggestion by Gill: taking the exponents of numbers and then calculating the results modulo some prime number.

Briefly, Diffie-Hellman works as follows:

• Both participants in the communication must first agree on two numbers. These numbers can be widely known or even published; it doesn't matter. Call them α and q.

- Each participant then chooses a secret number, X, and transmits to her partner the result of a mathematical formula that involves α, q, and X. Assume that the first participant picks the secret number X_1 and transmits the number Y_1. The second participant picks the secret number X_2 and transmits the number Y_2.

- Both participants can now compute a third number, K, by using a second mathematical formula. According to the mathematics discovered by Diffie and Hellman, the number K can be computed as a function of the numbers (X_1 and Y_2) or the numbers (X_2 and Y_1). However, it cannot be calculated from the numbers (Y_1 and Y_2).

An eavesdropper knows the numbers α, q, Y_1, and Y_2. However, the eavesdropper doesn't know the numbers X_1 or X_2 and therefore can't compute the number K. In practice, the number K is used as the session key for a private key encryption algorithm such as the DES.

For additional details and an example, see Appendix F, *The Mathematics of Cryptography*.

According to Diffie's paper:

> Marty and I immediately recognized that we had a far more compact solution to the key distribution problem than Merkle's puzzles and hastened to add it to both the upcoming National Computer Conference presentation and to "New Directions." The latter now contained a solution to each aspect of the public-key problem, though not the combined solution I had envisioned. It was sent off to the *IEEE Transactions on Information Theory* prior to my departure for NCC and like all of our other papers was immediately circulated in preprint.

The National Computer Conference was in June 1976. According to a telephone interview with Diffie in September 1994, the Diffie-Hellman encryption system was publicly demonstrated at the conference before an audience of more than two hundred people.

Stanford University filed for a patent on the key exchange algorithm on September 6, 1977. Patent number 4,200,700, "Cryptographic Apparatus and Method" was granted on April 29, 1980, to Martin E. Hellman of Palo Alto, California; Bailey W. Diffie of Berkeley, California; and Ralph C. Merkle of Palo Alto, California. Rights to the patent were assigned to Stanford University. The Canadian patent number 1,121,480 was awarded two years later, on April 6, 1982.

The Diffie-Hellman algorithm works great for two people who want to talk on the telephone. Unfortunately, this algorithm cannot be used as the basis for a workable email encryption system because it requires two active participants working together at the same time.

The Birth of RSA

In the spring of 1976, three young professors in the computational theory group at the MIT Laboratory for Computer Science read of the Diffie-Hellman paper "New Directions in Cryptography." They were Ronald Rivest, Adi Shamir, and Len Adleman. The three were intrigued by the idea of a multi-user cryptography system, and they decided to create one.

The three worked for months at MIT in a row of offices on the eighth floor of 545 Technology Square. Rivest came up with ideas; Adleman shot them down; Shamir traded sides, sometimes making codes, sometimes breaking them. It's a truism among cryptographers that you should never attempt to develop a new cryptography system until you have had significant experience in trying to find holes in others. One of the reasons for this rule is that it is currently mathematically impossible to prove that an encryption algorithm is "secure"; currently, we only know how to show that a code is insecure—by breaking it. (The only exception to this rule is the one-time pad described in Chapter 2.)

At one point, Rivest says, the group gave up looking for ways to create a public key system and instead tried to prove that such a system was not mathematically possible. "It just might be inherently contradictory," Rivest recalls thinking.

The discovery of the Diffie-Hellman key exchange system put an end to that line of investigation: clearly *some* kind of public key system was possible, because Whitfield Diffie and Martin Hellman had discovered one. The group of MIT professors pressed on with their quest. Developing a workable public key system and figuring out what makes it work neatly encapsulated many of the basic questions of theoretical computer science, which were their specialties.

In April 1977, Ron Rivest was at home in Belmont, Massachusetts, reading a book on group theory, when all of the ideas spinning around in his head suddenly jelled. (According to Bidzos, Rivest says that "He was lying on a couch, with a headache; suddenly, it hit him, and he got up and wrote it down. No, [Rivest] doesn't have the piece of paper. I asked him already.") The system that Rivest devised made use of the fact (noted by Knuth at Stanford) that it is easy to multiply two large prime numbers to create an even larger composite number, but it is very difficult to take that large composite number and find its prime factors.

The new algorithm, which today is known simply by the initials of its three inventors, RSA, satisfies the original Diffie-Hellman description of "multi-user cryptography" far better than even the Diffie-Hellman key exchange system, because RSA requires no active participation between the person performing the encryption and the person performing the decryption.

How does RSA work?

This section provides a brief summary of the RSA system. (RSA is described in greater detail in Chapter 6, *The Mathematics of Cryptography.*)

To use RSA, a person must create a *key pair* consisting of a public key and a secret key. To create a key pair, a person (in this example, Alice) must first chose two very large prime numbers, P and Q, at random. Next Alice multiplies the numbers to create N, the encryption modulus. Alice must also pick another number, e (the encryption key), which shares no common factors with the number (P–1)(Q–1).

Let's suppose that Alice picks the numbers 47 and 71 for her prime numbers. (In fact, all of the numbers you'd actually use for public key cryptography are very large, but this example will be a lot easier to follow if I stick to small numbers.)

P = 47

Q = 71

Alice can calculate the values N:

N = P × Q = 47 × 71 = 3337

And she knows that the encryption key must be relatively prime to (has no common factors with) the number 3220:

(P–1) × (Q–1) = (46) × (70) = 3220

Alice picks the number 79 as her encryption key.

Using the extended Euclid algorithm[†] and the prime numbers (which are known only to her), Alice can now compute the *decryption* key:

d = 79^{-1} (mod 3220) = 1019

Alice publishes her public key, which consists of the numbers N (3337) and e (79):

    Alice's RSA Public Key
    N = 3337
    e = 79

If Bob wants to encrypt the number 688 and send it to Alice, he simply goes to the public key registry and looks up Alice's numbers. Bob then takes the number he

---

† I don't describe this algorithm in this book, but it is in the PGP source code. It is also in Bruce Schneier's book, *Applied Cryptography*, which is where this example comes from.

wants to encrypt and raises it to the 79th power and takes the modulo 3337 of the result:

688^{79} mod 3337 = 1570[†]

When Alice gets the number 1570, she performs the same operation but uses the decryption key 1019:

1570^{1019} mod 3337 = 688

Intrigued with the breakthrough, Rivest, Shamir, and Adleman wrote a paper describing the invention and published it as an MIT Artificial Intelligence Laboratory Technical Report. Martin Gardner, a columnist for *Scientific American*, found out about the new encryption algorithm and contacted Rivest. Gardner wanted to publish a description of the algorithm in his "Mathematical Games" column. Gardner suggested that he publish, along with a description of the RSA algorithm, a challenge: a secret message encrypted with the algorithm that readers would be invited to crack.

Rivest, Shamir, and Adleman prepared a challenge for Gardner's column: a secret message that could be cracked by factoring the 129-digit encryption modulus:

```
N =
114,381,625,757,888,867,669,235,779,976,146,612,010,218,296,721,242,362,562,
561,842,935,706,935,245,733,897,830,597,123,563,958,705,058,989,075,147,599,
290,026,879,543,541
```

The public key for the message was the number 9007. The message itself was a single number converted to an English sentence by the simple technique of concatenating numbers representing each letter of the alphabet together, such that the letter *A* is 01, *B* is 02, and so on. (A space was represented as 00.) Thus, the words *HI MOM* would be encrypted as 080900131513. The encrypted ciphertext challenge printed in *Scientific American* was:

```
9686 9613 7546 2206
1477 1409 2225 4355
8829 0575 9991 1245
7431 9874 6951 2093
0816 2982 2514 5708
3569 3147 6622 8839
8962 8013 3919 9055
1829 9451 5781 5154
```

[†] You might have trouble doing this with your pocket calculator until you realize that you can take the modulo after each multiplication step, rather than first computing the 79th power of 688. That is, the number (688^{79} mod 3337) is equal to the number $((((688 \times 688) \text{ mod } 3337) \times 688^{77})$ mod 3337). So simply take the number 688×688, take (mod 3337), and repeat this operation 77 more times. The number you get is 1570.

The challenge appeared in Gardner's August 1977 column, under the title "A new kind of cipher that would take millions of years to break." The three MIT professors offered a hundred dollars to the first person who could factor the 129-digit composite number (which came to be known as RSA-129) and reveal the encrypted message. As proof that they did, in fact, have the secret key, they included the following digital signature:

167178611503808442460152713891683982454369010323583112178350384469290626554487 9 22371144905095786086556624965779748400040570 20373

When the digital signature is raised to the 9007th power and the result reduced modulo N, the resulting number is:

0609181920001915122205180023091419001514050008211404180504000415121201181 9

This number translates to "FIRST SOLVER WINS ONE HUNDRED DOLLARS". According to Gardner's column, "Rivest estimates that the running time required [to factor the modulus N and break the message] would be about 40 quadrillion years!" (with the factoring technology and computers of the time; actually, a far more accurate estimate appeared in the MIT Technical Memorandum described in the next section, although it was seen by fewer people). Even with just a hundred dollars on the table, it seemed that the money was safe.

Technical Memorandum #82

Unfortunately, there wasn't room in Gardner's column to explain the following three key ingredients of the RSA scheme:

- How to quickly pick a huge prime number.

- How to derive the decryption key from the encryption key and the encryption modulus.

- The shortcuts for performing the exponentiation and modulo arithmetic of very large numbers.

And so Gardner informed readers that the MIT technical memorandum describing the RSA public key system, MIT Technical Memorandum #82, dated April 1977, "is issued by the Laboratory for Computer Science, Massachusetts Institute of Technology, 545 Technology Square, Cambridge, Mass. 02139. The memorandum is free to anyone who writes Ronald Rivest at the above address enclosing a self-addressed, 9-by-12-inch clasp envelope with 35 cents in postage."

Rivest never anticipated the response that Gardner's column would generate. Soon after the August issue of *Scientific American* was published, the mail started flooding in. Eventually, says Rivest, more than 3000 letters were received, each asking for a copy of the paper. There was just one problem: Rivest didn't know if he was legally allowed to distribute the copies.

During the summer of 1977, Rivest, Shamir, and Adleman had planned to present the RSA cryptography scheme at a conference at Cornell University. Before the conference, an employee of the NSA contacted Rivest and gave him some chilling news. He warned Rivest that presenting the paper might violate the 1954 Munitions Control Act. Why? Because foreign nationals would be at the conference. By presenting the paper, Rivest might, in effect, be exporting knowledge about cryptography to a foreign country, which was forbidden by the 1954 act.

That same summer, George Davida, a professor of computer science at the University of Wisconsin, was informed that a patent application he had filed with the U.S. Patents and Trademarks Office had been suppressed with an Invention Secrecy Order—an order granted at the request of the NSA.

To academic researchers working on cryptography, the NSA appeared to be making a new and concerted effort to suppress the results of their research. In the short run, both the RSA case and the Davida case were resolved. The NSA maintained that the employee who had warned Rivest, Shamir, and Adleman had been acting on his own, without official sanction. Meanwhile, in Wisconsin, the chancellor of the University of Wisconsin appealed on behalf of Davida to the National Science Foundation (which had funded Davida's research). Two months later, the U.S. Patents and Trademarks Office rescinded the order suppressing Davida's patent application, saying that it had originally been granted as the result of a "bureaucratic snafu." MIT's lawyers decided that the MIT technical memorandum describing the RSA public key system could be distributed without infringing the 1954 Munitions Control Act. (After all, the *paper* wasn't munitions.)

Meanwhile, the head of the MIT Laboratory for Computer Science reviewed the RSA research and decided that the algorithm might be patentable. Under the terms of the U.S. research contract that funded the lab's work, MIT was obligated to file for a patent on patentable research. So that fall, Rivest worked with the MIT patent office to prepare a patent application for the RSA algorithm. The actual application was written by Mark Lappin, an attorney at an outside firm, and the application was filed on December 14, 1977. On September 20, 1983, the U.S. Patents and Trademarks Office granted patent number 4,405,829 for an invention entitled "Cryptographic Communications System and Method" to MIT and Ronald L. Rivest, of Belmont, Massachusetts; Adi Shamir, of Cambridge, Massachusetts; and Leonard M. Adleman of Arlington, Massachusetts. The patent gave MIT the right to stop anyone within the United States from making, using, selling, or importing devices that used the RSA algorithm. However, since the algorithm had been published before the patent application was filed, MIT could not secure foreign rights to the invention. (Under U.S. patent law, an inventor is allowed one year after the first publication of an invention to file for a patent, but under European and Japanese law, any publication before the application is filed makes an invention unpatentable.)

That December, Rivest, Shamir, and Adleman threw a big pizza party on the eighth floor of 545 Technology Square. Graduate students ate pizza and stuffed envelopes. For several months, Rivest had been getting telephone calls from angry *Scientific American* readers who had sent in their envelopes and were anxiously waiting for their papers. He was relieved that finally the papers were being sent.

One of them went to a computer science senior named Phil Zimmermann at Florida Atlantic University.

The Rise and Fall of Knapsacks

The same year that Rivest, Shamir, and Adleman developed their encryption algorithm, Ralph Merkle started working on another approach to public key cryptography—one that would demonstrate, perhaps more than any other example in the history of the field, the danger of trusting newly discovered cryptosystems.

Merkle's system was based on a mathematical game called the *knapsack problem*. Knapsack is an exercise in packing. Briefly, the puzzle involves a knapsack and an odd assortment of objects of different sizes. The goal is to pack the objects into the knapsack so no space is wasted. Obviously, for a given knapsack and a certain set of objects, there may be zero, one, or many solutions to the knapsack problem. You solve the puzzle by finding them.

Knapsack isn't a difficult problem if you have a small knapsack and a few objects, but it quickly becomes unwieldy when you have a large container and thousands of objects. To simplify the mathematics, Merkle's algorithm did not concern itself with wasted space but merely with the weight of the knapsack: given an infinitely large knapsack and a collection of objects of different weights, find the right combination of objects to put into the knapsack so it has a particular weight. As before, for any given knapsack problem there might be zero, one, or many solutions.

It turns out that there are broadly two kinds of knapsack problems: ordinary knapsacks, which are difficult to solve, and special kinds of knapsacks, called *superincreasing knapsacks*, which are simple to solve. Merkle devised a way to turn superincreasing knapsacks into knapsacks that were not superincreasing, thus turning an easy-to-solve problem into one that was nearly impossible. In conjunction with

Martin Hellman, Merkle also devised a way to encode information in a knapsack problem.[†]

How does the knapsack problem relate to public key cryptography? Let's return to Alice and Bob.

To use the knapsack encryption system, Alice creates a superincreasing knapsack that is, by definition, easy to solve. This knapsack is her secret key. From this knapsack Alice then creates a knapsack that is not superincreasing and is thus difficult to solve. The non-superincreasing knapsack is Alice's public key. Alice gives the non-superin-creasing knapsack to Bob. When Bob wishes to send Alice a message, he encodes it using the knapsack that she gave him. Bob (and anybody else who has the non-super-increasing knapsack) can't decrypt the message, because solving these kinds of knapsacks is difficult. But when Alice gets the message, she solves it with her superin-creasing knapsack. The mathematics of knapsacks are beyond the scope of this chapter, but you can find them in Diffie's paper and in Schneier's book.

On October 6, 1977, Martin E. Hellman, of Stanford, and Ralph C. Merkle, of Palo Alto, jointly filed for a patent on the algorithm. The patent, number 4,218,582, entitled "Public-Key Cryptographic Apparatus and Method," was granted on August 19, 1980, and assigned to the Board of Trustees of Stanford University. The patent holders claim that this patent covers the entire field of public key cryptography.

Merkle was so confident about the security of the knapsack system that he put a note in his office offering a hundred dollars to anyone who could break it.[‡] Indeed, on first consideration, knapsack looked like a good algorithm. But in 1978, T. Herlestam published an article entitled "Critical Remarks on Some Public-Key Cryptosystems" in which he noticed that a single bit of a message encrypted with knapsack could be revealed by a person who didn't know the superincreasing knapsack. The following year, 1979, Adi Shamir presented a paper at the 11th ACM Symposium on the Theory of Computing in which he showed that messages encrypted with knapsack could be broken under certain circumstances. Over the following three years, a number of other cryptographers found systematic problems with the knapsack algorithm, although no fatal flaws were revealed until the summer of 1982 at the Crypto '82 Conference.

Each year at the University of California at Santa Barbara, the world's crypto mavens get together for the annual Crypto Conference. For the 1982 conference, Whitfield

---

† Their paper, "Hidden Information and Signatures in Trapdoor Knapsacks," was published in *IEEE Transaction in Information Theory* in September 1978.

‡ Merkle actually offered a hundred dollars to anyone who could break a single iteration of the knapsack system. In actual practice, encrypting a message with knapsack involved iterating Merkle's algorithm many times. However, Merkle was so sure of the strength of knapsack that he felt confident offering the money to anyone who could break a single round.

Diffie had signed up to chair a session on cryptanalysis. As Diffie tells the story, "My original program ran into very bad luck, however. Of the papers initially scheduled only Donald Davie's talk on 'The Bombe at Bletchley Park' was actually presented. Nonetheless, the lost papers were more than replaced by presentations on various approaches to the knapsack problem."

Between the time that Diffie had signed up to chair the session and the start of the conference itself, Adi Shamir had announced to the world that he had broken the single-iteration knapsack encryption system based on new mathematics that had been recently discovered by Arjen Lenstra, H.W. Lenstra, Jr., and L. Lovácz at the Mathematische Centrum in Amsterdam. Three other cryptographers who announced similar findings after Shamir were Andy Odlyzko and Jeff Lagarias from AT&T Bell Laboratories and Len Adleman from MIT. Indeed, Adleman had done a lot more than the mathematical work; he had also programmed the solution on an Apple II computer (a popular personal computer of the time that was powered by a puny 6502 chip).

The beauty of using an Apple II was that the computer was portable. When the world's cryptography mavens converged on UCSB, Adleman brought his Apple II.

The first night of the Crypto '82 Conference, a knapsack puzzle was posted for the cryptographers to solve. When it came time for Diffie's session, cryptographer after cryptographer rose to present papers posing theoretical problems with the algorithm, but no one actually addressed the puzzle that had been presented.

No one, that is, until Len Adleman. Adleman was the last person on Diffie's program. According to Diffie, when Adleman rose to speak, he mumbled something about "the theory first, the public humiliation later." People were puzzled about what he meant. While Adleman explained his work, Carl Nicolai set up the accompanying demonstration. Writes Diffie:

> All the while the figure of Carl Nicolai moved silently in the background setting up the computer and copying a sequence of numbers from its screen onto a transparency. At last another transparency was drawn from a sealed envelope and the results placed side by side on the projector. They were identical. The public humiliation was not Adleman's, it was knapsack's.

Years later, Adleman insisted that the humiliation he spoke of was not Merkle's or knapsack's. "I meant my humiliation, thinking the Apple program might fail." he said.

Ralph Merkle was not present to see his algorithm go down in flames. Nevertheless, he did pay Shamir the hundred dollars in prize money that he had promised for breaking the code. But, strangely enough, Merkle's faith in his algorithm was unshaken. In a letter to *Time* magazine that was published in the November 15, 1982 issue, he offered a thousand dollars to anyone who could break a multiple iteration knapsack. Two years later, he had to pay the money to Ernie Brickell, who had solved a knapsack system of 40 iterations and 100 weights in an hour of time on a Cray-1 supercomputer.

Although Merkle's algorithms didn't result directly in workable systems, he was nevertheless a powerful catalyst to major and startling developments in both public key cryptography and secure hash algorithms. Merkle deserves at least a portion of the credit for these developments.

Taking Public Key to Market

After the initial discovery of public key cryptography, Rivest dedicated himself to the next task: making public key generally useful. That task required he put away his hat as a theoretical computer scientist and learn the basics of designing semiconductors.

For all of its wonderful properties, the RSA algorithm had a serious problem: working with 100-digit numbers required a lot of computational power. While the computational needs for RSA encryption and decryption were well within the power of the scientific computers available at the MIT Laboratory for Computer Science, the fastest computers that were generally available to the public in the late 1970s were four-function calculators: machines simply incapable of working with RSA-sized numbers.

Rivest's group at MIT decided to attack the problem by building special-purpose hardware. Their first development was a special-purpose circuit board that could perform an RSA encryption with a 100-digit modulus (two 50-digit primes) in a twentieth of a second.[†] The board was too expensive for general use, so Rivest started on the next project, an RSA chip.

Rivest planned that the RSA chip would be built with nMOS technology and be able to perform three RSA encryptions every second using 500-bit primes. (While the chip could perform RSA encryptions with great speed, the chip would do nothing to weaken the strength of the RSA cipher, because RSA encryption chips could not be used to factor the modulus used by RSA public keys. Unlike the DES, code making and code breaking with RSA are largely unrelated activities.) Such a chip would bring RSA encryption within the range of low-cost commercial applications, because the chip, once designed, could be mass produced very cheaply.

---

† At the same time, Sandia National Laboratories was building its own public key hardware. The goal was to use RSA-encrypted digital signatures to authenticate data sent to the United States from remote monitoring stations inside the Soviet Union that were allowed under the Limited Nuclear Test Ban Treaty of 1963. By using digital signatures, the U.S. government could be assured that the information being transmitted from the monitoring stations had not been tampered with by the Soviets, while the Soviet Union could be assured that the monitoring stations were transmitting only the information that the United States was allowed to acquire. For more information, see Simmons, G. J., "How to Insure that Data Acquired to Verify Treaty Compliance are Trustworthy," in "Authentication without secrecy: A secure communications problem uniquely solvable by asymmetric encryption techniques" *IEEE EASCON '79*, reprinted in *Contemporary Cryptography*, ed. G. Simmons, IEEE Press..

Unfortunately, Rivest's chip never worked properly. The problem wasn't the RSA encryption engine, but the chip's memory cells used to hold the numbers; the bits kept flipping, rendering the chip unusable for practical applications. (At the time, MIT lacked expertise in chip making. A similar effort by the MIT Artificial Intelligence Laboratory to make a chip that could run the Scheme programming language met with equal failure.) These problems were cured by the mid-1980s, when MIT opened a new building dedicated to research on microelectronics.

Rivest was not much more successful in getting companies outside the MIT laboratory to use the new encryption technology. A typical case, he says, was that of Pat Cremen, an engineer at LMI Erickson (a European telecommunications company), who had a dream of converting Ireland's cash economy to a system based on RSA-authenticated digital cash. "He was going to replace everybody's wallet with electronic wallets," Rivest recalls. But Cremen's dream was vetoed by higher-ups at Erickson, and the plan never went anywhere. Rivest also had discussions with Motorola and other companies, all with similar results.

Slowly it dawned on the inventors that if they wanted their invention to be used, they would have to do the really hard work themselves. "We decided in the end that [starting a company] was the only way that this technology was going to make it in the marketplace," Rivest recalls.

Rivest secured private funding from an investor in Reno, Nevada, who had an interest in seeing the widespread use of cryptography. Rivest, Shamir, and Adleman formed a company they called RSA Data Security, Inc. (RSADSI). An aspiring businessman in California signed on as the company's first president, and the company set up shop in Redwood City, California.

Rivest wasn't the only MIT professor to set up a company to commercialize his invention. Other professors, mostly from MIT's biology department, were having a go at what their own teachers would have called "crass commercialism" only a decade before. What made this all possible was a new university-wide policy encouraging professors throughout the institute to do exactly the same thing by promising them a share of the earnings from their inventions. MIT's reasoning was simple: who better to shepherd an invention on the perilous path from the laboratory to market than the original visionary? New technologies need champions to assure their success. They need small teams willing to work incredibly long hours for the promise of future payoff. They need small startups, not large companies where the technology might get lost. RSA Data Security fit the MIT vision. As was standard practice, RSA Data Security was given an exclusive license to the RSA patent.

Despite dedication and a brilliant idea, at first the fledgling cryptography company stumbled, as is so often the case with young startups. "The early days of the company were difficult" recalls Rivest. "We had the wrong initial team." RSADSI's management was accustomed to large corporations, not small startups. And there was another problem: "The technology was premature. When you are talking about encryption, you need a highly networked society. We had some interest, but it was scattered."

RSADSI made some early hires, but soon the company started shrinking. "Money was being spent and revenues were minuscule," says Rivest. One of the problems, Rivest says, was that the management couldn't make up its mind about what RSADSI should be doing:

- Should it develop encryption hardware (like Rivest's failed RSA chip)?

- Should it develop end-user software?

- Should it develop cryptography toolkits for other companies to embed in their products?

No one was sure, because no one had ever tried to start a new company on the strength of an encryption algorithm.

Working in his spare time from Massachusetts where he remained a professor at MIT, Rivest wrote a program for the IBM PC that demonstrated the unique possibilities of the RSA encryption system. The program was called MailSafe. (Len Adleman also worked on MailSafe.) Designed for computers running the DOS operating system, MailSafe allowed a computer user to create a public key/private key pair, encrypt messages, and convert encrypted messages into a form that could be sent via electronic mail. MailSafe also allowed people to sign messages electronically without encrypting them, as well as to sign other people's keys in order to assure their validity.

The program ran into much the same problem that RSADSI had been running into all along: in order to be useful, public-key encryption needed a large, interconnected network allowing electronic mail. Few people needed MailSafe. It was just too early for the technology, and time was running out.

"In this business, the sales cycle is very long," says Rivest. Sometimes, as much as three years would pass between the time that a company made its first contact with RSADSI and the time that the company decided to make a purchase. Three years was just too long. By 1986, the year MailSafe was first released, RSADSI was trimming back, letting people go, and desperately trying to cut costs. "The company practically folded."

That was the situation in 1986. But within the next few years, dramatic changes occurred—in the computer world and within RSADSI.

4

A Pretty Good History of PGP

I just fax'd you the letter I told you about. I hope this ends the bullshit over the "he has his side of the story, you have yours" discussions. He has his story, I have his signature. What will you do now? How long, and to how many people have you told the Zimmermann side of the story? Will you correct it now? It sure isn't as colorful as the version going around.

—Jim Bidzos in an email message to the author, April 7, 1994

PGP arouses passions like few other pieces of software. That's because PGP hits two raw nerves in the computer industry: the fight over encryption and privacy and the fight over software patents. And both of those fights are neatly encapsulated in the person of one computer scientist, turned peace activist turned cryptography outlaw, turned Cypherpunk spokesman: Phil Zimmermann.

Phil Zimmermann: On the Road to PGP

Phil Zimmermann doesn't fit the mold of the typical Cypherpunk. Married with two kids, Zimmermann lives in a small house in Boulder, Colorado, where he tries as best as he can to make a living as a full-time cryptography consultant. He feels more comfortable in a suit and tie than in a T-shirt and jeans. Zimmermann doesn't lead a glamorous, flamboyant life, but then cryptography isn't high-stakes poker. At least, it didn't used to be.

Zimmermann was born in Camden, New Jersey, in 1954, but his parents soon moved to southern Florida. He spent most of his formative years in Miami and Fort Lauderdale. When it was time for college, he picked Florida Atlantic University in nearby Boca Raton.

Phil Zimmermann, author of PGP
(photograph courtesy of Jerry Cleveland, the Denver Post)

In college Zimmermann first studied physics, but soon he was bitten by the bug and switched his major to computer science. He met one of the school's switchboard operators, fell in love, and got married on the spring equinox in 1977. He took a year off from school to get some real-world experience working at Harris Computer Systems Division in Fort Lauderdale, where he worked on a Fortran compiler, an interval arithmetic package, and some other compiler tools. When he graduated from college in late 1978, Phil and his wife packed up everything they owned and moved to Boulder, Colorado.

Phil didn't have a job waiting for him in the Rockies, but Boulder sounded like an interesting place to live. The mountains represented a big change from the life that the couple had known on the Florida coast. And Zimmermann's degree in computer science, combined with his year of work experience, meant that he didn't have to look long for work once he arrived. In short order, he became a freelance computer consultant working with a company that was designing devices for the upcoming consumer electronics bus (CEBus). Typical applications of the technology were controlling lights in a house by remote control or using a home's electrical wiring for an alarm system.

Things were looking up for the Zimmermann family, but clouds were on the horizon: mushroom clouds. In 1980, Ronald Reagan was elected to office, and Zimmermann began to get nervous. "Reagan was in the White House. Brezhnev was in the Kremlin. Our side was building weapons that were designed to launch a first strike," he later recalled. Day by day, Zimmermann and his wife worried more about the possibility of nuclear war; the birth of their first child in 1980 made matters all the more urgent. To the couple, there seemed to be only one logical solution: emigrate to New Zealand.

"We thought it would be a hard life in New Zealand after a nuclear war, but we thought it might be still livable," he says. It was better than the supposed alternative in post-war America.

Zimmermann started obtaining the necessary passports and immigration papers for himself and his family. Everything was in order and ready to go by early 1982, when the couple heard about a conference being held in Denver by a group calling itself the Nuclear Weapons Freeze Campaign. They decided to go.

Zimmermann remembers the conference as "sobering but empowering." He heard a lecture by Daniel Ellsberg, the man who gave the Pentagon Papers to the *New York Times*. Ellsberg left Zimmermann feeling hopeful. The United States, after all, is a democracy. "It seemed plausible that this was a political movement that had some chance of success, of turning things around," he recalls. "And so we decided to stay and fight."

Soon after the conference, Zimmermann started hunting for books about military policy and weapons. He discovered a particularly good bookstore at a nearby mall and spent several hundred dollars. Zimmermann was going to become a self-taught military policy analyst. As soon as he finished the books, he started teaching his own course called "Get Smart on the Arms Race" at the Community Free School, a nonaccredited adult education center in Boulder. He made the rounds as a public speaker and started to train lobbyists and political candidates on issues of military policy and weapons technology. He was even arrested, along with Carl Sagan, Daniel Ellsberg, and more than 400 other protesters, at the Nevada nuclear testing grounds. "Direct action," he called it.

Politically, Zimmermann's years with the antinuclear movement were a success. Zimmermann's group helped get Tim Wirth elected to the U.S. Senate and another Democrat, David Skaggs, elected to Congress. But financially, Zimmermann couldn't have picked a worse time: he had just given up his lucrative business as a computer consultant in favor of starting a computer company with some of his friends. And startup companies, especially in the computer field, have a way of not putting food on the table.

Metamorphic Systems

In 1980, the most exciting personal computer in the world was the Apple II, manufactured by a new company in Cupertino, California, called Apple Computer. The Apple II had a full-size keyboard, fantastic graphics, and a fairly speedy microprocessor, the 6502. But as time passed, the Apple's 6502 seemed to run slower and slower. When IBM launched its new personal computer in 1981, it didn't use the 6502, but a new chip from Intel, the 8088.

Zimmermann's startup had a simple premise: build a single-board computer with an Intel 8088 that could plug into the back of an Apple II. That way, Apple II users could get the speed of the 8088, without having to give up their existing software. Zimmermann and his friends gave their company an appropriate name, Metamorphic Systems. Its headquarters was located in the kitchen of one of the founders.

By day, Zimmermann would work in his friend's kitchen, writing the basic input/output system (BIOS) of the new Metamorphic computer. At night, he would study military policy at home. And at the bank, Zimmermann's savings were draining away.

One day, Metamorphic Systems got a telephone call from a computer programmer in Arkansas named Charlie Merritt. Zimmermann picked up the phone. Merritt had seen the advertisements for Metamorphic Systems' computer and was excited by the machine's speed. Merritt needed speed, he explained to Zimmermann, because he was writing programs to do public key cryptography with an algorithm called RSA, and RSA was a pig with CPU cycles. At the mention of cryptography, something clicked in Zimmermann's mind.

Charlie Merritt

Charlie Merritt got his start in cryptography in 1977 in Houston, where he was technical director of a microcomputer marketing company. A friend in Arkansas sent him a copy of the original MIT public key paper by Rivest, Shamir, and Adleman. The friend wanted to know if RSA could be implemented on a microcomputer. Merritt said, "Yes."

In 1980 Merritt moved to Fayetteville, where he formed a company with two other people to create an encryption system for Z80-based computers running the CP/M operating system. Merritt was right: RSA could run on the puny microcomputers of the time. It ran *s-l-o-w-l-y* but not as slowly as Merritt had feared. "We thought it would take a week or two to generate a 'pretty big' key. Encryption of a file might take 20 minutes," Merritt recalls. "Well, we did better than that. 256-bit keys generated in 10 minutes; a small file encoded in 20–30 seconds."

Merritt and his friends started selling a system called DEDICATE/32, which performed encryption using 32-byte (256-bit) keys. After a while he had a falling out with his two partners and set up a new company called Merritt Software, which contracted with Merritt's former company to market DEDICATE/32.

By 1983 Merritt Software was having a problem: "Most interest came from business people who wanted privacy from Banana Republic competitors that had bribed 'El Jefe' or were related to him," he says. The company also kept getting visits from NSA employees ("They always travel in pairs," Merritt says) who informed Merritt Software that their RSA programs were "munitions" and couldn't be legally exported to any country in the world except Canada. "We had few customers as close as Canada. Evil spies could buy crypto in the U.S. and sneak it 'over there' and copy the bee-Jesus out of it, but I couldn't make an honest $50 by selling it to a business person who wanted *privacy!*" Merritt complains.

Merritt's call to Metamorphic was actually a marketing gimmick. Merritt had bought a few computer magazines and was calling every single company that might be the least bit interested in having his RSA encryption package run on its computer. (At this time, RSA had no known patent restrictions. Although MIT had filed for the patent on the RSA encryption algorithm, the patent had not yet been issued.)

Zimmermann "was the most gee-whiz-whoopic enthusiastic character I had run into," recalls Merritt. "He didn't have a need for crypto, but as he told me, he had been interested in ciphers since the Boy Scouts had introduced him to the subject. He was the only person I had run into that knew nothing about public keys, and wanted *every single detail* on how to do it. The thought crossed my mind that he might be a practical joke inspired by a friend."

Zimmermann told Merritt that he was anti-Big Brother. Merritt liked that; he was really angry at the NSA for almost driving his company out of business with its policy against exporting cryptography. The two hit it off.

Indeed, Zimmermann had a lingering interest in cryptography since he had been a small boy; he simply hadn't had anyone to share it with and any practical knowledge of how to implement it. In fourth grade, Zimmermann found a copy of the book, *Codes and Secret Writing* by Herbert S. Zim, and read it cover to cover. "It was really cool," remembers Zimmermann. "I learned Morse code and Braille from it, and made invisible ink from lemon juice." A few years later, Zimmermann was making code wheels and transposition ciphers. He made codes in college with the school's computers. He even knew about the RSA algorithm that Merritt was using because he had written Ron Rivest asking for a copy of the RSA paper described in *Scientific American*.

Zimmermann had considered writing his own RSA implementation shortly after he received the original MIT paper but quickly gave up: microcomputers, Zimmermann thought, were just too slow. And here was Charlie Merritt, who had gotten RSA to work on a puny Z80. How did Merritt do it?

Merritt showed Zimmermann how. The Arkansas programmer had no formal training in mathematics, but he had taught himself the secrets of doing arithmetic with 100-digit numbers on a personal computer. Now he was teaching Zimmermann.

"He called more than once a week for [several] years," recalls Merritt. "He at first knew virtually nothing, but as time went on he began to grow quite formal. It was during this early time that he and I talked about his 8088 card for the Apple II and putting crypto on it. He studied the DES and gave me my first understandable explanation of why the cipher feedback would not melt down on a communication error. I realized that this guy was real, and that he had a vision I had given up. He had drive, I felt beat. He began talking about protocols, in *great detail*. For hours, on the phone. I hate protocols, that's for the Phone Company. But he needed a brick wall. Then he began asking exactly how math was implemented on a Z80. I mean detailed stuff about memory allocation, and adding two giant numbers and what about the carry bit. We were back in my territory."

Merritt's territory, it turned out, was programming computers in assembly language— the actual machine code used by the computer. Zimmermann was a C programmer. He wanted to program in a language that could be run on more than one computer. Merritt thought that C was some sort of "weird language that PRZ [Zimmermann] was hot on." Zimmermann sent Merritt a copy of Kernighan and Ritchie's C bible, with an inscription that said "Move into the 1980s." It was June 1985.

Phil Zimmermann Meets Public Key

Although the mathematics behind the RSA algorithm are theoretically simple, the difficulty of writing an RSA program is in performing the actual arithmetic. Making RSA work requires that you multiply numbers that are hundreds of digits long, then take those numbers to very high exponents, and finally perform modulo arithmetic. Most computer languages have multiplications, exponentiation, and modulo-division built in, but they are limited in their precision to 10, 15, or 20 digits. To make RSA work securely with 200-digit numbers, you must write your own multi-precision arithmetic functions. While you can easily find these algorithms in textbooks today, such algorithms were relatively obscure just ten years ago. They were also difficult to teach over the telephone, as Merritt and Zimmermann discovered.

By the summer of 1986, Merritt and Zimmermann decided to have their first face-to-face meeting. The stated purpose of the trip was to teach Zimmermann the fine details of performing multi-precision arithmetic on a computer. Zimmermann was thinking of starting on his own project: an implementation of RSA for the computer that seemed to be taking over the world, the IBM PC. Merritt would fly to Boulder and stay with Zimmermann and his family for a week.

For Merritt, there was a second purpose for the trip as well. For more than a year, Merritt had been doing contract work for RSA Data Security, the company that Ron Rivest, Adi Shamir, and Len Adleman had started back in 1983. In February of 1986, RSADSI had hired a new employee, Jim Bidzos, who had risen to become the company's president within a year, firing all of the company's other employees and hiring his own team in the process. Merritt wanted to meet Bidzos. As for Bidzos, he had business in Denver: it was a simple matter to cruise down to Boulder and see Merritt. Meeting Merritt in Boulder was a lot easier than flying to Arkansas. The meeting was set.

A few days before Merritt flew to Boulder, he touched base with Bidzos. Bidzos said that he knew one of the best steak houses in Boulder. Merritt and Bidzos planned to go "eat thick slabs of dead cow, drink, and smoke some fine cigars in a dim steak house," recalls Merritt. "What a good way to meet someone you had been doing business with." To Bidzos, the fact that he was also going to be meeting Phil Zimmermann was inconsequential.

Face to Face with Jim Bidzos

Boulder, Colorado. November 1986. From the first moment that Merritt, Bidzos, and Zimmermann met, the three were off to a rocky start. Merritt found himself in the middle. On the one hand, Merritt's politics were more in line with Zimmermann's: neither trusted the government. Merritt had protested against the war in Vietnam, whereas Zimmermann was in the middle of his crusade against the nuclear arms race. Bidzos, Merritt learned, had volunteered for the U.S. Marines despite his being a Greek citizen. And yet, Merritt was *working* for Bidzos—and on a military contract, at that. When Bidzos learned that Zimmermann was a programmer, he asked Zimmermann if he wanted to help on a contract for the United States Navy. The contract wasn't classified or relevant to weapons, but Zimmermann refused. Sure, he needed the money, but how could an anti-nuclear peace activist work on a military contract?

Bidzos brought with him two copies of RSA Data Security's new MailSafe product, the program Ron Rivest wrote to sign and encrypt electronic mail. In many ways, MailSafe was similar to the program that Zimmermann was thinking of writing.[†] Bidzos left a copy of the program with Zimmermann. They talked about encryption, and Zimmermann claims that during their meeting, Bidzos offered him a free license for the RSA algorithm—a claim Bidzos hotly disputes. The three then set their minds on dinner, and the evening continued to go downhill.

---

† Despite MailSafe's similarities to PGP, Zimmermann says that he doesn't remember much from the demonstration and that he promptly lost his copy of MailSafe after Bidzos left. Bidzos, on the other hand, claims that PGP is little more than a bad ripoff of the ideas that originated with MailSafe. It is true that the two programs have the same basic functionality, but they differ in two very important ways. The first has to do with the user interface: MailSafe has a graphical user interface, while PGP can be run only from the command line. The second is that MailSafe's system for encoding binary data as ASCII has a simple error-correction system that can correct some kinds of transmission errors—an important feature for people who are sending encrypted files by modem.

Jim Bidzos, president, RSA Data Security, Inc.
(photo courtesy Simson Garfinkel)

Zimmermann vetoed the idea of going to the steak joint: he didn't drink and didn't smoke and he wasn't much of a meat-eater. As the host of the evening, he had some influence on where the three men went for dinner. They ended up in the no smoking section of a well-lit restaurant that Merritt says was "PC before PC was PC."

"I was mixed up," recalls Merritt. "Jim and PRZ weren't. They flat out didn't get along. Jim kept pulling me aside, asking what was wrong with PRZ. PRZ kept giving me disgusted looks about the reactionary sitting with us." "Zimmermann kept saying he wanted to move to Canada so his tax dollars wouldn't go to military defense," recalls Bidzos. "I explained that Canadian tax dollars do the same."

Bidzos left for California the next day. Merritt stayed for a week at Zimmermann's house, teaching him everything he knew about doing fast arithmetic with huge numbers on a microcomputer. Phil's wife was a wonderful cook, Merritt recalls, and the house was a comfortable yuppie-ish place with a hippie crash-pad feel to it. "When I left, PRZ knew how my codes worked. He knew 95 percent of what I knew. He was now a 'real danger' to the national security machine."

The Rise of RSA Data Security

So, who was this Jim Bidzos, anyway?

Jim Bidzos says he was born in 1955 in a small mountainous Greek village near the Albanian border. The Italians invaded the village during World War II; then the Germans invaded. During the Greek civil war, the village was alternatively a home to rebels and to the Greek militia. "It wasn't a good place to raise a family," recalls Bidzos, "There was nothing there but farmers and soldiers." So Bidzos' father moved to the United States to find a new life. Starting without any money or knowledge of English, Bidzos Senior worked for a year and a half, sending what little earnings he had to Greece. Finally there was enough money for his wife and son to join him. The family settled in Ohio—"A good place to come from," says Bidzos.

Bidzos speaks numerous languages: English, Greek, Macedonian, German, and quite a bit of Japanese. He has a green card but has no intention of becoming a U.S. citizen. "I can see three benefits to becoming naturalized," he says. "One is that I could vote. The second is that I could leave the country for more than a year without jeopardizing my resident status. And the third reason," he says with a smile, "is that it is harder to get thrown out if you are a U.S. citizen. . . . But the down side is that Greece doesn't allow you to have dual citizenship. If I became a naturalized American citizen, I would have to give up my Greek passport and all the privileges of citizenship." For Bidzos, losing Greek citizenship would mean losing his membership in the European Community, which allows him to work and travel freely within Europe. "Why should I give that up? There's no difference with a green card: you pay taxes, you can be drafted, you can be jailed." And Bidzos is dedicated to his guest country—so much so that he enlisted in the U.S. Marine Corps.

In January 1986, RSA Data Security was on the verge of failing. "The company had no products, no customers, no revenue. It had taken some money from investors, and it had all disappeared," says Bidzos. Fewer than five people worked for the company. One of them, Bart O'Brien, was an old friend that Bidzos had worked with at Paradyne in Florida. Both were marketing executives. In 1983, they split up, with Bidzos going off to create an international technology marketing company, and O'Brien going out to California and eventually joining RSA Data Security. O'Brien called Bidzos and said that RSADSI needed help. O'Brien described the RSA technology and the patent. Bidzos started working there on February 1, 1986.

What saved RSADSI was a little company in eastern Massachusetts, Iris Associates, that was writing a program called Notes for the Lotus Development Corporation. "They didn't know that RSA was patented," says Bidzos. "They had played around with it and had finally gotten it to work, but [their implementation] was too slow. So they were actually delighted to know that there was a company called 'RSA.' They said, 'Gosh, maybe you can help us.'"

Bidzos committed to build an RSA encryption toolkit that Iris could drop into Notes. The toolkit was written mostly by Rivest and other members of the MIT faculty. Rivest also started work on MailSafe: a program that would serve two important purposes. It would supply RSADSI with a small revenue stream, and it would demonstrate the power of public key encryption. "It was perfect for showing people that it could work, how it worked, and that it could run fast enough on a personal computer," says Bidzos.

By the time that Bidzos met with Merritt and Zimmermann in Denver, things had already turned around for RSADSI. The deal with Lotus was closed in June 1986, giving RSADSI a large amount of prepaid royalties. The next big deal, with Motorola, used RSA for commercial secure telephones. The third deal, with Digital Equipment Corporation, involved the development of a secure network system. (The project was later killed because Digital couldn't export its secure software.) Next was Novell, which built RSA encryption into NetWare.

By 1991, says Bidzos, RSADSI was making substantially more money on toolkit royalties than it was on the sales of end-user programs. Bidzos boasts that even if RSADSI never licensed another company, RSADSI could have stayed in business indefinitely at its current strength. Of course, that didn't happen. New licenses continued to pour in. By 1993, more than 100 companies were incorporating RSADSI's toolkit into their products. By this time, Bidzos had also learned that a large, secret, and incredibly powerful government agency wanted him out of business.

Working with Big Jim

Bidzos is a strong man and a strong negotiator, and he drives a hard bargain. It's a style that might not work in some businesses. But RSA Data Security had a monopoly on public key cryptography: the MIT patent on RSA. Anyone in the United States who wants to use the RSA algorithm has to either make a deal with Bidzos or change their plans.†

Bidzos has a simple negotiating technique; no matter how well-informed the customer might be, Bidzos doesn't give a price until after he spends at least an hour educating his potential business partner about cryptography, public key, what a business can do with it, and various royalty models that RSA Data Security has for license fees. Finally he names a price. It's his goal, he says, for both RSADSI and the company that licenses the technology to make money with cryptography. "Everyone wanted it more or less for free," says Bidzos. "I believed it had more value, and I could be persuasive." Indeed, the fact that customers made deals with RSA to license the algorithms or software is a strong testimony to the truth of Bidzos' words.

"I put our customers into one of three categories," says Bidzos. "There are those like Lotus Notes users, who I think benefit immensely from the security that is there, and generally are aware of it. The second category really doesn't understand at all that it is there, and I think really doesn't need to, like Novell. And it is still for the benefit of the users. And then there is the case where [the users] don't know it, and our direct

---

† In 1987, representatives from Stanford University began to claim that RSA's patent rights could not be exercised without infringing on the Merkle-Hellman patent owned by Stanford. Eventually, MIT licensed the patent rights from Stanford. MIT, in turn, passed the rights to RSADSI. In exchange for the rights, MIT pays a portion of RSADSI's patent royalties to Stanford.

customer doesn't want their customers to know, or at least they don't want to broadcast the fact." An example of the third category, says Bidzos, is Atari, which uses RSA as the basis of its protection scheme on video game cartridges. Only cartridges that have been signed by the company's public key work in the company's video game machines.

Bidzos says that many people who don't contact him grossly overestimate the price of an RSA license. Newspaper accounts confirm this statement. According to an article by John Markoff in the *New York Times*, RSADSI's income is between $5 and $10 million a year on the sale of products, while between 2 and 4 million end-user software packages in the world include one of the company's algorithms. Court documents in a recent lawsuit imply that RSADSI's licenses might cost as little as a dollar per user for high-volume applications. Generally, Bidzos refuses to do deals in which RSA is sold to the end user as an option: he wants it embedded as part of the application program. "Users want absolute security, zero overhead, and no cost," says Bidzos. "We usually find a way to do that."

But patents aren't forever. RSADSI has been doing well, but an outside observer might wonder if RSADSI's reliance on its patents means that the company may face hard times. After all, patents last only 17 years; the RSA patent expires in the year 2000.

The reason that Bidzos isn't worried is that he isn't basing his company's future on the patents. In fact, RSA Data Security doesn't even license the patents anymore. On April 6, 1990, RSADSI and Cylink (holder of the Diffie-Hellman and Hellman-Merkle patents) formed a partnership called Public Key Partners, whose sole purpose is to acquire the rights to cryptography patents, write licenses, and collect license fees.

RSADSI has turned its attention to the development of cryptographic toolkits. The company's BSAFE 2.1 product, introduced in the summer of 1994, included implementations of many cryptographic algorithms: Bloom/Shamir Secret Sharing, RC2 Symmetric Block Cipher, RC4 Symmetric Stream Cipher, Pseudorandom Number Generators, RSA, DES, DESX, Triple-DES, MD5-With-XOR, RC4-With-MAC, Diffie-Hellman, and support for Privacy Enhanced Mail (PEM) by RFC 1422. The kit is designed for developers, costs $290 ($750 for a five-user license, $950 for a ten-user license), and includes a license for all of the relevant patents. Runtime fees are separately negotiated. (As mentioned, license fees for large customers might be as low as one dollar per user.)

"We have no unhappy customers," boasts Bidzos. "If they are unhappy, we give them their money back." So far, he says, he's never had to cancel a license agreement and refund a customer's money.

A Pretty Good Program

Although Zimmermann kept in touch with Bidzos on and off during the years following their meeting in Boulder, most of his time was spent devising his own solution to the problem of public key encryption on microcomputers. First Zimmermann wrote a paper describing standards and data structures for representing encryption keys, encrypted text, and signatures. The paper was eventually published in *IEEE Computer*. The paper gave Zimmermann the legitimacy in the eyes of the cryptography community to be able to call other cryptographers and not be instantly dismissed as a crank. Zimmermann next turned his attention to writing a working program that implemented the RSA public key system. He called his program PGP— short for Pretty Good Privacy. (Why? Zimmermann was a fan of Garrison Keillor's "Prairie Home Companion" radio program, in which one of the "sponsors" was "Ralph's Pretty Good Groceries.")

According to Bidzos, sometime during 1990, Phil Zimmermann called RSADSI asking for "a free license" to the RSA algorithm. "When I told him 'no,' he was really upset. He told me that he was behind on his mortgage payments and that he had invested years in writing this piece of software and needed to make money from it."

"I told him that what he should do is go find some larger company," recalls Bidzos. "He said that he was trying to help us by recommending RSA to companies. I said, 'Great! If you are working with them, *they'll buy a license!* It will be perfectly fine that you made something for them, and they buy the license. We won't try to keep you from making money. We don't begrudge anybody a living. We just can't give you a free license to go make money with.'"

Zimmermann went back to his keyboard. By the spring of 1991, the basic structure of PGP was beginning to take shape. Zimmermann's main interest was in distributing the program as "shareware." (People could freely copy the shareware program, but some critical component of it would not operate correctly unless the user sent the author a check to "register" his copy.) Shareware programs had taken off during the late 1980s; some people had become millionaires using the concept. Zimmermann's first attempt at shareware was a terminal program called PGT—Pretty Good Terminal. It was not very successful. But there was one hitch with either scheme: Zimmermann's PGP program violated the RSA patent held by RSA Data Security and later by Public Key Partners.

In April 1991, Zimmermann sent Jim Bidzos a one-page letter. "Dear Jim," the letter started, "Well, I'm finally getting around to writing you about requesting a royalty-free license for your RSA algorithm. We talked about this a few times since your 1986 visit to Boulder, when I developed my own RSA math library in C. Both you and Ron [Rivest] said then and later that you would grant me a free license to make and sell products with your algorithm. I appreciate that a lot. When we last spoke, you said you would need a letter telling you what products it's for. It was unclear whether this meant highly detailed firm product plans or just general fuzzy plans."

Zimmermann's letter goes on to describe two projects. The first project is a low-cost secure telephone, based on encryption and voice compression. The second project is a program to do RSA/DES encryption on a personal computer. "This would be somewhat analogous to your MailSafe or ComSafe products. I guess it would sort of compete with these products. I suspect these products are not the backbone of your company's cash flow, anyway. I just think they would be fun for me to do. I probably would not be developing that jointly with another company, but I may sell it through another company's marketing channels."

Bidzos was shocked by Zimmermann's letter: despite what Zimmermann thought, Bidzos maintains that he had never promised Zimmermann a "free license" of any kind.

"I said, 'We don't give those. It is not consistent with our business, and not consistent with licenses already granted,'" Bidzos recalls telling Zimmermann. "I promised to talk to our attorneys to explore the possibility, and did. I then wrote him a letter saying 'Nope, can't do it.' He later lied, claiming in some vague statement that I promised him a license."

Without the license, a shareware version of public key encryption wasn't possible. Zimmermann wasn't sure what to do. Then something happened that would change cryptography in the United States forever: the U.S. Senate discovered data encryption.

The Anti-Crime Bill S.266

An unexpected clause appeared in section 2201 of S.266, the Senate's 1991 omnibus anti-crime bill. The clause read:

> COOPERATION OF TELECOMMUNICATIONS PROVIDERS WITH LAW ENFORCEMENT
>
> It is the sense of Congress that providers of electronic communications services and manufacturers of electronic communications service equipment shall ensure that communications systems permit the government to obtain the plain text contents of voice, data, and other communications when appropriately authorized by law.

According to information in the Electronic Frontier Foundation's online newsletter *EFFector*, the language was inserted into S.266 at the behest of Senator Joseph R. Biden (Democrat-Delaware) and was written by John Bentivoglio, a staff member on the senator's Judiciary Committee. Others say that the text of Biden's amendment came from the FBI. In any event, the language in the Senate bill was intended to get communications providers to make it easier for law enforcement to tap cellular tele-

phones and new digital switches. Bentivoglio assured early opponents of the bill that
S.266 wasn't an outright attack on cryptography. "[Bentivoglio] also claims that this is
not the proverbial crack in the dike, and that the Senator has no intention of
following through with additional legislation to enforce a ban on secure cryptosystems," the *EFFector* reported.

Despite these reassurances, many civil liberties activists believed that S.266 would
have forced manufacturers of secure communications equipment to insert "trap doors"
into their products so that messages could be decrypted by the government.

Within a matter of months, RSA Data Security and the Washington office of Computer
Professionals for Social Responsibility had organized an industrywide offensive against
the wiretap language. The Electronic Frontier Foundation (EFF) later joined the
campaign. In early June 1991, members of the organizations met with the staff of
Senator Patrick Leahy (Democrat-Vermont) and voiced their objections. A week later,
the offending language was removed from the bill. Later that month, Computer Professionals for Social Responsibility, EFF, and RSA Data Security hosted an invitational
workshop on privacy and encryption in Washington D.C. That brought together the
leaders of the field, who were trying to figure out how to fight this onslaught on individual privacy.

The language was removed—for a while. But the concept wasn't dead, as Chapter 5
describes.

The Birth of PGP—Version 1.0

When Zimmermann heard about S.266, he flipped. Times were perilous. He had
missed five mortgage payments and was within an inch of losing his house. PGP was
going to be the big payoff. And now, whether the program was distributed either as
shareware or as a full-fledged product, the government wanted to make it illegal!

Zimmermann thought about PGP. Since he had spoken with Bidzos, he had taken out
the DES encryption (he didn't trust it) and replaced it with an encryption algorithm of
his own devising. Zimmermann called the cryptosystem Bass-O-Matic. Zimmermann
wrote: "Bass-O-Matic has not yet (in 89) been through a formal security review and
has had only limited peer review." Zimmermann wasn't sure whether Bass-O-Matic
was secure, but he was sure it was better than the DES.

The first file of the PGP package said the rest:

```
Pretty Good(tm) Privacy - RSA public key cryptography for the masses
Written by Philip Zimmermann, Phil's Pretty Good(tm) Software.
Beta test version 1.0 - Last revised 5 Jun 91 by PRZ
```

> PGP combines the convenience of the Rivest-Shamir-Adleman (RSA) public key
> cryptosystem with the speed of fast conventional cryptographic algorithms,
> fast message digest algorithms, data compression, and sophisticated key
> management. And PGP performs the RSA functions faster than most other
> software implementations. PGP is RSA public key cryptography for the masses.
> Uses RSA Data Security, Inc. MD4 Message Digest Algorithm for signatures.
> Uses the LZHUF algorithm for compression. Uses my own algorithm, Bass-O-Matic,
> for conventional encryption.
> (c) Copyright 1990 by Philip Zimmermann. All rights reserved. The author
> assumes no liability for damages resulting from the use of this software, even
> if the damage results from defects in this software. No warranty is expressed
> or implied.
> All the source code I wrote for PGP is available for free under the "Copyleft"
> General Public License from the Free Software Foundation. A copy of that
> license agreement is included in the source release package of PGP. The source
> code for the MD4 functions and the LZHUF functions were separately placed in
> the public domain by their respective authors. See the PGP User's Guide for
> more complete information about licensing, patent restrictions on the RSA
> algorithm, trademarks, copyrights, and export controls. Technical assistance
> from me is available for an hourly fee.
> ...
> The code in this source file (pgp.c) was hastily written, and it shows. It
> has a lot of redundant code, developed by ad-hoc "accretion" rather than by
> well-planned design. It isn't buggy, but it needs to be reorganized to make it
> cleaner, clearer, and more succinct. Maybe someday. Better and more typical
> examples of my programming style can be seen in the RSA library code in
> rsalib.c and keygen.c, and in the Bass-O-Matic conventional encryption
> routines in basslib.c and related files.

Talk about hasty! Zimmermann hadn't even remembered to change the copyright date
in his program. There simply wasn't time, he thought. Nor was there time to test everything properly. PGP had to be released—an emergency release, says a person who
was involved with the effort, and a preemptive strike on what Zimmermann viewed
as creeping government interference with cryptography and privacy. Zimmermann felt
that PGP had to get out before the government made cryptography illegal for individual citizens.

Zimmermann showed the program to Marc Rotenberg, head of the Washington D.C.
office of the Computer Professionals for Social Responsibility. Says Rotenberg, "A lot
of people knew about the patent issue and the battle with RSA. . . . I was more
concerned about the NSA and the information we were uncovering through the
Freedom of Information Act about the Agency's effort to undermine the Computer
Security Act [which forbade the NSA's involvement in making standards]. I had testi-
fied in Congress two years earlier that if the NSA was not watched carefully, it would
continue to restrict the ability of computer scientists in the U.S. to work freely. When
it became clear that the FBI was also involved in the development of the DSS and

later Clipper [see Chapter 5 and Chapter 6], the significance of Phil's program for 'computing freedom' became clear." Rotenberg endorsed PGP, saying "Pretty Good Privacy is a damn good idea."

Zimmermann then gave a copy of the program to a friend, who posted it to the Usenet, a worldwide network of UNIX computer systems. PGP was loose!

As soon as Bidzos discovered what had happened, he contacted Zimmermann and told him to stop distributing copies of PGP. According to Bidzos, at first Zimmermann denied that he had released the program and fingered his friend who Zimmermann said had actually done the dirty deed of putting PGP on the Internet. (Zimmermann says that the friend had told him that he was very willing to talk to Bidzos about his actions.) Bidzos called the friend, made sure that he would stop distributing the program, then called Zimmermann back with a deal: promise to stop distributing PGP, and Bidzos would promise that he wouldn't sue Zimmermann for willful patent infringement.

According to Bidzos, Zimmermann agreed. (Zimmermann says that the document he signed was not a promise not to distribute PGP but merely an assertion that RSADSI would not sue him if he did not distribute it.) Eventually, Bidzos sent Zimmermann two copies of a letter containing the same promise. At the bottom of each letter were places for two signatures: Zimmermann's and Bidzos'. Zimmermann signed his name at the bottom of one of the letters and sent it back. Zimmermann says that, since the time he signed his name to that letter, he has never distributed a copy of PGP. Nevertheless, PGP spread, and spread, and spread.

Bidzos probably wasn't too threatened by the PGP program itself. Although it did compete directly with RSA's MailSafe product, by 1991 MailSafe was only a minuscule part of RSA Data Security's income. According to Bidzos, MailSafe never sold more than a few tens of thousands of copies. No, the real problem with PGP was that, if Bidzos didn't aggressively attack the program, he would be at risk of forfeiting the valuable rights of the RSA patent; other companies that had not licensed the RSA patent could use the example of PGP as a reason not to pay patent royalties. Besides, Bidzos had a grudge against Zimmermann.

What followed could only be described as a low-intensity war by Bidzos against PGP and Zimmermann.

Bidzos' most effective weapon against the organized distribution of PGP was the RSA patent. Whenever Bidzos learned of an organization that was distributing copies of PGP, he wrote it letters demanding that it stop. CompuServe and America Online were both forced to take copies of PGP off their systems. Bidzos also went after universities, demanding that they not make PGP available to their students. According to Rotenberg, even the esteemed EFF took PGP off its FTP site.

The fight against Zimmermann himself was waged on various fronts as well. At every opportunity, in public, in private, Bidzos bad-mouthed Zimmermann. In email to the author, Bidzos wrote:

> Please do not use any *part* of this quote—please use it all. I've said Zimmermann is gutless and a liar. Why? 1. His enthusiastic willingness, when told putting PGP on the net violated both patent law and export law, to name his associate as the one "you need to talk to—he did it, not me, he did it"—clearly hiding behind this person. 2. His eagerness to cover his ass through an agreement with PKP just a few weeks later, which he did, but during which time he never bothered to seek protection for his associate, when all he had to do was ask. In other words, blaming someone else when it looked like he might get sued or charged, then forgetting that person ever existed while seeking protection for himself; his willingness to take credit later for what he tried to sacrifice someone else for. Yes, I call that gutless. He's an intellectual property thief as well. He offered to give away something that wasn't his to give.

There was just one problem for Bidzos: it was too late. The horse was already out of the barn and running around the world. PGP was out. . . .

. . . . but it wasn't free.

PGP Grows Up

PGP created a lot of excitement and in a lot of places that RSA Data Security had never visited. All over the world, people who picked up Zimmermann's program were intrigued by it, worried about the patent issues, and downright suspicious of Bass-O-Matic. Nobody quite knew what to make of it all. And all with good reason.

Bass-O-Matic

Every year in August, the world's leading cryptographers gather on the campus of the University of California at Santa Barbara for the annual Crypto Conference. The main conference consists mostly of highly mathematical papers given in a large auditorium. For a lot of the attendees, however, the real action at Crypto takes place in the hallways and outside the buildings, where the giants of cryptography swap gossip and try to discover as much classified information as they can from the conference's few military attendees.

In August of 1991, Zimmermann showed up at Crypto as he had in previous years. This time, though, he had a mission: he needed to get somebody to look over his Bass-O-Matic algorithm and tell him if it was any good. It wasn't just an academic curiosity; people were using it!

Zimmermann cornered Adi Shamir, the great cryptographer who had cracked Merkle's knapsacks back in 1982 and asked him if he could take a look at the routine. "He said 'send it to Israel[†] and I will spend 10 minutes looking at it.'" says Zimmermann. "I suppose if I had followed through I would have been violating some export laws."

After striking out with Shamir, Zimmermann found Eli Biham, another very good cryptographer from the Weizmann. Biham was more open than Shamir; he suggested that they look at the algorithm over lunch at the university's cafeteria, just a short walk from where the conference was being held.

After Biham and Zimmermann got their food and sat down, Zimmermann took out a few pages of computer listings. Within minutes, Biham was finding fundamental flaws in Bass-O-Matic. Some of the flaws were subtle—weaknesses that made the algorithm susceptible to differential cryptanalysis, which was Biham's speciality. Others were more embarrassing, like a conceptual error in Zimmermann's algorithm that prevented the last bit of each byte from being properly encrypted. After ten minutes of Biham's onslaught, Zimmermann realized that Bass-O-Matic was a lost cause. He also realized something he had kind of known all along but never really acknowledged: only world-class cryptographers can make encryption algorithms that are any good. Anybody else who tries is either an undiscovered genius or a fool. Zimmermann had learned his lesson.

The Real Thing—PGP Version 2.0

Not long after its release in the United States, PGP started turning up on computers overseas. By numerous accounts, the program was exported separately by many different people. Since all that is involved in "exporting" a computer program is for someone in the United States to send it to someone overseas in an electronic mail message, it is not hard to see how easily PGP could leave the country. A variety of sites within the United States even made PGP available for anonymous FTP from anywhere on the Internet.

Throughout the fall of 1991 and 1992, an informal team of programmers across the world assembled to create the second release of PGP, PGP Version 2.0. The most important change in Version 2.0 was the replacement of Zimmermann's Bass-O-Matic encryption algorithm with a new cipher created in Switzerland called IDEA (International Data Encryption Algorithm). Another important change was the modification of PGP so that it could automatically translate its prompts from one language to another (with the aid of an appropriate file containing language translations).

---

† Shamir had gone to the Weizmann Institute from MIT.

The major people who worked on the international PGP Version 2.0 were Branko Lankester in the Netherlands and Peter Gutmann in New Zealand. Other people helped, such as Jean-loup Gailly, a computer programmer in France, who wrote the compression algorithm and also did the French translation for the program. Miguel Gallardo, a lecturer in computer science in Alcala University, helped with the Spanish translation. Gallardo also wrote some articles about PGP and Phil Zimmermann for publication in Spain. "I first got PGP 1.0 [from] a friend who told me he downloaded it from CompuServe," says Gallardo. Peter Simons worked on the Amiga port of PGP, writing a few assembly language routines. Zimmermann says that he helped guide the effort but that he did not actually write any of the code.

Branko Lankester and Peter Gutmann released Version 2.0 simultaneously in the Netherlands and New Zealand. The program soon filtered back into the United States. It quickly went through a number of minor revisions. In the spring of 1993, PGP Version 2.0 seemed to finally settle down to a stable version, 2.3a.

The Cypherpunks

In the fall of 1992, a group of crypto-rebels was forming. Calling themselves "Cypherpunks," the group organized itself loosely around the principle that the technologies of freedom—strong cryptography, anonymous communications, and electronic signatures—should be made available throughout the world.

The founders of the Cypherpunk group were Tim May, an engineer who had retired from Intel in his mid-thirties, and Eric Hughes, a Berkeley-based computer consultant who worked part-time for a company on the East Coast. The Cypherpunks group set up an electronic mailing list, created an FTP site at the University of California at Berkeley, and met regularly to teach themselves cryptography and to talk about developments in the field. The group's first meeting in Oakland occurred a week after the release of PGP Version 2.0. "We found out about [PGP Version 2.0] after we scheduled the meeting," recalls Hughes. "We handed out diskettes at the meeting." This fortunate confluence of 30 crypto-rebels hastened the spread of PGP Version 2.0. People in the group realized that the program was a good start but that it had fundamental problems, not the least of which was its use of the RSA patent without a license, and they set about contacting Zimmermann to find out what he was going to do about the problems.

PEM, RSAREF, and RIPEM

PGP's popularity was growing, but its patent problems were still keeping many individuals and corporations from using the program. In the spring of 1993, Cypherpunk Eric Hughes started a private campaign on the secret *pgp-dev* mailing list to convince Phil Zimmermann to work out his differences with Bidzos and produce a version of

PGP that didn't violate the PKP patents. For the first time since PGP's creation, it looked as if such an agreement might be possible.

When PGP was first released, Jim Bidzos didn't think that there could ever be any value for his company in the creation of a noncommercial version of the program that could be distributed royalty free. But in the years that followed, he changed his mind. Following the release of PGP, RSA Data Security created a second implementation of RSA called RSAREF (RSA Reference), which was distributed by anonymous FTP as source code. RSAREF included a patent license that allowed use of the patents in noncommercial programs.

Why do this? The purpose of RSAREF was to allow academics and others to experiment with the RSA algorithm. One important motivation behind the release of RSAREF was the emerging Internet standard for Privacy Enhanced Mail (PEM). After years of negotiation, the PEM standard was completed a few weeks before Zimmermann released PGP. But there is a big difference between completing a standard and releasing working application programs. By the time that important programs that understood PEM were finally available, PGP already had a year's head start.

PEM had another problem. The standard relied on a system of centralized key certification. Before anyone could use PEM, she needed to have her keys signed by a "certificate granting authority." One of the side effects of this situation was that it made it easy to charge for each public key that was granted, because only keys that were officially signed could be used with the system.[†]

According to Bidzos, one of the conditions of having PEM adopted as an Internet standard was that RSA Data Security had to create a freely redistributable implementation of the standard that could be used royalty free for noncommercial purposes. This was the reason behind RSAREF, a toolkit that implemented the RSA algorithms (although not as efficiently as the company's commercial security toolkit product), which could be used by anyone to create a noncommercial program that used the RSA algorithms.

Before RSAREF was released, Mark Riordan, a programmer from Michigan, had written a program similar to PGP called RPEM. Although RPEM did not use the RSA algorithm, Bidzos claimed that RPEM infringed upon PKP's patents and threatened to sue Riordan if he didn't stop distributing the program. Riordan stopped, then rewrote the program with RSAREF. The resulting program, called RIPEM, is now distributed by RSA Data Security as a reference implementation of the PEM protocols.

---

† Largely in response to PGP, the PEM standard was eventually changed so that it no longer required a central authority. Called PEM 2, the new standard was completed approximately six months before the release of PGP Version 2.6, although application programs that implement the new standard were still not widely available when PGP Version 2.6 was released.

If such an approach could work for RIPEM, Hughes asked, then why not for PGP? If Bidzos was willing to allow one free, noncommercial implementation of RSA, why not two?

Zimmermann wasn't convinced. According to those involved at the time, Zimmermann thought it would be just fine if PGP remained an underground program. At the same time, Zimmermann was terrified that PEM would become more popular than PGP because PEM had no patent problems. Eventually, he relented and agreed to help the legitimizing effort.

It turned out that there was a problem with using RSAREF with PGP—a nit with the RSAREF license that almost seemed to have been placed there on purpose. An anti-PGP nit. The provision allowed developers to use only certain, specified functions denoted by particular entry points within the RSAREF package. And those functions were the ones that did PEM-style encryption. The functions needed by PGP were buried deep within the program, where they couldn't be used under the RSAREF license agreement. A second anti-PGP clause forbade a license for RSAREF to anyone who had previously infringed RSADSI's patents. The best way to rectify these problems, thought Hughes, was to negotiate a special license for PGP with Bidzos.

In the spring of 1993, Hughes traveled from Berkeley to Redwood City to meet with Bidzos. He found Bidzos to be a reasonable negotiator. For example, Hughes was thinking about working on an encrypting *telnet* program for the Internet, but to do it properly, he needed RSA to put a patent-friendly version of the Diffie-Hellman key exchange algorithm into RSAREF. Bidzos thought about the request and agreed to grant it. (Diffie-Hellman key exchange appeared in RSAREF Version 2.0.)

Unfortunately, there was still one stumbling block to a deal between the Cypherpunks and Bidzos. That stumbling block was Zimmermann himself. According to people familiar with circumstances at the time, Zimmermann would not agree to Bidzos' terms: creating a version of PGP that was incompatible with the patent-infringing version that had already been released.

ViaCrypt

Instead of working with Bidzos back in 1993, Zimmermann went another route. In the spring of that year, Zimmermann posted a message on the Usenet saying that he was trying to find a company to work with—a company that had a valid license for the RSA algorithm. Leonard E. Mikus, a software entrepreneur in Phoenix, saw the message and replied. Mikus' company, Lemcom, had a division called ViaCrypt that already had a license from Public Key Partners for the RSA algorithms that, Mikus said, allowed ViaCrypt to sell a commercial version of PGP. In August 1993, the deal was finalized, and ViaCrypt PGP Version 2.4 was released that November.

ViaCrypt PGP was based on PGP Version 2.3a, with Zimmermann's RSA encryption engine ripped out and another RSA engine, which ViaCrypt had previous developed, dropped in its place. Some people thought that Zimmermann was selling out by licensing PGP to ViaCrypt. Not so, says Zimmermann; he was simply trying to find a way to make the program available to as many people as possible. Many businesses refuse to use free software unless it is supported by a legitimate company. Still others didn't want to touch PGP while there were unresolved questions about the program's patent infringement. By going with ViaCrypt, Zimmermann found a way to legitimize PGP, at least for people who were willing to pay a hundred dollars to buy a commercial copy of it.

"I'm going to try to safeguard PGP, and that means making compromises," said Zimmermann at the 1994 USENIX Conference in Boston. "The only way I could get the deal with ViaCrypt was if I made it an exclusive commercial deal. That was the only way. And they were the only company that would come to me at the time."

MIT Steps in

Toward the end of the summer of 1993, another group contacted Zimmermann to try to develop a noncommercial version of PGP that used RSAREF. This time, the group was from MIT, the original home of the RSA patent. Contacting Zimmermann were two MIT people who were very interested in computer security: Jeffrey Schiller, MIT's network manager, and James Bruce, a professor and the vice president for information systems at MIT.

"MIT had the strong belief that heavy-duty cryptography, or the ability to encrypt something so that it remains private, needed to be in the hands of the general public," recalls Bruce. "As we looked about, PGP was there, and we believed that it met that need."

In January 1994, nothing came of a meeting at MIT with Bidzos, Schiller, MIT Professor Ronald Rivest, and John Preston, who oversees the MIT Technology Licensing Office. A month later, Phil Zimmermann met with Schiller and Bruce. Again, nothing came of it.

Then came the breakthrough. Or perhaps it was a mistake.

Like Eric Hughes and dozens of other people, Schiller and Bruce had realized that using the RSAREF encryption package was probably the way to make PGP freely available for noncommercial use inside the United States. They faced the same problem that Hughes had faced before—the PEM-oriented "hooks" in the toolkit code. But then, on March 16, 1994, RSA released RSAREF Version 2.0, which revealed the necessary programmatic hooks needed by PGP. "It became clear that you could build PGP on top of [RSAREF 2.0]," says Bruce, who is convinced that Bidzos never intended for RSAREF to be used for legitimizing PGP.

Seizing the opportunity, the MIT crew contacted Zimmermann again with an elegant proposition: take the encryption engine from RSAREF 2.0 and drop it into PGP. If PGP used RSAREF, RSAREF's license, allowing use of the RSA algorithm in noncommercial applications, would apply to PGP.

By then, Zimmermann had been convinced of the necessity of legitimizing PGP. He took PGP Version 2.3a, ripped out the patent-violating software, and plugged in RSAREF's patent-friendly code, producing PGP Version 2.5. (In the process, he also had to remove the "copyleft" license agreement and replace it with one allowing only noncommercial use.)

In early May, Schiller sent out a message on the Internet announcing that MIT "will shortly distribute PGP Version 2.5, incorporating the RSAREF 2.0 cryptographic toolkit under license from RSA Data Security, Inc. . . . PGP 2.5 strictly conforms to the conditions of the RSAREF 2.0 license of March 16, 1994." By that time, the MIT group had expanded to include Professor Hal Abelson and graduate students Brian LaMacchia and Derek Atkins.

The message that Schiller sent out was quickly forwarded to the Cypherpunks mailing list, and from there to many other mailing lists. The full text is as follows:

> The Massachusetts Institute of Technology announces that it will shortly distribute PGP version 2.5, incorporating the RSAREF 2.0 cryptographic toolkit under license from RSA Data Security, Inc., dated March 16, 1994. In accordance with the terms and limitations of the RSAREF 2.0 license of March 16, 1994, this version of PGP may be used for non-commercial purposes only. PGP 2.5 strictly conforms to the conditions of the RSAREF 2.0 license of March 16, 1994. As permitted under its RSAREF license, MIT's distribution of PGP 2.5 includes an accompanying distribution of the March 16, 1994 release of RSAREF 2.0. Users of PGP 2.5 are directed to consult the RSAREF 2.0 license included with the distribution to understand their obligations under that license.

> This distribution of PGP 2.5, available in source code form, will be available only to users within the United States of America. Use of PGP 2.5 (and the included RSAREF 2.0) may be subject to export control. Questions concerning possible export restrictions on PGP 2.5 (and RSAREF 2.0) should be directed to the U.S. State Department's Office of Defense Trade Controls.

Bidzos went ballistic.

In the flurry of telephone calls, email messages, protracted negotiations and false starts that followed, Bidzos asserted that if MIT distributed PGP Version 2.5, it would be inducing people with older versions of PGP to infringe upon PKP's patents. The MIT team said that people with earlier versions of PGP would naturally upgrade to get the newest version of the software. But Bidzos wanted a guarantee that users would be forced to upgrade.

Two weeks later, the two sides reached a compromise. Instead of Version 2.5, MIT would release a new, "improved" Version 2.6. The big change: after September 1, 1994, PGP Version 2.6 would place the number *3* next to its cryptographic signatures. Copies of PGP Version 2.6 or later would be able to read these signatures without a problem, but earlier versions of PGP—the ones that infringed upon PKP's patents— would be locked out.

The compromise was just that: a midway position between Bidzos' demand that MIT not release a version of PGP that interoperated with previous versions (those that violated PKP's patents) and MIT's contention that a newer version of PGP could not possibly induce people to violate PKP's patents by using older versions. (Indeed, a new, noninfringing version that included bug fixes was probably the best way to get people to stop using the earlier versions that did violate the patents.)

"Jim Bidzos insisted on backwards incompatibility," recalls Abelson. "His position is that full interoperation with earlier versions of PGP would be sanctioning infringe-ment of the RSA patents. The September 1 date is there to give people time to switch. I don't remember whose idea it was, but it was agreed upon in discussions with Bidzos.

"There were a lot of people who wanted to use PGP, but didn't want to get into patent hassles. We'd like to see more widespread use of PGP, and more effort going into support for it (e.g., better user interfaces and key server support). For example, we hope to provide systematic PGP support for email throughout MIT, starting some time in the fall. The patent hassles were preventing this kind of effort from going into PGP on a large scale," Abelson added.

Some people wondered if the required incompatibility was simply another way for Bidzos to create hassles for Zimmermann. But RSADSI's president denies this asser-tion. "Making trouble for Zimmermann is not the reason," Bidzos said, when asked why he forced MIT to make the change. "If [Version 2.6] won't talk to infringing versions, you can't use it to induce infringement."

Zimmermann feels otherwise: "I don't think that it was necessary to do it, but we did it anyway as an olive branch to Bidzos," he said.

Schiller's conclusion: "Finally we have been able to bring to the public a noncommer-cial version of PGP which really does not have any sword of Damocles hanging over its head or over the heads of its users. Anybody in the U.S. can get a copy of this, and RSA is not going to object."

On May 26, 1994, MIT issued the following press release:

FOR IMMEDIATE RELEASE, May 26, 1994

Contact: Ken Campbell, Director, MIT News Office

(617 253-2703 or 2700)

NON-COMMERCIAL USE

MIT Issues Software Codes To Promote Internet Privacy

The Massachusetts Institute of Technology has issued—for non-commercial use—a free public software package that will allow people to send private coded messages on electronic networks in the United States. The release provides non-commercial U.S. users of the Internet with the ability to obtain secure communication and data protection. Commercial versions have been licensed to over four million users. The software, known as PGP Version 2.6 (for "pretty good privacy") uses the RSAREF(TM) Cryptographic Toolkit, supplied by RSA Data Security, Inc. of Redwood City, Calif. It is being released by MIT with the agreement of RSADSI. PGP 2.6 is fully licensed, for U.S. non-commercial users, to use public-key technology that has been licensed by MIT and Stanford University to RSA Data Security and Public Key Partners. Public-key technology gives users of electronic mail the ability to sign messages in an unforgeable way, as well as the ability to send confidential messages that can be read only by the intended recipients, without any prior need to exchange secret keys. "This agreement solves the problem of software being distributed on the Internet which potentially infringed the intellectual property of MIT and the licensee, RSA," said Professor James D. Bruce, vice president for information systems. Although prior versions of PGP have been available on the Internet, the potential infringement of MIT and Stanford University patents has prevented it from coming into widespread adoption. END

KDC 5/26/94

For Jim Bidzos, the whole PGP battle is a relatively unimportant sidebar in his fight to get cryptography (along with PKP's patented algorithms and RSA's proprietary implementations) publicly accepted as a worldwide cryptography standard. Ironically, PGP may be the best advertisement for public key encryption that has ever been created.

Throwing PGP into the Wind

Within days following the release of PGP Version 2.6, the MIT version was available on European FTP servers: the only way it could have ended up there was if someone inside the United States had exported it to Europe or had made it available for anonymous FTP so that someone in Europe could have picked it up. This is strictly forbidden by U.S. export laws.

How did PGP get to Europe? Nobody knows. Or, rather, few will admit to performing the act. "Honestly, I don't know how PGP first came to Europe. But even if I knew I wouldn't tell you, sorry," writes Jean-loup Gailly in an email message.

Others are willing to admit to the exporting as long as their names are kept secret. Michael Froomkin, a professor at the University of Miami Law School, received the following electronic message from someone in Europe about the export of PGP Version 2.6:

> I got my copy of PGP 2.5 from *ftp.dsi.unimi.it* after it appeared there with the permissions apparently set so that you could not download it. There must have been something wrong with their ftp server because anyone could get it, and many did.

> I got my copy of PGP 2.6 from *ftp.informatik.uni-hamburg.de*, in Vesselin's *pub/virus/crypto* directory. It also resides at the *black.ox.ac.uk* ftp server. I know that the admins of archives like these receive PGP as unsolicited mail via anonymous remailers, encrypted with the admin's public key that can be got from the key servers.

> More interestingly from your point of view, a friend of mine from this same institution obtained PGP 2.6 merely hours after its release by using a U.S. based free-internet provider. The free access account was used to get PGP from the export-controlled archive (not MIT, by the way). Once PGP was at the free-access account it was a simple matter of ftp'ing it abroad and deleting it from the free-access account afterwards.

> It is also interesting to note how PGP 2.6 got all around the world's ftp archives by accident. Someone uploaded it to an incoming directory at a popular Linux archive site (*sunsite.unc.edu*). Overnight the many sites around the world that mirror sunsite faithfully did so, unwittingly distributing PGP worldwide.

> There is also a mail server at *star.houston.tx.us* (I think) that will send you anything from its archive via an automated e-mail response program. This archive contains export-restricted programs such as Secure Drive and does not check where it is sending things.

> I now use PGP 2.6ui and have consigned MIT 2.6 to the archives.

> Please do not publish my name and details, the originating address on this mail should be sufficient to validate my origins.

Vesselin Bontchev, a Bulgarian antivirus researcher enrolled as a graduate student at VTC-Hamburg in Germany, puts it this way: "I am 100% certain that Phil Zimmermann has not exported it himself—although I suspect that he was not surprised that somebody who has got it has exported it—it was an inevitable thing to happen." Bontchev runs an FTP site that is the home to both PGP 2.6 and 2.6ui. ("ui" stands for "Unoffi cial International," a version of PGP 2.3 that interoperates with PGP 2.6 but does not include the RSAREF encryption toolkit or the RSAREF noncommercial restrictions.)

"According to the download statistics of our FTP site," continues Bontchev, "MIT-PGP 2.6 is not very popular. The other sites that have it seem to confirm this. Most people prefer to use the European version, even people in the States. I suspect that this is caused mainly by ignorance and paranoia. The MIT version is very good and secure, but it doesn't have the taste of 'forbidden freeware' any more, so people don't trust it. Which is a pity. I know that Phil participated in this project, and MIT PGP 2.6 is a very good, secure, and trustworthy product."

Despite this opinion, most Europeans would do well to stay away from PGP 2.6; that's because this new version of PGP includes the restriction requiring noncommercial use. Version 2.6ui has no such restrictions.

The Federal Investigation of Zimmermann

There remains for Phil Zimmermann one last legal problem arising from PGP: a pending federal investigation aimed at discovering how PGP Version 1.0 left the country in the first place.

Shortly after PGP was released in the United States, it turned up on bulletin board systems all over the world. Certainly, exporting PGP was illegal. But the U.S. government cannot search every floppy disk taken overseas, it cannot wiretap every overseas telephone call or intercept and decode every piece of electronic mail over high-speed international links. And, of course, once a single copy of PGP made its way overseas, the program could be easily copied and copied again. Even the copies could be copied. It was probably for this reason that Zimmermann called PGP "guerrilla freeware."

But PGP wasn't a true guerrilla movement for one reason: Phil Zimmermann hadn't gone underground. Indeed, after PGP's release, Zimmermann continued to lead a very public life, attending conferences and talking about the need for encryption in a free society. When PGP started showing up overseas, he became an easy target for people in the U.S. government who wanted to demonstrate that there are teeth after all in the U.S. export control laws.

In February 1993, two investigators from the U.S. Customs Department came to visit Phil Zimmermann in his hometown of Boulder, Colorado. The investigators had recently met with Bidzos in California and had come away from that meeting convinced, "that PGP was stolen property. That it was owned by PKP. And indeed, there was some significance to the fact that PGP and PKP had some similarities to their names, differing only by the middle letter," says Zimmermann, recalling the meeting.

Slowly Zimmermann realized that the inspectors weren't concerned with the possible violation of the export regulations but with the shipping of stolen property overseas. "I explained to them that PGP was by no means stolen property, that it was written from scratch, and that there was a controversy involving patents." The idea of software patents itself is a controversy within the industry. "Disputes involving patents," Zimmermann said, "are supposed to be resolved by civil action between the patent holder and the alleged infringer, not between Customs and me!"

The investigators seemed woefully uninformed, Zimmermann reported. "They spent as much time asking questions about patents and stolen property as they did about the export control laws. In fact, they spent slightly more time talking about the former than the latter. . . . They told us at the meeting that I was not the target of the investigation, and, indeed, that there was no target. They just said that they wanted to hear about PGP and collect information."

A few months later, Austin Code Works, a company that sells floppy disks containing public-domain source code, was slapped with a subpoena demanding all of its business records pertaining to the overseas sale of PGP.[†] (The feds didn't get anything from ACW; there had been no overseas sales.) A second subpoena went to ViaCrypt; the government wanted copies of all the correspondence between ViaCrypt and Zimmermann. Presumably, since ViaCrypt had just licensed PGP from Zimmermann, this subpoena was more successful.

Following the issuance of the subpoenas, the federal prosecutor told Zimmermann that he was the target of an investigation.

Interestingly enough, RSA Data Security is not the target of any investigation, even though its RSAREF data encryption toolkit is available on many international FTP servers and thus has also been exported illegally. And no subpoenas were ever issued against companies such as Netcom, which have FTP servers that can be contacted from outside the United States and used to download PGP.

At the present time, the federal investigation is still pending. With that excess of caution that results from being the subject of a federal criminal investigation, and to avoid any appearance of impropriety, Zimmermann has refused to allow anyone outside the United States or Canada to participate in the development of the next release of PGP, Version 3.0. But the exclusion of Europeans from the 3.0 development effort has caused many ill feelings in Europe and Australia.

---

† Ironically, Austin Code Works didn't even know that Phil Zimmermann had written PGP. The program, which appeared on a disk called "Moby Crypto," had been furnished to Austin Code Works by someone named Grady Ward.

Whither PGP?

Where is PGP going internationally?

In September 1994, Phil Zimmermann met at MIT with Jeff Schiller and Hal Abelson, and Schiller and Abelson then got together with Ron Rivest and Jim Bidzos. The upshot of those meetings was that MIT would submit the PGP file formats as an Internet standard. The drive behind this decision was the widening split between United States and European PGP development. Zimmermann needed some way of assuring that the files produced by the slowly diverging versions of PGP would continue to be compatible. The only way to assure that compatibility was by passing a standard. Until Version 2.5, compatibility between European and U.S. versions has been assured by the fact that they were the same program; that might no longer be possible. Thus, the standard, which Zimmermann reasoned would allow both the United States and the Europeans to continue to develop their own versions.

Zimmermann plans to continue working on PGP Version 3.0 without the standard. When a standard is finally produced, a later version of PGP (probably 3.1 or 4.0) would implement it.

And what about the federal prosecutor? Only time will tell.

RSA-129 Solved!

How secure is PGP? After all this hullabaloo, is the program a worthwhile way to protect email messages and files?

There are three ways to decrypt a message encrypted with PGP Versions 2.0 through 2.6.1: crack the IDEA encryption, factor the encryption modulus that is part of the recipient's public key, or steal the recipient's secret key.

IDEA uses a 128-bit key. Unless a fundamental flaw is discovered in IDEA, the only way to break a message that is encrypted with IDEA is by an exhaustive key search. At 128 bits, there simply is not enough time before the sun explodes to crack an IDEA-encrypted message. (Of course, IDEA is still a relatively new cipher; such a flaw might be found one day.)

A more exciting point of attack is the RSA public key itself. PGP Version 2.3 allowed the user to specify a 384-, 512-, or 1024-bit public key. PGP Version 2.5 increased the length of the public key to 512, 768, or 1024 bits. To "break" the key, just factor the number.

What's going on in the RSA factoring area? In 1993, an international team of volunteers coordinated by Arjen Lenstra at Bellcore (the research arm of the U.S. local telephone companies), Derek Atkins, Michael Graff, and Paul Leyland decided to pick up the challenge that Rivest, Shamir, and Adleman had thrown down so long ago when Martin Gardner first described the RSA algorithm to *Scientific American* readers back in 1977.

What made the effort conceivable today were faster computers and breakthroughs in the science of factoring numbers. Volunteers from all over the world were invited to FTP files from Atkins' computer, set up the software on their own computers, and start it running. (The software was written in such a way that the system did not consume computer time when the computers were being used by others.) Each volunteer was given a different part of the factoring problem to work on. Each program ran independently and continuously and emailed its output back to MIT, where all the results were tabulated.

By April 1994, more than 600 volunteers had signed up. They came from Australia, Belgium, Brazil, Canada, Chile, Denmark, Finland, France, Germany, Holland, Ireland, Israel, Italy, Japan, New Zealand, Norway, Portugal, South Africa, Spain, Sweden, Switzerland, the United Kingdom, the United States, and Venezuela. In total, more than 1600 workstations, mainframes, and supercomputers spent eight months attacking the number.

On April 26, 1994, the solution was announced at a celebratory meeting in New York City. The two factors of the number:

```
N =
114,381,625,757,888,867,669,235,779,976,146,612,010,218,296,721,242,362,562,
561,842,935,706,935,245,733,897,830,597,123,563,958,705,058,989,075,147,599,
290,026,879,543,541
```

are:

```
3,490,529,510,847,650,949,147,849,619,903,898,133,417,764,638,493,387,843,990,
820,577
```

and:

```
32,769,132,993,266,709,549,961,988,190,834,461,413,177,642,967,992,942,539,798,
288,533
```

Is your PGP public key safe? The 129-digit RSA modulus could be represented by a binary number 429 bits long. That's considerably longer than the original 384-bit modulus for the smallest keys in PGP Version 2.3. Indeed, it's nearly 512 bits, although the time to factor a number approximately doubles for every additional ten bits in length with the factoring algorithm used by the group. (Faster factoring algorithms have since been discovered.) And while it is unlikely that such a large international effort could be assembled to crack a random person's public key, it is not unthinkable that a company with a thousand workstations might devote the computer's spare time to cracking the public key of one of its competitors.

Phil's Pretty Good Pizza has reason to worry! With a 512-bit public key, the pizza parlor may be vulnerable in a few years.

As a consequence of this breakthrough, I now recommend that people use PGP's maximum 1024-bit keys. Such long keys seem reasonably safe for a *very long time.* (All of the computers in the world working together could not crack a 1024-bit number within the lifespan of anyone reading this book.) But you never know; there might be a breakthrough in factoring or in computer speed. For this reason, future versions of PGP will probably allow public keys to be considerably longer than 1024 bits.

What about the hundred dollars that Rivest promised for breaking the code? The international effort promised to give the money to the Free Software Foundation. Originally, Lenstra wanted Richard Stallman, the foundation's founder and president, to accept the money in person. However, Stallman is also the founder of the League for Programming Freedom, an organization dedicated to the abolition of software patents. Project organizers feared that Stallman would use the event as a podium to attack software patents, such as the RSA patent itself, for thwarting the progress of computer science and creating a danger for those who wish to program freely, without legal threats. The organizers didn't want their announcement to be subverted by Stallman for his own ends, so they barred him from the event and gave the money to the Free Software Foundation *in absentia.*

And what about the message that was encrypted in that *Scientific American* article? One of the people most surprised by this turn of events was Ron Rivest, who was sure that he would never again see the words he had encrypted back in 1977. (Rivest has allegedly admitted that he simply made up the figure "40 quadrillion years" as the time necessary to factor the RSA-129 number. Even so, the number turned out to be an approximate count of the number of *instructions* that needed to be executed in order to find the result.) Seventeen years later, he read them again:

THE MAGIC WORDS ARE SQUEAMISH OSSIFRAGE

5

Privacy and Public Policy

The day after the memorandum [a War Department request for a bureau of code and cipher experts, probably the first American example of a secret intelligence budget] was submitted, it was approved by Frank L. Polk, the Acting Secretary of State; and on May 20, 1919, as the ink from the signature of Chief of Staff General Peyton C. March began drying, America's Black Chamber was born. . . . To hide even further the true nature of the work (as well as to earn a few extra dollars), Yardley formed a commercial code business called Code Compilation Company, and operated it from the first floor of the brownstone. If anyone ventured in through the front door, he would find an apparently legitimate company. The firm did produce a commercial code, the University Trade Code, which it was able to sell profitably."

—James Bamford in *The Puzzle Palace*, 1982

PGP is a program that arouses strong emotions. Civil rights advocates see PGP as the first step toward an electronic future in which personal information and the privacy of communications are sacrosanct. Some software developers—particularly those who create free software—see PGP as an example of the damaging effects of software patents. Other software developers—such as those who hold software patents—see PGP as out-and-out theft.

And some see PGP as a threat. Law enforcement officials and the intelligence agencies are terrified by PGP and its promise of widely available, easy-to-use, military-grade encryption. Because ubiquitous cryptography threatens to dramatically increase the cost of police investigations and intelligence gathering, law enforcement and intelligence organizations are fighting it.

This chapter looks at the larger context in which the battles between PGP and U.S. government policy on individual privacy are playing themselves out.[†] Chapter 6, *Cryptography Patents and Export*, looks at public policy as it affects and is affected by patents on cryptography.

Wiretapping and the U.S. Government

The history of cryptography and information security is full of examples of the struggle between technology, individual privacy, government controls, and attempts to strike a balance between conflicting rights and requirements.[‡] Each new communications advance is followed closely by encryption inventions aimed at protecting those communications. And each new type of protection inevitably is followed by governmental attempts to intercept those communications.

As soon as Samuel F.B. Morse introduced the telegraph back in 1845, people started worrying about the confidentiality of the messages being transmitted with the new device. Within a year, a commercial encryption code had been developed to protect telegraphed messages. A few years after that, the U.S. governnment sought ways to tap into the protected messages.

The first widely known wiretappings occurred during the Civil War when both Union and Confederate troops intercepted electronic messages by setting up rudimentary taps on enemy telegraph lines, thereby gaining intelligence on troop movements and strengths. Codes and especially ciphers were widely employed on both sides in an attempt to mask the meaning of the communications. The Civil War was not only the first time electronic messages and wiretaps were employed on a large scale; it was also the first time codebreaking became a common weapon of war. The rebel forces also used ciphers to mask their diplomatic communications with foreign capitals— particularly Great Britain. (In Washington, D.C., the State Department did not adopt ciphers to protect diplomatic communications until 20 months after Lee's surrender.)

After the Civil War, some law enforcement officials continued to use wiretaps as a means of investigating suspected criminal activity, but there was a catch: no laws addressed wiretapping. Some states passed their own wiretap statutes; others did not. Some states allowed wiretapping; others did not. Complicating matters still further was the fact that telephone and telegraph wires crossed state lines; which state's laws had jurisdiction over an interstate cable?

---

† Much of this chapter was written with the help of Brock M. Meeks.
‡ The information in this history is partially based on *Codes, Keys, and Conflicts: Issues in U.S. Crypto Policy*, report of a special panel of the Association of Computing Machinery, and on *United States Diplomatic Codes and Ciphers, 1775–1938* by Ralph E. Weber.

The federal government passed its first wiretap law in 1918. The law permitted wiretaps but strictly as a counterespionage tool during the First World War. Wiretapping proved so effective, however, that law enforcement continued to use it after the war to fight bootleggers and crack down on the rampant crime spawned during the era of Prohibition. It didn't take long for this use of wiretapping to be challenged in the courts.

In 1928, the Supreme Court ruled in the case of Olmstead v. United States that the Fourth Amendment prohibition against unreasonable searches and seizures covered only material items. Conversations, the Court said, weren't material goods. As a result, snagging conversations during a wiretap *didn't* amount to unconstitutional search under the Fourth Amendment. In this divided opinion, Justice Brandeis dissented, delivering his famous opinion that the Constitution implicitly gives Americans a right to privacy, the right "to be let alone" by their government. Today the majority opinion in the Olmstead case is long forgotten, and Brandeis' dissent has been taken as the basis for laws and public policy on privacy.

In 1934, Congress passed the Federal Communications Act. The statute contained specific language that forbade the interception of wire or radio communications. Eventually, the Supreme Court ruled that information obtained by a wiretap that was not backed by a court order could not be used as evidence in court.

During World War II, Congress once again authorized wiretapping as a means of tracking spies. Meanwhile, the Supreme Court decided in a series of cases that conversations intercepted by other electronic means and without a court order *could* be allowed as evidence. In 1942, the Court ruled in the government's favor in the case of Goldman v. United States, in which law enforcement agents had rented an office adjacent to the office of the suspect, drilled a hole in the wall, and inserted an electronic bugging device. (Such devices were called "spike mikes" and were widely used at the time.) The Court ruled that the agents had not actually trespassed into the suspect's office; thus, the Fourth Amendment's prohibition on unreasonable search had not been breached. In the 1954 case, Irvine v. California, the Court extended this notion to include microphones hidden in the walls of a suspect's home.

The Court reversed itself in 1961, ruling in the case of Silverman v. United States that information obtained from a spike mike was inadmissible. In 1967, the Court ruled in the case of Katz v. United States that public telephone booths could not be tapped without a warrant, because, despite the fact that public phones are in public places, such phones carry with them a reasonable expectation of privacy.

This case led to the rewriting of the federal wiretap laws in the 1968 Omnibus Crime Control Act, which was passed at the time to deal with the emerging specter of organized crime. Wiretaps were seen as the only effective way to breach the closed organized crime societies of the time.

What's behind the Court's reversal of legal protection against wiretaps and other forms of electronic surveillance? It is hard to say. One possibility is that between 1928 and 1961, members of the Court steadily became more familiar with communication technologies and the invasiveness of electronic communications. Actions that did not seem to violate the Fourth Amendment in the early part of this century might be viewed as constitutionally dubious in the latter half.

In the two decades that followed, wiretaps became an accepted tool for law enforcement—a tool credited with the destruction of major organized crime networks throughout the United States. For example, information obtained from wiretapes was crucial in obtaining convictions of alleged mobsters John Gotti and John Stanfa. Nevertheless, the statistics in the following table show that the actual number of court-ordered wiretaps is fewer than a thousand a year over the past decade:

Year	Federal Wiretaps	State Wiretaps[†]
1984	289	512
1985	243	541
1986	250	504
1987	236	437
1988	293	445
1989	310	453
1990	324	548
1991	356	500
1992	340	579
1993	450	526

[†] Source: *Wiretap Report*

In the early 1990s, the FBI and other federal agencies claimed that they were beginning to notice increasing delays in the execution of wiretap orders, in part due to the newer telecommunications systems of the day. Cellular telephones presented a particular challenge. In New York City, for example, no provision had been made for wiretapping in the cellular telephone systems that the city's cellular telephone carriers had installed. The FBI was alarmed that this might be the start of a trend.

Although cellular telephone conversations can easily be picked up by a hand-held scanner, zeroing in on a particular cellular telephone conversation is more difficult. The computers that route conversations between the cellular and conventional telephone networks could monitor specific phone calls only at special "technical ports" located on the telephone switch itself. One of the systems installed in New York City, an AT&T Autoplex 1000, which could handle 150,000 subscribers, had just *seven* technical ports. According to then-FBI engineering chief James K. Kallstrom, if John Gotti had used a cellular telephone, some of the conversations that led to his conviction might have gone unheard and unrecorded by law enforcement agents.

The revolution in telecommunications was allegedly causing other problems for law enforcement as well. Most wiretaps require the insertion of a special recording device across the wires of a suspect's telephone line. With call-forwarding, a suspect could have his calls automatically redirected to another telephone number—across town, across the country, or across the world, simultaneously bypassing the wiretap and possibly changing jurisdiction as well. Digital ISDN telephone, moreover, required special digital wiretaps. When ISDN was first deployed, such equipment was not available for law enforcement agencies. Anybody using a digital phone was all but guaranteed an untappable line.

The FBI's Digital Telephony Plan

The FBI's plan to stem the tide of technology made its first public debut in the spring of 1992 at the second Conference on Computers, Freedom, and Privacy. At the conference, a photocopied document that had been leaked a few days earlier slowly made its way around the hall. On the first page of the document the words "Digital Telephony" were printed in simple block letters. On the second page was the seal of the FBI, followed by many pages of proposed legislation. Conference participants soon realized that the Digital Telephony proposal was an official policy initiative from the highest levels of the bureau.

The Digital Telephony proposal would have required every communications system in the nation to install "easy access" software to facilitate wiretaps. Developers of systems that did not comply would be fined $10,000 per day. The plan would have allowed the FBI to eavesdrop on any kind of electronic communication, from voice to email to faxes. The plan applied to both public and private networks. The FBI argued that the proposal was necessary simply to maintain the status quo, but experts familiar with the actual step-by-step procedure of obtaining a wiretap court order and setting up a wiretap said that the Digital Telephony proposal would have made the mechanics of wiretapping dramatically easier for law enforcement—and possibly far easier to abuse.

One of the key elements of the Digital Telephony plan was to allow remote monitoring of communications networks without the active involvement of the network's own operators. According to law enforcement officials, remote monitors are crucial because it is currently very difficult to wiretap a crime boss, for example, who has bribed employees of the phone company. The plan further required that the telecommunication networks be designed in such a way that the users of the system not be able to determine that they are being monitored—no flashing lights, no tell-tale clicks, and no change in performance.

The Digital Telephony plan met with strong industry opposition organized by the Computer Professionals for Social Responsibility and the Electronic Frontier Foundation. Major corporations contacted members of Congress, and the FBI's proposal never reached the floor of the House.

How could the FBI have so grossly miscalculated public and corporate opinion?

The Washington, D.C. office of the Computer Professionals for Social Responsibility (now renamed the Electronic Privacy Information Center, or EPIC) tried to find out. Using previously classified documents obtained through the Freedom of Information Act, it was able to trace the policy decisions that led to the doomed proposal.

The more than 180 pages of previously classified documents obtained by EPIC make it clear that the FBI introduced its digital wiretap legislative proposal only after concluding that the telephone industry would not go along voluntarily with the Digital Telephony plan.

EPIC reported that the FBI:

- Tried to get the telephone industry to voluntarily write digital wiretap "trap doors" into future specifications for central office switches.

- Tried to convince the industry to cooperate voluntarily by indicating that the FBI wouldn't be able to protect network security.

- Developed a cost analysis study of the financial impact of digital wiretap access on the telephone industry, though it later claimed that no such study existed.

According to an internal FBI memo dated February 8, 1991, the bureau tried to induce telephone companies to develop "immediate and interim solutions" for digital wiretap access. The memo also said that FBI agents, in conversations with industry executives, "stressed the necessity to incorporate these monitoring requirements in future specifications for central office switches." But the companies were reluctant to go along unless they were forced to do so by new legislation. Another internal FBI memo dated August 21, 1991, quotes an unidentified PacBell official as saying "The only viable solution for this problem would be through legislative action as technical solutions alone would be cost prohibitive and ineffective." The PacBell official also is quoted as saying that legislation "would ensure the equal commitment of all providers."

The following year, the FBI started a two-year secret campaign, code-named "Operation Root Canal," to win quiet telephone industry agreement that would give the agency easy wiretap access to all digital conversations. The FBI also started a one-on-

one lobbying effort from its highest levels to win the heart of every member of Congress.

In a September 22, 1992, letter to Charles Bowsher (former Comptroller General), then-FBI Director William Sessions said that when FBI efforts to gain industry's voluntary compliance failed "to achieve prompt action," the industry reached consensus that "legislative mandate was both needed and desired." An FBI source is quoted as saying that legislation "was the Bureau's court of last resort."

But when the FBI introduced its legislative plan, the telephone companies cut the bureau off at the knees by vocally opposing the bill. This stance confused the FBI, which thought it had full industry endorsement. Telephone industry executives, meanwhile, continue to deny that they encouraged the FBI to introduce the wiretap bill.

Digital Telephony was temporarily stopped in its tracks. It wasn't dead, though. It was just . . . sleeping.

The Untold Cost of Digital Telephony

The FBI gained a powerful ally early in 1994 when the Clinton administration gave its backing to the controversial FBI plan. But the administration's support was based, in large part, on severely flawed data, according to a story first reported by *CyberWire Dispatch*, an Internet news bulletin distributed by Brock Meeks, a former reporter for *Communications Daily.*

Using a confidential FBI cost analysis document, *CyberWire Dispatch* reported that the agency estimated it would take some $300 million to implement the mandatory wiretap access scheme. But government and industry sources at the time said that the actual cost of implementation could quickly escalate to more than $1 billion. One reason: The FBI's own cost analysis didn't consider the price of mandatory compliance for the newer technologies—computer networks, cable TV operations, digital cellular systems, and emerging personal communication systems.

The FBI's answer to the digital wiretap problem lies in developing a software program that could be loaded into a telephone switch. But the cost for developing this software is "difficult to estimate absent specific feasibility studies," FBI documents say. It is known that at least four different versions of the program would have to be written to cover the installed base of telephone switches in the United States.

The FBI's cost estimate also didn't factor in the cost of maintaining the software. Currently, the Baby Bells and major independent telephone companies spend more than $1 billion a year in new switch and application upgrade software, according to the National Association of Regulatory Utility Commissioners.

Quality control and the integrity of the nation's telephone network is a very serious matter to the communications industry, and software is an important factor in today's automated switching systems. Telephone company executives remember all too well being criticized by House Telecommunications Subcommittee Chairman Ed Markey (Democrat-Massachusetts) in 1990 during intense Congressional hearings aimed at discovering the cause of a massive failure of the telephone system involving half of the East Coast. The cause, it was later admitted, was a "3-bit bug" software coding error. The switch's software revision hadn't undergone sufficiently rigorous testing before being installed in the local network.

Who picks up the tab for revising the wiretap software to make sure it's compatible with each new calling feature and modification to switch software? At first, the FBI wanted American citizens to pay for all this work through higher local telephone rates. That idea drew such withering fire from consumer groups and industry that the FBI deleted that language from its original bill. Now the legislation has approved some $500 million over four years to pay for the initial upgrades. So Americans still end up paying but through the "back door" of taxes.

Return of Digital Telephony

Through FBI Director Louis Freeh's intense lobbying of nearly every member of Congress, the FBI succeeded in having its digital wiretap proposal introduced as an official piece of legislation in 1994—a feat thought impossible when the bureau first introduced the severely flawed bill. Ironically, the bill was introduced by leading Congressional privacy advocates, Senator Patrick Leahy (Democrat-Vermont) and Representative Don Edwards (Democrat-California), who claimed the bill is a "good compromise," compared with what the FBI originally wanted.

Close inspection of the 1994 bill revealed that it essentially turned control of the nation's communications network over to the Justice Department. At a cost of more than $500 million, it's a move that virtually nationalizes all telephone technology— something unprecedented in U.S. history, except during time of war.

Although private companies retain control over profits and revenues, the 1994 bill puts them at the technological beck and call of the Justice Department. The bill gives the Justice Department the authority to make technological demands on the nation's communications networks that must be complied with, at the risk of severe penalties for noncompliance. The bill specifically states that law enforcement agencies can't dictate a "specific design or system configuration," but that's little comfort.

The Leahy-Edwards bill gives the government the authority to dictate—forever— specific capabilities that each communications company has to meet. Companies that can't meet the government's demands for easy wiretap access to their customers' conversations, electronic mail messages, faxes, or file transfers, will be fined as much as $10,000 a day.

The bill also dramatically expands the scope of "common carriers" (which are mainly your local and long distance telephone companies) to a new category of "telecommunications carriers." This new category, penciled in at the insistence of the telephone companies facing the threat of having to bear the entire burden for making the FBI's job easier, includes "any person or entity engaged in the transmission or switching of wire or electronic communications for value for unaffiliated persons, but does not include persons or entities engaged in providing information services."

The bill requires the Attorney General to draw up a kind of easy wiretap access battle plan and present it to the industry. Included in that plan must be a written notice of the maximum capacity required to "accommodate all the communications interceptions, pen registers, and trap-and trace-devices" the Attorney General estimates the government will need.

All telecommunications carriers then have three years to comply with those requests. The catch is that the Justice Department can "periodically" provide updates to that original plan, which "increases the maximum capacity" first stated. For each upgraded estimate, the industry has three years to cooperate or get hammered.

If a carrier fails to comply, the Justice Department can order compliance, up to and including ordering manufacturers to redesign their products so they can be installed on U.S. communications networks (including the U.S. portion of the Internet).

The bill also forces the Federal Communications Commission (FCC) into a new position of policing wiretap standards for law enforcement agencies. Under this bill, the FCC is made out to be the court of last resort for any wiretap standards disputes. "[I]f industry associations or bodies fail to issue specifications or standards, any person may petition" the FCC to "establish . . . specifications or standards" that implement easy wiretap access, the bill says.

Because the FCC is not presently equipped to write standards, the bill allows the FCC to assess and collect fees that it will levy against telecommunications carriers to increase its technical staff.

Where's the Beef?

Perhaps the oddest, yet the most significant, aspect of the FBI's wiretap bill was that, despite FBI insistence that digital technologies have the potential to thwart investigation, the bureau has never actually provided proof to support these claims. The bureau has tried, but so far, it hasn't been able to.

Documents released to EPIC, in fact, indicate that the opposite appears to be true. FBI field report documents show that the bureau received no support from its field officers to back up the claims of problems caused by digital technologies. In previously classified memos, field offices repeatedly reported no difficulty in carrying out electronic surveillance. A December 3, 1992, report from the Newark office is typical. It reported the following:

- The Drug Enforcement Administration (DEA) "advised that as of this date, the DEA has not had any technical problems with advanced telephone technology."

- The New Jersey attorney general's office said that it hasn't had any problems "since the last contact."

- The IRS reported no problems with "advanced telephone matters."

- The New Jersey state police said that "as of this date" the agency has had no problems with technology's hindering investigations.

An examination of all of the documents released turned up no reports of technology's hampering investigations. And during a November 16, 1994, appearance on Wisconsin Public Radio, FBI Special Agent James Kallstrom also contradicted previous FBI claims, admitting during a debate with EPIC's legal counsel, David Sobel, that digital technologies hadn't yet hampered FBI investigations.

An Information Superhighway that's "Wired for Sound"

In early 1994, a law enforcement panel addressing the administration's Information Infrastructure Task Force Working Group on Privacy told a public meeting that it wanted to "front load" the National Information Infrastructure (NII) with trap door technologies that would allow easy access to digital conversations, either by eavesdropping on conversations or by capturing electronic communications midstream.

Panel members representing the Justice Department, the FBI, and the U.S. Attorney General's office said that they took Vice President Gore's promise that the White House would work to ensure that the NII would "help law enforcement agencies thwart criminals and terrorists who might use advanced telecommunications to commit crimes," as tacit approval of their proposals to push for digital wiretap access and government-mandated encryption policies. (Gore buried those remarks in a speech he made in Los Angeles in 1994, in which he outlined the administration's plan to rewrite the rules for communications in a newer, perhaps more enlightened, age.)

From the government's viewpoint, installing interception technologies all along the information superhighway is simply "proactive" law enforcement policy, in the words of Kent Walker, Assistant U.S. Attorney, Northern District of California. Designing these technologies into future networks, which include all telephone systems, would ensure that law enforcement organizations "have the same capabilities that we all enjoy right now," Walker said.

For Walker, privacy issues weighed against law enforcement needs are black and white, or rather "good guys vs. bad guys." For example, he said that the rapid rise of private (nongovernment) encryption technologies such as PGP didn't mean law enforcement would have to work harder. On the contrary, "it only means we'll catch less criminals," he said.

David Sobel, legal counsel for EPIC, sees things differently. "Because of law enforcement's concerns (regarding digital technologies), we're seeing an unprecedented involvement by federal security agencies in the domestic law enforcement activities." Sobel is also concerned that, for the first time in history, the NSA "is now deeply involved in the design of the public telecommunications network." Another move he calls "unprecedented" is that if the NSA, FBI, and other law enforcement organizations have their way with the standardization of telecommunications technology, the design of the national telecommunications network will end up classified and withheld from the public.

Walker thinks individual citizens agree with the government's stand. "There has to be a balance between privacy needs and law enforcement needs to catch criminals," he says. "If you ask the public, 'Is privacy more important than catching criminals?' They'll tell you, 'No.' "

This must be the logic that the FBI used in the closing days of the 1994 Congress, when the U.S. Senate passed the FBI's wiretap bill by unanimous consent. President Clinton signed it a few days later. "Digital Telephony" is now the law of the land.

The NSA's Clipper Chip

Strong encryption could render the entire Digital Telephony law irrelevant: if gangsters use encrypting telephones, law enforcement officials won't be able to understand the conversations that they intercept. So the logical second half of the U.S. government's data communication strategy for the 1990s is to stamp out the use of encryption that it cannot break.

Encrypting telephones and voice scrambling technology are older than the NSA itself. Bell Laboratories developed early voice scrambling systems in the 1930s. During World War II, Franklin Roosevelt used a voice scrambler to speak with Winston Churchill. These systems never troubled law enforcement, however; government security, high cost, and low availability kept them out of the hands of the public—until now.

Largely motivated by recent well-publicized cases of industrial espionage, American businesses are interested in using cryptography to protect their business communications. Unfortunately for the U.S. government, technology that could prevent the government of France from listening in on the conversations of Boeing executives could also be used by organized crime to render wiretaps useless. The solution was simple: a code that France couldn't break, but that the FBI could.

Thus, while the FBI pushed its Digital Telephony proposal in public, the super-secret National Security Agency was busy designing its own encryption algorithm to replace the aging, battle-scarred Data Encryption Standard. But, whereas the DES had been adopted only after extensive public review, work on and discussion of the new algorithm was shrouded in secrecy.

The NSA's secret plan is to have its own home-grown encryption technology widely adopted as a public standard and installed on every type of communications network in the United States. On April 16, 1993, the White House first unveiled the NSA's secret encryption standard, affectionately known as the "Clipper chip."

Inside Clipper

The Clipper chip contains a classified algorithm called Skipjack. Clipper was intended to encode voice communications on digital telephones and fax machines. Data, email, and other kinds of communications were to be handled by something called the Fortezza card, a PCMCIA card suitable for plugging into most laptop computers.

Clipper is a moderately priced ($10–$30) encryption/decryption chip that can be installed in virtually any digital communications device. By all accounts, the encryption used by Clipper is excellent; no one has cracked the code yet. Skipjack is an 80-bit encryption algorithm that is supposedly 16 million times harder to crack than the DES. And it's even harder to crack, the government says, because the NSA is keeping the Clipper encryption algorithm secret. Anything encrypted with a Clipper chip is very secure for years to come.

There's just one exception to this security: the U.S. government can read any message that is encrypted with Clipper because the government already has the keys.

Each Clipper chip is programmed with two unique codes: a serial number (sort of like the chip's social security number) and a master encryption key. You, the user of the chip, can't view either of these two codes. Clipper is a tamper-proof chip; if you try to discover the chip's secret number, the chip destroys the data.

Every time a Clipper chip encrypts a message, it takes a copy of the session key needed to decrypt the message and encrypts that key with the chip's own master encryption key. It then collects both the encrypted session key and the chip's serial number and sends them along with every encrypted message.

Clipper uses the Diffie-Hellman key exchange algorithm to exchange keys.

The government's plan, called the Escrowed Encryption Standard (EES), is to create a master database containing the serial number of each Clipper chip and that chip's master encryption key. Actually, the government plans to create two databases, each one containing the chip numbers and *half* of the encryption key. Each half key will be held by a different "escrow agent." One half is held by the National Institute for Standards and Technology (NIST), the other half by the Automated Systems Division of the Department of the Treasury. Both of these groups are in the executive branch of the U.S. government. In June 1994, Steven Levy reported in the *New York Times Sunday Magazine* that each half-database resides on two sets of floppy disks kept in a double-walled safe. At that time, 20,000 "key splits" were on file.

Who Gets the Keys?

A U.S. Department of Justice February 4, 1994, memorandum, entitled "Authorization Procedures for Release of Encryption Key Components in Conjunction with Intercepts Pursuant to Title III," outlines the following procedure by which the keys will be released:[†]

1. "In each case, there shall be a legal authorization for the interception. . . ." (That is, there must be a court-ordered wiretap or an authorization that can legally bypass the in-court procedure.)

2. If the authorization is in the form of a court order, it must contain provisions for "after-the-fact minimization." (That is, if the agent picks up information that is not within the scope of the warrant, that information must not be used.)

3. If federal law enforcement agents discover during the course of a lawfully authorized interception that they are receiving encrypted communications, they need to obtain certification from their investigative agency or the U.S. Attorney General's office that: a) identifies the agency and the person providing the certification; b) certifies that necessary legal authorization has been obtained to conduct electronic surveillance; c) specifies the termination date of the period for which interception has been authorized; d) identifies by docket number or some other suitable method the source of the authorization; e) certifies that communications covered by the authorization are being encrypted with a key-escrow encryption method; f)

---

† The following points are loosely excerpted from the DOJ's memorandum.

specifies the identifier (ID) number of the key escrow encryption chip providing such encryption; g) specifies the serial number of the key escrow decryption device that will be used by the law enforcement agency or other authority for decryption of the intercepted communications.

4. The agency conducting the interception shall submit this certification to each of the designated key component escrow agents.

5. Upon receiving the request, each key escrow agent shall release the necessary key component to the requesting agency. "The key components shall be provided in a manner that assures they cannot be used other than in conjunction with the lawfully authorized electronic surveillance for which they were requested."

6. Each of the key escrow agents shall retain a copy of the certification of the requesting agency.

7. Upon completion of the electronic surveillance, the ability of the requesting agency to decrypt intercepted communications shall terminate, and the requesting agency may not retain the key components.

8. The Department of Justice shall, in each case: a) ascertain the existence of authorizations for electronic surveillance; b) ascertain that key components for a particular key-escrow chip are being used only by the investigative agency authorized to conduct electronic surveillance; c) ascertain that the ability of the requesting agency to decrypt intercepted communications is terminated.

9. A report of the key release shall be made to the Administrative Offices of the U.S. Courts. (This office tracks all wiretap-related facts in its annually published *Wiretap Report*.)

In other words, when a law enforcement agency (which could be your local sheriff's department) wants to wiretap a conversation that's been encrypted by Clipper, the agency applies to each of the escrow agents. The agents send their respective keys, electronically, to a "black box" operated by the law enforcement agency. As encrypted conversations stream into the box, they come out decrypted. The keys from the escrow agents are equipped with expiration codes; when the warrant expires, the black box stops decrypting conversations.

When Clipper was introduced, the White House said its use was to be a "voluntary program to improve the security and privacy of telephone communications while meeting the legitimate needs of law enforcement." As part of the plan, the escrow agents would not turn over their keys unless the applicant had first obtained a court-approved wiretap. This, the administration says, is where your privacy is protected. "We're not going to use Clipper to listen in on the American public," said Raymond Kammer, NIST's deputy director. Clipper will be used only to catch criminals.

However, the last paragraph of the government procedures states that, "These procedures do not create, and are not intended to create, any substantive rights for individuals intercepted through electronic surveillance, and noncompliance with these procedures shall not provide the basis for any motion to suppress or other objection to the introduction of electronic surveillance evidence lawfully acquired." In other words, if the government "lawfully" intercepts communication and manages to get hold of the decryption keys without following its nine-step procedure, the evidence is still valid in a court of law.

What the government hasn't said is whether the NSA will have access to the escrow database or perhaps to a second, functionally identical database. It's hard to believe that the NSA would allow itself to be placed in a position of having to get court orders to access the keys. It's important to note the government has stated that devices containing Clipper will be allowed to be exported. Remember that the NSA has the legislative right and the executive mandate to eavesdrop on any electronic communication originating or received outside the United States. If Clipper-equipped radios were being used by Iraqi fighter pilots, the NSA would want to listen in. Although the NSA hasn't said so publicly, it is doubtful that the agency would jeopardize national security in order to play along with the escrow system.

One way that the NSA could neatly subvert the entire process is by preempting the programming of the Clipper chips themselves. As of this writing, Clipper chips are manufactured by only one company, Mykotronx, which has had extensive classified dealings with the Department of Defense. The design of the Clipper chip itself is classified. Also classified is the exact manner in which each chip's master key is created. The NSA might know all of the master keys even before they are stamped into the chips themselves. Since almost everything about Clipper is classified, no one who knows all of the facts of the case is allowed to state them publicly.

The Battle over Clipper and the EES

The introduction of Clipper raised a firestorm of protest. NIST sought public comment on the EES proposal, but it wasn't prepared for the response. Overwhelmingly, the public responded negatively. NIST received hundreds of comments; only three were positive.

This public outcry should have been enough to warn the administration that it had bought into a bad dog. It wasn't. Despite the fact that the Clipper plan was inherited by the Clinton administration from the Bush administration, it was embraced wholeheartedly. Indeed, to this day, the Clinton administration has never given a straightforward answer as to why it so easily bought into the idea of Clipper.

On February 4, 1994, after months of internal government review, the White House approved Clipper and the EES.

The White House endorsement of the EES represents a sea change in how the government deals with individual privacy. The initiative that embodies the EES involved the creation of "new products to accelerate the development and use of advanced and secure telecommunications networks and wireless telecommunications links," the White House said. In other words, law enforcement and intelligence agencies now have an easy way to access any and all forms of spoken or electronically transmitted communications.

Clipper is voluntary. You don't have to sign on to it. You don't have to use government-approved encryption devices. But if you plan to do any business with the government, you have to use them. In this manner, the government hopes that Clipper devices will make the EES a de facto standard.

Some opponents of Clipper fear that if you don't use the government standard, you'll be branding yourself a Crypto-rebel. Big deal? Maybe, maybe not. But think for a moment about how things could evolve over time. Perhaps someday, some agency will be able to check your "crypto-approval rating." Perhaps those favorable bank loans, mortgage rates, or low insurance premiums will go only to those with high crypto-approval ratings. Paranoia? There are some who don't think so.

While the White House stresses that the EES is voluntary, there is a niggling bit of background information to contend with. Buried deep in the original April 16, 1993, Clipper background information papers was an official policy statement from the White House that said that no U.S. citizen "as a matter of right, is entitled to an unbreakable commercial encryption product."

The Cypherpunks and civil liberties groups go ballistic over this statement on encryption, which they read as a first step toward what could, one day, be a policy of outlawing private encryption schemes.

The government says that Clipper is beneficial for all citizens except those engaged in illegal activities. It gives individual citizens the type of powerful cryptography that was previously available only to the military and to the largest corporations. It gives law enforcement the ability to solve and prevent crimes. Vice President Al Gore says this about the administration's endorsement of the EES: "Encryption is a law and order issue since it can be used by criminals to thwart wiretaps and avoid detection and prosecution. . . . Our policy is designed to provide better encryption to individuals and businesses while ensuring that the needs of law enforcement and national security are met."

The administration won't say why it expects Americans to simply hand over all their privacy safeguards to the government. "Listen, if you knew what we knew about criminal activity, this issue wouldn't even be debated," said Mike Nelson of the Office of Science and Technology Policy and co-chair of the Working Group on Data Security, a newly created interagency task force. (Nelson is also famous for admitting that the horrendous policy issues surrounding the EES made it the "Bosnia of telecommunications.")

Just Forget About Clipper

What about those wily criminals? Would they ever use devices that contain Clipper chips? Once they get wind of this, won't they seek another type of encryption? The FBI doesn't think so. In fact, the FBI thinks that criminals have the brains of trout and are likely to forget all about the fact that Clipper even exists.

"I predict that few criminals will remember years from now what they've read in the *Wall Street Journal* about how these devices were installed in telephones," said FBI's James Kallstrom. Others disagree, pointing out that these are the same criminals who are putting together multi-million dollar drug deals, not to mention risking arrest, every time they make a call. They may not be brilliant, but they're likely to pay *some* attention.

Problems with Clipper

Matthew Blaze, a researcher for AT&T Bell Labs, was just doing his job in 1994 when he rocked the entire intelligence community of the United States. His job was to nose around inside the government's encryption code to see if he could break it.

You might say that Blaze failed: he couldn't find a way to decrypt a Clipper-encrypted message. In fact, he found a way to make these messages even more secure, by disabling the key escrow encryption scheme.

What Blaze discovered was a design flaw in Clipper's technological "back door": the Law Enforcement Access Field (LEAF). The LEAF contains an encoded copy of the session key that can be used to read encrypted data. Using the LEAF, law enforcement agencies can obtain the appropriate copies of Clipper's two keys held by the key escrow agents in their digital vaults.

Blaze discovered that if you can corrupt the LEAF, law enforcement can't unscramble a Clipper-encoded message. The LEAF is protected by a 16-bit checksum, which is a kind of self-checking mathematical equation. But it turns out that any random sequence of bits has a 1 in 65,536 shot of passing that checksum test.

Generating that many numbers is a simple hack for even a pedestrian programmer. Blaze found it possible to generate a seemingly valid yet "rogue" checksum in about

42 minutes. This means that law enforcement agencies could be fooled into thinking they had a valid LEAF, only to find, when presenting it to the key escrow agents, that they actually held a bogus LEAF.

The NSA tried to downplay the news of Blaze's discovery. "Anyone interested in circumventing law enforcement access would most likely choose simpler alternatives," said Michael Smith, the agency's planning director. "More difficult and time-consuming efforts, like those discussed in the Blaze paper, are very unlikely to be employed."

And he's right. Those "simpler alternatives" include everything from private encryption methods to not using a Clipper-equipped phone or fax in the first place. (At the same time, the FBI says that criminals won't use any of this simpler technology because they are too dumb.)

Despite the NSA's attempt to blow off Blaze's findings, the agency is grinding its gears. One NSA source said that the Blaze paper is "a major embarrassment for the program." But the situation is "containable" he said. "There will be a fix."

Expect Son of Clipper to debut sometime in 1995.

6

Cryptography Patents and Export

> *9. Cylink is informed and believes and on that basis alleges that the [RSA] patent is invalid, unenforceable, and void. . . .*
>
> —Complaint for Declaratory Judgment and Injunctive Relief and Demand for Jury Trial, Attorneys for Plaintiff, CYLINK CORPORATION, in the case of Cylink Corporation v. RSA Data Security, Inc., C94 02332

Many people believe that both U.S. export restrictions and patent policies have limited the spread of strong cryptography. This chapter looks at current U.S. government policy in these areas and at the general area of cryptographic patents and the recent attacks on those patents in the courts.

Patents and Policy

The U.S. Data Encryption Standard (DES) was published in 1975 and formally adopted as an American standard in 1976. The RSA public key cryptography system was published in *Scientific American* in 1977; within a few years, reasonably fast implementations of RSA were available on low-cost personal computers. Nevertheless, strong cryptography is still relatively rare in mass-market computer programs, both within the United States and abroad. Why?

Certainly, the U.S. restrictions on the export of cryptography have been a major stumbling block to the integration of strong cryptography into shrink-wrapped software. Most programmers who learn about cryptography soon find to their dismay that the software is export-controlled. The hassle of maintaining separate versions of a program for the United States and for export, combined with the uncertainty imposed by export and the severe penalties for breaking the rules, stop many companies from including strong cryptography in their products. Export problems have effectively kept such cryptography out of many mainstream software packages, such as word processors, electronic address books, and spreadsheets.

The patents on public key cryptography have also contributed to the overall uncertainty surrounding the technology. Until recently, few people were familiar with how these patents worked. Many firms that knew of the patents on public key cryptography didn't even think to contact the patent holders to arrange a license; they simply changed their plans and avoided putting public key cryptography into their products. Table 6-1 summarizes all of the patents on public key cryptography.

Table 6-1. The public key cryptography patents

Title and Patent #	Covers Invention	Inventors	Assignee	Dates
Cryptographic Apparatus and Method (4,200,770)	Diffie-Hellman key exchange	Martin E. Hellman, Bailey W. Diffie, Ralph C. Merkle	Stanford University	Filed: 9/6/77 Granted: 4/29/80 Expires:4/29/97
Public Key Cryptographic Apparatus and Method (4,218,582)	Knapsack and possibly all of public key cryptography	Martin E. Hellman, Ralph C. Merkle	Stanford University	Filed: 10/6/77 Granted: 8/19/80 Expires: 8/19/97
Exponentiation Cryptographic Apparatus and Method (4,424,414)		Martin E. Hellman, Stephen C. Pohlig	Stanford University	Filed: 5/1/78 Granted: 1/3/84 Expires: 1/3/2001
Cryptographic Communications System and Method (4,405,829)	RSA encryption	Ronald L. Rivest, Adi Shamir, Leonard M. Adleman	MIT	Filed: 12/14/77 Granted: 9/20/83 Expires: 9/20/2000
Method for Identifying Subscribers and for Generating and Verifying Electronic Signatures in a Data Exchange System (4,995,082)	Digital Signature Standard	Claus P. Schnorr	—	Filed: 2/23/90 Granted: 2/19/91 Expires: 2/19/2008

Recently, this situation has been changing. Thanks in part to programs like PGP, knowledge about encryption has become far more widespread. Increasingly, users are asking for encryption to be a standard part of the application programs that they purchase. Since some companies start to offer encryption, other companies are forced to do likewise or risk losing sales. The tide has started to turn.

Export: 40 Bits is not Enough!

In 1992, the U.S. government softened its position on the export of cryptography for the first time, thanks to a deal between the Software Publishers Association (SPA) and the Bush administration. Under the terms of the deal, software publishers were guaranteed a "fast-track" review of mass-market programs that used encryption and were promised exportability if those programs used RSA Data Security's RC2 or RC4 ciphers with a key length limited to 40 bits.

Many people attacked the deal between SPA and the U.S. government, saying that a cipher that used a 40-bit key was trivial to crack. Whitfield Diffie said point-blank that any cryptography algorithm that uses a 40-bit key is not secure. RSA's president Jim Bidzos was slightly more charitable: he said that even though the RC2 and RC4 ciphers encrypt and decrypt information very quickly, setting up the internal crypto engine for each new key requires a significant amount of time. As a result, Bidzos said, it would take an attacker who possessed the RC2 or RC4 algorithms 200 MIPS-years to perform a key search attack on a piece of text encrypted with RC2 or RC4.

In practical terms, 200 MIPS-years is the computing power of a single 200-MIPS workstation running for one year, or 200 1-MIPS workstations running for a year. In practice, a company with a network of 50 SPARCStation II workstations or 66 MHz 486 PCs could perform an exhaustive key search attack of a 40-bit key in 2.4 months. An engineer, working at night without authorization, could break a message encrypted by his company's CFO in four months. This isn't particularly secure. Bidzos argued that simply extending the key size from 40 to 48 bits would have dramatically improved the security, increasing the time required to crack an encrypted message from a few months to 64 years with current technology. (Adding 8 bits would increase the complexity of the problem by a factor of 256.)

On the other hand, the government's deal represented real progress over the status quo of the time, which flatly prohibited the export of serious encryption. The feeling at the time was that 40 bits was a start and that a change in the key length could be negotiated later. There was also a feeling, on the part of SPA and members of the Computer Professionals for Social Responsibility, that if negotiations over increasing the size of the key broke down, it would be a simple matter to petition Congress to change the size of the key by legislative action. (Such hopes may have been premature: a proposed bill by Representative Maria Cantwell (Democrat-Washington) in 1994 that would have eased restrictions on the export of cryptography by moving jurisdiction of export control from the State Department to the Commerce Department was killed by a unanimous vote of the Senate Intelligence Committee.)

The Digital Signature Standard

On August 30, 1991, the National Institute of Standards and Technology (NIST) published a proposed Federal Information Processing Standard (FIPS) for the Digital Signature Standard (DSS) in the *Federal Register*. NIST said that the DSS used a public key algorithm that "the government has applied to the U.S. Patent office for a patent on" as well as a message digest function that had yet to be determined. NIST also said "We believe this technique is patentable and that no other patents would apply to the DSS, but we cannot give firm assurances to such effect in advance of issuance of the patents."

According to the notice in the *Federal Register*, NIST expected the DSS to be widely implemented in everything from smart cards used in personal computers to mainframes. It further said that it expected to make the patent available for use by the public on a royalty-free basis.

For the DSS, NIST did not propose RSA digital signatures, which were being steadily adopted by the industry at the time. Instead, NIST proposed a new algorithm that had never been seen before: the Digital Signature Algorithm (DSA). Originally, NIST said that it had developed the DSA itself. Eventually, NIST admitted that DSA had been developed by scientists at the National Security Agency.

The Battle over the DSS

RSA Data Security was among the first to publicly criticize NIST's DSS proposal. RSA had lobbied heavily for the government to adopt digital signatures based on the RSA algorithm as a national standard. RSA had complained that a "common modulus" algorithm might allow the government to forge signatures. MIT professor Ron Rivest was particularly vocal in his criticism of the DSS, which has a modulus size of 512 bits. Rivest showed that the government (through NSA) has enough computer power to precompute sufficient information about the standard DSS factors to allow the government to forge DSS signatures at will.

Other companies also voiced opposition against the DSS. According to Bruce Schneier, "[the opposition] was more political than academic. . . . Companies such as IBM, Apple, Novell, Lotus, Northern Telecom, Microsoft, DEC, and Sun had already spent large amounts of money implementing the RSA algorithm. They were not interested in losing their investment."

NIST received 109 comments on the DSS by the end of the first comment period in February 1992. The criticisms focused on the following seven important points:

- The DSS could be used only for digital signatures and not encryption. Indeed, this was one of the purposes of the proposal: to adopt a standard that could be freely exported without any restrictions. NIST later admitted that one of the primary attractions of the DSS was that the algorithm was not RSA.

- DSA was developed by NSA, and the algorithm could have a secret "trap door" that allows nefarious uses. To date, no such trap doors have been found, although it is possible to hide secret information in DSS signatures without the knowledge of the signer.

- DSA is significantly slower than RSA.

- RSA was the de facto standard, both nationally and internationally, and had been proposed as an international standard as ISO/IEC 9796. Supporters of the DSS attacked Rivest, saying that his criticism of the DSS was solely motivated by his financial stake in RSA Data Security. NIST responded that RSA was covered by patents, whereas DSA could be used royalty-free.

- DSA was selected by a secret committee.

- DSA may infringe upon other patents.

- The key size (512 bits) specified for DSA in the DSS was too small. (NIST responded by making the key size variable, from 512 to 1024 bits.)

In January 1992, NIST published in the *Federal Register* its proposal for the DSS's message digest algorithm, the Secure Hash Algorithm (SHA). "For applications not requiring a digital signature, the SHA is to be used whenever a secure hash algorithm is required for Federal applications." Although the algorithm was clearly inspired by Ron Rivest's MD4 message digest algorithm (RSADSI's Jim Bidzos went so far as to call SHA the "Stolen Hash Algorithm"), many people felt that SHA was superior because it had a hash value of 160 bits, compared to 128 for MD4. Nevertheless, SHA was designed in secret by the NSA, and it is possible that the algorithm might contain a trap door or other hidden fault known only to its creators. In addition, the published algorithm was changed, without explanation, in 1994.

The DSS and Patents

Public Key Partners claimed that DSA infringed upon three patents: Diffie-Hellman (expires April 29, 1997), Merkle-Hellman (expires August 19, 1997), and Schnorr (expires February 19, 2008).

The Schnorr patent (U.S. patent number 4,995,082, "Method for Identifying Subscribers and Generating and Verifying Electronic Signatures in a Data Exchange System," issued to C.P. Schnorr on February 19, 1994) was the most troubling to the government for a number of reasons. First, it was valid for the longest period of time. Second, the algorithm had been developed without any government money, and therefore, unlike the two Hellman patents, the government was not entitled to use it royalty-free. Third, Schnorr, an eminent German mathematician, had obtained world-wide patent rights for his algorithm. According to Schneier, "Even if the U.S. courts rule in favor of DSA, it is unclear what courts around the world will do. Is an international company going to adopt a standard that may be legal in some countries but infringe on a patent in others?"

Realizing the value of the Schnorr patent in his upcoming battle with the government, Jim Bidzos acquired the patent for Public Key Partners in early 1994.

In June 1993, NIST proposed to resolve these problems by giving Public Key Partners an exclusive patent license on DSA and requiring that all other users of DSA in the United States pay patent royalties to PKP. Although no agreement was ever reached, one amount that was widely discussed was the royalty of one dollar per user per year. Bruce Schneier called this arrangement "the worst of both worlds:" it would not give users a royalty-free digital signature algorithm, and, at the same time, it would prevent the creation of a worldwide digital signature standard. If DSA turned out to be covered by patents after all, why not just adopt RSA as the standard?

The patent license announcement was the big payoff that everyone involved with Public Key Partners had hoped for over the years. For example, since the IRS was considering requiring the use of the DSS to sign electronically filed federal tax returns, this deal alone would have meant a tidy profit for PKP (more than $200 million per year until the year 2008).

This deal soon fell apart, however. According to sources close to NIST, decision makers at NSA were proud of DSA and wanted it adopted as an international standard. This was not likely to happen if the algorithm was exclusively licensed to PKP. Foreign governments refused to use an algorithm for which patent rights were held by a U.S. company. On May 19, 1994, NIST published its final approval of the DSS in the *Federal Register* as Federal Information Processing Standards Publication (FIPS PUB) 186. As part of the publication, NIST noted wryly, "The Department of Commerce is not aware of any patents that would be infringed by this standard." The standard is scheduled to become effective on December 1, 1994.

The Fall of PKP?

Not long after NIST announced its acceptance of DSA as a federal standard, Public Key Partners itself began to unravel.

The Cylink Lawsuit

Despite the fact that Public Key Partners was a partnership, the second partner, Cylink, of Sunnyvale, California, had always been something of a silent partner. Indeed, Cylink wasn't even really a partner of PKP; the real partner was the Caro-Kann Corporation, a Cylink subsidiary created specifically for the purpose of entering into the agreement with RSA Data Security (and, some people say, for further obscuring Cylink's involvement).

Cylink was founded, shortly after RSA Data Security, by James Omura, a University of California (Los Angeles) professor who was one of the nation's leading experts on spread-spectrum radio technology. The company licensed the Diffie-Hellman and Merkle-Hellman patents from Stanford University, then used them to develop a series of communications devices that provided end-to-end encryption. Headquartered just a few miles from RSA Data Security, Cylink was different from Bidzos' company in a few important ways. Whereas RSADSI specialized in encryption software, and particularly toolkits, Cylink concentrated on encryption hardware. And, whereas RSADSI pursued both civilian and government contracts, Cylink's products were sold primarily to governments around the world. (Later the company branched out and closed a few deals with large financial institutions.)

In the mid 1980s, Stanford University complained that RSA Data Security needed a license on the Hellman patents in order to use the RSA patent from MIT. (Under U.S. patent law, a patent does not actually give a patent holder the right to practice an invention; instead, it actually confers a right to prevent other people from practicing the invention. It is possible that a particular invention might actually be covered under several patents—for example, a basic patent and an improvement patent. In such a case, licenses from all of the relevant patents would be required to practice the invention.) Fortunately for RSA Data Security, Cylink's licenses for the Hellman patents were not exclusive licenses; MIT was able to negotiate a license from Stanford and convey a license, in turn, to RSA Data Security. Negotiations were concluded and the license was signed, according to Bidzos, in 1988.

According to an article in *Information Law Alert* by Mark Voorhees, "Cylink, formed shortly after RSA and one of the few other license holders of the Stanford patents, was not pleased by the development. . . . Chief executive Lew Morris threatened to sue RSA unless Cylink was able to purchase RSA, according to Bidzos. Instead, the two companies agreed to work together and pool the licensing rights of the three Stanford patents and one MIT patent. The product of this compromise and conception was, of course, PKP." The date of the initial agreement, says Bidzos, was October 17, 1989, the day of the Loma Prieta earthquake in the San Francisco Bay area.

While Bidzos was named president of PKP, day-to-day operations were managed by Robert Fougner, who was PKP's director of licensing, Cylink's general counsel, and Caro-Kann's president.

By 1993, the two partners were increasingly at odds over the terms of their relationship. The problem, according to Cylink's side of the story, revolved around two points: the license arrangements of RSA Data Security's BSAFE toolkit and implementations of the RSA algorithm built into integrated circuits for use on PCMCIA and smart cards.

Fougner felt that PKP and, by extension, Cylink, was not getting its due share of royalties from companies that had purchased toolkits from RSA Data Security. According to court records later filed by Fougner, PKP has given RSA Data Security only two royalty distributions since its creation, the last distribution in 1992. It is reasonable to suspect that Cylink received distributions on a similar schedule—this, despite the fact that RSA Data Security was allegedly grossing between $5 and $10 million per year.

The second Cylink argument arose over licensing silicon implementations of RSA. According to Voorhees, RSA had been working with National Semiconductor to develop the software for National's iPower PCMCIA card, a wallet-sized circuit card that would allow users to shop, sign documents, and store encrypted information. But Cylink had developed a similar chip for use in PCMCIA cards. "These disagreements and antagonisms did not, however, reach the boiling point until last December, when RSA told Cylink it was violating the RSA patent. In April Cylink filed a demand for arbitration in order to win the RSA license that it has been expecting to receive," wrote Voorhees. Fougner told Voorhees that Bidzos wouldn't give Cylink the same license that he had given other companies; Bidzos told Voorhees that Cylink wanted a license that was considerably more generous than that granted to other companies.

Bidzos has a different explanation for the fallout between the two partners. According to Bidzos, Cylink's main interest was to use the PKP partnership as a means of denying licenses on the Diffie-Hellman and RSA patents to its competitors. Bidzos says that companies like Newbridge and Motorola wanted to expand their licenses to the algorithms to uses other than secure telephones, but that Cylink thwarted these attempts because they would compete with Cylink's main product line. So these companies, and others, bypassed the PKP partnership—and Cylink's veto—by licensing software from RSADSI. Furthermore, says Bidzos, Cylink wanted "to sell a low-cost single-fee license to NIST/NSA for DSS and Clipper. RSA resisted, seeing this as a sellout both financially and politically."

During the first four years of the partnership, Bidzos claims that RSADSI paid more than nine times as much to the PKP bank account in license fees than Cylink, "yet Cylink's sales of public key products were ten times RSA's."

According to Fougner, Cylink's cryptography products during the first four years of the PKP partnership used Diffie-Hellman key exchange but did not use the RSA algorithm. Fougner says that, as the fourth anniversary of the PKP partnership approached, Cylink sought to exercise a clause of the contract and have RSADSI issue a license to Cylink to practice the RSA algorithm. (According to Fougner, California contract law places a four-year statute of limitations on exercising these kinds of contract provisions.) Bidzos balked, not liking the terms that Cylink proposed. Fougner says that Cylink soon started making products that used the RSA algorithm to satisfy customer demands.

On June 29, 1994, Bidzos wrote Fougner, saying that RSA intended to sue Cylink for infringing the RSA patent. The next day, Cylink filed suit against RSA in federal court in San Jose. Among other things, Cylink claimed that it had new evidence proving that the RSA patent was invalid. Bidzos was incensed at this revelation, saying that it was potentially fraudulent and unethical for Cylink to have been collecting royalties on the RSA patent if the company knew that the patent was invalid all along.

Later that same summer, Cylink filed papers in California to have the PKP partnership forcibly dissolved. Fougner also contacted members of the standards committees that were considering the adoption of RSA as a data protection standard, telling them that PKP could no longer guarantee licenses on fair and uniform terms, one of the requirements for adopting patented technologies as national and international standards.

The Schlafly Lawsuit

Meanwhile, Roger Schlafly, a mathematician based in Santa Cruz, California, had filed his own law suit against Public Key Partners. In the mid 1980s, Schlafly was sued by RSA Data Security for making and selling a program called CRYPTMASTER—a program that, like MailSafe and PGP, performed public key encryption, digital signatures, and key management. Under a 1988 consent decree, Schlafly agreed to cease production of his product. His current lawsuit against PKP pertains to an RSA implementation that Schlafly has written for an AT&T product called Secret Agent. PKP claimed that Schlafly's contribution to Secret Agent violated PKP's patents on public key cryptography. Schlafly's response was to sue, charging that the two Hellman patents are invalid.[†]

---

† As an interesting side note, in 1993 Schlafly sued NIST to prevent the federal agency from granting an exclusive license on DSA to PKP. That suit was dismissed.

Schlafly's lawsuit against PKP may have been precipitated by Cylink's against RSA: one of Schlafly's exhibits is the PKP partnership agreement, which Schlafly presumably got from Cylink's court filings. Schlafly also notes that Cylink claims to have evidence that the RSA patent is invalid.

Schlafly's lawsuit raises two interesting questions about the Hellman patents that have apparently never before been litigated in court. The Merkle-Hellman patent on the knapsack algorithm and, by extension, on all of public key cryptography, is invalid, Schlafly argues, because the knapsack algorithm doesn't work. The patent says that the secret key cannot be derived from the public key when, in fact, it can. (Recall that the secret key was derived from the public key on the stage of the Crypto '82 conference by an Apple II computer.) As further proof, Schlafly notes that Merkle was forced to pay $100, and later $1000, to people who had cracked knapsack problems.

Schlafly's challenge against the Diffie-Hellman patent is based on Diffie's public demonstration of the Diffie-Hellman encryption algorithm at the June 1976 National Computer Conference. Under U.S. patent law, an inventor loses the right to patent an invention if the invention is publicly disclosed more than 12 months before the patent application is filed. The Diffie-Hellman patent application was filed in September 1977.

It is true, says Whitfield Diffie, who has seen less royalties on public key patents than perhaps any of the other inventors, that the Diffie-Hellman exponential key exchange was precisely described at the conference. "There must have been 200 witnesses," he said in a telephone interview in September 1994. Nevertheless, Diffie added, he was told that patent law views disclosure in printed publications differently from disclosure in talks. "Lectures have much less impact than publications." Furthermore, because of the timeliness of the discovery, the mathematics for exponential key exchange did not appear in the conference's printed proceedings.

When ambiguity surrounds the validity of a patent, it is usually up the federal courts to make a decision. But patent litigation is among the most expensive kind of litigation in the United States. That's why for many companies it has been cheaper to simply license software, which comes with a license for the relevant patents, from RSA Data Security than to fight RSA Data Security or Public Key Partners in court over the validity of the patents.

As time runs out for the patents on public key cryptography, an observer might wonder what good Schlafly's lawsuit might possibly do at this point. Filed during the summer of 1994, the case almost certainly won't come to trial until 1996 at the earliest. The Merkle-Hellman and Diffie-Hellman patents are very likely to expire before the case of Schlafly v. Public Key Partners is decided—assuming that Public Key Partners is still in existence by the time that the case is heard.

Using PGP

This part of the book explains everything you need to know about using PGP. It contains the following chapters:

- Chapter 7, *Protecting Your Files*, shows you how to encrypt and decrypt files with the same key, using private key cryptography.

- Chapter 8, *Creating PGP Keys*, explains how to create public and secret keys.

- Chapter 9, *Managing PGP Keys*, explains how to give others a copy of your public key, how to obtain others' public keys (a must before you can send them encrypted mail), and how to perform other key management functions.

- Chapter 10, *Encrypting Email*, explains how to encrypt a message with PGP and send it. It also explains how to read the encrypted mail that you receive.

- Chapter 11, *Using Digital Signatures*, describes digital signatures and explains how to electronically sign a document and how to verify a digital signature attached to a document.

- Chapter 12, *Certifying and Distributing Keys*, explains how you can sign a PGP key with its own digital signature so that when you send it to someone, the recipient knows it is an authentic key.

- Chapter 13, *Revoking, Disabling, and Escrowing Keys*, explains how you can revoke your key, disable someone else's key, and set up a manual key escrow system.

- Chapter 14, *PGP Configuration File*, explains how you can customize PGP.

- Chapter 15, *PGP Internet Key Servers*, explains how you can register your PGP key with the PGP Internet key servers and how you can get someone else's key.

7

Protecting Your Files

> *I talked with a guy at the American Association for the Advancement of Science, a human rights worker in a Central American country, who documents atrocities from death squads. His documents are interviews with witnesses. If government troops were to capture these documents, they would find his witnesses and kill them. So he encrypts them with PGP.*
>
> —Phil Zimmermann,
> summer 1994 USENIX Conference

The simplest thing you can do with PGP is to encrypt a file so that no one else can read it. Using PGP in this fashion turns your computer into a safe—a safe so strong that all of the world's lock pickers and safe crackers working together can't break inside.

As the above quotation illustrates, there are some very compelling reasons why people might want this type of security. Even if you aren't opposing a totalitarian government or planning a corporate takeover, you might want to encrypt data on your own computer for one of the following reasons:

- You might be sharing your computer with a spouse or a child, and your computer might contain personal information that you don't want the other person to see.

    Years ago, when I was in high school, my father accidentally left a copy of his will on the kitchen table. I'm sure that it was an accident, and that he didn't want me to read it. . . . These days, when do-it-yourself will preparation packages are readily available for personal computers, it's a simple matter for kids to read your will, your financial records, and anything else that's on your computer's hard disk. The only way around this problem is to use encryption.

- You might have information on your system that you don't want accessible to the general public in the event that your computer is lost or stolen.

An astronomer friend of mine once left his laptop computer in the back of a taxi. He thought he would never get it back. The next day, he got a phone call from the taxi driver. The driver had figured out how the laptop worked and searched through its files, looking for personal information that he could use to return the computer. (The minute the laptop was returned, my friend put his name and phone number on the computer's case.)

Another taxi driver might not have been so kind—or so ethical. He might have gone through my friend's files looking for credit card numbers, bank accounts, or information that might be useful for other nefarious purposes. What kind of information is on your computer's hard disk?

- You might have stored extremely sensitive information on your computer's hard disk without the knowledge of your organization's information services staff.

Several years ago, an office that is part of the Federal Witness Protection program sold some of its personal computers on the open market. Unknown to the people who arranged the sale, the computers still had files on them listing the real names of protected witnesses and the names under which they were living in hiding. Fortunately, the computers were recovered without incident, but the information on the hard disks never should have been left there unencrypted in the first place.

Encrypting and Decrypting Files

This chapter describes the PGP options that let you encrypt and decrypt files:

- Typing **pgp** **−c** encrypts a file.

- Typing **pgp** (with no options) decrypts an encrypted file.

Figure 7-1 illustrates how PGP encrypts and decrypts a file.

Encrypting a File

Encrypting a file with a password is one of the simplest things that you can do with PGP. To encrypt a file, simply run PGP with the −c option followed by the name of the file that you are encrypting. PGP prompts you for a pass phrase and performs the requested encryption. ("The Pass Phrase" section later in this chapter provides the details of selecting this pass phrase.)

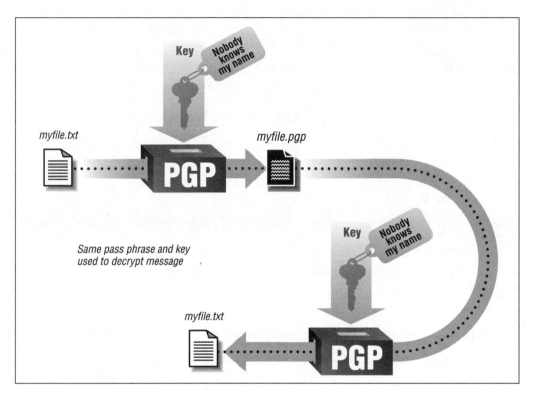

Figure 7-1. Encrypting and decrypting a file

The following is a file that you might reasonably wish to encrypt:

```
C:\WORK> type accounts
Safe deposit box: #402, East Street Savings Bank.
Combination lock code: 16-30-5
Mother's maiden name: Logsdon
Swiss bank account number: 4321-3324-9323-3442 A
C:\WORK>
```

You can encrypt this file using PGP. PGP prompts you to enter the pass phrase you want to use to protect the file. (Note that this pass phrase is not echoed on the display screen.)

```
C:\WORK> pgp -c accounts
Pretty Good Privacy(tm) 2.6 - Public-key encryption for the masses.
 (c) 1990-1994 Philip Zimmermann, Phil's Pretty Good Software. 23 May 94
Distributed by the Massachusetts Institute of Technology.  Uses RSAREF.
Export of this software may be restricted by the U.S. government.
Current time: 1994/06/26 21:47 GMT

You need a pass phrase to encrypt the file.
```

```
Enter pass phrase: Nobody knows my name.
Enter same pass phrase again: Nobody knows my name.Just a moment...

Ciphertext file: accounts.pgp
C:\WORK>
```

Never Write Down Your Pass Phrase

The security of the information in your file depends entirely on your pass phrase. Be sure to pick a pass phrase that you can remember, and *never* write it down.

- Do not write your pass phrase on a Post-It note that you put on your terminal.

- Do not write your pass phrase on a piece of paper and put it in your wallet.

- Do not put your pass phrase in a file on your computer.

- Do not put your pass phrase in a file on your computer even if you later encrypt that file.

- Do not write your pass phrase in your address book.

- Do not write down your pass phrase at all.

Don't even think about writing it down.

As the program output indicates, PGP encrypts the *accounts* file and writes it to the output file *accounts.pgp*.

Let's compare the two files. Notice that the encrypted file does not bear any resemblance to the unencrypted file :

```
C:\WORK> dir accounts.*

 Volume in drive C has no label
 Volume Serial Number is 2945-1403
 Directory of C:\WORK

ACCOUNTS TXT        166 06-26-94   2:42p
ACCOUNTS PGP        181 06-26-94   2:52p
        2 file(s)            347 bytes
                   9,885,696 bytes free

C:\WORK> type accounts.pgp
```

```
~®B?q9‡3?†Á_`96–c‡'òoÇ~d"  +Úúe??æÙ˜w'‡]!I?…í^Æ¥w†z?éi??*¥?óí"\¯ê8†ò–
CsÁù‡i˝?6j^??Ô{:èduÉ4Ãflyí-˘¥]Íê?Ô22»`?ÉÄ,*î1>&u"ÉCq?è†^ÌJ £Úéœ AdÚÔÛ£4,?…dE?
tfl,?bFV„¿Ç
C:\WORK>
```

Making a Mistake

If you accidentally type your pass phrase differently the first and second times, you
see the following error message:

```
C:\WORK> pgp -c accounts
Pretty Good Privacy(tm) 2.6 - Public-key encryption for the masses.
 (c) 1990-1994 Philip Zimmermann, Phil's Pretty Good Software. 23 May 94
Distributed by the Massachusetts Institute of Technology.  Uses RSAREF.
Export of this software may be restricted by the U.S. government.
Date: 1994/06/26 21:47 GMT

You need a pass phrase to encrypt the file.
Enter pass phrase: Nobody knows my name.
Enter same pass phrase again: Nobody knew my name.Just a moment...
Error: Pass phrases were different.  Try again.
C:\WORK>
```

Erasing the Original File (-w Option)

Once you've created your encrypted file, you should erase the original one, which is
a little more difficult than it may seem at first. If you are using DOS, you can simply
use the *del* command to delete the file. However, if you do, a person who steals your
computer can simply use the *undelete* command to get it back! This is because the
DOS *del* command doesn't really delete the file—it simply removes the file from the
directory that contains it. Programs like *undelete* look for the disembodied file and
reconnect it.

The situation is only a little better with UNIX, which doesn't have a *delete* command
but leaves the undeleted file on the disk for prying eyes to find.

The solution is the –w (wipe) option in PGP. If you specify this option during PGP
encryption, it causes PGP to delete (wipe) the unencrypted file from the disk.

PGP's wiping process is extensive: instead of just deleting the plaintext file, PGP first
overwrites the file with random data. In most cases, this magnetically changes the
physical bits on the computer's hard disk. (PGP overwrites the data with random bits,
rather than all 1s or all 0s, in order to make disk compression systems such as
dblspace truly overwrite the old file. Using random data also makes it harder to
recover the plaintext of the file using sophisticated laboratory techniques.)

To encrypt the file and erase your plaintext, simply replace the –c option with –cw:

```
C:\WORK> pgp -cw accounts
Pretty Good Privacy(tm) 2.6 - Public-key encryption for the masses.
 (c) 1990-1994 Philip Zimmermann, Phil's Pretty Good Software. 23 May 94
Distributed by the Massachusetts Institute of Technology.  Uses RSAREF.
Export of this software may be restricted by the U.S. government.
Current time: 1994/06/26 21:47 GMT

You need a pass phrase to encrypt the file.
Enter pass phrase: Nobody knows my name.
Enter same pass phrase again: Nobody knows my name.Just a moment...

File accounts wiped and deleted.
C:\WORK>
```

When Wiping Isn't Enough

Wiping your data isn't always enough. Under certain circumstances, you should take extra precautions to be sure that your data is destroyed:

- If your data is automatically backed up, wiping does not delete the copy on the backup tapes.

- If you are using write-once media, wiping does not erase the old sectors.

Retrieving Your Encrypted File (Default Option)

After you encrypt a file, how do you read it? With PGP, the answer is easy; just run PGP with the name of the encrypted file as the sole parameter. PGP reads the file, automatically determines that it has been encrypted with conventional private key encryption, prompts you for the pass phrase, decrypts the file, and writes the decrypted text into a separate file.

For example, to read your encrypted file, just type the following:

```
C:\WORK> pgp accounts.pgp
Pretty Good Privacy(tm) 2.6 - Public-key encryption for the masses.
 (c) 1990-1994 Philip Zimmermann, Phil's Pretty Good Software. 23 May 94
Distributed by the Massachusetts Institute of Technology.  Uses RSAREF.
Export of this software may be restricted by the U.S. government.
Current time: 1994/06/26 22:17 GMT
```

```
File is conventionally encrypted.
You need a pass phrase to decrypt this file.
Enter pass phrase: Nobody knows my name. Just a moment....Pass phrase
appears good.

Plaintext filename: accounts
C:\WORK>
```

The data is in the *accounts* file:

```
C:\WORK> type accounts
Safe deposit box: #402, East Street Savings Bank.
Combination lock code: 16-30-5
Mother's maiden name: Logsdon
Swiss bank account number: 4321-3324-9323-3442 A

C:\WORK>
```

The Pass Phrase

Like many other security systems, PGP uses passwords to control access. But whereas most systems use the password directly as the encryption key, PGP uses the password to generate a 128-bit code.

The algorithm that PGP uses to generate the 128-bit code is called a *hash function*. The hash function accepts an input string of any length; the string can contain spaces, periods, uppercase and lowercase characters, and any other symbols you can type from the keyboard. Since the input can be of any length, it is called a "pass phrase" (and not a "password").

PGP uses pass phrases to encrypt both files and the secret keys on your secret key ring.

Should You Use a Different Pass Phrase for Every File?

Probably not. If you are encrypting more than a few files, either you won't remember the pass phrase (and you'll have to write it down—a bad idea, as I've discussed) or you'll be tempted to base the pass phrase in some way on the filename (for example, encrypting the file *thesis* with the pass phrase "this is the file thesis").

Certainly, you are much better off using a single pass phrase and not writing it down, than you are using a thousand phrases and writing down each one of them.

Basing your pass phrase on the filename isn't a good idea. The reason for this has to do with the fact that the encryption that PGP uses for its files is IDEA—an algorithm with a 128-bit key. *No one* is going to initiate a brute force attack on the IDEA key used to encrypt a file that you have protected with conventional encryption. Instead, a potential adversary is going to search for the pass phrase that you've used, trick you into typing it into a program that is not PGP, or pick it off the wire with some type of wiretap. It will be easier for him to discover the pass phrase if it's based on the filename of an encrypted file.

By far, the safest alternative is simply to use a few long pass phrases for your files and not write them down.

NOTE

Do *not* use the same pass phrase for your files that you use for your secret key. (See "Picking Your Pass Phrase" in Chapter 8.)

How to Pick a Pass Phrase

There's no secret to picking a good pass phrase: simply use a long phrase or sentence that other people are not likely to guess and that you are not likely to forget. If someone guesses your pass phrase, she can decrypt your encrypted files. (Of course, she also needs copies of the encrypted files.) Therefore, you should choose a pass phrase that other people are not likely to guess.

If you forget your pass phrase, you are lost: you won't be able to read your encrypted files.

A good pass phrase is one that is easy to remember. One benefit of PGP pass phrases is that spaces, punctuation, uppercase and lowercase characters, and (most) control characters are all significant. That is, PGP considers the following pass phrases to be different:

```
I could tell you my pass phrase, but then I would have to kill you.
I could tell you my pass phrase. But then, I would have to kill you.
i could tell you my pass phrase, but then i would have to kill you.
```

I can't tell you what to put in *your* pass phrase; if I did, that would make it a useless pass phrase![†] But I can make some suggestions (see the next section), and I can tell you what to avoid. Since the following are easily guessed, you should generally avoid picking pass phrases that consist solely of one of these items:[‡]

*   Your name

*   Your spouse's name

[†] I might also have to kill you!
[‡] This list is from the book *Practical Unix Security* (O'Reilly & Associates, 1991), but it applies to all types of passwords and pass phrases, not just UNIX ones.

- Your parents' names

- Your pet's name

- Your child's name

- Names of close friends or coworkers

- Names of your favorite fantasy characters

- Your boss' name

- Anyone's name

- The name of the operating system you're using

- The hostname of your computer

- Your phone number

- Your license plate number

- Any part of your social security number

- Anyone's birth date

- Other information that is easily obtained about you

- Words such as *wizard, guru, gandalf,* and so on

- Any username on a computer in any form (as is, capitalized, doubled, and so on)

- A single word (English or foreign)

- A place name

- A proper noun

- Groupings of all the same letter

- Simple patterns of letters on the keyboard, like *qwerty*

- Any of the above spelled backwards

- Any of the above followed or preceded by a single digit

If you think this list is ridiculous, you probably haven't heard about password-cracking dictionaries. They contain hundreds of thousands of words drawn from the above categories, and they are very useful to people who are trying to break into computers or to decrypt encrypted files. Password-cracking dictionaries are readily available.

Good Pass Phrases

If you had a photographic memory and could type very accurately, you could use pass phrases that are virtually impossible to guess, such as the following:

```
M^`#_-!`\`!+O[@`&S1G_P```!`(K@`$_QA@_P```9((([@`$_QA@
34fo3560j1213kfvkjKL(*1kj1k3450g[]ask4j5jfs((*()..as9332ffASSD
98735431876968778569856254125875669875563398547854
```

Unfortunately, most people don't have memories that are this good. Thus, such pass phrases aren't actually very useful ones.

You might want to mull over the following ideas when you are creating your pass phrase. Use a pass phrase that:

*   Contains the first line from one of your favorite books:

    `To many people, "UNIX security" may seem to be an oxymoron.`

*   Lists some words from the dictionary:

    `food chain food poisoning food processor food stamp food stuff`

*   Is a funny phrase that you can remember:

    `He had been mistaken for a police spy.`

*   Contains your first ten favorite numbers (repeats are okay):

    `5 21 67 7 12 65 9 9 9 9`

Just remember: no matter what you pick, be sure that you can remember it without writing it down!

NOTE

Feel free to use the ideas suggested in this section for creating your own pass phrase, but *do not, under any circumstances, actually use one of these phrases.* Since they have been printed in this book, they are no longer difficult to guess.

Why Use a Long Pass Phrase?

Potential attackers could decrypt a PGP-encrypted file in one of several ways. The following two kinds of attacks could theoretically be effective against a file that is encrypted with the IDEA algorithm:

*   *Brute force attacks against the IDEA key itself,* in which attackers try to figure out the key with which the file was encrypted by trying every possible key, one after another. Brute force attacks, although theoretically possible, are very unlikely to work with good cryptography. PGP Version 2.0 uses the IDEA

algorithm, a very strong algorithm indeed. IDEA has a 128-bit key. With a 128-bit key, there are billions of possible keys. (There are precisely 2^{128}=340,282,366,920,938,463,463,374,607,431,768,211,456 different keys.)

Clearly, the brute force attack would not be the first choice of someone who is contemplating breaking this code.

- *Brute force attacks against the PGP pass phrase.* Instead of searching for your actual encryption key, attackers can search for the pass phrase that you type into PGP to encrypt your files. ("Breaking the Code" in Chapter 2 describes a number of different types of attacks.) The difficulty of a pass phrase attack depends on the length of the pass phrase that you type into PGP. Theoretically, a key search is as difficult as a brute force attack, but if you use a pass phrase that is composed of only two lowercase letters, there are only 26×26=676 different keys to try. This makes it dramatically easier for someone who intercepts your messages to decode them. Thus, it is to your advantage to use a long pass phrase. (I recommend at least ten characters.)

Resourceful attackers might try the following other ways to retrieve the unencrypted contents of your encrypted files:

- They could scan your hard disk for an unencrypted copy of your file. Even if you delete the file, it is possible that an unencrypted copy is among your disk's blocks. (I've explained in "Erasing the Original File (–w Option)" how to guard against this threat.)

- They could booby-trap your copy of PGP. That is, your copy of PGP might have been modified by an attacker, so that it places a copy of each key (or the unencrypted file itself) in a hidden directory. Or your PGP program might not encrypt the file at all, or it might encrypt it with a key that is different from the one you provide. How can you guard against this threat? I explain in Appendix A, *Getting PGP*, how you can obtain a copy of PGP and how you can be sure it is a secure copy.

- Your attacker might kidnap and imprison you, threatening you with death unless you reveal your encryption key. This threat is beyond the scope of this book! Frankly, I don't know how to advise you to protect yourself against this threat. What you do probably depends on what you have encrypted.

For most PGP users, these last three attacks are not too likely to occur. In any event, they represent threats that are beyond the scope of the PGP program itself.

8

Creating PGP Keys

If you would wish another to keep your secret, first keep it yourself.
—Seneca in *Hippolytus*, c. 60 A.D.

If you would keep your secret from an enemy, tell it not to a friend.
—Benjamin Franklin in *Poor Richard's Almanac*, 1741

A secret may be sometimes best kept by keeping the secret of its being a secret.
—Henry Taylor in *The Statesman*, 1836

In the last chapter, we learned how to encrypt a file using PGP's conventional cryptography. This technique is effective when you are using encryption only to protect data on your hard disk, but you will probably use encryption more often to exchange messages with people. Using encryption, you can send a message and be sure that no one but the intended recipient can fathom its meaning.

There's just one problem: in order to send someone a message with the sort of private key (conventional) encryption I described in the previous chapter, you and that person must use the same key, and both of you would need to be sure that no one else is using that key. You would need *a secure way to deliver the key to the message.* And there's the rub: if you have a secure way to deliver a key to someone, why not simply use that same means to send her the message itself?

Public key encryption solves this problem by using two keys: one to encrypt the message, the second to decrypt the message. If you want to send someone a message, simply call that person on the phone and get her public key. Or she could send you her public key on a postcard. Or she could write it on billboards. Or you could pick it up on the Internet using one of the PGP key servers (see Chapter 15, *PGP Internet*

Key Servers). It doesn't matter: people who have your public key can send you encrypted mail, but they can't read encrypted mail that other people have sent to you.

This chapter describes how you create the public and secret keys you need to encrypt and sign your email. You do this by typing **pgp –kg** and responding to the program's prompts.

Making Public Key Cryptography Work

To use public key encryption, you and your correspondent must do the following:

*   Agree on a cryptography system.

*   Create a key pair consisting of a public key and a secret key.

*   Obtain the other's public key.

The first requirement should be obvious, but frequently it isn't. In order to exchange encrypted messages with someone, you and that person need to agree on some ground rules—a unified means for sharing public keys, for applying the keys to ASCII text, and for representing the text of encrypted messages. This requirement is analogous to exchanging files between two different kinds of word processors; both must be able to read and write the same file format.

Never assume, just because two encryption programs use the same algorithm, that they have compatible encryption formats: even two different versions of the same program can have their incompatibilities. (For example, PGP Version 1.0 cannot read files generated by PGP Version 2.0, even though both use RSA encryption.) The simplest way to guarantee file compatibility, of course, is for all parties to use the same encryption program.[†]

The second and third requirements are somewhat less obvious: with public key encryption, you can receive encrypted mail if:

*   You have created your public key.

*   The person sending you mail has a copy of that public key.

*   That person has encrypted the message with your public key.

    This is a slightly different problem from the key exchange problem posed by private key (conventional) systems. With private key systems, you have to be sure that you share the key with your correspondent and that no one else has a copy

---

† Another way to guarantee file compatibility is to use agreed-upon standards. Unfortunately, you can't use a standard to encrypt your email: you need a program that implements the standard. And, all too often, programs that claim to implement the same standard end up being incompatible. *Caveat emptor!*

of the key. But with public key systems, you simply need to have your correspondent's public key (and she yours). You can find out about each other's keys independently—for example, by getting them off the Internet or by looking them up in a phone book.

- You need to be sure that the public key you have really belongs to the person that you think it does.

  Verifying that the public key you have *really belongs to the person that you think it does* is a problem with no easy solution. For now, we're going to assume that you can hand your public key to your friend on a floppy disk, and vice versa. I discuss additional solutions in Chapter 12, *Certifying and Distributing Keys*.

The Theory Behind the Keys

As I explained in Part I of this book, the heart of PGP is the RSA public key encryption system. RSA gets its security from a mathematical puzzle that is easy to create but very difficult to solve; the puzzle involves the factoring of large numbers.

You may remember from your school days that one way of classifying numbers is by how many factors they have. Numbers such as 3, 5, and 7 are called *prime numbers* because they cannot be evenly divided by any integers other than themselves and the number 1. Numbers such as 4, 27, and 28,507 are called *composite numbers* because they can be evenly divided by other integers (4÷2=2; 27÷3=9; 28,507÷29=983).

It's an easy matter to multiply two prime numbers and produce a composite number. On the other hand, it's difficult to determine the factors of a large composite number.

To demonstrate this problem, consider the number 91: it has two factors, 7 and 13. Given the numbers 7 and 13, it's easy to calculate their product: simply multiply them (7×13=91). But given the number 91, it's more difficult to figure out that its only factors are 7 and 13.

Now, consider the number 18,933,907. Is it prime? Well, it's not divisible by 3, 5, 7, 9, 11, 13, 17, or 23. In fact, 18,933,907 is not divisible by any number under 1000. But it is perfectly divided by 4201 and 4507, both of which are prime. Therefore, the number 18,933,907 is not prime.

Your secret and public keys each consist of two large numbers that PGP creates for you. To make your key pair, PGP randomly chooses two very large prime numbers and multiplies them. PGP then uses the product, *n*, of the two primes to generate two other numbers, one of which, together with *n*, makes up your public key. The other generated number, together with *n*, serves as your secret key. The security of the RSA algorithm comes from the fact that it is difficult to factor the large number into the original primes.

If you are interested in the math that's behind RSA, you can find it in Appendix F, *The Mathematics of Cryptography.*

Using PGP to Create Keys (-kg Option)

To create your pair of secret and public keys, use the –kg (key generate) option. I've shown the entire key creation process in the following example, and it is followed by a step-by-step description.

The following is PGP's complete key generation process:

```
unix% pgp -kg
Pretty Good Privacy(tm) 2.6 - Public-key encryption for the masses.
(c) 1990-1994 Philip Zimmermann, Phil's Pretty Good Software. 23 May 94
Distributed by the Massachusetts Institute of Technology. Uses RSAREF.
Export of this software may be restricted by the U.S. government.
Current time: 1994/07/07 23:03 GMT
Pick your RSA key size:
   1)   512 bits- Low commercial grade, fast but less secure
   2)   768 bits- High commercial grade, medium speed, good security
   3) 1024 bits- "Military" grade, slow, highest security
Choose 1, 2, or 3, or enter desired number of bits: 3

You need a user ID for your public key. The desired form for this
user ID is your name, followed by your E-mail address enclosed in
<angle brackets>, if you have an E-mail address.
For example: John Q. Smith <12345.6789@compuserve.com>

Enter a user ID for your public key:
Simson Garfinkel <simsong@acm.org>

You need a pass phrase to protect your RSA secret key.
Your pass phrase can be any sentence or phrase and may have many
words, spaces, punctuation, or any other printable characters.
Enter pass phrase: Nobody knows my name.
Enter same pass phrase again: Nobody knows my name.

We need to generate 624 random bits. This is done by measuring the
time intervals between your keystrokes. Please enter some random text
on your keyboard until you hear the beep:
   624 .Nobody really cares what I type as long as I do not hold down the repeat
key or take too long between my key presses. PGP is a wonderful program and
Phil Zimmermann is a fantastic person. Buy more O'Reilly Books.
```

```
    0 * -Enough, thank you.
Note that key generation is a VERY lengthy process.
.....................++++ ............++++
Key generation completed.
unix%
```

Now let's look at the prompts, responses, and operations step by step.

Choosing the Length of Your Public Key

PGP first asks you to choose the length of the public key you wish to use:

```
Pick your RSA key size:
   1)   512 bits- Low commercial grade, fast but less secure
   2)   768 bits- High commercial grade, medium speed, good security
   3) 1024 bits- "Military" grade, slow, highest security
Choose 1, 2, or 3, or enter desired number of bits: 3
```

The longer your key, the more secure your message, but more time is required for PGP to generate your keys and to encrypt and decrypt files.

I recommend that you use an RSA key length of 1024 bits. While RSA encryption with a 1024-bit key is nearly four times slower to use than encryption with a 512-bit key, remember that PGP doesn't use RSA to encrypt your file; it uses RSA only to encrypt the file's *session key*. The file itself is encrypted with IDEA, and this process takes the same amount of time, regardless of whether you use a 512-bit, 768-bit, or 1024-bit key. Thus, while using a 1024-bit key means that you spend more time generating your initial public key, you probably won't notice too much of a difference in the amount of time required to encrypt your files.

You cannot change the length of your key after you have created it. If at some future point in time you want a longer key, you must create a new one from scratch and distribute it to your associates. Most people I know who started with 512-bit keys now have 1024-bit keys.

Entering Your User ID

PGP next asks you to type a user ID for your public key. This is the ID that appears as a comment, alongside your public key, whenever it is shown. Carefully consider what you type. Many people who use PGP with electronic mail use their complete email addresses as their IDs, but there is no requirement that you follow this convention. The following are sample PGP IDs:

```
John Q. Random <jqr@computer.company.com>
jqr@computer.company.com
John Q. Random, 1212 Templeton Street, Providence, RI, 94321
John Q. Random, 401/555-1212
```

Why Not Use a 10,000-bit Key?

Since longer keys are more secure, why stop at a 1024-bit key? Wouldn't a 2048-, a 4096-, or even a 10,240-bit key be more secure?

Probably not. The reason has to do partially with common sense and partially with the way that PGP works.

From a common sense point of view, the reason that long prime numbers make better RSA keys has to do with the mathematical problem of factoring. Larger numbers are generally harder to factor than smaller ones. Thus, it takes longer to find the factors of a composite number that is 2048 bits long than to factor a number that is 1024 bits.

But how much longer? With today's fastest computers, it would take approximately 3×10^{11} years to factor a 1024-bit number that is the product of two 512-bit primes. Factoring a 2048-bit number that is the product of two 1024-bit primes would take approximately 4×10^{27} years. Sure, using a 2048-bit key would be more secure, but a 1024-bit number is probably secure enough for most humans.

Of course, factoring is not a fully understood science: it is possible that some breakthrough in math might let people factor very large numbers very quickly. If such a breakthrough should take place, it might render 2048- or 4096-bit numbers as easy to factor as 1024-bit ones.

The second reason that longer primes aren't necessarily better has to do with the way that PGP encrypts messages. PGP doesn't use RSA to encrypt messages; it encrypts the messages with the IDEA cipher and a random session key that is encrypted with RSA. PGP does this because RSA encryption is 1000 times slower than IDEA. It would take a prohibitively long time to encrypt messages with RSA itself. Since the actual message is encrypted with IDEA, at some point it is easier to search for the IDEA session key (or try to reverse-engineer PGP's random number generator) than it is to factor the RSA public key.

Don't get too hung up over choosing your ID: you can change it later. On the other hand, while you can change the ID that is stored with the public key on your computer, you can't easily change it on your friend's computer, on all of your friends' friends' computers, on a public key server, or in a printed phone book of public keys. It is therefore a good idea to be careful when you pick an ID—just don't obsess over it.

```
You need a user ID for your public key. The desired form for this
user ID is your name, followed by your E-mail address enclosed in
<angle brackets>, if you have an E-mail address.
For example: John Q. Smith <12345.6789@compuserve.com>

Enter a user ID for your public key:
Simson Garfinkel <simsong@acm.org>
```

Picking Your Pass Phrase

In the next part of the key generation process, PGP asks you to type a pass phrase. As I've discussed, this pass phrase is used to encrypt the copy of your secret key that is stored on your computer's hard disk.

You must pick a pass phrase for PGP that is difficult for an attacker to guess. In Chapter 7, *Protecting Your Files,* I discussed pass phrases and suggested some guidelines for picking them. (See the section called "How to Pick a Pass Phrase" in that chapter.) Ideally, you should pick a phrase that is different from every other computer password. Don't pick the same pass phrase that you use to protect any of your encrypted files. Why? Because your secret key pass phrase is the most important password that you will ever create. If any of your other passwords is compromised, someone may be able to log into your computer and read some of your files. But if someone guesses (or discovers) your PGP secret key pass phrase, that person can read all of your encrypted email (the very email that you are trying to protect), now and forever more.

```
You need a pass phrase to protect your RSA secret key.
Your pass phrase can be any sentence or phrase and may have many
words, spaces, punctuation, or any other printable characters.
Enter pass phrase: Nobody knows my name.
Enter same pass phrase again: Nobody knows my name.
```

Creating Randomness

PGP needs only one more piece of input before it can create your key: randomness, which only you can provide.

Most computer programs are deterministic: run the program two times with the exact same input, and you are guaranteed to get the same results. This characteristic is true of every program, from the simplest word processor to the most sophisticated video game.

Computer games achieve their seemingly random behavior in two ways. One is a process called pseudo-random number generation. A pseudo-random number generator is a function whose output isn't really random but looks as if it is. Such a generator might have the following output:

    rand(100) = 34 78 33 61 09 83 47 68 23 13 16 10 99 98 55 47

That looks random, doesn't it? The problem with pseudo-random number generators is that, if you run them long enough, they eventually give you the same pattern a second time:

    rand(100) = 22 23 64 ... 34 78 33 61 09 83 47 68 23 13 16 10 99 98 55 47

Most such generators even let you set them at a particular location, so you can generate the same sequence of "random" numbers again and again. This is called "seeding" the pseudo-random number generator with a particular value. If you can seed a pseudo-random number generator with a truly "random" value, the sequence of numbers that you get from it are unpredictable

Many video games use a variety of approaches to seed the random number generator. One such approach is to simply seed the random number generator with the current time and date. The problem with this approach for cryptography is that people could presumably determine the seed value of your random number generator by figuring out when your key was created.

Another approach to generating random numbers is to rely on the user to provide the random seed input. As long as you do this in a sufficiently random way, you get "good" random numbers—that is, numbers that are largely unpredictable.

You can't just ask the user to provide a random number. It should be clear why not: pick a random number. Did you guess 7? How about 3? 5? Perhaps you picked 2 or 1, or maybe 6, 8, 9, 10, 11, 13, 17, or 21. Why didn't you pick 952,763? Asking users to enter random numbers doesn't produce unpredictable random numbers: people don't tend to pick numbers randomly. If there is a chance that a person might pick one from a million possible random numbers, an attacker could simply try all of those million possible numbers. Computers are fast, and a million isn't very many. (Most computers can count from 1 to a million in less than a second.)

A better way to chose random numbers is to measure the time a person takes to perform some sort of standardized task. Everyone is a little different; with the computer, you can measure and amplify those differences and use them as the basis for a true random number generator.

PGP takes this approach. After you enter your pass phrase, you are asked to generate a number of random bits by typing randomly on the keyboard. PGP displays a number; after you press each key, the number decreases. (Don't hold down the keys and make the keys repeat. Doing so produces regular keystrokes at precise, predefined intervals, rather than the haphazard and seemingly random timings of human typists.)

PGP is measuring the time between each of your keystrokes. PGP computes the randomness generation by asking you to type on the keyboard and timing the intervals between your keystrokes until it has a sufficient random sampling.

Here's how I did it. The three lines with strikeouts are the lines I typed to generate the random numbers; it took about 20 seconds of typing:

```
We need to generate 624 random bits. This is done by measuring the
time intervals between your keystrokes. Please enter some random text
on your keyboard until you hear the beep:
 624 .Nobody really cares what I type as long as I do not hold down the repeat
key or take too long between my key presses. PGP is a wonderful program and
Phil Zimmermann is a fantastic person. Buy more O'Reilly Books.
```

As you type on the keyboard, the number displayed on the last line counts down to 0. (If PGP displays a question mark, you are typing too fast—slow down.)

After a minute or two, PGP displays the following:

```
 0 * -Enough, thank you.
Note that key generation is a VERY lengthy process.
.....................++++ ............++++
Key generation completed.
unix%
```

What If PGP Won't Generate Keys?

Newer versions of PGP have a special built-in feature that prevents you from generating key pairs unless the PGP manual is present on the same disk as the PGP program. Phil Zimmermann included this feature as a result of his frustration with some PGP users. Phil reports that hundreds of people called him to ask the most basic questions about how the program worked. He would tell them to "read the manual." They would answer "I haven't got the manual." Why not? In many cases, people have distributed copies of PGP without the supporting documentation. Finally, Phil decided to change the software. So now PGP won't let you create keys unless you have the manual.

PGP displays the following if it can't find a copy of the manual on your disk:

```
% pgp -kg
Pretty Good Privacy(tm) 2.6 - Public-key encryption for the masses.
(c) 1990-1994 Philip Zimmermann, Phil's Pretty Good Software. 23 May 94
Distributed by the Massachusetts Institute of Technology. Uses RSAREF.
Export of this software may be restricted by the U.S. government.
Current time: 1994/07/06 15:16 GMT
```

```
Error: PGP User's Guide not found.
PGP looked for it in the following directories:
    "$PGPPATH"
    ""
    "pgp"
    "pgp25"
    "/usr/local/lib/pgp/"
    "$HOME/.pgp"
    "$HOME"
    "$HOME/pgp"
    "$HOME/pgp25"
    ".."
```
and the doc subdirectory of each of the above. Please put a copy of
both volumes of the User's Guide in one of these directories.

Under NO CIRCUMSTANCES should PGP ever be distributed without the PGP
User's Guide, which is included in the standard distribution package.
If you got a copy of PGP without the manual, please inform whomever you
got it from that this is an incomplete package that should not be
distributed further.

PGP will not generate a key without finding the User's Guide.
```
unix%
```

If you get this message, get the manual—or a whole new copy of PGP—from an official site (see Appendix A, *Getting PGP*). Put a copy of the manual in the file specified by your PGPPATH environment variable. Don't forget to give your friends a copy of the manual when you give them copies of PGP. (Note that you can get PGP to generate keys without having the documentation online by using PGP's NOMANUAL configuration variable. For more information, see Chapter 14, *PGP Configuration File*.)

PGP Key Rings: A Place for Your Keys

Once it creates your public and secret keys, PGP puts them into a special file called a *key ring*. As I introduced in Chapter 1, *Introduction to PGP*, PGP uses two key rings by default, although you can create more of each type:

Public key ring
This key ring holds the PGP public keys of everyone with whom you exchange messages. Think of it as an address book. By default, PGP stores this key ring in a file called *pubring.pgp*.

Secret key ring
This key ring holds your PGP secret key. If you have more than one secret key, it holds them all. By default, PGP stores this key ring in a file called *secring.pgp*.

Since anyone who has access to your secret key can decrypt your secret messages, you need to protect your secret key ring with the greatest care. PGP protects the key ring the best way known—with encryption. Specifically, each key on your secret key ring is encrypted using a pass phrase, using the same conventional encryption technique PGP uses to encrypt ordinary files. Fortunately, PGP automates this process so you never see it. But you can sleep comfortably knowing that PGP is providing special protection for your secret keys.

9

Managing PGP Keys

Time and chance reveal all secrets.
—Mary De La Riviere Manley in *The New Atlantis*, II, 1709

In the last chapter we created a secret key and a matching public key. In this chapter, I show you how to give your public key to an associate, how to add a colleague's public key to your key ring, and how to use a variety of other key management capabilities. *Key management* is a generic term for any operation performed on a key.

This chapter describes the following PGP options that let you perform key management:

- The –kv (key view) option lets you view the keys on a key ring.

- The –kx (key extract) option extracts a key from a key ring so that you can give it to an associate.

- The –ka (key add) option adds new keys to a key ring.

- The –kr (key remove) option removes keys from a key ring.

- The –ke (key edit) option edits a key ring, letting you change the user ID of your public key, add alternative user IDs, or delete user IDs.

Chapter 11 and Chapter 12 explain additional key management functions that you can use to sign keys and check signatures.

If you can't wait to try your new key, you might want to skip ahead to Chapter 10, *Encrypting Email.*

Secret and Public Key Rings

After you create your first public and secret keys (as described in Chapter 8, *Creating PGP Keys*), you'll discover that PGP has created three new files in your PGP directory:

```
C:\PGP> dir

   Volume in drive C has no label
   Volume Serial Number is 12D9-1B44
   Directory of C:\PGP

.                <DIR>           06-26-94    1:48p
..               <DIR>           06-26-94    1:48p
PGP      EXE     200,034 03-07-93    1:09a
CONFIG   TXT       3,986 05-21-94    6:06p
SECRING  PGP         311 07-01-94    1:01p
PUBRING  PGP         138 07-01-94    1:01p
RANDSEED BIN          24 06-30-94    9:10p
       7 file(s)        204,493 bytes
                      4,063,232 bytes free
C:\PGP>
```

PGP creates the following files during key generation:

secring.pgp
>   This key ring contains your secret key.

pubring.pgp
>   This key ring contains your public key.

randseed.bin
>   This file contains a random "seed" that PGP creates when you type random text; you do not need to concern yourself with the contents of the file *randseed.bin*, which PGP uses internally, but you must keep it secret.

Since the key rings contain binary information, you can't view or manipulate their contents directly. Instead, you use PGP itself, which contains a number of sophisticated utilities for managing key rings..

Getting Help with Keys

The –k (key) option lists all of the key management functions currently available in PGP. PGP Version 2.6 implements the following key management functions:

```
unix% pgp -k
Pretty Good Privacy(tm) 2.6 - Public-key encryption for the masses.
 (c) 1990-1994 Philip Zimmermann, Phil's Pretty Good Software. 23 May 94
Distributed by the Massachusetts Institute of Technology.  Uses RSAREF.
Export of this software may be restricted by the U.S. government.
Current time: 1994/08/13 22:55 GMT


Key management functions:
To generate your own unique public/secret key pair:
   pgp -kg
To add a key file's contents to your public or secret key ring:
   pgp -ka keyfile [keyring]
To remove a key or a user ID from your public or secret key ring:
   pgp -kr userid [keyring]
To edit your user ID or pass phrase:
   pgp -ke your_userid [keyring]
To extract (copy) a key from your public or secret key ring:
   pgp -kx userid keyfile [keyring]
To view the contents of your public key ring:
   pgp -kv[v] [userid] [keyring]
To check signatures on your public key ring:
   pgp -kc [userid] [keyring]
To sign someone else's public key on your public key ring:
   pgp -ks her_userid [-u your_userid] [keyring]
To remove selected signatures from a userid on a keyring:
   pgp -krs userid [keyring]
unix%
```

Viewing Keys (–kv Option)

The simplest key management function is to list the keys that a key ring contains. You can list them using the –kv (key view) option in PGP. The following sections show you how you can view keys on your public key ring, your secret key ring, or any other key ring you wish to view.

Viewing Keys on Your Public Key Ring

Type the –kv option by itself to list the keys on your public key ring:

```
C:\WORK> pgp -kv
Pretty Good Privacy(tm) 2.6 - Public-key encryption for the masses.
 (c) 1990-1994 Philip Zimmermann, Phil's Pretty Good Software. 23 May 94
Distributed by the Massachusetts Institute of Technology.  Uses RSAREF.
Export of this software may be restricted by the U.S. government.
Current time: 1994/08/13 22:39 GMT

Key ring: 'c:\pgp\pubring.pgp'
Type bits/keyID    Date        User ID
pub  1024/903C9265 1994/07/15 Simson L. Garfinkel <simsong@acm.org>
1 key(s) examined.
C:\WORK>
```

In this example, PGP is telling me that my public key ring contains one key. The key is a public key that is 1024 bits long, was created July 15, 1994, has a single user ID "Simson L. Garfinkel <simsong@acm.org>", and has a key identification code "903C9265."

There is no way to tell if this key was really created by Simson Garfinkel; all I know is that the person who created the key typed in the user ID "Simson L. Garfinkel <simsong@acm.org>" when he was prompted for a user ID by the PGP program. You too could create a key for Simson L. Garfinkel—you could masquerade as me— although your key would probably have a different key ID. You will see later on that this is an important characteristic of PGP; some people think that it's a flaw in the program. Fortunately, the possible danger of user fraud can be minimized by using key fingerprints and digital signatures, as I describe in Chapter 11 and Chapter 12.

Viewing Keys on Your Secret Key Ring

By default, the –kv (key view) option lists the keys in your public key ring. It is a simple matter, though, to list the keys in your secret key ring. All you have to do is specify the name of your secret key ring after the –kv option:

```
C:\WORK> pgp -kv secring.pgp
Pretty Good Privacy(tm) 2.6 - Public-key encryption for the masses.
 (c) 1990-1994 Philip Zimmermann, Phil's Pretty Good Software. 23 May 94
Distributed by the Massachusetts Institute of Technology.  Uses RSAREF.
Export of this software may be restricted by the U.S. government.
Current time: 1994/08/13 22:39 GMT
```

```
Key ring: 'secring.pgp'
Type bits/keyID     Date        User ID
sec  1024/903C9265 1994/07/15 Simson L. Garfinkel <simsong@acm.org>
1 key(s) examined.
C:\WORK>
```

Notice the differences between this output and the output from the previous (public key ring) example:

- In the previous example, the key ring was type "pub". This time, the key ring is type "sec"—that is, this time I am listing a secret key ring.

- In the previous example, PGP listed the key ring *c:\pgp\pubring.pgp*—that is, PGP displayed the complete pathname of the file. In the second example, PGP listed the keys in the key ring *secring.pgp*. The reason for the difference is that, in the previous example, PGP found the public key ring *pubring.pgp* by using the PGPPATH environment variable. In the second example, PGP found the key ring *secring.pgp* by looking for the file whose name I had typed on the command line. (If you are using the UNIX version of PGP, you may need to specify the full path of your secret key ring by typing $*PGPPATH/secring.pgp* instead of simply typing *secring.pgp*.)

- The two keys shown in the two examples represent a single key pair, one public and one secret. They also have the same key ID and the same user ID, which won't always be the case because you can change a user ID after a key is generated. Generally, though, if two keys have the same key ID, it is likely that they are a matched pair.

Viewing Keys on Other Key Rings

In PGP you can have as many key rings as you wish. Each ring resides in a separate file. You can use the –kv option to view the contents of any key ring.

In this example, the company Last Computers, Inc.[†] has distributed a key ring consisting of the names of the company's nine employees, their PGP public keys, their telephone extensions, and their email addresses. In this way, the key ring doubles as the company's address book.

```
unix% pgp -kv company.pgp
Pretty Good Privacy(tm) 2.6 - Public-key encryption for the masses.
(c) 1990-1994 Philip Zimmermann, Phil's Pretty Good Software. 23 May 94
Distributed by the Massachusetts Institute of Technology.  Uses RSAREF.
Export of this software may be restricted by the U.S. government.
Current time: 1994/08/26 13:27 GMT
```

---

† "We make the last computers you'll ever need."

```
Key ring: 'company.pgp'
Type bits/keyID     Date        User ID
pub  1024/89AF3289 1993/09/23 Peter Aagiorou, x100 <aagiorou@last.com>
pub  1024/AA331034 1994/07/07 David ben Aaron, x103 <dba@last.com>
pub  1024/AB3824FF 1994/05/12 Sally Chesnais, x104 <sc@last.com>
pub  1024/C8348EFA 1994/05/12 Elsa Chassell, x102 <ec@last.com>
pub  1024/328A3845 1994/05/12 Lisa Harris, x108<harris@last.com>
pub  1024/88394F38 1994/05/12 Brian Hawley, x105 <bh@last.com>
pub  1024/9883FB21 1994/07/07 Tina Hess, x109 <tina@last.com>
pub  1024/1123FA98 1994/07/07 Warren Johns, x107 <wj@last.com>
pub  1024/49345842 1994/05/26 Xiaj Lee, x110 <xiaj@last.com>
9 matching keys found.
unix%
```

If your company has a computer network or a shared file server, you could put the company key ring in a location that can be accessed by everyone in the company. If your company has only non-networked personal computers, you can put copies of the key ring on a floppy disk and copy it onto each computer.

Getting More Information about Keys (–kvc Option)

You can get even more information about your keys by using the –kc (key check) and –kvc (key view and check) options:

```
unix% pgp -kc
Pretty Good Privacy(tm) 2.6 - Public-key encryption for the masses.
(c) 1990-1994 Philip Zimmermann, Phil's Pretty Good Software. 23 May 94
Distributed by the Massachusetts Institute of Technology.  Uses RSAREF.
Export of this software may be restricted by the U.S. government.
Current time: 1994/08/13 23:01 GMT

Key ring: '/Net/next/Users/simsong/Library/pgp/pubring.pgp'
Type bits/keyID     Date        User ID
pub    512/43744F09 1994/07/07 Phil's Pretty Good Pizza <phil@pgp.com>
pub  1024/903C9265 1994/07/15 Simson L. Garfinkel <simsong@acm.org>
                              Simson L. Garfinkel <simsong@mit.edu>


  KeyID     Trust     Validity  User ID
  43744F09 undefined undefined Phil's Pretty Good Pizza <phil@pgp.com>
* 903C9265 ultimate   complete  Simson L. Garfinkel <simsong@acm.org>
                      complete   Simson L. Garfinkel <simsong@mit.edu>


unix%
```

```
unix% pgp -kvc
Pretty Good Privacy(tm) 2.6 - Public-key encryption for the masses.
(c) 1990-1994 Philip Zimmermann, Phil's Pretty Good Software. 23 May 94
Distributed by the Massachusetts Institute of Technology.  Uses RSAREF.
Export of this software may be restricted by the U.S. government.
Current time: 1994/08/13 23:00 GMT

Key ring: '/Net/next/Users/simsong/Library/pgp/pubring.pgp'
Type bits/keyID    Date        User ID
pub   512/43744F09 1994/07/07 Phil's Pretty Good Pizza <phil@pgp.com>
        Key fingerprint =  24 38 1A 58 46 AD CC 2D  AB C9 E0 F1 C7 3C 67 EC
pub  1024/903C9265 1994/07/15 Simson L. Garfinkel <simsong@acm.org>
        Key fingerprint =  68 06 7B 9A 8C E6 58 3D  6E D8 0E 90 01 C5 DE 01
                           Simson L. Garfinkel <simsong@mit.edu>
2 matching keys found.
unix%
```

I explain these options in Chapter 12 when I discuss how to certify and distribute keys.

Changing Your Key Certificate (-ke Option)

In PGP you can make a number of different types of changes to your secret and public key certificates after you have created them:

- You can change your pass phrase.

- You can add another user ID to your public key.

- You can delete a user ID from your public key.

To make these changes, run PGP with the –ke (key edit) option and specify the user ID for the key you are editing. (If you do not type a user ID after the –ke option, PGP prompts you for one.)

Changing Your Pass Phrase

Why would you change your pass phrase? You might be concerned that the one you originally selected was not secure enough, or you might fear that someone has guessed your pass phrase. To change your pass phrase, run PGP with the –ke (key edit) option and specify your user ID on the command line. PGP asks you if you wish to edit your pass phrase. Type **y** and then type the new pass phrase:

```
unix% pgp -ke simson
Pretty Good Privacy(tm) 2.6 - Public-key encryption for the masses.
(c) 1990-1994 Philip Zimmermann, Phil's Pretty Good Software. 23 May 94
Distributed by the Massachusetts Institute of Technology.  Uses RSAREF.
Export of this software may be restricted by the U.S. government.
```

```
Current time: 1994/08/28 17:36 GMT

Editing userid "simson" in key ring: '/Users/simsong/Library/pgp/pubring.pgp'.

Key for user ID: Simson L. Garfinkel <simsong@acm.org>
1024-bit key, Key ID 903C9265, created 1994/07/15

You need a pass phrase to unlock your RSA secret key.
Key for user ID "Simson L. Garfinkel <simsong@acm.org>"

Enter pass phrase: Nobody knows me. Pass phrase is good.
Current user ID: Simson L. Garfinkel <simsong@acm.org>
Do you want to add a new user ID (y/N)? n

Do you want to change your pass phrase (y/N)? y

Enter pass phrase: Nobody reads this stuff anyway.
Enter same pass phrase again: Nobody reads this stuff anyway.
Secret key ring updated...
(No need to update public key ring)
unix%
```

Changing Your User ID (-ke Option)

When you use PGP for more than a few months, you may find that you need to change the user ID that is embedded in your public and secret keys. There are lots of reasons why you might need to make such a change:

- You might have made a mistake when you originally typed your user ID.

- Your email address might have changed.

- You may wish to add information, such as your telephone number, to your user ID.

- You may have been married or divorced and want to change your last name.

- You may have had a sex change and want to change your first name!

To change your user ID, you also use the –ke (key edit) option. If you don't specify a user ID on the command line, PGP prompts you for one. In the following example, I am adding an alternative email address to the list of user IDs on my public key:

```
unix% pgp -ke
Pretty Good Privacy(tm) 2.6 - Public-key encryption for the masses.
(c) 1990-1994 Philip Zimmermann, Phil's Pretty Good Software. 23 May 94
Distributed by the Massachusetts Institute of Technology.  Uses RSAREF.
Export of this software may be restricted by the U.S. government.
Current time: 1994/08/13 22:49 GMT
```

```
A user ID is required to select the key you want to edit.
Enter the key's user ID: simson

Editing userid "simson" in key ring: '/Users/simsong/Library/pgp/pubring.pgp'.

Key for user ID: Simson L. Garfinkel <simsong@acm.org>
1024-bit key, Key ID 903C9265, created 1994/07/15

You need a pass phrase to unlock your RSA secret key.
Key for user ID "Simson L. Garfinkel <simsong@acm.org>"

Enter pass phrase: Nobody knows my name.Pass phrase is good.
Current user ID: Simson L. Garfinkel <simsong@acm.org>
Do you want to add a new user ID (y/N)? y

Enter the new user ID: Simson L. Garfinkel <simsong@mit.edu>

Make this user ID the primary user ID for this key (y/N)? n

Do you want to change your pass phrase (y/N)? n

Secret key ring updated...
Public key ring updated.
unix%
```

Now I use the –kv (key view) option to verify that the second user ID was in fact
added to the key:

```
unix% pgp -kv
Pretty Good Privacy(tm) 2.6 - Public-key encryption for the masses.
 (c) 1990-1994 Philip Zimmermann, Phil's Pretty Good Software. 23 May 94
Distributed by the Massachusetts Institute of Technology.  Uses RSAREF.
Export of this software may be restricted by the U.S. government.
Current time: 1994/08/13 22:50 GMT

Key ring: '/Users/simsong/Library/pgp/pubring.pgp'
Type bits/keyID     Date       User ID
pub    512/43744F09 1994/07/07 Phil's Pretty Good Pizza <phil@pgp.com>
pub   1024/903C9265 1994/07/15 Simson L. Garfinkel <simsong@acm.org>
                               Simson L. Garfinkel <simsong@mit.edu>
2 matching keys found.
unix%
```

Notice that the new user ID does not replace the original user ID; instead, PGP adds it
to the list, which makes it easier to decrypt messages that you (or other people) have
received that were encrypted with the older key.

You may end up with a number of distinct user IDs associated with a particular public key on your key ring, but only one is considered the "primary" user ID. "Primary" simply means that this is the user ID that PGP displays when it encounters the key ID in a signed message. Because I answered **n** to the question, "Make this user ID the primary user ID for this key (y/N)?", the original user ID (simsong@acm.org) is listed first. If I had answered **y** to this question, the new user ID (simsong@mit.edu) would have been listed first:

```
unix% pgp -kv
Pretty Good Privacy(tm) 2.6 - Public-key encryption for the masses.
 (c) 1990-1994 Philip Zimmermann, Phil's Pretty Good Software. 23 May 94
Distributed by the Massachusetts Institute of Technology.  Uses RSAREF.
Export of this software may be restricted by the U.S. government.
Current time: 1994/08/13 22:52 GMT


Key ring: '/Users/simsong/Library/pgp/pubring.pgp'
Type bits/keyID    Date        User ID
pub    512/43744F09 1994/07/07 Phil's Pretty Good Pizza <phil@pgp.com>
pub   1024/903C9265 1994/07/15 Simson L. Garfinkel <simsong@mit.edu>
                               Simson L. Garfinkel <simsong@acm.org>
2 matching keys found.

unix%
```

Editing with Options

You can speed the editing process by specifying on the command line the user ID you wish to edit:

```
unix% pgp -ke simson
Pretty Good Privacy(tm) 2.6 - Public-key encryption for the masses.
 (c) 1990-1994 Philip Zimmermann, Phil's Pretty Good Software. 23 May 94
Distributed by the Massachusetts Institute of Technology.  Uses RSAREF.
Export of this software may be restricted by the U.S. government.
Current time: 1994/08/13 22:49 GMT


Editing userid "simson" in key ring: '/Net/next/Users/simsong/Library/pgp/
pubring.pgp'.

Key for user ID: Simson L. Garfinkel <simsong@acm.org>
1024-bit key, Key ID 903C9265, created 1994/07/15

You need a pass phrase to unlock your RSA secret key.
Key for user ID "Simson L. Garfinkel <simsong@acm.org>"

Enter pass phrase: Nobody knows my name.Pass phrase is good.
Current user ID: Simson L. Garfinkel <simsong@acm.org>
```

```
Do you want to add a new user ID (y/N)? y

Enter the new user ID: Simson L. Garfinkel <simsong@mit.edu>

Make this user ID the primary user ID for this key (y/N)? n

Do you want to change your pass phrase (y/N)? n

Secret key ring updated...
Public key ring updated.
unix%
```

You can also edit the keys stored in a different key ring by specifying on the command line both the user ID and the name of the desired key ring. (See the next section for a description of how to do this.)

Changing Your User ID (-ke and -kr Options)

You've seen how you can use the –ke option to add a user ID to a key certificate. To change your user ID completely, you must first use the –ke (key edit) option to add a new user ID and then use the –kr (key remove) option to remove an old one.

For example, if Jane at Last Computers wanted to change her telephone extension, she would first add the new user ID with the new extension via the –ke option:

```
unix% pgp -ke Jane company.pgp
Pretty Good Privacy(tm) 2.6 - Public-key encryption for the masses.
(c) 1990-1994 Philip Zimmermann, Phil's Pretty Good Software. 23 May 94
Distributed by the Massachusetts Institute of Technology.  Uses RSAREF.
Export of this software may be restricted by the U.S. government.
Current time: 1994/08/26 15:00 GMT

Editing userid "Jane" in key ring: 'company.pgp'.

Key for user ID: Jane Weise, x111 <jane@last.com>
1024-bit key, Key ID BEEFCC19, created 1994/08/26

You need a pass phrase to unlock your RSA secret key.
Key for user ID "Jane Weise, x111 <jane@last.com>"

Enter pass phrase: my name is jane. Pass phrase is good.
Use this key as an ultimately-trusted introducer (y/N)? n

Current user ID: Jane Weise, x111 <jane@last.com>
Do you want to add a new user ID (y/N)? y

Enter the new user ID: Jane Weise, x113 <jane@last.com>
```

```
Make this user ID the primary user ID for this key (y/N)? y

Do you want to change your pass phrase (y/N)? n

Secret key ring updated...
Public key ring updated.
unix%
```

Next Jane would remove her old extension with the –kr (key remove) option:

```
unix% pgp -kr Jane company.pgp
Pretty Good Privacy(tm) 2.6 - Public-key encryption for the masses.
(c) 1990-1994 Philip Zimmermann, Phil's Pretty Good Software. 23 May 94
Distributed by the Massachusetts Institute of Technology.  Uses RSAREF.
Export of this software may be restricted by the U.S. government.
Current time: 1994/08/26 15:02 GMT

Removing from key ring: 'company.pgp', userid "Jane".

Key for user ID: Jane Weise, x113 <jane@last.com>
1024-bit key, Key ID BEEFCC19, created 1994/08/26
Also known as: Jane Weise, x111 <jane@last.com>

Key has more than one user ID.
Do you want to remove the whole key (y/N)? n
Remove "Jane Weise, x113 <jane@last.com>" (y/N)? n
Remove "Jane Weise, x111 <jane@last.com>" (y/N)? y

User ID removed from key ring.
unix%
```

Be careful. If you remove all of the user IDs, PGP removes your key.

Giving Your Public Key to Someone

With PGP, you can't read encrypted email (even email sent only to you) unless the sender first encrypts the mail with your public key. For the sender to do so, you need to be sure that she has a copy of your public key.

As I've mentioned, many public keys are stored in PGP's public key servers. If you use PGP frequently, you probably should add your key to the servers as well. (See Chapter 15, *PGP Internet Key Servers*, for information on how to do this.)

Copying Your Public Key Ring

There are many other ways to give someone a copy of your public key. The easiest way is to copy your entire public key ring onto a floppy disk, which you can do by typing the following:

```
C:\PGP> copy pubring.pgp a:simson.pgp
        1 file(s) copied
C:\PGP>
```

I don't recommend that you do this. It's smarter to extract just your own public key from your public key ring.

Extracting Your Public Key (-kx Option)

Although there is technically nothing wrong with making someone a copy of your entire public key ring, there are several reasons why you may wish to avoid doing so:

- You might get confused and give your colleague a copy of your secret key ring by accident. If you do, he won't be able to send you any messages. This is unlikely, but it has happened.

- If you don't change the name of the *pubring.pgp* file, your colleague might accidentally copy your public key ring over his public key ring (because the files have the same names), which would make it difficult for him to exchange encrypted mail with other people. Again, it's unlikely, but I've seen it happen.

- If your public key ring should fall into the wrong hands, your enemies would be able to determine the names of everyone with whom you exchange encrypted mail and how much you trust each person. In the world of computer security, this is what is called *traffic analysis*. Although your enemy wouldn't be able to read any of the encrypted email, you may wish to keep the identities of your correspondents secret.

For all of these reasons, *you should not simply give your friends copies of your public key ring.* Instead, you should use the –kx (key extract) option.

In the following example, I am extracting only my own public key from my public key ring (the first "simson" in the example identifies the user ID on that key) and creating a new file called *simson.pgp* (the *.pgp* extension is supplied by default):

```
C:\PGP> pgp -kx simson simson
Pretty Good Privacy(tm) 2.6 - Public-key encryption for the masses.
(c) 1990-1994 Philip Zimmermann, Phil's Pretty Good Software. 23 May 94
Distributed by the Massachusetts Institute of Technology.  Uses RSAREF.
Export of this software may be restricted by the U.S. government.
Current time: 1994/08/13 22:38 GMT
```

```
Extracting from key ring: 'c:\pgp\pubring.pgp', userid "simson".

Key for user ID: Simson Garfinkel <simsong@acm.org>
512-bit key, Key ID 73A907, created 1994/07/01

Key extracted to file 'simson.pgp'.
C:\PGP> dir simson.pgp

 Volume in drive C has no label
 Volume Serial Number is 12D9-1B44
 Directory of C:\PGP

SIMSON   PGP           132 07-01-94   1:52p
       1 file(s)               132 bytes
                      4,046,848 bytes free
C:\PGP>
```

The –kx option creates a file that has a single key in it—the key that I extracted. This file contains a copy of my public key. My own public key ring still contains my original public key. The *simson.pgp* file is called a *key file*. It is like a key ring, except it does not contain "trust" information. (See Chapter 12, *Certifying and Distributing Keys*, for details about trust.) Like the key ring, the key file is in binary, which means that you cannot decode its contents simply by typing the filename on your screen. If you do, you see garbage similar to the following:

```
C:\PGP> type simson.pgp
ÛM.v6ñÕË*Û,p9$H???õ4Üûñ "Ø.?QÔ¸Êê–ú?ÿ"§–fLs›nNLËÓB5s'·2Simson Garfinkel
<simsong@acm.org>
C:\PGP>
```

The most straightforward way to give this key file to a colleague is to copy it onto a floppy disk and physically hand it to her:

```
C:\PGP> copy simson.pgp a:
        1 file(s) copied

C:\PGP>
```

Because your colleague gets the disk from you, she knows for sure that the key on it is really your key. In security jargon, this procedure is known as *positive authentication using biometric indicators*. In this case, the biometrics are sight, smell, touch, and behavior—your friend sees you and recognizes you.

If you cannot physically hand the floppy disk containing your key to your colleague, you can send it in the mail, but this procedure is somewhat less secure. Since it is your *public key* and not your *secret key*, it doesn't matter if someone else intercepts it. You could even publish your public key in the phone book.

Extracting Printable Keys with ASCII Armor (-kxa Option)

There's one potential problem with publishing the key file described in the previous section: it's in binary. Because the file is in binary, it's fast for the PGP program to open it and read its contents. Unfortunately, while binary keys are great for storing on a computer's hard disk and copying to a floppy, they're lousy for sending through electronic mail or publishing in a printed directory.

PGP has a built-in system for converting binary information into a printable ASCII representation and for converting that ASCII representation back into binary. The system is called *ASCII armor,* and I introduced it in Chapter 1, *Introduction to PGP.* ASCII armor is enabled by adding the letter *a* to the PGP option. The format of ASCII armor is called Radix 64 because the representation uses 64 different symbols, allowing each 8-bit character to represent 6 binary bits. ASCII armor thus takes up one-third more space than its binary equivalent. Non-printable characters are included in Radix 64.

PGP Compression

Despite ASCII armor, encrypting your files with PGP does not make them notice-ably bigger because PGP compresses encrypted files and keys with the ZIP com-pression algorithm. Long text files (such as encrypted messages) are very compressible; for example, the PGP documentation file *pgpdoc1.txt*, which takes up 79K, is just 30K after compression (and 40K with ASCII armor).

The –kxa (key extract ASCII) option lets you extract a printable ASCII key from your public key ring. You can then include this key in an email message, post it to the Usenet, or print it on your business card:

```
unix% pgp -kxa simson simsong
Pretty Good Privacy(tm) 2.6 - Public-key encryption for the masses.
(c) 1990-1994 Philip Zimmermann, Phil's Pretty Good Software. 23 May 94
Distributed by the Massachusetts Institute of Technology.  Uses RSAREF.
Export of this software may be restricted by the U.S. government.
Current time: 1994/08/13 22:40 GMT

Extracting from key ring: '/Users/simsong/Library/pgp/pubring.pgp', userid
"simson".
```

```
Key for user ID: Simson L. Garfinkel <simsong@acm.org>
1024-bit key, Key ID 903C9265, created 1994/07/15

Transport armor file: simsong.asc

Key extracted to file 'simsong.asc'.
unix%
```

The following is what the ASCII-armored key looks like. Note that the file containing the ASCII-armored key has a default extension of *.asc*.

```
unix% cat simsong.asc
-----BEGIN PGP PUBLIC KEY BLOCK-----
Version: 2.6

mQCNAi4mq/gAAAEEAPcbmtIyFTyqdpwU3HFP7XEIBGu1CXKZpzxDgDY21gKwy5uJ
nxsSbTaz//AxrHE6R1LXZXnZgEFJWp/AIr1PdwjKciRJFIvqdqooyZHSPFQ9r8oS
3Fq+0xPpOCEyPDb9+Ghv9HYcIepLwJJrcORinor5ZdzfWRyW13D7CbCQPJJ1AAUR
tCVTaW1zb24gTC4gR2FyZmlua2VsIDxzaW1zb25nQGFjbS5vcmc+
=un1L
-----END PGP PUBLIC KEY BLOCK-----
unix%
```

Notice that the last line is significantly shorter than the other four. This last line contains the CRC (cyclic redundancy check) code for the key. CRC is a number that is calculated by a mathematical formula. When PGP created the file *simsong.pgp*, it calculated the CRC and put it at the end of the file. When PGP reads the file back in, it recalculates the CRC and compares the result with the number included at the end of the file. If the two CRCs match, PGP knows that the file hasn't been corrupted during transmission. If they do not match, PGP displays the following message:

```
ERROR: Bad ASCII armor checksum

Error: Transport armor stripping failed for file simson.asc
```

Using Filter Mode (-f Option)

If you are going to be sending the extracted key by electronic mail, you can skip the intermediate step of putting the public key into a file and simply use the –f (filter) option. The filter option causes PGP to print its output to the program's *standard output*. You can then pipe this output into the UNIX *mail* program's *standard input*. The filter option works as follows:

```
unix% pgp -kxaf simson | mail -s "my public key" associate@business.com
Pretty Good Privacy(tm) 2.6 - Public-key encryption for the masses.
(c) 1990-1994 Philip Zimmermann, Phil's Pretty Good Software. 23 May 94
Distributed by the Massachusetts Institute of Technology.  Uses RSAREF.
```

```
Export of this software may be restricted by the U.S. government.
Current time: 1994/09/03 13:03 GMT

Extracting from key ring: '/Users/simsong/Library/pgp/pubring.pgp', userid
"simson".

Key for user ID: Simson L. Garfinkel <simsong@acm.org>
1024-bit key, Key ID 903C9265, created 1994/07/15

Key extracted to file 'pgptemp.$00'.
unix%
```

Extracting Multiple Keys into a Single ASCII-Armored File

You can put several PGP keys into a single ASCII-armored file. If you send this file by email, anyone who receives it can add all of the keys to his own public key ring with a single operation.

To create an ASCII file that contains several public keys, follow this two-step process:

1. Create a PGP key file that contains the keys for every person that you want to include.

2. Convert this file to ASCII by using the –a option by itself.

For example, suppose I wanted to create a file with the public keys for Phil's Pretty Good Pizza, Dawn's Fabulous French Fries, and Tim's Tasty Tacos. I could start with this PGP key ring:

```
unix% pgp -kv
Pretty Good Privacy(tm) 2.6 - Public-key encryption for the masses.
(c) 1990-1994 Philip Zimmermann, Phil's Pretty Good Software. 23 May 94
Distributed by the Massachusetts Institute of Technology.  Uses RSAREF.
Export of this software may be restricted by the U.S. government.
Current time: 1994/09/17 19:14 GMT

Key ring: '/Users/simsong/Library/pgp/pubring.pgp'
Type bits/keyID    Date        User ID
pub   768/763FD321 1994/08/27 Dawn's Fabulous French Fries <dawn@fff.com>
pub   512/873FA3FF 1994/08/27 Tim's Tasy Tacos <tim@taco.com>
pub   512/43744F09 1994/07/07 Phil's Pretty Good Pizza <phil@pgp.com>
pub  1024/903C9265 1994/07/15 Simson L. Garfinkel <simsong@acm.org>
4 matching keys found.
unix%
```

Now I use the –kx (key extract) option to extract the keys into a single file called
restaurants.pgp:

```
unix% pgp -kx phil restaurants.pgp
...
unix% pgp -kx dawn restaurants.pgp
...
unix% pgp -kx tim restaurants.pgp
...
```

If I were using a DOS computer, I could have combined all of these key additions in
a single command line as follows:

```
c:\> for %a in (phil dawn tim) do pgp -kx %%a rkeys.pgp
```

Likewise, if were using the UNIX C shell, I could have used the following command:

```
unix% foreach i (phil dawn tim)
? pgp -kx $i rkeys.pgp
? end
```

Next I use the –a (ASCII armor) option to armor the *restaurants.pgp* file:

```
unix% pgp -a restaurants.pgp
Pretty Good Privacy(tm) 2.6 - Public-key encryption for the masses.
(c) 1990-1994 Philip Zimmermann, Phil's Pretty Good Software. 23 May 94
Distributed by the Massachusetts Institute of Technology.  Uses RSAREF.
Export of this software may be restricted by the U.S. government.
Current time: 1994/09/06 01:53 GMT

Input file 'resturants.pgp' looks like it may have been created by PGP.
Is it safe to assume that it was created by PGP (y/N)? y

Transport armor file: restaurants.asc
unix%
```

The public keys are now in the file *restaurants.asc*. When I email this file, the recipients can incorporate it into their public key rings.

Adding Keys to Key Rings (-ka Option)

The following sections describe how you add keys to your public key ring and to
other key rings.

Adding Someone's Key to Your Public Key Ring

When you receive a public key from a friend or colleague, you need to add it to your
public key ring before you can use it. To do this, use the –ka (key add) option. You

can use the same –ka option to add either PGP binary files (with a *.pgp* extension) or PGP ASCII-armor files (with a *.asc* extension).

For example, suppose that Phil has given me a floppy disk containing a copy of his public key so I can safely order pizza. The following example shows how I would add it to my *pubring.pgp* key ring:

```
C:\PGP> dir a:

 Volume in drive C has no label
 Volume Serial Number is 12D9-1B44
 Directory of A:\

PHIL     PGP           90 07-01-94   9:35p
        1 file(s)              90 bytes
                        3,964,928 bytes free
C:\PGP>


C:\PGP> pgp -ka a:phil
Pretty Good Privacy(tm) 2.6 - Public-key encryption for the masses.
 (c) 1990-1994 Philip Zimmermann, Phil's Pretty Good Software. 23 May 94
Distributed by the Massachusetts Institute of Technology.  Uses RSAREF.
Export of this software may be restricted by the U.S. government.
Current time: 1994/08/13 22:42 GMT

Looking for new keys...
pub    512/43744F09 1994/07/07  Phil's Pretty Good Pizza <phil@pgp.com>

Checking signatures...

Keyfile contains:
   1 new key(s)

One or more of the new keys are not fully certified.
Do you want to certify any of these keys yourself (y/N)? n
C:\PGP>
```

In this example I asked PGP to add the key file *phil.pgp* to my public key ring. PGP complained that Phil's key wasn't fully "certified" and gave me a chance to certify Phil's key. (Certification is described fully in Chapter 12, *Certifying and Distributing Keys*. For now, I believe that the key is okay, and I type **n** and press Return.) PGP adds Phil's key, uncertified, to my public key ring. I then type **pgp –kv** to view the key ring. It now contains two public keys: my own and the one for Phil's Pretty Good Pizza.

You can verify that a key has been put on your key ring by using the –kv (key view) option:

```
C:\PGP> pgp -kv
Pretty Good Privacy(tm) 2.6 - Public-key encryption for the masses.
 (c) 1990-1994 Philip Zimmermann, Phil's Pretty Good Software. 23 May 94
Distributed by the Massachusetts Institute of Technology.  Uses RSAREF.
Export of this software may be restricted by the U.S. government.
Date: 1994/06/26 21:47 GMT


Key ring: 'c:\pgp\pubring.pgp'
Type bits/keyID      Date       User ID
pub   512/43744F09 1994/07/07  Phil's Pretty Good Pizza <phil@pgp.com>
pub  1024/903C9265 1994/07/01  Simson Garfinkel <simsong@acm.org>
2 key(s) examined.
C:\PGP>
```

As we can see, Phil's Pretty Good Pizza has a PGP key that is only 512 bits long. That's not terribly secure, but it's probably good enough for ordering double cheese, double mushroom. Notice that Phil's key also has a different key ID and was created on a different date from when mine was created.

Adding a Key to a Specified Key Ring

You can also add a key to a specified key ring by including the name of the key ring on the command line following the name of the file containing the key you wish to add.

For example, suppose that Jane Weise has joined Last Computers and you are charged with adding her public key to the company key ring. Jane makes her PGP key and gives it to you in a file called *jane.pgp*. The following example shows how you would add her key to the *company.pgp* file:

```
unix% pgp -ka jane.pgp company.pgp
Pretty Good Privacy(tm) 2.6 - Public-key encryption for the masses.
 (c) 1990-1994 Philip Zimmermann, Phil's Pretty Good Software. 23 May 94
Distributed by the Massachusetts Institute of Technology.  Uses RSAREF.
Export of this software may be restricted by the U.S. government.
Current time: 1994/08/26 14:09 GMT

Looking for new keys...
pub  1024/BEEFCC19 1994/08/26  Jane Weise, x111 <jane@last.com>

Checking signatures...
```

```
Keyfile contains:
   1 new key(s)

One or more of the new keys are not fully certified.
Do you want to certify any of these keys yourself (y/N)? n
unix%
```

Impatient? Use a Smaller Key Ring.

If it seems to you that your version of PGP is slowing down the more you use it, you may be right. PGP Version 2.6 has a very inefficient algorithm for managing key rings, which doesn't work very well if the key ring is larger than a few hundred public keys. (According to Phil Zimmermann, it can take a typical PC more than *two days* to add a key ring containing 10,000 keys.)

PGP Version 3.0 will fix this problem. That version will need just two minutes to add 10,000 keys. Until Version 3.0 is available, you can make things easier for yourself by keeping your key rings small and manageable.

If you frequently correspond with just a few people, I *strongly recommend* keeping their public keys on your main public key ring and keeping all of the others that you may correspond with on a second key ring.

No Duplicates Allowed

PGP won't allow you to add a key to a key ring if it is already there. The following is what happens if you try to add Jane's public key a second time:

```
unix% pgp -ka jane.pgp company.pgp
Pretty Good Privacy(tm) 2.6 - Public-key encryption for the masses.
(c) 1990-1994 Philip Zimmermann, Phil's Pretty Good Software. 23 May 94
Distributed by the Massachusetts Institute of Technology.  Uses RSAREF.
Export of this software may be restricted by the U.S. government.
Current time: 1994/08/26 14:14 GMT

Looking for new keys...
No new keys or signatures in keyfile.
unix%
```

Removing Keys from Key Rings (-kr Option)

The following sections describe how you remove keys from your public key ring and from other key rings.

Removing Keys from Your Public Key Ring

If you are sure that you are never going to want a particular public key again, you can delete it from your key ring using the –kr (key remove) option:

```
unix% pgp -kr phil
Pretty Good Privacy(tm) 2.6 - Public-key encryption for the masses.
 (c) 1990-1994 Philip Zimmermann, Phil's Pretty Good Software. 23 May 94
Distributed by the Massachusetts Institute of Technology.  Uses RSAREF.
Export of this software may be restricted by the U.S. government.
Current time: 1994/08/13 22:46 GMT

Removing from key ring: '/Users/simsong/Library/pgp/pubring.pgp', userid
"phil".

Key for user ID: Phil's Pretty Good Pizza <phil@pgp.com>
512-bit key, Key ID 43744F09, created 1994/07/07

Are you sure you want this key removed (y/N)? y

Key removed from key ring.
unix%
```

Removing Keys from a Specified Key Ring

You can remove keys from any key ring that you wish. Simply specify the name of the key ring on the command line following the user ID of the person whose key you wish to remove.

For example, if Elsa is fired from Last Computers, I could easily remove her public key from the company's key ring:

```
unix% pgp -kr Elsa company.pgp
Pretty Good Privacy(tm) 2.6 - Public-key encryption for the masses.
 (c) 1990-1994 Philip Zimmermann, Phil's Pretty Good Software. 23 May 94
Distributed by the Massachusetts Institute of Technology.  Uses RSAREF.
Export of this software may be restricted by the U.S. government.
Current time: 1994/08/26 14:20 GMT

Removing from key ring: 'company.pgp', userid "Elsa".

Key for user ID: Elsa Chassell, x102 <ec@last.com>
512-bit key, Key ID C8348EFA, created 1994/05/12

Are you sure you want this key removed (y/N)? y

Key removed from key ring.
unix%
```

A Starter Set of Public Keys

PGP comes with the file called *keys.asc,* which contains the public keys for various people involved with the creation of PGP. I can add these keys to my public key ring with the –ka option:

```
unix% ls -l pgp26/pgp26/keys.asc
-r--r--r--  1 simsong      4886 May 23 18:40 pgp26/pgp26/keys.asc
unix% pgp pgp26/pgp26/keys.asc
Pretty Good Privacy(tm) 2.6 - Public-key encryption for the masses.
(c) 1990-1994 Philip Zimmermann, Phil's Pretty Good Software. 23 May 94
Distributed by the Massachusetts Institute of Technology.  Uses RSAREF.
Export of this software may be restricted by the U.S. government.
Current time: 1994/07/12 23:51 GMT

File contains key(s).  Contents follow...
Key ring: 'pgp26/pgp26/keys.$00'
Type bits/keyID    Date       User ID
pub   512/4D0C4EE1 1992/09/10 Jeffrey I. Schiller <jis@mit.edu>
sig       C7A966DD            Philip R. Zimmermann <prz@acm.org>
sig       8DCBB1C3            (Unknown signator, can't be checked)
sig       71946BDF            (Unknown signator, can't be checked)
sig       7396D3B7            (Unknown signator, can't be checked)
sig       8CB4B951            (Unknown signator, can't be checked)
pub  1024/0778338D 1993/09/17 Philip L. Dubois <dubois@csn.org>
sig       C7A966DD            Philip R. Zimmermann <prz@acm.org>
pub  1024/FBBB8AB1 1994/05/07 Colin Plumb <colin@nyx.cs.du.edu>
sig       C7A966DD            Philip R. Zimmermann <prz@acm.org>
sig       865AA7F3            (Unknown signator, can't be checked)
sig       FBBB8AB1            Colin Plumb <colin@nyx.cs.du.edu>
pub  1024/C7A966DD 1993/05/21 Philip R. Zimmermann <prz@acm.org>
sig       C7A966DD            Philip R. Zimmermann <prz@acm.org>
sig       FF67F70B            (Unknown signator, can't be checked)
pub   709/C1B06AF1 1992/09/25 Derek Atkins <warlord@MIT.EDU>
sig       C7A966DD            Philip R. Zimmermann <prz@acm.org>
pub  1024/8DE722D9 1992/07/22 Branko Lankester  <branko@hacktic.nl>
sig       C7A966DD            Philip R. Zimmermann <prz@acm.org>
sig       8DE722D9            Branko Lankester  <branko@hacktic.nl>
pub  1024/9D997D47 1992/08/02 Peter Gutmann <pgut1@cs.aukuni.ac.nz>
sig       C7A966DD            Philip R. Zimmermann <prz@acm.org>
pub   510/DC620423 1992/08/27 Jean-loup Gailly <jloup@chorus.fr>
pub  1024/28748E05 1992/09/06 Hugh A.J. Kennedy <70042.710@compuserve.com>
9 matching keys found.

Do you want to add this keyfile to keyring '/Net/next/Users/simsong/Library/
pgp/pubring.pgp' (y/N)? y

Looking for new keys...
```

```
pub    512/4D0C4EE1 1992/09/10  Jeffrey I. Schiller <jis@mit.edu>
pub   1024/0778338D 1993/09/17  Philip L. Dubois <dubois@csn.org>
pub   1024/FBBB8AB1 1994/05/07  Colin Plumb <colin@nyx.cs.du.edu>
pub   1024/C7A966DD 1993/05/21  Philip R. Zimmermann <prz@acm.org>
pub    709/C1B06AF1 1992/09/25  Derek Atkins <warlord@MIT.EDU>
pub   1024/8DE722D9 1992/07/22  Branko Lankester  <branko@hacktic.nl>
pub   1024/9D997D47 1992/08/02  Peter Gutmann <pgut1@cs.aukuni.ac.nz>
pub    510/DC620423 1992/08/27  Jean-loup Gailly <jloup@chorus.fr>
pub   1024/28748E05 1992/09/06  Hugh A.J. Kennedy <70042.710@compuserve.com>

Checking signatures...
pub    512/4D0C4EE1 1992/09/10 Jeffrey I. Schiller <jis@mit.edu>
sig!        C7A966DD 1994/05/07  Philip R. Zimmermann <prz@acm.org>
pub   1024/0778338D 1993/09/17 Philip L. Dubois <dubois@csn.org>
sig!        C7A966DD 1993/10/19  Philip R. Zimmermann <prz@acm.org>
pub   1024/FBBB8AB1 1994/05/07 Colin Plumb <colin@nyx.cs.du.edu>
sig!        C7A966DD 1994/05/07  Philip R. Zimmermann <prz@acm.org>
sig!        FBBB8AB1 1994/05/07  Colin Plumb <colin@nyx.cs.du.edu>
pub   1024/C7A966DD 1993/05/21 Philip R. Zimmermann <prz@acm.org>
sig!        C7A966DD 1994/05/07  Philip R. Zimmermann <prz@acm.org>
pub    709/C1B06AF1 1992/09/25 Derek Atkins <warlord@MIT.EDU>
sig!        C7A966DD 1994/05/07  Philip R. Zimmermann <prz@acm.org>
pub   1024/8DE722D9 1992/07/22 Branko Lankester <branko@hacktic.nl>
sig!        C7A966DD 1994/05/07  Philip R. Zimmermann <prz@acm.org>
sig!        8DE722D9 1993/11/06  Branko Lankester  <branko@hacktic.nl>
pub   1024/9D997D47 1992/08/02 Peter Gutmann <pgut1@cs.aukuni.ac.nz>
sig!        C7A966DD 1994/02/06  Philip R. Zimmermann <prz@acm.org>

Keyfile contains:
   9 new key(s)

One or more of the new keys are not fully certified.
Do you want to certify any of these keys yourself (y/N)? n
unix%
```

I know many of these people, and many of these people have signed each other's keys. For now, I've answered **n** to the question, "Do you want to certify any of these keys yourself?" To learn how to certify these keys, turn to the section called "Certifying the Keys in keys.asc (Version 2.6.1)" in Chapter 12.

10

Encrypting Email

> *PGP will encrypt files so not even crazy people with supercomputers can decrypt them. You write e-mail on a word processor, encrypt it using someone's public key, and send it off. They use their private key to decrypt it. . . . Phil Zimmermann's PGP is the grassroots alternative to the Clipper Chip, which gives the government your secret key.*
>
> —Xenon (*na4813@anon.penet.fi*)

In the last chapter you learned how to create PGP key pairs—a vital prelude to the ability to send encrypted email, which is the central purpose of PGP.

This chapter describes the following PGP options that let you encrypt and decrypt email:

- The –e (encrypt) option encrypts a message.

- Typing **pgp** (followed by no options) decrypts a message.

This chapter also describes how you can combine the following additional options with encryption or decryption options:

- The –a (ASCII armor) option puts ASCII armor on messages.

- The –f (filter) option reads messages from standard input and writes to standard output.

- The –m (more) option indicates that a message should only be displayed and not saved to disk.

- The –t (text) option tells PGP to use the text mode conventions for the computer you are using.

Sending Encrypted Email

Sending encrypted email with PGP is a four-step process, consisting of the following steps:

1. Create the message that you wish to send.

2. Get the public key of the person to whom you're sending the message.

3. Encrypt the message using that person's public key.

4. Send the encrypted message via your traditional electronic mail program.

I'm sure that a new generation of electronic mail applications will combine these functions automatically within the next few years. Sophisticated systems will maintain the public keys in an address book; when you send email to a person in your book, the message will automatically be encrypted. Nevertheless, these newer systems will at least internally follow the steps listed above.

Figure 10-1 illustrates how PGP encrypts email.

Step 1: Creating the Message

Before you can send your encrypted message, you must first create it. With PGP, you have three choices:

- You can create the message with a word processor. (If you don't know for sure that your recipient has the same word processor that you have, save the file as ASCII.)

- You can copy your keystrokes directly into a file using commands such as *copy* (DOS) or *cp* (UNIX).

- You can use PGP in filter mode (with the –f option) and type your message directly into the program.

Each of these techniques has certain advantages. Using a word processor allows you to carefully consider and edit your thoughts. Copying your keystrokes directly into a file is quick, and it allows you to edit the message if you make a mistake. And using PGP in filter mode may be more secure, because you don't ever have a plaintext copy of the message on your hard disk.[†]

---

† If you are running PGP under Windows or UNIX, your computer's virtual memory system might swap PGP onto the computer's hard disk. When the program swaps in, a copy of PGP and your unencrypted secret key and the plaintext of your message might be left behind.

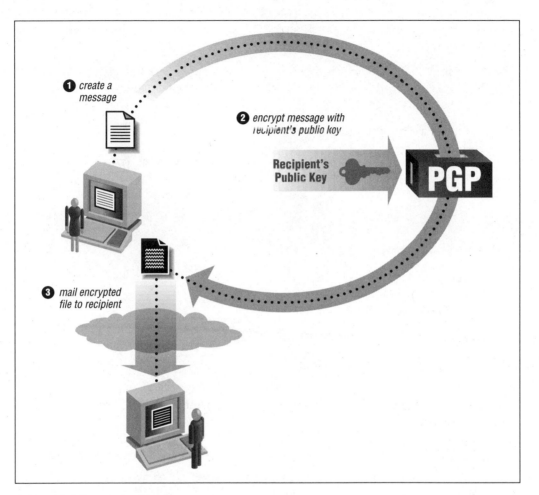

Figure 10-1. Encrypting email

Creating a message with your word processor

The documentation for your word processor should provide detailed information on how to create an ASCII text file. If you use Microsoft Word, for example, choose the Save As option and specify ASCII With Line Breaks as your file type when you save the file (unless you specifically want to send a Word document to someone who can read Word files).

Creating a message from the keyboard

With many email systems, you don't have much of a choice when you create a message: you simply type your message, line by line, and when you are finished, you type a special line and the message is sent. While this way of creating a message is great for just dashing off a quick note, it doesn't lend itself to the deliberative exchange of thoughts.

You can mimic such systems with PGP. In DOS, simply use the *copy* command to copy from the keyboard to a file. End your message by typing Control-Z on a separate line:

```
C:\WORK> copy con message
Phil,
     I would like a double-cheese pizza with olives to go at 8pm.
-Simson
^Z

        1 file(s) copied

C:\WORK> dir message

 Volume in drive C has no label
 Volume Serial Number is 17EA-102D
 Directory of C:\WORK

MESSAGE              98 07-04-94   1:51p
        1 file(s)             76 bytes
                      54,910,976 bytes free
C:\WORK>
```

You can do the same in UNIX by using the *cat* command. In UNIX, end your message with Control-D:

```
unix% cat > message
Phil,
     I would like a double-cheese pizza with olives to go at 8pm.
-Simson
^D
unix% ls -l message
-rw-r--r--  1 simsong       78 Jul  4 13:46 message
unix%
```

Running PGP in filter mode

Because running PGP in filter mode involves a combination of all of the steps mentioned in this chapter, I've described the approach later in the section "Typing, Encrypting, and Sending at the Same Time."

Step 2: Getting the Recipient's Public Key

Before you encrypt your message, you need to be sure that you are encrypting it with the correct public key for the person to whom you're sending the message. Encrypting a message with the wrong key can lead to two undesired consequences:

- The intended recipient won't be able to read the message.

- Someone else might be able to read the message instead.

In Chapter 11, I talk about the cryptographic methods that PGP uses for signing keys. For now, though, assume that the public key for Phil's Pretty Good Pizza is, in fact, an authentic key.

Let's look at the key ring containing the public keys of people I correspond with regularly:

```
C:\WORK> pgp -kv
Pretty Good Privacy(tm) 2.6 - Public-key encryption for the masses.
 (c) 1990-1994 Philip Zimmermann, Phil's Pretty Good Software. 23 May 94
Distributed by the Massachusetts Institute of Technology.  Uses RSAREF.
Export of this software may be restricted by the U.S. government.
Current time: 1994/08/15 03:47 GMT

Key ring: '/simsong/Library/pgp/pubring.pgp'
Type bits/keyID    Date        User ID
pub   512/43744F09 1994/07/07 Phil's Pretty Good Pizza <phil@pgp.com>
pub  1024/903C9265 1994/07/15 Simson L. Garfinkel <simsong@acm.org>
2 matching keys found.
C:\WORK>
```

Step 3: Encrypting the Message (-e Option).

Once you have a key, you can use it to encrypt a message. In theory, all you need to type is **pgp -e** (encrypt option). However, you might want to use the –ea (encrypt ASCII) or the –eat (encrypt ASCII text) options instead. The –e option tells PGP to encrypt; the –a option means that PGP should encrypt into ASCII, which you need to use if you want to send the message by electronic mail; and the –t option tells PGP that you are encrypting a *text* file.

In the following example, *message* is the name of the file I'm encrypting (PGP assumes a default extension of *.pgp*), and "phil" is sufficient to identify the user ID for Phil's Pretty Good Pizza:

```
C:\WORK> pgp -eat message phil
Pretty Good Privacy(tm) 2.6 - Public-key encryption for the masses.
 (c) 1990-1994 Philip Zimmermann, Phil's Pretty Good Software. 23 May 94
Distributed by the Massachusetts Institute of Technology.  Uses RSAREF.
```

```
Export of this software may be restricted by the U.S. government.
Current time: 1994/08/15 03:48 GMT


Recipients' public key(s) will be used to encrypt.
Key for user ID: Phil's Pretty Good Pizza <phil@pgp.com>
512-bit key, Key ID 43744F09, created 1994/07/07

WARNING:  Because this public key is not certified with a trusted
signature, it is not known with high confidence that this public key
actually belongs to: "Phil's Pretty Good Pizza <phil@pgp.com>".

Are you sure you want to use this public key (y/N)? y
.
Transport armor file: message.asc
C:\WORK>
```

Notice that PGP warns me that the key that I am using to encrypt the file hasn't been certified. What does this mean? When I added Phil's key to my key ring in the last chapter, I chose not to certify it. PGP is telling me that I have no way of knowing that this public key is really the public key for Phil's Pretty Good Pizza.[†]

Text Mode (–t Option)

Each of the three most popular kinds of computers that PGP runs on—PCs, Macs, and UNIX workstations—represent the ends of lines in text files in slightly different ways.

Fortunately, PGP knows about these differences. When you specify the –t option for encrypting and decrypting files, PGP automatically translates characters so they are correct for the kind of computer you are using.

You don't need to use the –t option if you are exchanging encrypted messages only with people using the same kind of computer that you are, because no end-of-line translation is needed.

Don't use the –t option if you are sending word processor files, spreadsheets, or other kinds of files that contain binary data. (If you do accidentally use the –t option with a binary file, PGP should realize your mistake and turn off the text option anyway, but why take the risk?)

If I were sending secret messages containing Swiss bank account numbers or the names of U.S. agents operating inside Moscow and St. Petersburg, I might want to

---

† Confused about certification? It's all explained in Chapter 12.

reconsider my plans and not send the message encrypted with this questionable key. But, hey, I'm just sending an order for pizza! That's why, when PGP asks if I really want to encrypt the message with this key, I tell PGP to go ahead.

Finally, PGP tells me that it has encrypted the message and put the result in the file *message.asc*.

Let's see what this file looks like:

```
C:\WORK>type message.asc
-----BEGIN PGP MESSAGE-----
Version: 2.6

hEwCJ19DTkN0TwkBAgCeIlvWCpx9zd3jYXWukoTK01Gu51GjBwsXfchZFf/H9a45
WCoEDnH7KB451cJ1nE1C236JV1dMvHYObKQbmSvnpgAAAHCW/5hiPGjjEAGKFt0V
jGKzTqKZGSPmnffNv68R7Hc8P9KWDIiVjIvcdGMuZPyy1u1/CIQAV07i6nnwzCK1
dRJDb89h5XwF2jolmWHNrxKpC5fquQmG+Ps3qo9UsNQ8anuVDuW5pstHts3c4UJ4
+SIP
=rckA
-----END PGP MESSAGE-----
C:\WORK>
```

This message can be decrypted only with Phil's secret key. Looking at the message, I can tell that it is encrypted with PGP Version 2.6, but I can't tell anything else. I can't read this file back, even though I encrypted it! Since I encrypted the message with the public key of Phil's Pretty Good Pizza, only someone who has the secret key for Phil's can decrypt it. The public key isn't sufficient. If I try to read it, I see the following:

```
C:\WORK> pgp message.asc
Pretty Good Privacy(tm) 2.6 - Public-key encryption for the masses.
 (c) 1990-1994 Philip Zimmermann, Phil's Pretty Good Software. 23 May 94
Distributed by the Massachusetts Institute of Technology.  Uses RSAREF.
Export of this software may be restricted by the U.S. government.
Current time: 1994/08/15 03:50 GMT

File is encrypted.  Secret key is required to read it.
This message can only be read by:
   Phil's Pretty Good Pizza <phil@pgp.com>

You do not have the secret key needed to decrypt this file.

For a usage summary, type: pgp -h
For more detailed help, consult the PGP User's Guide.
C:\WORK>
```

If it seems absurd that I can't read something I just composed, rest assured that there is a way around this problem of not being able to read the messages that you yourself encrypt: you can simply encrypt every message so that both you and your intended recipient can read it. (I show you how to do that in "Adding Yourself to the Mailing List" later in this chapter.)

For Your Eyes Only (-m Option)

The –m option can be helpful in encryption, although it is most often used in decryption (as described later in this chapter). If you specify this option, PGP automatically pages through the file and does not save it to the hard disk. This is a handy way to ask the receiver not to leave the decrypted file around.

But beware: the –m option is easily defeated by the person reading the encrypted message. A person viewing a file with the –m option could simply use a cut-and-paste system for saving the PGP-decrypted message to a file. Or, to make matters even easier, she could simply redirect the output to a file by using the greater than (>) character and a command such as the following:

```
unix% pgp secrets.pgp > secrets.txt
```

The first time I used Phil's uncertified public key to encrypt a message, PGP gave me a warning and asked if I really wanted to encrypt the file. If I try to encrypt another message to Phil, however, PGP remembers that I'm willing to use this uncertified key and won't ask the question again. Note also that in the following example, PGP prompts me for the recipient's user ID because I didn't type Phil's user ID on the command line.

```
C:\WORK> type message2
Phil,
      My doctor has told me to cut down on my fat intake. Do you
have fat-free onion rings?
-Simson

C:\WORK> pgp -eat message2
Pretty Good Privacy(tm) 2.6 - Public-key encryption for the masses.
(c) 1990-1994 Philip Zimmermann, Phil's Pretty Good Software. 23 May 94
Distributed by the Massachusetts Institute of Technology.  Uses RSAREF.
Export of this software may be restricted by the U.S. government.
Current time: 1994/08/15 03:52 GMT


Recipients' public key(s) will be used to encrypt.
A user ID is required to select the recipient's public key.
Enter the recipient's user ID: phil

Key for user ID: Phil's Pretty Good Pizza <phil@pgp.com>
512-bit key, Key ID 43744F09, created 1994/07/07
```

```
WARNING:  Because this public key is not certified with a trusted
signature, it is not known with high confidence that this public key
actually belongs to: "Phil's Pretty Good Pizza <phil@pgp.com>".
But you previously approved using this public key anyway.
.
Transport armor file: message2.asc
C:\WORK> type message2.asc
-----BEGIN PGP MESSAGE-----
Version: 2.6

hEwCJ19DTkN0TwkBAf47QvmKqs0mPiJD5C2Ix19zsZHsVZdaeN6+gSsU/NeO78V5
mKrscXrDwIrFnTkY52haLE+VzyFHsct6Lhl20ESnpgAAAH7b8B38M+iRdvic6V2L
/YzXAqecU6wFODfQ5/AKn0BK7w2Hc7mSvPsU2X+YVDIX7MnQHyj4+db4cXtWFj/T
Jo9Xd1Mx7UG3oqktvosqdmS+DSHDm0LbVBrb+i7FlvcVFv86FpD71ZmnX3UfyXfg
jz/xUTgOqeQYgjYzh9kQCO0=
=RfIS
-----END PGP MESSAGE-----
C:\WORK>
```

It's Different!

Even if you encrypt two messages that are exactly the same for exactly the same recipient, the resulting encrypted messages will be *completely different*. This is because PGP encrypts each message with a random session key.

Having the identical message encrypt differently on different occasions adds to the overall security of PGP: it makes it impossible for an attacker looking only at the message ciphertext to tell if you are sending the same messages or different ones.

Step 4: Sending the Message

Once you have successfully encrypted your message, you can send it to its intended destination.

There are many different ways that you can send your message, depending on the system, network connection, and electronic mail program you use. If you are using PGP on a UNIX system, you can simply send the message from the command line using the standard UNIX mail program. (You can do this even if you use a more sophisticated electronic mail program, such as *elm*, *pine*, or *xmh*, to read your mail.) Just use the shell's redirection facility:

```
% mail phil@pizza.com < message.asc
%
```

If you are sending email via America Online, Prodigy, CompuServe, or some other service, read your documentation to find out how to upload a text file and send the file as a message.

Should I Send Encrypted Files as Attachments?

Some online services, such as CompuServe, MCI Mail, and America Online, allow you to send files using the same service as "attachments." Attachments are great for sending word processor files from one online user to another user: they come through as clean, binary files without any damage.

You can send PGP-encrypted files as attachments but remember that they can be received and decrypted only by people who happen to be using the same online service that you are.

When MIME is universally adopted as a standard for sending attachments, PGP's armor function will become unnecessary. Perhaps we will be very lucky, and the MIME standard will eventually include PGP encryption as well.

Doing It All at Once (-f Option)

One of the powerful features of the UNIX operating system is the ability to chain together long commands on a single line. Both PGP and the *mail* program have provisions for this feature. Using the –f (filter) option in PGP causes the program to write its output to *standard output*, instead of to a file. By default, *mail* reads its messages from *standard input*. This opens numerous possibilities, which I describe in the following sections.

Encrypting and Sending a Message at the Same Time

Using the –f option, you can encrypt and send, in a single step, a message that you have previously prepared:

```
unix% pgp -eatf phil < message | mail phil@pizza.com
Pretty Good Privacy(tm) 2.6 - Public-key encryption for the masses.
(c) 1990-1994 Philip Zimmermann, Phil's Pretty Good Software. 23 May 94
Distributed by the Massachusetts Institute of Technology.  Uses RSAREF.
Export of this software may be restricted by the U.S. government.
Current time: 1994/08/26 16:32 GMT

Key for user ID: Phil's Pretty Good Pizza <phil@pgp.com>
512-bit key, Key ID 43744F09, created 1994/07/07

WARNING:  Because this public key is not certified with a trusted
```

signature, it is not known with high confidence that this public key
actually belongs to: "Phil's Pretty Good Pizza <phil@pgp.com>".
But you previously approved using this public key anyway.
unix%

Typing, Encrypting, and Sending at the Same Time

You can even combine typing, encrypting, and sending your message all at the same
time with the following command line:

```
unix% pgp -eatf phil | mail phil@pizza.com
Pretty Good Privacy(tm) 2.6 - Public-key encryption for the masses.
(c) 1990-1994 Philip Zimmermann, Phil's Pretty Good Software. 23 May 94
Distributed by the Massachusetts Institute of Technology. Uses RSAREF.
Export of this software may be restricted by the U.S. government.
Current time: 1994/08/26 16:35 GMT
Phil,
Send me a large pizza with double-cheese, double-mushrooms,
and double-anchovy. I know that these pizzas cost about $50.
-Simson
^D
Key for user ID: Phil's Pretty Good Pizza <phil@pgp.com>
512-bit key, Key ID 43744F09, created 1994/07/07

WARNING:  Because this public key is not certified with a trusted
signature, it is not known with high confidence that this public key
actually belongs to: "Phil's Pretty Good Pizza <phil@pgp.com>".
But you previously approved using this public key anyway.
unix%
```

Note that PGP won't prompt you for a message, and you need to terminate your input
by typing Control-D on a separate line.

The method shown in the example may be the most secure means for sending a PGP-
encrypted message from a UNIX workstation, because the plaintext of your message
is never written to a file. (Nevertheless, you still must worry about people looking at
your screen, reading the memory of your PGP process, intercepting your keystrokes,
and scavenging through your machine's virtual memory system.)

Receiving Encrypted Email

Decrypting messages that have been encrypted with PGP is much simpler than
encrypting them. If you receive a PGP-encrypted message, all you need to do is save
it to a file and specify that filename as an argument to the PGP program.

Figure 10-2 illustrates how PGP decrypts email.

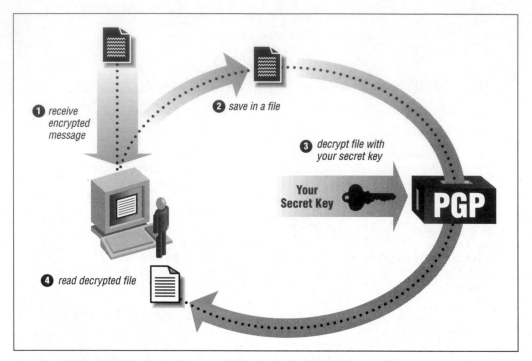

Figure 10-2. Decrypting email

Decrypting Email

For example, suppose Phil's Pretty Good Pizza received my encrypted message and sent me a response that I saved to a file *reply.asc*. The following is the file:

```
C:\WORK> dir reply.*

 Volume in drive C has no label
 Volume Serial Number is 17EA-102D
 Directory of C:\WORK

REPLY     ASC          451 07-04-94   8:13p
       1 file(s)              451 bytes
                   54,829,056 bytes free
C:\WORK>
```

To decrypt this file, I simply process it with PGP. PGP automatically applies my secret key to the file. If the message is truly meant for me, it decrypts properly.

```
C:\WORK> pgp reply.asc
Pretty Good Privacy(tm) 2.6 - Public-key encryption for the masses.
(c) 1990-1994 Philip Zimmermann, Phil's Pretty Good Software. 23 May 94
```

```
Distributed by the Massachusetts Institute of Technology.  Uses RSAREF.
Export of this software may be restricted by the U.S. government.
Current time: 1994/08/15 03:57 GMT

File is encrypted.  Secret key is required to read it.
Key for user ID: Simson Garfinkel <simsong@acm.org>
1024-bit key, Key ID 903C9265, created 1994/07/15
Also known as: Simson L. Garfinkel <simsong@mit.edu>

You need a pass phrase to unlock your RSA secret key.
Enter pass phrase: Nobody knows my name.Pass phrase is good.  Just a
moment......
Plaintext filename: reply
C:\WORK>
```

Note that PGP prompted me for my pass phrase so it could decrypt my secret key. I can use the DOS *dir* command to see that both *reply.asc* (the original ciphertext) and *reply* (the plaintext file) are on my hard disk:

```
C:\WORK> dir reply.*

 Volume in drive C has no label
 Volume Serial Number is 17EA-102D
 Directory of C:\WORK

REPLY     ASC          451 07-04-94    8:13p
REPLY                  203 07-04-94    8:14p
        2 file(s)             654 bytes
                  54,829,056 bytes free

C:\WORK>
```

I use the DOS *type* command to view the contents of the file:

```
C:\WORK> type reply
Simson,
    We have some fat-free onion rings under development, but they
haven't received FDA-approval. I would be happy to whip you up some,
but---whatever you do---please don't export them.

    -Phil

C:\WORK>
```

Changing the Output File (-o Option)

If you want, you can use the –o (output) option to save the output to a different file. Just specify –o and the name of the file on the command line:

```
C:\WORK> pgp reply.asc -o from-phil
Pretty Good Privacy(tm) 2.6 - Public-key encryption for the masses.
(c) 1990-1994 Philip Zimmermann, Phil's Pretty Good Software. 23 May 94
Distributed by the Massachusetts Institute of Technology.  Uses RSAREF.
Export of this software may be restricted by the U.S. government.
Current time: 1994/08/15 04:20 GMT


File is encrypted.  Secret key is required to read it.
Key for user ID: Simson Garfinkel <simsong@acm.org>
1024-bit key, Key ID 903C9265, created 1994/07/15
Also known as: Simson L. Garfinkel <simsong@mit.edu>


You need a pass phrase to unlock your RSA secret key.
Enter pass phrase: Nobody knows my name.Pass phrase is good.  Just a
moment......
Plaintext filename: from-phil
C:\WORK>
```

Viewing the Decrypted File (-m Option)

You can view the decrypted file directly using the –m (more) option. PGP uses its built-in file-viewing subsystem to display the file. When you use this option, PGP fills a page of text and displays the following message:

```
More -- 0% -- Hit space for next screen, Enter for new line, 'Q' to quit --
```

Press the space bar to see the next screen. When you have seen the entire file (or when you type **Q**), PGP displays the following:

```
Save this file permanently (y/N)?
```

If you type **y** and press Return, PGP prompts you for the filename:

```
Save this file permanently (y/N)? y
Enter filename to save file as: from-phil
C:\WORK>
```

You can also use the –m option when you are encrypting email, as described in the previous section "Step 3: Encrypting the Message (–e Option).."

User Unknown

Remember that PGP can't decrypt a message if you don't have the secret key corresponding to the public key that was used to encrypt the message. If you don't have that secret key, you're out of luck. End of story. Please don't call Phil Zimmermann to decrypt a message for which you do not have the secret key because it is mathematically impossible to do so. As I've mentioned, this is true even if you encrypted the message yourself.

Later in this chapter, I show you how to get around this restriction by adding yourself to the mailing list.

Sending and Receiving Huge Documents

Some electronic mail providers place strict limits on the maximum size of a particular email message. Phil Zimmermann uses one of these services.

Largely because Phil has a restrictive email provider, he added a PGP feature that automatically splits large files into smaller ones. This file splitting occurs automatically as part of the ASCII armor process.

For example, suppose you are vacationing in St. Petersburg when you learn that Last Computers has decided to drop its line of computer hardware and go into the business of selling stylish black chatchkas. You pull out your laptop, fire up your copy of LastCAD, and design some nifty ones. Now you want to send the file to Jane in the United States, but you've got two problems: you know your hotel telephone line is tapped, and your Russian email provider won't let you send email messages longer than 64K.

You sit at your screen, staring at the file:

```
unix% ls -l fashions.cad
-rw-r--r--  1 simsong   432134 Aug 26 16:05 fashions.cad
unix%
```

No problem, you realize. Just use PGP:

```
unix% pgp -eat fashions.cad Jane
Pretty Good Privacy(tm) 2.6 - Public-key encryption for the masses.
(c) 1990-1994 Philip Zimmermann, Phil's Pretty Good Software. 23 May 94
Distributed by the Massachusetts Institute of Technology.  Uses RSAREF.
Export of this software may be restricted by the U.S. government.
Current time: 1994/08/26 20:06 GMT


Recipients' public key(s) will be used to encrypt.
Key for user ID: Jane Weise, x111 <jane@last.com>
1024-bit key, Key ID BEEFCC19, created 1994/08/26
```

```
Transport armor files: fashions.cad.as1, fashions.cad.as2, fashions.cad.as3,
fashions.cad.as4, fashions.cad.as5, fashions.cad.as6
unix%
```

And here are the encrypted files:

```
unix% ls -l fashions.cad.*
-rw-------  1 simsong      46899 Aug 26 16:06 fashions.cad.as1
-rw-------  1 simsong      46886 Aug 26 16:06 fashions.cad.as2
-rw-------  1 simsong      46886 Aug 26 16:06 fashions.cad.as3
-rw-------  1 simsong      46886 Aug 26 16:06 fashions.cad.as4
-rw-------  1 simsong      46886 Aug 26 16:06 fashions.cad.as5
-rw-------  1 simsong       9406 Aug 26 16:06 fashions.cad.as6
unix%
```

"Aha!" you exclaim, "Not only won't they get my valuable designs; I'll even save half my transmission time by sending these files split and encrypted, because PGP automatically compresses my files as well!"

Now, how can Jane, back in the States, put your split message together again? At the beginning and end of each PGP file are a few lines that identify the part of the message to which they belong. The following are the first ten lines of the first message:

```
unix% head fashions.cad.as1
-----BEGIN PGP MESSAGE, PART 01/06-----
Version: 2.6

hIwC3Y7xHL7vzBkBA/4/bod4lv22pGlm0SlPGIMu8dV1PvnroZH9Y68Nx3Qixzjd
x4BNPjj3WGDIv5J6eX/GKW2MQE1vASXzqJQhEZaX2bJJ8I16U5uPShwvyJDB1zus
NrISwFZIdMH9Qi4vYMy3tSxMa1sAx2IIDW1Zq2FpMj0nP1i3ZjSn1c1xVd4sf6YA
AqNYp331I1Cjv9icPitX+QTgOmn8DMy8oT+pCZ3KHDnsX9CfVE2ypj/vCpcgLJlJ
1naWrOyCAFKuFAnwV3cLDnGJZ07LeDu9HM8I3W6NQp8OLvMizmwT+SIMAFW5ROL2
TdFwynAoh81ZKchN249NhQlY8HC09NXwVDJbX4xrZ/PAj+vY2a2aQ219mGCILK5t
DbZ2OpC1cHHiDtErKSUkOykPh7NoUQKPe7vSvd0SFI/sV8wqJ5lvdU5gsfucmRi5
unix%
```

And the following are the last ten lines of the last message:

```
unix% tail fashions.cad.as6
APxpXnIT+AzJ9I0RXwzDeK6PjiYxJIr+ta/CvwFVDwE3GrvWDJRhBqjfpXwOr/L6
nEyvX1NNH/NU6gX2FSCvZ7c4wHv2Z13g0SJP043Z8QfCn+RypBsJYM61D/jsiQUP
Rama3khH2KgY4mK+WY9iDS56ujhDj41NZErLmgKSYvCaIL0CmMXONHa5EwVBgwlR
9oc0Dz46hZIc4TdUf1frBhBPjwQTgA006DOCcnDcNnKuYs/zNNyVu+yIzeeUMU7n
```

```
    doPWN2pa1h9Qu7+E5nrO46izFAHEsVqPaaAduYkXBDgbmyoXNFRCJuprNC7Xp+xR
    YEqDRu5KTsptXpYUfvYqL861VVbu9FuthzvG4xgdKWx5hR7ttAmyzAbhgw62twIg
    quYok5e5UG3RtcihDZSFrWZVh54dG938wuN1
    =dbLN
    -----END PGP MESSAGE, PART 06/06-----

    unix%
```

You send all of the files to Jane:

```
    unix% foreach i ( fashions.cad.as?)
    ? mail -s $i jane@last.com < $i
    ? echo $i
    ? end
    fashions.cad.as1
    fashions.cad.as2
    fashions.cad.as3
    fashions.cad.as4
    fashions.cad.as5
    fashions.cad.as6
    unix%
```

At the receiving end, Jane easily recombines all of the PGP files using the UNIX *cat* command:

```
    unix% ls -l
    total 231
    -rw-------  1 jane        46899 Aug 26 16:06 fashions.cad.as1
    -rw-------  1 jane        46886 Aug 26 16:06 fashions.cad.as2
    -rw-------  1 jane        46886 Aug 26 16:06 fashions.cad.as3
    -rw-------  1 jane        46886 Aug 26 16:06 fashions.cad.as4
    -rw-------  1 jane        46886 Aug 26 16:06 fashions.cad.as5
    -rw-------  1 jane          406 Aug 26 16:06 fashions.cad.as6
    unix% cat fashions.cad.as? > fash.cad.asc
    unix% ls -l
    total 471
    -rw-r--r--  1 jane       234849 Aug 26 16:17 fash.cad.asc
    -rw-------  1 jane        46899 Aug 26 16:06 fashions.cad.as1
    -rw-------  1 jane        46886 Aug 26 16:06 fashions.cad.as2
    -rw-------  1 jane        46886 Aug 26 16:06 fashions.cad.as3
    -rw-------  1 jane        46886 Aug 26 16:06 fashions.cad.as4
    -rw-------  1 jane        46886 Aug 26 16:06 fashions.cad.as5
    -rw-------  1 jane          406 Aug 26 16:06 fashions.cad.as6
    unix% pgp fash.asc
    Pretty Good Privacy(tm) 2.6 - Public-key encryption for the masses.
    (c) 1990-1994 Philip Zimmermann, Phil's Pretty Good Software. 23 May 94
    Distributed by the Massachusetts Institute of Technology.  Uses RSAREF.
    Export of this software may be restricted by the U.S. government.
    Current time: 1994/08/26 20:18 GMT
```

```
File is encrypted.  Secret key is required to read it.
Key for user ID: Jane Weise, x113
1024-bit key, Key ID BEEFCC19, created 1994/08/26
Also known as: Jane Weise, x111 <jane@last.com>

You need a pass phrase to unlock your RSA secret key.
Enter pass phrase: My name is Jane.Pass phrase is good.  Just a moment......
Plaintext filename: fash.cad
unix%
```

And Jane is left with the original file:

```
unix% ls -l fash.cad
-rw-------  1 jane        432134 Aug 26 16:18 fash.cad
unix%
```

Changing the Size of Armored Files

By default, PGP makes its armored sections 720 lines long. You can change this length by editing the ARMORLINES configuration variable in the PGP configuration file *config.txt*. (See Chapter 14, *PGP Configuration File*, for a discussion of all of the configuration options.)

For example, if your mailer allows you to send files that are up to 256K in length, you might want to set ARMORLINES to 2880. Edit the file *config.txt* and change the last line in the following example:

```
# ArmorLines is the maximum number of lines per packet when creating a
# transport armored file.  Set to 0 to disable splitting in parts.
Armorlines = 720
```

to this:

```
# ArmorLines is the maximum number of lines per packet when creating a
# transport armored file.  Set to 0 to disable splitting in parts.
Armorlines = 2880
```

Before you do so, make sure that everyone with whom you exchange messages can receive messages longer than 64K.

Sending an Encrypted File to a Mailing List

In all of the examples in this chapter so far, messages were encrypted and sent to a single person. With PGP, it's easy to encrypt a message for more than one recipient at a time. It's also easy to add yourself to the list of recipients, either for a single message or, automatically, for all the messages you send.

Encrypting and Sending to Multiple People

Suppose I am planning the Great Pizza Price Fix of 1995;[†] with the help of Phil's Pretty Good Pizza and Andy's Pizza Pad, I plan to raise prices to $15 for a small pie. To prevent consumer groups from getting wind of my plans, I encrypt my messages with PGP.

First I need to make sure that I have all of the required public keys:

```
unix% pgp -kv
Pretty Good Privacy(tm) 2.6 - Public-key encryption for the masses.
(c) 1990-1994 Philip Zimmermann, Phil's Pretty Good Software. 23 May 94
Distributed by the Massachusetts Institute of Technology.  Uses RSAREF.
Export of this software may be restricted by the U.S. government.
Current time: 1994/08/26 21:03 GMT


Key ring: '/Users/simsong/Library/pgp/pubring.pgp'
Type bits/keyID    Date        User ID
pub   512/AD045B15 1994/08/26 Andy's Pizza Pad <andy@pizza-pad.com>
pub  1024/903C9265 1994/07/15 Simson L. Garfinkel <simsong@acm.org>
pub   512/43744F09 1994/07/07 Phil's Pretty Good Pizza <phil@pgp.com>
4 matching keys found.
unix%
```

Next I create my message:

```
unix% cat > message
Phil & Andy,
        Let's change our plans and charge $300 for a small pie! This way
we will be sure to take over the Pizza world!
unix%
```

This time I specify both Phil's and Andy's public keys during the encryption step:

```
unix% pgp -eat message phil andy
Pretty Good Privacy(tm) 2.6 - Public-key encryption for the masses.
(c) 1990-1994 Philip Zimmermann, Phil's Pretty Good Software. 23 May 94
Distributed by the Massachusetts Institute of Technology.  Uses RSAREF.
Export of this software may be restricted by the U.S. government.
Current time: 1994/08/26 21:06 GMT


Recipients' public key(s) will be used to encrypt.
Key for user ID: Phil's Pretty Good Pizza <phil@pgp.com>
512-bit key, Key ID 43744F09, created 1994/07/07

Key for user ID: Andy's Pizza Pad <andy@pizza-pad.com>
```

---

† This example is not a violation of U.S. anti-trust laws because Phil and Andy do not have a controlling interest of the U.S. pizza market.

```
512-bit key, Key ID AD045B15, created 1994/08/26

Transport armor file: message.asc
unix%
```

Notice that a message that is encrypted for two people doesn't look particularly different from a message encrypted for a single person:

```
unix% cat message.asc
-----BEGIN PGP MESSAGE-----
Version: 2.6

hEwCJ19DTkN0TwkBAfoDBikpoPL2V9sHk93k+hKkPzMEedzIZlU+UmCzkT5LO7oA
Oj/+SvaOWoCGpBG81Nuzv9dovuU/KqiLVmrSaTVyhEwCaelIs60EWxUBAf9Z7wNq
+zVO5LJgOdrwGrrSgvyFWepPjbqzsuA0aAjP0KpVldsZqrBNkeOoQCFGGyKEFls6
vTIyzOqVsf9FHiWMpgAAAI9rtgXapnV9jn0XQHiWWzLTa5vBB5kL+DM3Vd7/of1B
kNTFET25AcGAodp8Yv+ZWxCSW8HfhmevvC+XcK4d0g4+pASCIO9CivabKrcvPvEA
UQH961x29KaIP8DMMTcZkgpUmCU+UGQzXQUyoB/lQ2eIO4kKKn2QdHrb3g9SsCfu
cAhUvoBhY9haRev6BGP1gg==
=eJ0b
-----END PGP MESSAGE-----
unix%
```

When PGP encrypts for multiple recipients, it encrypts the message only once, but it encrypts a separate copy of the IDEA session key for each recipient. (Actually, PGP pads the session key with random data to avoid a known weakness in RSA that occurs when the same message is encrypted with different public keys for different recipients.) If you know how PGP encrypts its files, you can determine that this message has been encrypted for two recipients, but you can't figure out who they are unless you have their public keys.

Adding Yourself to the Mailing List

Being able to encrypt a message for more than one person creates an important possibility. Remember that, earlier in this chapter, I pointed out that you can't normally read a file that you've encrypted. Because you've encrypted it with someone else's public key, only that someone can decrypt the message.

However, by adding yourself to the list of message recipients, you can encrypt PGP messages so that you are able to decrypt the message that you send.

To add myself to the list of recipients, I simply specify my user ID on the PGP command line. The following message goes to Phil, Andy, and yours truly:

```
unix% pgp -eat message phil andy simson
Pretty Good Privacy(tm) 2.6 - Public-key encryption for the masses.
 (c) 1990-1994 Philip Zimmermann, Phil's Pretty Good Software. 23 May 94
Distributed by the Massachusetts Institute of Technology.  Uses RSAREF.
```

```
Export of this software may be restricted by the U.S. government.
Current time: 1994/08/26 21:06 GMT


Recipients' public key(s) will be used to encrypt.
Key for user ID: Phil's Pretty Good Pizza <phil@pgp.com>
512-bit key, Key ID 43744F09, created 1994/07/07

Key for user ID: Andy's Pizza Pad <andy@pizza-pad.com>
512-bit key, Key ID AD045B15, created 1994/08/26

Key for user ID: Simson L. Garfinkel <simsong@acm.org>
1024-bit key, Key ID 903C9265, created 1994/07/15

Transport armor file: message.asc
unix%
```

Adding Yourself Automatically to the List

If you want to be able to read every PGP file that you encrypt, you can tell PGP to automatically send you a copy of every message. You do this by setting the PGP ENCRYPTTOSELF configuration variable in the PGP configuration file (see Chapter 14 for a summary of all of these variables).

```
# Add my key to every message encrypted
EncryptToSelf = ON
```

Encrypting each message for yourself is a wonderful way to prevent you from producing an encrypted file that you can't read. However, it's not PGP's default. Why? There are several reasons why you might not want to add yourself automatically to the encryption list:

- The second encryption takes time.

  When you are encrypting short files, more than half of the time needed to encrypt a message is taken up by the RSA encryption of the session key. If you perform this RSA encryption twice, it can take more than 50 percent longer to encrypt a short message.

- Encrypting for additional recipients increases the vulnerability of your message (and possibly yourself).

  If only one person can decrypt your message, only one secret key can be compromised to reveal the contents of your message. If you encrypt every message so it can be read by both the intended recipient and yourself, you yourself become another point of vulnerability.

For some people, this additional point of vulnerability may be unacceptable. Suppose you are sending messages containing military intelligence. If you can decrypt every message you send and if your host country discovers that you are sending encrypted messages that you yourself can decrypt, you might possibly find yourself at a higher risk of capture and torture. That is why ENCRYPTTOSELF is not the default setting.

11

Using Digital Signatures

We intend to begin on the first of February unrestricted warfare. We shall endeavour in spite of this to keep the United States of America neutral. In the event of this not succeeding, we make Mexico a proposal of alliance on the following basis: Make war together, make peace together, generous financial support, and an understanding on our part that Mexico is to reconquer the lost territory in Texas, New Mexico and Arizona. The settlement in detail is left to you. You will inform the President [of Mexico] of the above most secretly, as soon as the outbreak of war with the United States of America is certain and add the suggestion that he should, on his own initiative, invite Japan to immediate adherence and at the same time mediate between Japan and ourselves. Please call the President's attention to the fact that the ruthless employment of our submarines now offers the prospect of compelling England in a few months to make peace.

Zimmermann

—The Zimmermann Telegram, which promised Mexico the states of Texas, New Mexico, and Arizona in exchange for supporting Germany in the First World War. The decryption of the telegram, and subsequent publicity, was one of the major factors that pushed the United States into the war.

In this chapter, you will learn about digital signatures. Like their analog counterparts, digital signatures are used as a form of identification: you can look at a digital signature and determine whether it was signed by someone you know. But unlike a signature created with pen on paper, digital signatures cannot be forged.

This chapter describes these PGP options:

- The –s option (sign) signs a message with your secret key. You can specify this option by itself or in conjunction with the –e (encrypt) option.

- The –sb (sign by itself) option creates a signature that is detached from the message it signs.

- The –u (user) option lets you select a particular key to use for signing your message.

How Do Digital Signatures Work?

A digital signature is nothing more than a number—a special number that is cryptographically produced and digitally verified.

PGP digital signatures can perform two different functions, both very important to the security of your communications:

- **Integrity**—A digital signature tells you whether a file or a message has been modified.

- **Authentication**—A digital signature makes it possible for you to mathematically verify the name of the person who signed the message.

Before I use a signature and show you how you use PGP to create one, I want to show you how a digital signature works.

The MD5 Message Digest Function

Digital signatures are based on a kind of mathematical function known as a *message digest*. A message digest function distills the information contained in a file (small or large) into a single large number.[†]

There are many message digest functions available today. All of them work in roughly the same way, but they differ in speed and specific features. PGP's digital signatures are based upon the MD5 message digest function, which was developed by Ronald Rivest, is distributed by RSA Data Security, and may be used freely without license costs.

The MD5 message digest function produces a 128-bit number from a block of text of any length. The 128-bit number is usually expressed as a 32-digit string of hexadecimal digits.

The following example shows the MD5 function at work:

```
MD5(There is $1500 in the blue box.)=05f8cfc03f4e58cbee731aa4a14b3f03
MD5(The meeting last week was swell.)=050f3905211cddf36107ffc361c23e3d
MD5(There is $1100 in the blue box.)=d6dee11aae89661a45eb9d21e30d34cb
```

Notice that all of these messages have dramatically different MD5 codes. Even the first and the third messages, which differ only by a single character (and, within that character, only by a single binary digit), have completely different message digests. The message digest appears almost random, but it's not. Let's look at a few more message digests and see why:

---

† Message digest functions are one-way functions: there is no way to use the message digest number to reconstruct the original file.

```
MD5(There is $1500 in the blue bo)=  f80b3fde8ecbac1b515960b9058de7a1
MD5(There is $1500 in the blue box)= a4a5471a0e019a4a502134d38fb64729
MD5(There is $1500 in the blue box.)=05f8cfc03f4e58cbee731aa4a14b3f03
MD5(There is $1500 in the blue box!)=4b36807076169572b804907735accd42
MD5(There is $1500 in the blue box..)=3a7b4e07ae316eb60b5af4a1a2345931
```

Look at the MD5 code for the third line in the above example: you see that it is *exactly the same* as the first MD5 code shown previously. This is because *the same text always produces the same MD5 code.*

Other Message Digests

MD5 isn't the only message digest function around. Others include traditional "checksum" functions, the CRC (cyclic redundancy check), Snerfu, MD4, and the Secure Hash Algorithm (SHA).

Mathematically, it's easy to see that billions and billions of messages have the same MD5 result, because the MD5 function produces only 128 bits of output—just sixteen 8-bit digits. So theoretically, if a message is only 17 characters in length, there would probably be 256 different messages that have the same MD5 code (because there would be 256 more possible messages than possible MD5 codes, which means that some codes would have to be reused).

So why does MD5 seem so secure? Because 128 bits allows you to have 2^{128}=340,282,366,920,938,463,463,374,607,431,768,211,456 different possible MD5 codes. That is a number that is billions of times larger than the total number of documents that will ever be created by the human race for the next thousand years. So even though many different documents have the same MD5 code, human beings aren't likely to find many of them in their lifetimes.

NOTE

The message digest function is a powerful tool for detecting very small changes in very large files or messages; simply calculate the MD5 code for your message and set it aside. If you think that the file has been changed (either accidentally or on purpose), just recalculate the MD5 code and compare it with the MD5 that you originally calculated. If they match, there is an excellent chance that the file was not modified. (Of course, there is a theoretical possibility that two files might have the same MD5 code. So far, however, no two files with the same MD5 code have ever been found.)

Message Digests and Public Key

Given the way that MD5 works, you can understand why it makes a wonderful authentication system for anyone distributing digital documents; simply publish your documents electronically, distribute them on the Internet, and for each document also publish its MD5 key. Then, if you want to be sure that the copy of the document you download from the Internet is an unaltered copy of the original, simply calculate the document's MD5 code and compare it with the one for the document that you published. If they match, you know you've got the real McCoy.

In fact, CERT (Computer Emergency Response Team) does this via the Internet when it distributes patches and bug fixes for security-related problems. The following is a portion of a 1994 message from CERT advising recipients to replace the *ftp* programs on their computers with more secure versions:

```
Date: Thu, 14 Apr 94 16:00:00 EDT
Subject: CERT Advisory CA-94:08.ftpd.vulnerabilities
To: cert-advisory-request@cert.org
From: cert-advisory@cert.org (CERT Advisory)
Organization: CERT Coordination Center
Address:        Software Engineering Institute
                Carnegie Mellon University
                Pittsburgh, Pennsylvania 15213-3890
=======================================================================
CA-94:08                    CERT Advisory
                           April 14, 1994
                         ftpd Vulnerabilities
-----------------------------------------------------------------------

The CERT Coordination Center has received information concerning two
vulnerabilities in some ftpd implementations.  The first is a
vulnerability with the SITE EXEC command feature of the FTP daemon
(ftpd) found in versions of ftpd that support the SITE EXEC feature.
This vulnerability allows local or remote users to gain root access.
The second vulnerability involves a race condition found in the ftpd
implementations listed in Section I. below.  This vulnerability allows
local users to gain root access.

Sites using these implementations are vulnerable even if they do not
support anonymous FTP.


                            . . .


II.  Impact
```

Anyone (remote or local) can gain root access on a host running a
vulnerable FTP daemon. Support for anonymous FTP is not required
to exploit this vulnerability.

III. Solution

Affected sites can solve both of these problems by upgrading to
the latest version of ftpd. These versions are listed below. Be
certain to verify the checksum information to confirm that you
have retrieved a valid copy.

If you cannot install the new version in a timely manner, you
should disable FTP service until you have corrected this problem.
It is not sufficient to disable anonymous FTP. You must disable
the FTP daemon.

For wuarchive ftpd, you can obtain version 2.4 via anonymous
FTP from wuarchive.wustl.edu, in the "/packages/wuarchive-ftpd"
directory. If you are currently running version 2.3, a patch
file is available.

File	BSD Checksum		SVR4 Checksum		MD5 Digital Signature
wu-ftpd-2.4.tar.Z	38213	181	20337	362	cdcb237b71082fa23706429134d8c32e
patch_2.3-2.4.Z	09291	8	51092	16	5558a04d9da7cdb1113b158aff89be8f

                                        . . .

As you can tell from the tone of the message, CERT considers the security problem to
be extremely serious: anyone on the Internet could break into a computer running a
particular *ftpd* program and become the superuser! CERT had a fix for this bug but
rather than distribute it to each site individually, they placed the fix on a computer
(*wuarchive.wustl.edu*) and advised people to download it.

Why does CERT use MD5 codes? So people can verify the authenticity of the patch
before they install it. After receiving the message from CERT and downloading the
patch, system administrators are supposed to compute the MD5 of the binary, which
provides two indications. First, if the MD5 of the binary matches the one published in
the CERT message, a system administrator knows the file wasn't damaged during the
download; and second, and more importantly, if the two MD5 codes match, a system
administrator can be sure hackers haven't broken into the computer
wuarchive.wustl.edu and replaced the patch with a program that contains security
holes.

By the way, although CERT's interest in security is commendable, there is unfortunately an important flaw in this approach. Nothing guarantees that the CERT message itself isn't forged. In other words, any hacker with sufficient skill to break into an anonymous FTP repository and play switcheroo with the binaries might also be able to break into CERT's computers and send a forged message. (Indeed, it is possible to forge electronic mail to make it look like it originated from CERT without even breaking into CERT's systems.) The hackers could then construct an email message telling system administrators to install new (and faulty) software and send the message to CERT's mailing lists. Unsuspecting administrators would receive the email message, download the patch, check the MD5 codes, and install the software— creating a new security hole for the hackers to exploit.

CERT's problem, then, is this: while the MD5 code in the email message is a signature for the patch, *there is no signature for the message from CERT itself!* There is no way to verify that the CERT message is authentic.

CERT is aware of the problem that alerts can be forged. For this reason, CERT makes the detached ASCII-armored signatures for all its alerts available via anonymous FTP from the computer *ftp.cert.org*. For each alert, you find a file with an *.asc* file extension, which contains the signature. (I can't figure out why CERT doesn't put the PGP signatures at the end of the alert messages.)

RSA Digital Signatures

The MD5 message digest function is only half of the solution to creating a reliable digital signature. The other half is RSA public key encryption itself—only this time, it's RSA encryption run in reverse.

Recall that when I introduced RSA encryption in Part II of this book, I said that the RSA algorithm depends on two keys:

public key
    You use John's public key to encrypt a message intended for him.

secret key
    John uses his secret key to decrypt the message you've encrypted for him.

By using a little bit of mathematical gymnastics, it is possible to run the RSA algorithm in reverse. That is, it is possible to encrypt messages with your secret key; these messages can then be decrypted by anyone who possesses your public key.

Why would anyone want to do this? Each RSA public key has one and only one matching secret key. If a particular RSA public key can decrypt a message, you can be sure that the matching secret key was used to encrypt it. And that is how PGP's digital signatures work.

When you apply your secret key to a message, you are signing it. By using your secret key and the MD5 message digest function, PGP calculates a digital signature for the message you're sending.

PGP's Digital Signatures

First in Figure 11-1 and then in some PGP examples, I'll show you how digital signatures work in practice.

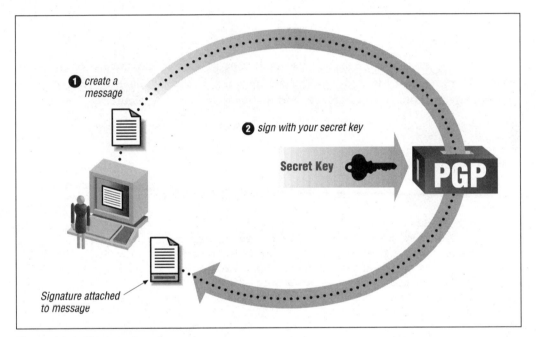

Figure 11-1. Signing a message

Signing a Message (-s Option)

To add your digital signature to the end of a message, use the –sta option (*s* for sign, *t* for text, and *a* for ASCII output). For example, to sign a file *text*, I type the following command:

```
unix% pgp -sta text
Pretty Good Privacy(tm) 2.6 - Public-key encryption for the masses.
(c) 1990-1994 Philip Zimmermann, Phil's Pretty Good Software. 23 May 94
Distributed by the Massachusetts Institute of Technology.  Uses RSAREF.
Export of this software may be restricted by the U.S. government.
Current time: 1994/07/07 13:04 GMT
```

```
A secret key is required to make a signature.
You specified no user ID to select your secret key,
so the default user ID and key will be the most recently
added key on your secret keyring.
You need a pass phrase to unlock your RSA secret key.
Key for user ID "Simson Garfinkel <simsong@acm.org>"

Enter pass phrase: Nobody knows my name. Pass phrase is good.
Key for user ID: Simson Garfinkel <simsong@acm.org>
1024-bit key, Key ID 903C9265, created 1994/07/15
Just a moment....
Clear signature file: text.asc
unix%
```

I had to type my pass phrase because PGP uses my secret key (which is encrypted with my pass phrase) to sign my digital signature. If I didn't have to type my pass phrase, anyone could sign my name, and that wouldn't be very secure.

The following is the resulting file, with the text signed by my secret key:

```
unix% cat text.asc
-----BEGIN PGP SIGNED MESSAGE-----

- From where I stand, this is one of the most important tenets in US law:

    4th Amendment
        The right of the people to be secure in their persons, houses,
    papers, and effects, against unreasonable searches and seizures,
    shall not be violated; and no warrants shall issue, but upon
    probable cause, supported by oath or affirmation, and
    particularly describing the place to be searched and the persons
    or things to be seized.

What do you think?
- -Simson

-----BEGIN PGP SIGNATURE-----
Version: 2.6

iQB1AgUBLhwFvnOD8bPZas15AQF4VwL+NfmyMPYDmlXs7j0AoWPecC1I0b5fpGZa
SQx3bHV1sdEaLF7eEQVTa+C85cjPMmXi9c0yDmv/IB4xrX8q652IGWuAwn+xa2EF
5xE9QEOIfhpfaC9UVVZCykU4SjVrWuyU
=2Qe4
-----END PGP SIGNATURE-----
unix%
```

Notice what I've done in this example. I've signed the message, but I have *not* encrypted it. In many cases, you won't be concerned about protecting the privacy of a message, but you will be very concerned about its integrity (has it arrived without alteration?) and its authenticity (was it really sent by the person claiming to send it?).

The first part of the message in the example is regular ASCII text. The message is followed by a PGP signature block. The signature block is actually the MD5 message digest code for the preceding text block, which has then been encrypted with my PGP secret key.

If you use PGP to verify the signature of this block, PGP calculates for itself the MD5 code for the text. It uses my public key to decrypt the encrypted signature block. If the two MD5 codes match, the signature is verified. (In order to make this work, you need to have a copy of my public key.)

You can verify the digital signature of a document by running PGP over the signed file, which extracts a copy of the original, unsigned message. You may notice that the original message is slightly different from the signed message because PGP makes minor changes to a file before signing it. These changes do not affect the text in any way, but they do prevent the PGP messages from being damaged by certain mail-handling systems on the Internet. (Remember, if a message is damaged in any way, it won't verify.)

Notice that I don't need to specify any options on the PGP command line; I simply type the name of the file in which I've saved the signed message:

```
unix% pgp text
Pretty Good Privacy(tm) 2.6 - Public-key encryption for the masses.
(c) 1990-1994 Philip Zimmermann, Phil's Pretty Good Software. 23 May 94
Distributed by the Massachusetts Institute of Technology.  Uses RSAREF.
Export of this software may be restricted by the U.S. government.
Current time: 1994/07/07 13:38 GMT

File has signature.  Public key is required to check signature. .
Good signature from user "Simson Garfinkel <simsong@acm.org>".
Signature made 1994/07/07 13:34 GMT

Plaintext filename: text
unix% cat text
From where I stand, this is one of the most important tenets in US law:

    4th Amendment
       The right of the people to be secure in their persons, houses,
    papers, and effects, against unreasonable searches and seizures,
    shall not be violated; and no warrants shall issue, but upon
    probable cause, supported by oath or affirmation, and
    particularly describing the place to be searched and the persons
    or things to be seized.
```

```
What do you think?
-Simson
unix%
```

As I've said, the modifications made to improve email handling are quite minor. The line in the signed message that began "- From" reads "From" in the above example, and the line that previously was "- -Simson" is just "-Simson" in the above example.

Verifying a Digital Signature

Signing digital messages electronically is much better than signing paper messages with pen and ink. A skillful person can lift a signature from one document and put it on another. You can't do this with digital signatures because different files have different message digests. Likewise, a good forger can change the number on a check or a key phrase in a document. You can't do this with digital signatures, because if you make one change in a document, the signature won't verify. Let's prove this by making a surreptitious change to the signed message in the example:

```
unix% cat text.asc
-----BEGIN PGP SIGNED MESSAGE-----

- From where I stand, this is one of the most important tenets in US law:

    4th Amendment
       The right of the people to be secure in their persons, houses,
    papers, and effects, against unreasonable searches and seizures,
    is limited in the digital age; and warrants shall issue, upon
    probable cause, supported by oath or affirmation, and
    particularly describing the place to be searched or the persons
    or things to be seized.

What do you think?
- -Simson

-----BEGIN PGP SIGNATURE-----
Version: 2.6

iQB1AgUBLhwFvnOD8bPZas15AQF4VwL+NfmyMPYDmlXs7j0AoWPecC1I0b5fpGZa
SQx3bHV1sdEaLF7eEQVTa+C85cjPMmXi9c0yDmv/IB4xrX8q652IGWuAwn+xa2EF
5xE9QEOIfhpfaC9UVVZCykU4SjVrWuyU
=2Qe4
-----END PGP SIGNATURE-----
unix% pgp text.asc
Pretty Good Privacy(tm) 2.6 - Public-key encryption for the masses.
(c) 1990-1994 Philip Zimmermann, Phil's Pretty Good Software. 23 May 94
Distributed by the Massachusetts Institute of Technology.  Uses RSAREF.
Export of this software may be restricted by the U.S. government.
```

```
Current time: 1994/07/07 13:51 GMT

File has signature.  Public key is required to check signature. .
WARNING: Bad signature, doesn't match file contents!

Bad signature from user "Simson Garfinkel <simsong@acm.org>".
Signature made 1994/07/07 13:40 GMT

Plaintext filename: text
unix%
```

As you can see, PGP has foiled this attempted change in the Bill of Rights! The signature doesn't verify because the changed message has a different MD5 message digest code from that of the original message. (Even so, PGP still made a copy of the modified plaintext in the file *text*.)

Figure 11-2 illustrates how signature verification works with PGP.

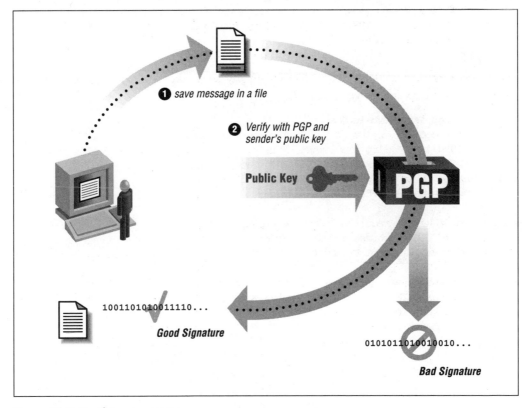

Figure 11-2. Verifying a message

Selecting from Multiple Secret Keys (–u Option)

If you have more than one secret key on your PGP secret key ring, PGP automatically signs files with the last key that was added (and the first displayed). You can force PGP to use a different key by specifying the –u (user) option.

For example, suppose I have the PGP secret key for both Simson L. Garfinkel and Joe Friday on my secret key ring:[†]

```
unix% pgp -kv $PGPPATH/secring.pgp
Pretty Good Privacy(tm) 2.6 - Public-key encryption for the masses.
(c) 1990-1994 Philip Zimmermann, Phil's Pretty Good Software. 23 May 94
Distributed by the Massachusetts Institute of Technology.  Uses RSAREF.
Export of this software may be restricted by the U.S. government.
Current time: 1994/08/26 23:46 GMT

Key ring: '/Users/simsong/Library/pgp/secring.pgp'
Type bits/keyID    Date         User ID
sec  1024/903C9265 1994/07/15 Simson L. Garfinkel <simsong@acm.org>
sec   512/A741B8AD 1994/08/26 Joe Friday <joe@pleasant.cambridge.ma.us>
2 matching keys found.
unix%
```

With this key ring, PGP signs messages with my secret key unless I specifically tell it to use Joe's. I can do this very easily:

```
unix% pgp -sta text -u joe
Pretty Good Privacy(tm) 2.6 - Public-key encryption for the masses.
(c) 1990-1994 Philip Zimmermann, Phil's Pretty Good Software. 23 May 94
Distributed by the Massachusetts Institute of Technology.  Uses RSAREF.
Export of this software may be restricted by the U.S. government.
Current time: 1994/08/26 23:48 GMT

A secret key is required to make a signature.
You need a pass phrase to unlock your RSA secret key.
Key for user ID "Joe Friday <joe@pleasant.cambridge.ma.us>"

Enter pass phrase: ~~The story you are about to read~~Pass phrase is good.
Key for user ID: Joe Friday <joe@pleasant.cambridge.ma.us>
512-bit key, Key ID A741B8AD, created 1994/08/26
Just a moment....
Clear signature file: text.asc
unix%
```

---

† Notice that I specified the location of the PGP secret key ring by typing *$PGPPATH/secring.pgp*. This sort of notation works only on the UNIX versions of PGP. With other versions, you would need to specify the entire path of the secret key ring.

Signing and Encrypting a Message (-se Option)

Earlier in this chapter, you saw how to sign a message. In many cases, that's all you'll want to do—sign a message to prove that it's been sent by you without modification. In other cases, though, the privacy of the message is important as well, and you'll want to sign *and* encrypt. You sign the message with your secret key, and you encrypt it with the public key of the person to whom you're sending the message.

Signing and encrypting messages is the most secure way that you can send electronic mail; the message can be read only by the recipient, who can tell with absolute assurance that it was you who sent the message. Figure 11-3 illustrates how PGP signs and encrypts a message.

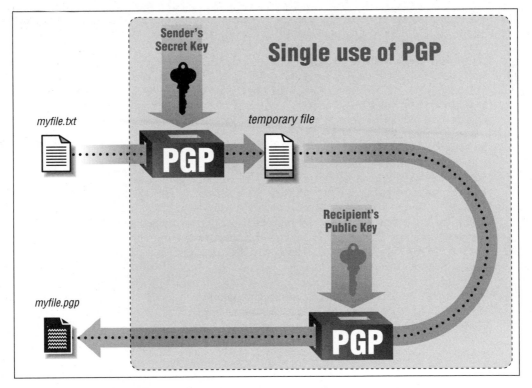

Figure 11-3. Signing and encrypting a message

To sign and encrypt a message with PGP, you need to use the –se option. To also make a file that is suitable for sending by electronic mail, you'll use the –seat options (*s* is for sign, *e* is for encrypt, *a* is for ASCII, and *t* is for text). For example, suppose I am going to send a message to a freedom fighter in Africa. First, I need to make sure I have the freedom fighter's public key.

```
unix% pgp -kv
Pretty Good Privacy(tm) 2.6 - Public-key encryption for the masses.
(c) 1990-1994 Philip Zimmermann, Phil's Pretty Good Software. 23 May 94
Distributed by the Massachusetts Institute of Technology. Uses RSAREF.
Export of this software may be restricted by the U.S. government.
Current time: 1994/07/07 19:00 GMT

Key ring: '/Users/simsong/Library/pgp/pubring.pgp'
Type bits/keyID    Date       User ID
pub  1024/FB704769 1994/08/26 Freedom Fighter <ff@freedom.net>
pub   512/A4171B2D 1994/05/12 Terrence Talbot <tjt@dtw.com>
pub  1024/903C9265 1994/07/15 Simson L. Garfinkel <simsong@acm.org>
3 matching keys found.
unix%
```

Next, I sign and encrypt the message; "freedom" identifies the freedom fighter and tells PGP to encrypt the message with this user's public key:

```
unix% pgp -seat message freedom
Pretty Good Privacy(tm) 2.6 - Public-key encryption for the masses.
(c) 1990-1994 Philip Zimmermann, Phil's Pretty Good Software. 23 May 94
Distributed by the Massachusetts Institute of Technology. Uses RSAREF.
Export of this software may be restricted by the U.S. government.
Current time: 1994/08/26 23:23 GMT

A secret key is required to make a signature.
You need a pass phrase to unlock your RSA secret key.
Key for user ID "Simson L. Garfinkel <simsong@acm.org>"

Enter pass phrase: Nobody knows my name.Pass phrase is good.
Key for user ID: Simson L. Garfinkel <simsong@acm.org>
1024-bit key, Key ID 903C9265, created 1994/07/15
Just a moment....

Recipients' public key(s) will be used to encrypt.
Key for user ID: Freedom Fighter <ff@freedom.net>
1024-bit key, Key ID FB704769, created 1994/08/26
.
Transport armor file: message.asc
unix%
```

Receiving Signed Mail

I described in Chapter 10 how to decrypt encrypted mail that you receive. The process is exactly the same for signed mail or for signed encrypted mail. PGP figures out what it needs to do based on what the sender has requested for the mail (encrypt only, sign only, or sign and encrypt) and handles it automatically. Figure 11-4 illustrates how this works.

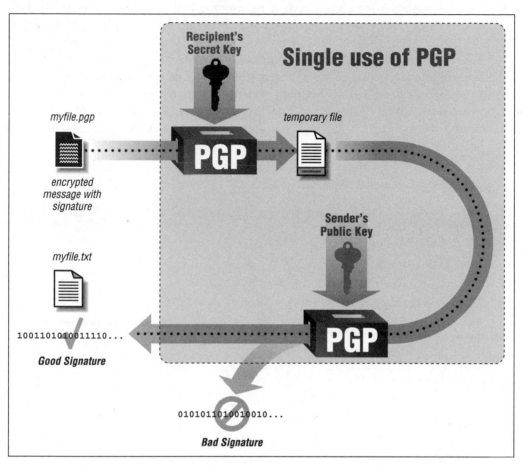

Figure 11-4. Decrypting and verifying a signature

All of the options described in "Receiving Encrypted Email" apply to both signed encrypted and signed unencrypted mail].

Creating Detached Signatures (-sb Option)

When you sign a file, PGP gives you two choices of where you can place the signature:

- To create a new file that contains the original file and the signature, simply run PGP with the –s (sign) option. If you need to be able to send the combined file by electronic mail, run PGP with the –sa (sign ASCII) option. Note that your recipient needs a copy of PGP to read the contents of this file.

- You can create a *detached signature* by running PGP with the −sb (sign by itself) option. A detached signature is simply a PGP signature that is placed in a separate file. Why create a detached signature? You might want to sign a very large file and then mail the signature to someone who has a copy of the large file but doesn't know whether to trust the copy. Or you might sign a message, send the unsigned message to the recipient, and hold onto the signature yourself. If you ever need to verify the signature in the future, you supply the entire file to the person who requires it; otherwise, if you never need to verify your signature, you keep the file confidential.

12

Certifying and Distributing Keys

Up to this point, I have finessed a critical problem with public key cryptography: key authentication.

When you want to send someone encrypted electronic mail, you need a copy of that person's public key. Without it, you won't be able to encrypt a message for him. Likewise, when someone sends you mail that is electronically signed, you need that person's public key to verify the signature.

How do you know whether you've got the right public key? After all, if you have an adversary who is determined to invade your privacy or to send forged documents with your name on them, that villain is probably smart enough to create his own PGP public and private keys with *your user ID* associated with them. Horrifying but true! How can you and the people with whom you are communicating tell these bogus PGP keys from the real ones?

This chapter describes the PGP options that help you certify keys:

- The –ka (key add) option adds a key with a signature to your key ring.

- The –kc (key check) option checks the signatures on a key; –kvv (key view verbose) provides additional information.

- The –kvc (key view and check) option checks a key's fingerprint.

- The –ke (key edit) option lets you change your level of trust in a person.

- The –ks (key sign) option lets you sign a key; adding the –u (user) option lets you select which key to use for signing.

- The –krs (key remove signature) option removes a signature from a key.

Forged Keys

You, or anyone else, can easily sit down at your keyboard and create public and secret key pairs for anyone you wish. For example, the following is a public key for President Bill Clinton:

```
Type bits/keyID    Date        User ID
pub   512/F1CA1B4D 1994/08/27 Bill Clinton <president@whitehouse.gov>

-----BEGIN PGP PUBLIC KEY BLOCK-----
Version: 2.6

mQBNAi5fTeoAAAECAL+4e5EKBCIdQDrtFHnkMhxDToiz9MibTilcAtxxXcXLJTMnU
GllwcYghnBNMtBiISMGV7cTkjBVE7x0JXPHKG00ABRG0J0JpbGwgQ2xpbnRvbiA8
cHJlc2lkZW50QHdoaXRlaG91c2UuZ292Pg==
=NEiO
-----END PGP PUBLIC KEY BLOCK-----
```

And this is the corresponding secret key:

```
Type bits/keyID    Date        User ID
sec   512/F1CA1B4D 1994/08/27 Bill Clinton <president@whitehouse.gov>

-----BEGIN PGP MESSAGE-----
Version: 2.6

lQEAAi5fTeoAAAECAL+4e5EKBCIdQDrtFHnkMhxDToiz9MibTilcAtxxXcXLJTMnU
GllwcYghnBNMtBiISMGV7cTkjBVE7x0JXPHKG00ABREBAxTErSi2AP0B/cOpzSC6
usY83FyNh3QAhksjV4/lyVqqgZNhqknK1zKzx/DBb8esPLndeot/xrs/0WVuLg4t
C7Yd7Xevm2qFc6YBAFfdoYvnzArQzI9LOEn63TD7A4jpI8nAz37V1DV8HNMtAQBX
EWJ398HapAVjIBfLgWNJNEJniqkXcl4gv1csXsPIawD/VBcovATuCRSFZw64Vzwq
sMUkMdMtoO8LqNhFz8E5uQRRt7QnQmlsbCBDbGludG9uIDxwcmVzaWRlbnRAd2hp
dGVob3VzZS5nb3Y+
=DUEs
-----END PGP MESSAGE-----
```

These PGP keys work perfectly: you can type the public key and use it to encrypt email messages. You can decrypt those email messages with the secret key. (The PGP pass phrase for the secret key is "bill".) There's just one problem: these keys don't belong to President Bill Clinton. They belong to me. And they belong to you. Anyone with a copy of this book can read messages that are encrypted with these keys.

There is one person who can't use this PGP key: President Bill Clinton himself. (That is, unless Clinton has a staff member buy a copy of this book and type the key.)

Forged keys like these are the bane of public key cryptography. Clearly, if people can create their own public keys, there needs to be a mechanism for certifying the names on those keys—for knowing if a key with a particular name on it *really, truly* belongs to the person that it claims to belong to.

This mechanism is called *key certification,* and it is an integral part of PGP.

The Web of Trust

Most of us start life knowing just a few people—the members of our immediate family, perhaps a babysitter, and some playmates. As we grow older, we meet more people. Some of them are trustworthy: we can count on them not to steal our possessions, not to hurt us, and to help us up when we fall down. Other people aren't too trustworthy (and the less said about these people, the better).

How do we know whether to trust the new people that we meet? Most children trust everyone. But as they grow older, they become suspicious. After just a few years, when kids meet new people, kids look to their parents and their friends—people they already trust—to figure out whether they should trust the newcomers.

PGP works the same way. Each key certificate on your PGP public key ring has the following two parameters:

validity
> An indication of whether you believe that the key you have in your possession actually belongs to the person to whom it says it belongs.

trust
> A measure of how much you believe the honesty and judgment of the person who created the key. The more you trust a key, the more you trust the person who created the key to certify other people's keys.

The idea behind validity and trust is relatively simple: if you believe that a key is valid, you believe that only the person who created the key will be able to read a message encrypted with the key. If you believe that a person who creates a key is trustworthy and you find that person's signature on a third person's key certificate, you are likely to believe that the third person's key is itself valid.

Figure 12-1 illustrates the PGP web of trust.

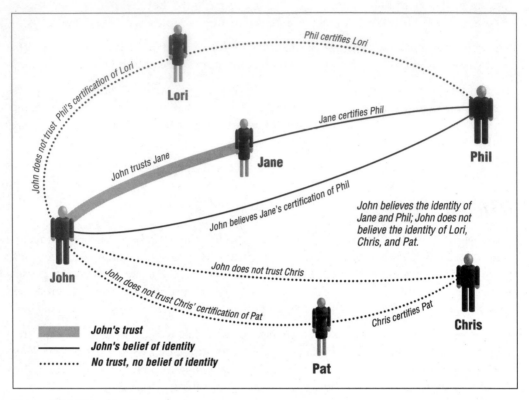

Figure 12-1. The web of trust

Adding a Key with Signatures (-ka Option)

In the following examples, I show how to add a key that you certify yourself. The first example shows a key that I know is valid but that I don't trust. The second example shows a key that is both trusted and valid. The third example adds something new; in this example, I add the key of a person I have never met directly but whose key has been certified by another key that is on my key ring.

Adding a Key for Phil's Pretty Good Pizza

On the counter at Phil's Pretty Good Pizza, next to the menus and the paper napkins, is a stack of floppy disks. Last week Phil got his Internet connection, and he's going to start accepting orders electronically. He doesn't want people to send him their credit card numbers in the clear. "Take one," says Phil, "they've got my PGP public key on them."

I take the floppy disk home and put it in the floppy disk drive of my PC. Then I type the following to add Phil's PGP public key to my key ring:

pgp -ka a:phil.pgp

Since I *know* that it's Phil's key (Phil himself gave me the floppy), I certify the validity of the key myself.

```
C:WORK\> pgp -ka a:phil.pgp
Pretty Good Privacy(tm) 2.6 - Public-key encryption for the masses.
(c) 1990-1994 Philip Zimmermann, Phil's Pretty Good Software. 23 May 94
Distributed by the Massachusetts Institute of Technology.  Uses RSAREF.
Export of this software may be restricted by the U.S. government.
Current time: 1994/08/27 17:13 GMT

Looking for new keys...
pub   512/43744F09 1994/07/07  Phil's Pretty Good Pizza <phil@pgp.com>

Checking signatures...


Keyfile contains:
   1 new key(s)

One or more of the new keys are not fully certified.
Do you want to certify any of these keys yourself (y/N)? y

Key for user ID: Phil's Pretty Good Pizza <phil@pgp.com>
512-bit key, Key ID 43744F09, created 1994/07/07
Key fingerprint =  24 38 1A 58 46 AD CC 2D  AB C9 E0 F1 C7 3C 67 EC
This key/userID association is not certified.

Do you want to certify this key yourself (y/N)? y

Looking for key for user 'Phil's Pretty Good Pizza <phil@pgp.com>':

Key for user ID: Phil's Pretty Good Pizza <phil@pgp.com>
512-bit key, Key ID 43744F09, created 1994/07/07


READ CAREFULLY:  Based on your own direct first-hand knowledge, are
you absolutely certain that you are prepared to solemnly certify that
the above public key actually belongs to the user specified by the
above user ID (y/N)? y

You need a pass phrase to unlock your RSA secret key.
Key for user ID "Simson L. Garfinkel <simsong@acm.org>"
```

```
Enter pass phrase: Nobody knows my name. Pass phrase is good.  Just a moment....
Key signature certificate added.

Make a determination in your own mind whether this key actually
belongs to the person whom you think it belongs to, based on available
evidence.  If you think it does, then based on your estimate of
that person's integrity and competence in key management, answer
the following question:

Would you trust "Phil's Pretty Good Pizza <phil@pgp.com>"
to act as an introducer and certify other people's public keys to you?
(1=I don't know. 2=No. 3=Usually. 4=Yes, always.) ? 2
C:WORK\>
```

When PGP starts up, it first reads the public key in the file *a:phil.pgp*. PGP then notices that Phil's key is not certified and asks me if I want to certify it for myself. I type **y** because I know that the key is good!

The fingerprint

After I tell PGP that I want to certify a key, PGP prints that key's fingerprint:

```
Key for user ID: Phil's Pretty Good Pizza <phil@pgp.com>
512-bit key, Key ID 43744F09, created 1994/07/07
Key fingerprint =  24 38 1A 58 46 AD CC 2D  AB C9 E0 F1 C7 3C 67 EC
This key/userID association is not certified.

Do you want to certify this key yourself (y/N)? y
```

Look carefully at the fingerprint. You'll see that it is a collection of 16 hexadecimal numbers, each one exactly one byte in length. That's 128 bits. You remember from Chapter 11, *Using Digital Signatures*, that 128 bits is the length of an MD5 message digest. And, sure enough, that is what the PGP key fingerprint actually is: it is an MD5 message digest for the public key I am going to certify.

Just as every file has a unique MD5 signature, every PGP key has a unique signature as well. PGP prints the key's fingerprint so that I can verify that the key I am about to certify is *really* the key that I think it is.

How does this apply to Phil's key?

When I picked up the floppy disk (along with a veggie, hold the onions) at Phil's Pretty Good Pizza, I noticed a sign advertising Phil's new Internet connection:

Order your Pizza by the Internet

Send your orders to:

pizza@pgp.com

Be sure to include your
VISA or MasterCard Number

Our PGP key's fingerprint is

24 38 1A 58 46 AD CC 2D AB C9 AB C9 E0 FI C7 3C 67 EC

Luckily, I made a note of the key fingerprint. Now sitting at my computer, I look at the floppy disk and notice that the fingerprint printed on the external label matches both the fingerprint that is on Phil's sign and the fingerprint displayed on the screen. Since everything matches, I know that the public key I am about to add to my key ring is the same public key that Phil made back in July when he first started playing around with PGP. So I type **y** in response to the query, "Do you want to certify this key yourself (y/N)?"

Now suppose that Ollie from Ollie's Pizza Pad and Credit Doctor had surreptitiously left a stack of floppy disks on Phil's countertop with a different set of public keys. Say it was Ollie's plan to intercept the messages bound for Phil, to steal the credit card numbers, and to resend the messages encrypted with Phil's original PGP key. Well, this plan wouldn't work, because when I inserted one of Ollie's disks into my floppy disk drive and ran PGP, the user ID might be the same, but the key's fingerprint wouldn't match:[†]

```
Key for user ID: Phil's Pretty Good Pizza <phil@pgp.com>
512-bit key, Key ID 65FD3223, created 1994/07/07
Key fingerprint =  43 65 F3 AD 32 34 66 12 2A 54 CD BB AA 87 43 FD
This key/userID association is not certified.

Do you want to certify this key yourself (y/N)? n
```

---

† The key ID doesn't match either, but if Ollie was very patient and knew a lot about cryptography and C programming, he could perhaps have come up with a key that did have the same key ID.

The certification

After I tell PGP that I want to certify the key myself, PGP asks me The Big Question:

```
Looking for key for user 'Phil's Pretty Good Pizza <phil@pgp.com>':

Key for user ID: Phil's Pretty Good Pizza <phil@pgp.com>
512-bit key, Key ID 43744F09, created 1994/07/07


READ CAREFULLY:  Based on your own direct first-hand knowledge, are
you absolutely certain that you are prepared to solemnly certify that
the above public key actually belongs to the user specified by the
above user ID (y/N)? y
```

PGP is formal about this question because of the import of what the program is about to do: it is going to put my electronic signature on my copy of Phil's key. That signature is my promise to anyone who gets this key that this is a valid key for Phil's Pretty Good Pizza.

PGP next asks me for my pass phrase to certify the public key that I am going to add to my key ring:

```
You need a pass phrase to unlock your RSA secret key.
Key for user ID "Simson Garfinkel <simsong@acm.org>"

Enter pass phrase: Nobody knows me. Pass phrase is good.  Just a moment....
Key signature certificate added.

Make a determination in your own mind whether this key actually
belongs to the person whom you think it belongs to, based on available
evidence.  If you think it does, then based on your estimate of
that person's integrity and competence in key management, answer
the following question:

Would you trust "Phil's Pretty Good Pizza <phil@pgp.com>"
to act as an introducer and certify other people's public keys to you?
(1=I don't know. 2=No. 3=Usually. 4=Yes, always.) ?
C:WORK\>
```

This question may seem a little grandiose for a pizza parlor. Remember, though, that Phil's Pretty Good Pizza has a fully working copy of PGP just as I do and just as the freedom fighter, the financier, and maybe even the president does. Phil can receive encrypted messages, and he can also sign his digital signature across other people's keys (just as you and I can).

This question is asking how much I *trust* Phil's Pretty Good Pizza. That is, if I found Phil's signature written on someone else's key, would I *trust* that key to be valid?

I wouldn't. That's why I typed **2** in response to PGP's query. I trust Phil with my Visa card number and my stomach, but I don't trust Phil to certify other peoples' keys. Sorry, Phil!

Should You Trust Phil Zimmermann?

Every copy of PGP comes with a copy of Phil Zimmermann's public key. Nearly everyone I have spoken with unconditionally trusts Phil Zimmermann's signature to sign other keys. I have no idea why this is the case. Phil Zimmermann has no idea why this is the case. Should you trust Phil Zimmermann's signature? Beats me. Would you trust him with your wallet?

Adding a Key for Terrence Talbot, Esq.

Terry isn't my lawyer, but he is a friend, and he did just graduate from Boston University Law School. Terry is especially interested in intellectual property law.

A few weeks ago, I asked Terry for a copy of his PGP public key. He sent it to me in the following mail message:

```
From: Terrence Talbot <tjt@dtw.com>
Date: Fri, 26 Aug 94 17:04:05 -0500
To: "Simson L. Garfinkel" <simsong@next>
Subject: pgp 2.6 public key

Here it is:

-----BEGIN PGP PUBLIC KEY BLOCK-----
Version: 2.6

mQBNAi3SnoIAAAECAMMsV42lk5jurLRHVJ5MrlaumbaXeWvKFVyu9TjXHEJJR6mC
5QOXgkzxyEAQoblxTvbpf2VKQQnRgeJ92aQXGy0ABRG0HVRlcnJlbmNlIFRhbGJv
dCA8dGp0QGR0dy5jb20+
=HeG1
-----END PGP PUBLIC KEY BLOCK-----
```

To add Terry's key to my public key ring, I saved his email message in a file *terry.asc* (it's okay to save the mail headers):

```
unix% ls -l terry.asc
-rw-r--r--  1 simsong      398 Aug 27 15:28 terry.asc
unix%
```

Next I added Terry's key to my public key with –ka (key add) option. Adding Terry's key is similar to adding the key for Phil's Pretty Good Pizza, except that I trust Terry to introduce other people's keys:

```
unix% pgp -ka terry.asc
Pretty Good Privacy(tm) 2.6 - Public-key encryption for the masses.
(c) 1990-1994 Philip Zimmermann, Phil's Pretty Good Software. 23 May 94
Distributed by the Massachusetts Institute of Technology.  Uses RSAREF.
Export of this software may be restricted by the U.S. government.
Current time: 1994/08/28 10:40 GMT

Looking for new keys...
pub   512/A4171B2D 1994/05/12  Terrence Talbot <tjt@dtw.com>

Checking signatures...


Keyfile contains:
   1 new key(s)

One or more of the new keys are not fully certified.
Do you want to certify any of these keys yourself (y/N)? y

Key for user ID: Terrence Talbot <tjt@dtw.com>
512-bit key, Key ID A4171B2D, created 1994/05/12
Key fingerprint =  45 3B 25 66 3F 97 D3 CF  B9 41 B4 B4 C1 99 DD 7F
This key/userID association is not certified.

Do you want to certify this key yourself (y/N)? y

Looking for key for user 'Terrence Talbot <tjt@dtw.com>':

Key for user ID: Terrence Talbot <tjt@dtw.com>
512-bit key, Key ID A4171B2D, created 1994/05/12


READ CAREFULLY:  Based on your own direct first-hand knowledge, are
you absolutely certain that you are prepared to solemnly certify that
the above public key actually belongs to the user specified by the
above user ID (y/N)? y

You need a pass phrase to unlock your RSA secret key.
Key for user ID "Simson L. Garfinkel <simsong@mit.edu>"

Enter pass phrase: Nobody knows my name.Pass phrase is good.  Just a moment....
Key signature certificate added.
```

```
Make a determination in your own mind whether this key actually
belongs to the person whom you think it belongs to, based on available
evidence.  If you think it does, then based on your estimate of
that person's integrity and competence in key management, answer
the following question:

Would you trust "Terrence Talbot <tjt@dtw.com>"
to act as an introducer and certify other people's public keys to you?
(1=I don't know. 2=No. 3=Usually. 4=Yes, always.) ? 4
unix%
```

Traffic Analysis

When you certify a person's public key, your electronic signature is signed at the bottom of the key. If you later extract that key from your key ring (using the –kx option) and give the key to someone else, your signature is still on the key—it's there for anyone in the world to see.

Leaving your signature on the other person's key is the way that PGP builds its web of trust. If I give you Terry's key, you get a key that's *signed by me*. If you trust me to sign keys, you've got a key from Terry that you consider valid.

The problem is that you might give Terry's key to a third party, someone, perhaps, who I'd rather not know that Terry and I have been corresponding.

While my signature at the bottom of Terry's key isn't *proof* that we have been corresponding, it's pretty darn close. You might consider such a signature at the bottom of a key to be a violation of your privacy.

Information about *who* is communicating with *whom*, rather than *what* they are communicating about, is used by a branch of military intelligence called traffic analysis.

If you are concerned about leaving your signature on other peoples' public keys, you should be sure to remove the signatures before you distribute copies. To remove your signature, use the –krs (key remove signature) option, described later in this chapter. And be extra careful with your public key ring, since the signatures on it are not encrypted.

How did I verify the MD5 message digest of Terry's key? I didn't. I've exchanged a lot of email with Terry in the past, I know him well, and I sincerely doubt that anyone is intercepting his messages and replacing them with others.

That's my call. You might do things differently. However, if I were in the middle of negotiating the takeover of IBM, I probably would have been more cautious. In a situation like that, I might call Terry and ask him to read me the fingerprint for his key over the phone.

Business Card Authentication

Another way to let people verify your PGP public key fingerprint is to print it on your business cards. That's what Eric Hughes did for the Third Conference on Computers, Freedom, and Privacy held in San Francisco during the spring of 1993. I met Eric in the hotel lobby; he told me that I could pick up a copy of his PGP public key from the Internet PGP key servers (see Chapter 15 for more information), and he handed me a copy of his business card with the PGP fingerprint for his public key printed along the bottom.

Levels of trust

Let's look at the last question PGP asked:

```
Would you trust "Terrence Talbot <tjt@dtw.com>"
to act as an introducer and certify other people's public keys to you?
(1=I don't know. 2=No. 3=Usually. 4=Yes, always.) ?
```

How I answer this question determines how PGP behaves when I try to add to my key ring public keys that have been certified by the person whose key I am adding:

- If I answer `1=I don't know`, PGP asks me each time a key is added with Terry's signature.

- If I answer `2=No`, PGP ignores certification by this person on other peoples' public keys.

- If I answer `3=Usually`, PGP rates Terry as "marginal." If PGP, in its default configuration, discovers two signatures from people who are marginally trusted, that's just as good as getting one signature by someone who is completely trusted. (Chapter 14, *PGP Configuration File*, describes how you can change this configuration.)

- If I answer `4=Yes, always`, PGP always accepts that person's signature as gospel.

Adding a Key for Sam Spade

Terry decided not to go into law after all but joined the Sam Spade Detective Agency. (The one Sam set up with the money he made from recovering the real Maltese Falcon.) Terry says that he is going to London for a few months and, because of the impending takeover of Last Computers, he has emailed me Sam's PGP public key:

```
unix% pgp -ka sam.pgp
Pretty Good Privacy(tm) 2.6 - Public-key encryption for the masses.
(c) 1990-1994 Philip Zimmermann, Phil's Pretty Good Software. 23 May 94
Distributed by the Massachusetts Institute of Technology.  Uses RSAREF.
Export of this software may be restricted by the U.S. government.
Current time: 1994/08/27 21:31 GMT

Looking for new keys...
pub   768/3F1DEA81 1994/08/27  Sam Spade <smokey@bureau.com>

Checking signatures...
pub   768/3F1DEA81 1994/08/27 Sam Spade <smokey@bureau.com>
sig!      A4171B2D 1994/05/12 Terrence Talbot <tjt@dtw.com>


Keyfile contains:
   1 new key(s)

Make a determination in your own mind whether this key actually
belongs to the person whom you think it belongs to, based on available
evidence.  If you think it does, then based on your estimate of
that person's integrity and competence in key management, answer
the following question:

Would you trust "Sam Spade <smokey@bureau.com>"
to act as an introducer and certify other people's public keys to you?
(1=I don't know. 2=No. 3=Usually. 4=Yes, always.) ? 3
unix%
```

Notice that PGP didn't ask me to certify Sam's key: Terry had already done it for us, and I trust Terry to certify keys for me. (If I didn't trust Terry to sign keys, PGP would have told me that the key was signed, but it still would have asked if I wanted to certify Sam's key myself.)

PGP did ask me whether I trust Sam as an introducer to certify other people's public keys. I do.

Viewing Signatures

There are two different ways to view the signatures of all of the PGP keys on your key rings. The first is by using the –kc (key check) option. The second is by using the PGP option –kvv (key view verbose). These two options give you somewhat different information.

You can also check all of the key's fingerprints with the –kvc (key view and check) option.

Checking Your Keys and Signatures (-kc Option)

The –kc (key check) option shows you each of the keys on your key ring and then, for each key, shows you who is attesting to its validity.

Let's run the –kc option to see what my public key ring presently looks like:

```
unix% pgp -kc
Pretty Good Privacy(tm) 2.6 - Public-key encryption for the masses.
(c) 1990-1994 Philip Zimmermann, Phil's Pretty Good Software. 23 May 94
Distributed by the Massachusetts Institute of Technology.  Uses RSAREF.
Export of this software may be restricted by the U.S. government.
Current time: 1994/08/27 21:39 GMT

Key ring: '/Users/simsong/Library/pgp/pubring.pgp'
Type bits/keyID    Date        User ID
pub   768/3F1DEA81 1994/08/27 Sam Spade <smokey@bureau.com>
sig!      A4171B2D 1994/05/12  Terrence Talbot <tjt@dtw.com>
pub   512/A4171B2D 1994/05/12 Terrence Talbot <tjt@dtw.com>
sig!      903C9265 1994/08/27  Simson L. Garfinkel <simsong@acm.org>
pub   512/43744F09 1994/07/07 Phil's Pretty Good Pizza <phil@pgp.com>
sig!      903C9265 1994/08/27  Simson L. Garfinkel <simsong@acm.org>
pub  1024/903C9265 1994/07/15 Simson L. Garfinkel <simsong@acm.org>

   KeyID    Trust     Validity  User ID
   3F1DEA81 marginal  complete  Sam Spade <smokey@bureau.com>
c           complete            Terrence Talbot <tjt@dtw.com>
   A4171B2D complete  complete  Terrence Talbot <tjt@dtw.com>
c           ultimate            Simson L. Garfinkel <simsong@acm.org>
   43744F09 untrusted complete  Phil's Pretty Good Pizza <phil@pgp.com>
c           ultimate            Simson L. Garfinkel <simsong@acm.org>
* 903C9265 ultimate  complete  Simson L. Garfinkel <simsong@acm.org>
unix%
```

The block of lines that follows PGP's startup display text shows the four public keys currently on my key ring: one for Sam Spade, one for Terry Talbot, one for Phil's Pretty Good Pizza, and one for Simson Garfinkel (this is the public key that matches my secret key). Notice that the keys are displayed in the opposite order from the order in which I added them to the key ring.

The lines in the block labeled *pub* represent signatures. These lines say that Terry signed Sam's key and that Simson signed both Terry's key and the key for Phil's Pretty Good Pizza.

The last block of lines shows how I trust the various keys and signatures that are on my key ring. Sam's trust is marginal (I said that I would "usually" trust him to introduce other keys), but the validity is complete because his key is signed by Terry, who I trust completely.

Terry's key is trusted completely, and it is completely valid, because I signed it.

The key for Phil's Pretty Good Pizza isn't trusted at all, but its validity is complete because I signed the key. Remember that I trusted Phil's key enough to use it but not enough to have him vouch for other keys.

And what's so special about my signature? Well, it's mine. The trust in my signature is "ultimate" and the validity "complete" because I made that key myself. Your version of PGP always trusts your own public keys.

The following is a complete list of the different kinds of trust that a PGP key can have, based on how you answered the question "Would you trust *so and so* to act as an introducer and certify other people's public keys to you?"

If your answer to the question, "Would you trust...?" is:	PGP considers your trust:
I don't know	undefined
No	untrusted
Usually	marginal
Yes	complete

Checking Your Keys and Signatures (-kvv Option)

You can also view the contents of your key ring with the –kvv (key view verbose) option. The option shows you the signatures, but it doesn't show you the levels of trust or validity on each key:

```
unix% pgp -kvv
Pretty Good Privacy(tm) 2.6 - Public-key encryption for the masses.
(c) 1990-1994 Philip Zimmermann, Phil's Pretty Good Software. 23 May 94
Distributed by the Massachusetts Institute of Technology.  Uses RSAREF.
Export of this software may be restricted by the U.S. government.
Current time: 1994/08/27 21:56 GMT
```

```
Key ring: '/Users/simsong/Library/pgp/pubring.pgp'
Type bits/keyID     Date        User ID
pub   768/3F1DEA81 1994/08/27 Sam Spade <smokey@bureau.com>
sig       A4171B2D Terrence Talbot <tjt@dtw.com>
pub   512/A4171B2D 1994/05/12 Terrence Talbot <tjt@dtw.com>
sig       903C9265             Simson L. Garfinkel <simsong@acm.org>
pub   512/43744F09 1994/07/07 Phil's Pretty Good Pizza <phil@pgp.com>
sig       903C9265             Simson L. Garfinkel <simsong@acm.org>
pub  1024/903C9265 1994/07/15 Simson L. Garfinkel <simsong@acm.org>
4 matching keys found.
unix%
```

Checking all the Fingerprints for Your Keys (-kvc Option)

The –kvc (key view check) option shows me the MD5 fingerprints for every key on my public key ring:

```
unix% pgp -kvc
Pretty Good Privacy(tm) 2.6 - Public-key encryption for the masses.
(c) 1990-1994 Philip Zimmermann, Phil's Pretty Good Software. 23 May 94
Distributed by the Massachusetts Institute of Technology.  Uses RSAREF.
Export of this software may be restricted by the U.S. government.
Current time: 1994/08/28 18:34 GMT

Key ring: '/Users/simsong/Library/pgp/pubring.pgp'
Type bits/keyID     Date        User ID
pub   512/33681029 1994/08/28 Nosmis Noel, Secret Agent <nn@nsa.gov>
        Key fingerprint =  B4 42 4F A4 15 67 FA FD  84 DD 43 E7 3F E7 09 45
pub   768/3F1DEA81 1994/08/27 Sam Spade <smokey@bureau.com>
        Key fingerprint =  FA 80 83 A5 F4 9F 48 EF  67 C6 1C 20 2F 4F 65 1E
pub   512/A62474F5 1994/08/27 Terrence Talbot <tjt@dtw.com>
        Key fingerprint =  98 67 F3 71 D7 57 7D 30  F4 82 7C 76 84 91 90 4C
pub   512/43744F09 1994/07/07 Phil's Pretty Good Pizza <phil@pgp.com>
        Key fingerprint =  24 38 1A 58 46 AD CC 2D  AB C9 E0 F1 C7 3C 67 EC
pub  1024/903C9265 1994/07/15 Simson L. Garfinkel <simsong@acm.org>
        Key fingerprint =  68 06 7B 9A 8C E6 58 3D  6E D8 0E 90 01 C5 DE 01
5 matching keys found.
unix%
```

You can view an alternative key ring by specifying the name of the file containing it on the command line following the –kvc option as follows:

```
unix% pgp -kvc anotherRing.pgp
```

Changing Your Trust in a Person (-ke Option)

You can use the –ke (key edit) option to change the level of trust you have in a public key stored on your key ring.

For example, to change the trust of Terry's key from "complete" to "marginal," I would type the following:

```
unix% pgp -ke tjt
Pretty Good Privacy(tm) 2.6 - Public-key encryption for the masses.
(c) 1990-1994 Philip Zimmermann, Phil's Pretty Good Software. 23 May 94
Distributed by the Massachusetts Institute of Technology.  Uses RSAREF.
Export of this software may be restricted by the U.S. government.
Current time: 1994/08/15 04:43 GMT


Editing userid "tjt" in key ring: '/simsong/Library/pgp/pubring.pgp'.


Key for user ID: Terrence Talbot <tjt@dtw.com>
512-bit key, Key ID A4171B2D, created 1994/05/12


No secret key available.  Editing public key trust parameter.


Key for user ID: Terrence Talbot <tjt@dtw.com>
512-bit key, Key ID A4171B2D, created 1994/05/12
This user is completely trusted to certify other keys.
This key/userID association is fully certified.
   Axiomatically trusted certification from:
   Simson L. Garfinkel <simsong@acm.org>
Current trust for this key's owner is: complete


Make a determination in your own mind whether this key actually
belongs to the person whom you think it belongs to, based on available
evidence.  If you think it does, then based on your estimate of
that person's integrity and competence in key management, answer
the following question:


Would you trust "Terrence Talbot <tjt@dtw.com>"
to act as an introducer and certify other people's public keys to you?
(1=I don't know. 2=No. 3=Usually. 4=Yes, always.) ? 3
Public key ring updated.
unix%
```

Notice that PGP doesn't ask me for my pass phrase before making this change. This has important implications if you are sharing a computer with other people. Without needing to know your pass phrase, someone could add a key to your key ring with minimal trust. They could then use this key to add other keys to your key ring— perhaps even adding public keys that have the same user IDs for people with whom you already communicate. While the validity of these keys would be "unknown" (because they would not be signed with your secret key), their trust might very well say "trusted." For this reason, if other people have access to your computer, it is a good idea to use the –kc option every now and then to make sure that the public keys you are using are really the ones that you think they are.

This is a good idea even if you think that other people don't have access to your computer. After all, if your communications are so valuable that you need to be using encryption, you can't rule out the possibility that someone might surreptitiously use your computer without your knowledge and make unauthorized modifications to your key ring.

Signatures and the -ke Option

A signature on your key certifies that a particular user ID belongs to a particular key. Thus, if you use the –ke (key edit) option to add a new user ID to a key that has been signed, that new user ID won't be signed. (After all, the people who signed your key didn't sign the new user ID, because the user ID wasn't on the key when they signed it.)

Be careful when you use the –kr (key remove) option to remove user IDs from your keys; if you remove the user ID that has all of your signatures (usually your primary user ID), you are left with an unsigned key!

Why Change the Level of Trust?

There are many reasons why you might want to change the level of trust you have noted on a person's key:

- The person might be indiscriminately signing any key that she receives. In this case, you would probably want to stop trusting the person, because that person's judgment appears suspect.

- You might discover that the person signed a key that belongs to an imposter, in which case you might not trust any other keys that he has signed.

- You might want to upgrade your trust again after the person returns from a five-day course in key certification protocols and now thoroughly understands what it means to sign a key.

- You might have recently met the person and, based on that meeting, decide that you trust them more than you did when you first received his key.

Finally, if a person's key is stolen, you probably want to do more than change your level of trust in that person's key: you probably want to delete the person's key altogether. You do this with the –kr (key remove) option (described in Chapter 9) or by adding a –kd (key disable) option for that person's key (described in Chapter 13).

Specifying a Different Key Ring

As with most of the PGP key management options, you can specify a different key ring for the –ke (key edit) option by specifying the key ring on the command line following the user ID of the key that you are editing:

```
unix% pgp -ke tjt anyKeyRing
```

Signing a Key (-ks Option)

When you add a key to your key ring and certify its validity, PGP automatically signs it for you. You can also manually sign keys that you did not certify when they were first added.

To sign a key, use the –ks (key sign) option. Before you sign a key, you should be absolutely sure that it belongs to the person that you think it does.

For example, the following is my key ring:

```
unix% pgp -kvv
Pretty Good Privacy(tm) 2.6 - Public-key encryption for the masses.
(c) 1990-1994 Philip Zimmermann, Phil's Pretty Good Software. 23 May 94
Distributed by the Massachusetts Institute of Technology.  Uses RSAREF.
Export of this software may be restricted by the U.S. government.
Current time: 1994/08/28 18:01 GMT

Key ring: '/Users/simsong/Library/pgp/pubring.pgp'
Type bits/keyID    Date       User ID
pub   768/3F1DEA81 1994/08/27 Sam Spade <smokey@bureau.com>
sig       A62474F5            Terrence Talbot <tjt@dtw.com>
pub   512/A62474F5 1994/08/27 Terrence Talbot <tjt@dtw.com>
sig       903C9265            Simson L. Garfinkel <simsong@acm.org>
pub   512/43744F09 1994/07/07 Phil's Pretty Good Pizza <phil@pgp.com>
sig       903C9265            Simson L. Garfinkel <simsong@acm.org>
pub   1024/903C9265 1994/07/15 Simson L. Garfinkel <simsong@acm.org>
4 matching keys found.
unix%
```

I've signed Terry's and Phil's keys, but only Terry has signed Sam's key. If I want to sign Sam's key as well, I can do so with the –ks option:[†]

```
unix% pgp -ks sam
Pretty Good Privacy(tm) 2.6 - Public-key encryption for the masses.
 (c) 1990-1994 Philip Zimmermann, Phil's Pretty Good Software. 23 May 94
Distributed by the Massachusetts Institute of Technology.  Uses RSAREF.
Export of this software may be restricted by the U.S. government.
Current time: 1994/08/28 18:05 GMT

A secret key is required to make a signature.
You specified no user ID to select your secret key,
so the default user ID and key will be the most recently
added key on your secret keyring.

Looking for key for user 'sam':

Key for user ID: Sam Spade <smokey@bureau.com>
768-bit key, Key ID 3F1DEA81, created 1994/08/27


READ CAREFULLY:  Based on your own direct first-hand knowledge, are
you absolutely certain that you are prepared to solemnly certify that
the above public key actually belongs to the user specified by the
above user ID (y/N)? y

You need a pass phrase to unlock your RSA secret key.
Key for user ID "Simson L. Garfinkel <simsong@acm.org>"

Enter pass phrase: Pass phrase is good.  Just a moment....
Key signature certificate added.
unix%
```

I can now verify that my signature is on the key by using the –kvv option once again:

```
unix% pgp -kvv
Pretty Good Privacy(tm) 2.6 - Public-key encryption for the masses.
 (c) 1990-1994 Philip Zimmermann, Phil's Pretty Good Software. 23 May 94
Distributed by the Massachusetts Institute of Technology.  Uses RSAREF.
Export of this software may be restricted by the U.S. government.
Current time: 1994/08/28 18:07 GMT
```

---

† Although I don't need to sign Sam's key in order to use it, I might want to give a copy of it to an associate who trusts me but does not trust Terry. I should sign Sam's key only after I have verified that the key actually belongs to Sam.

```
Key ring: '/Users/simsong/Library/pgp/pubring.pgp'
Type bits/keyID    Date       User ID
pub   768/3F1DEA81 1994/08/27 Sam Spade <smokey@bureau.com>
sig       903C9265            Simson L. Garfinkel <simsong@acm.org>
sig       A62474F5            Terrence Talbot <tjt@dtw.com>
pub   512/A62474F5 1994/08/27 Terrence Talbot <tjt@dtw.com>
sig       903C9265            Simson L. Garfinkel <simsong@acm.org>
pub   512/43744F09 1994/07/07 Phil's Pretty Good Pizza <phil@pgp.com>
sig       903C9265            Simson L. Garfinkel <simsong@acm.org>
pub  1024/903C9265 1994/07/15 Simson L. Garfinkel <simsong@acm.org>
4 matching keys found.
unix%
```

As you can see, my signature is added to Terry's signature. A key can have any number of signatures.

Signing with a Different Secret Key (-u Option)

If my key ring contains more than one secret key, I can specify the PGP –u (user) option to pick which key to use for creating the signature.

For example, let's say that I have created a secret key for my alter ego, Nosmis Noel, and I want Nosmis to sign Sam's key.

This is the key ring:

```
unix% pgp -kvv
Pretty Good Privacy(tm) 2.6 - Public-key encryption for the masses.
(c) 1990-1994 Philip Zimmermann, Phil's Pretty Good Software. 23 May 94
Distributed by the Massachusetts Institute of Technology.  Uses RSAREF.
Export of this software may be restricted by the U.S. government.
Current time: 1994/08/28 18:10 GMT

Key ring: '/Users/simsong/Library/pgp/pubring.pgp'
Type bits/keyID    Date       User ID
pub   512/33681029 1994/08/28 Nosmis Noel, Secret Agent <nn@nsa.gov>
pub   768/3F1DEA81 1994/08/27 Sam Spade <smokey@bureau.com>
sig       A62474F5            Terrence Talbot <tjt@dtw.com>
pub   512/A62474F5 1994/08/27 Terrence Talbot <tjt@dtw.com>
sig       903C9265            Simson L. Garfinkel <simsong@acm.org>
pub   512/43744F09 1994/07/07 Phil's Pretty Good Pizza <phil@pgp.com>
sig       903C9265            Simson L. Garfinkel <simsong@acm.org>
pub  1024/903C9265 1994/07/15 Simson L. Garfinkel <simsong@acm.org>
5 matching keys found.
unix%
```

The following example shows how I sign the key with the "nosmis" secret key:

```
unix% pgp -ks sam -u nosmis
Pretty Good Privacy(tm) 2.6 - Public-key encryption for the masses.
 (c) 1990-1994 Philip Zimmermann, Phil's Pretty Good Software. 23 May 94
Distributed by the Massachusetts Institute of Technology.  Uses RSAREF.
Export of this software may be restricted by the U.S. government.
Current time: 1994/08/28 18:12 GMT


Looking for key for user 'sam':

Key for user ID: Sam Spade <smokey@bureau.com>
768-bit key, Key ID 3F1DEA81, created 1994/08/27



READ CAREFULLY:  Based on your own direct first-hand knowledge, are
you absolutely certain that you are prepared to solemnly certify that
the above public key actually belongs to the user specified by the
above user ID (y/N)? y

You need a pass phrase to unlock your RSA secret key.
Key for user ID "Nosmis Noel, Secret Agent <nn@nsa.gov>"

Enter pass phrase: Eat more oats! Pass phrase is good.  Just a moment....
Key signature certificate added.
unix%
```

And the following is proof that the key is signed:

```
unix% pgp -kvv
Pretty Good Privacy(tm) 2.6 - Public-key encryption for the masses.
 (c) 1990-1994 Philip Zimmermann, Phil's Pretty Good Software. 23 May 94
Distributed by the Massachusetts Institute of Technology.  Uses RSAREF.
Export of this software may be restricted by the U.S. government.
Current time: 1994/08/28 18:13 GMT


Key ring: '/Users/simsong/Library/pgp/pubring.pgp'
Type bits/keyID    Date        User ID
pub   512/33681029 1994/08/28 Nosmis Noel, Secret Agent <nn@nsa.gov>
pub   768/3F1DEA81 1994/08/27 Sam Spade <smokey@bureau.com>
sig       33681029            Nosmis Noel, Secret Agent <nn@nsa.gov>
sig       A62474F5            Terrence Talbot <tjt@dtw.com>
pub   512/A62474F5 1994/08/27 Terrence Talbot <tjt@dtw.com>
sig       903C9265            Simson L. Garfinkel <simsong@acm.org>
pub   512/43744F09 1994/07/07 Phil's Pretty Good Pizza <phil@pgp.com>
sig       903C9265            Simson L. Garfinkel <simsong@acm.org>
pub  1024/903C9265 1994/07/15 Simson L. Garfinkel <simsong@acm.org>
5 matching keys found.
unix%
```

Should You Sign Your Own Keys?

The short answer is yes. After you create a key, you should use that key to sign itself. The easy way to do this is by typing the following:

```
unix% pgp -ks yourUserID -u yourUserID
```

You need to sign your own keys because of a subtle security problem that arises from keys that are completely unsigned.

This is the long answer:

PGP signatures certify that a given user ID in fact belongs to a given RSA public key. That's important because, as we have seen, anyone can create a public key that has any user ID on it. If a public key is unsigned, then any person who encounters the public key can use the –ke (key edit) option to change the user ID on the key, and the key looks just the same.

A bad guy could still edit your user ID, removing the one that you created and adding one of his own. But if he does, the one that he adds won't be signed, because the bad guy doesn't have your secret key.

Thus, if you come upon a self-signed key, you know that the person who created the key gave it the user ID that it currently has. A key that isn't self-signed might possibly have been modified without the creator's knowledge.

Removing a Signature (-krs Option)

You can remove a signature on a key by using the –krs (key remove signature) option. You can remove *any* signature from a key—you do not need to be the person who wrote the signature.

For example, I can easily remove the signatures of Nosmis and Simson from Sam Spade's key:

```
unix% pgp -krs sam
Pretty Good Privacy(tm) 2.6 - Public-key encryption for the masses.
(c) 1990-1994 Philip Zimmermann, Phil's Pretty Good Software. 23 May 94
Distributed by the Massachusetts Institute of Technology.  Uses RSAREF.
Export of this software may be restricted by the U.S. government.
Current time: 1994/08/28 18:33 GMT

Removing signatures from userid 'sam' in key ring '/Users/simsong/Library/pgp/
pubring.pgp'
```

```
Key for user ID: Sam Spade <smokey@bureau.com>
768-bit key, Key ID 3F1DEA81, created 1994/08/27

Key has 2 signature(s):
sig        33681029              Nosmis Noel, Secret Agent <nn@nsa.gov>
Remove this signature (y/N)? y
sig        A903C9265             Simson L. Garfinkel <simsong@acm.org>
Remove this signature (y/N)? y

2 key signature(s) removed.
unix%
```

Unknown Signers

While I was working on this book, I received an email message from Jeremiah S. Junken that contained a guide he was writing about PGP. I noticed that there were two PGP keys at the end of the file he sent. One key was very short; the other was quite long. Those keys and the story behind them illustrates an important point about signatures on keys, and I thank Jeremiah and Peter (Jeremiah's keymate) for their permission to include their keys.

This Jeremiah's key:

```
-----BEGIN PGP PUBLIC KEY BLOCK-----
Version: 2.3a.3

mQCNAi3+N/sAAAEEAKg5XtFem9nM1zU9LxwHIWqvsPaESFjkyxTPtX5YLj5ugvQr
818hgXqXwdG8415ZbJNMYP9qRA5u44NNCGhEDI1jkj4E5w4CB3JXu/GruaZ+1zAO
9hCAYzajenfCeM2Y3xSO2eiN4nuHWzwV0EW2y1mGD0EXspBRpEVyiiRQvPXpAAUR
tDM8SmVyZW1pYWggUy5KdW5rZW4+IGpqdW5rZW5AbmF0aW9ucy51Y3MuaW5kaWFu
YS51ZHU=
=WT8H
-----END PGP PUBLIC KEY BLOCK-----
```

This is Peter's key:

```
-----BEGIN PGP PUBLIC KEY BLOCK-----
Version: 2.3a.3

mQCNAiyg9DgAAAEEAMnWa12Ub+g8uzR/GByKjpMiNsHZygQ4pw2Bjix+WjyEVsHH
JV8DRqdnYBs+MPrhvou1dDXEkhC641klC23xlawI2yaXBtKadKgEEOdKLF9tVibP
SFqgxT/TNw1l0cDDeCkeQmSXtY2/MpK0tXCRAvFb/dnaHkKDew9HL1s0103BAAUR
tCFQZXRlciBTaW1vbnMgPHNpbW9uc0BwZXRpLkdVTi5kZT6JAFUCBRAtsEbiIfI/
FvoHHfkBAYp4AgCn8M8fUp4AWyGpbra+kSy200LMX6z2kR8cSYfnbqo7DQzJnBGM
LPuDz08J3bCj8HXdy2zXZr6FgMJy8PwnBXS0iQBVAgUQLbsqO5vaUYPwhBsRAQFA
```

zQIAhxJafc2vxF6FQ7+BR73GU0E3uPSOZzbQfkU/7RFlp4iuOjA5cB1DQyv0IqHN
P8VGQi0aubGR4kh5OGw1vnrp54kAlQIFEC1muGWtei73+sUbeQEBCB0D/2JJ/rnB
pXdKCKcsTzwQuH6TjofkYvDjL+Y2QZ0X+nziYgAyuGSOMo9KfP9exv7y+A16e/ve
2NrfC4aBKLJPqqaDw/Mpmu7VN7qRSMPYYnBz7PMnn9FMyq5KorRFHQm3D83M90D5
ff+fi0X5xWJiI/cEdFFnskX4gcp+cDoCqvfEiQBVAgUQLVVp0v2YSvmy1vClAQEH
RAIAyElndiq8/yu42bzGGgImJV91xViZN0RV/ogH0k+rPJRgHcdTwHHrw8AoIMXp
rfxRRYWsaIXCpE/zE3k/yXaao4kAVQIFEC1Utjzlc12j2z/KwQEB9y8B/05B0rVS
h8T2Sqg/fhwNvsHYgljZMnR88UpJLkqrBPoZVFJnqTPO0/minYeSHwSeTTqn7BuD
48FJZloTEQKpuEuJAFUCBRAtU+s6ERkJHPqUz38BAVi0Af4mE/oIbeU7UKViul/z
0Tcw4sQ+vTVBIs83BudsWk32Pxcas80E+++HRHyAhHrqO1swdCvpfT7DDrbxJ+Ti
frqLiQBVAgUQLN/aRLVpsU3/KyuPAQEWegIA1quUkJ6hlOZ+jO7Fh+VW7bxk5xdQ
k4SYlcqiw4r10gkktYOUvkQ9o+mL8rHtrObV7bSeD9eYwlory2mo10p9WYkAVQIF
ECzfpSDiivn9aZDvXQEBsr8B/RSPPjgsrz/GObDCvoXKnADPlgOnqPF9AN+JIMPT
ov935pnMrfajTBvMktrpGKp2RxqoOUyk0e3bhthREDhpkRCJAJUCBRAtUvWsE3I3
96iLPhkBAa0qA/wMIiIxTabG8wfifPFI+ddni05vrH2i+luft0vJ7IPsaI78UQLY
d1j8ClyultEheHwbu5rPhKyT3r0qNCdNgt/ldKgZlfIakJHxyhYsjimr5C0JWzz8
HtqzI4IgUnJB9ew3Bm9gtOem/+jcq7oGqDjAN6zDzUxlbYvYEAP9bLAp6okAlQIF
EC1S7wHQ+XRbkhtylQEBa8MD+wSClbilT1wdK5TRdAnzSTqQY0VeO/oruKAO7BgL
ZgWxRFqF0rrTet1E2Xpluk2rtHOKCSdVMRkwk2xv6O8n254AUb2b1y7QeE/wjBHo
+r7FPt6fPiy+MVxPr3YhLjIN2pOr1XBGxDO9hsfvWVXGp/rQrIYYtS3vthsVDsy/
FvyriQCVAgUQLVNPm0hfqy8j2SvjAQF26wQAjM2ejxovriRtifTXhCZ/D8KUZJP+
8w971Dryk0yuTZWR7ICMDxpXpdL+4JrewnjOL7SWwXMw48wQvEBBU3nAsrEHMoA4
0Mfxfgal8benmgnWJzkI7sgozU/+6eq9APqC39/ePDYyUr8qo+46H1KW4e+rodlM
tQiIaQelgR8V2beJAFUCBRAtUvhac5JDRKnQpMMBARgWAf46hG/L6tZ4AuP9jK1f
41AFG5xW5qbOo9ylMWDAR7pJRWknFOLR+NJ9rsguZYTCUYMImxi79nolyyDPJjDr
nl2NiQBVAgUQLVNKMXmMGAx7t12JAQGR2QH8DMLIptuojGjKTiHGvlilh9zVwhnH
r0XSbBBKzx4sTD3FDrBfO7DjRbbP0NnTrlaNyaG1IYwZEbXqsa5EuCEAU4kARQIF
EC1S8y91nsSrAn0L2QEBR+gBfj9WKNWGhJ7v1djo/gklSfDR86MgaV7AlXK26okR
dhYZ96ugDuzM0/f1Sm4itKbtookAlQIFEC0y75F76nchDdGcwQEBXNgEAJGIC+9+
51FPKHczyZQ130mug7v91UxFYou2xeb4MYy+w/3Gp7QiWZFL/Mk8YTzECHuHdIZQ
7LCBQlOS+XOEZ2wbjv8w7JiRU6tTgywj305tX2c0KPCgEuEcT4EiqM+rAn7HIm82
Hy/9jzSJK76I54VataY0xO5XCnEn2Z1PDWS+iQCVAgUQLKtBN61MOADdzRPBAQHL
yAQAxPm8IDV15lt8IqVL7BCFeHq95VO/hXlb/6XY3cJFIj7goCK0zkFluTxaBH0V
5cH1cRnedIxVYihB4CXT7UXIriSETfvP6cL4XV4u3oaOVkiccw6BvHmFnSSgm8wQ
v6CxMkPQMfLR8Tn2rZn3O2ffKRB8nFLiiwThfPKUc9NPYlaJAJUCBRAs7468OxwH
hXg8g/EBAViMBACWap0CD/iX+kaFsyBtHF4qpq8XO11zTGuHI7Z/HaOwxyEuPeOX
JbM+7pbhRyzRQ7nhyhEQ27hF3wsD07IKSaE6QMFHtObOBmGYPIHkBCGyvlmh545r
N+KNCJkDM9GQ6UgDEwieoTYjNju51NrxNlco0eJ21hzB6gE/Iu8ml1LxZ4kAlQIF
ECzlQrTSJ29yPs8yJQEBgAUEAIYrigbBZ8ocSJCNyb2F39QVMV/kkQM+Gm3UU4tb
GrB2f/yW+wB8xgu5VHEBCALN3GoJZ5Jo58oDKEICKJy0CIBxUYGTaTTTaTdCOX2i
qgfFbdglzQJ5O1oc8I57KKL20DgW6zxCS01VUCfB7K1F90mqIDkxLEFGwvjqeGVu
lmG5iQCVAgUQLMOaw6Da852xEaRBAQFTSAP/WeEmX6CCYnxtPweReQbiOPH0e15H
RA05gFGn8xOrGV4SQ+SN3qHVkDbEos3QCNPO2EN68PwSXHmpqSERR9aro29SSeu5
rBRoujODI/pVEesZGJlafgXljmBKMNEBbkJo8Av0Iig6nLEPJ1BoSTrWLGBPAx5O
L/W9UIg3fT7/JZuJAFUCBRAspUMs6phj4SBVVVcBAc13AfwPq4zYjTX1wNaJPXvc
Gie43TXNVVTDFQM0SQaMJCUggVgpLLpCExGHy8eZVNLHT/oXUNDMub62y9tI/62s
zG54iQBVAgUQLLPH5MXXeS9/020BAQEeVgIAm/QuutqE/PEDU7cALELs8dDKS/2i

```
G0ixgP5INdQtusRxRPOTLJr7obmiehxCdpMZlmSqYQ+Sxocl7ePBkuDLkIkAlQIF
ECyokzreJzX92ofAxwEBUMgEAIQmc4aobPOPX3STKiwqif/Yad4vBzrGMCXyhEz6
86o5C3C3TjVNapDz673Lt3vsDv4gwfEKfIPkO2qa0Mnw1HIlko3Ep3PBpRNXmkQl
WmstBT1b4//NbqImb301OUi88ZDrbA7ECpRQkpbJlLjKB6YMuX9Vhmw/goSl+5L2
r1DciQBFAgUQLKhZdBddOICR7WnVAQFhMAF9F66RpmQSiBYYQKwLfwcWQvZTDMvY
7/2voVdW0SvkLyigvjPPSih1KRg8NqW7QGr8iQBVAgUQLKRhFIGIYXUhejq5AQFA
qAH+OE0BRKa2D6a22GPqHQKqLJi+H/2PkCWh5jvDfnl5FnuBG51k1GlkPI+qSY/f
YoS9CZ+/EBAwn4UwIeB6vTcn6A==
=rJ6m
-----END PGP PUBLIC KEY BLOCK-----
```

I was curious about what was actually in these two keys, so I saved each one to a file—the first to a file *Jeremiah.asc,* and the second to a file *Peter.asc:*

```
unix% ls -l *.asc
-rw-r--r--  1 simsong      364 Jul 12 19:21 Jeremiah.asc
-rw-r--r--  1 simsong     4025 Jul 12 19:21 Peter.asc
unix%
```

Next I used the –ka (key add) option to save both keys to a key ring *temp.pgp:*

```
unix% pgp -ka Jeremiah.asc temp.pgp
Pretty Good Privacy(tm) 2.6 - Public-key encryption for the masses.
(c) 1990-1994 Philip Zimmermann, Phil's Pretty Good Software. 23 May 94
Distributed by the Massachusetts Institute of Technology.  Uses RSAREF.
Export of this software may be restricted by the U.S. government.
Current time: 1994/07/12 23:43 GMT

Looking for new keys...
pub  1024/50BCF5E9 1994/06/14   <Jeremiah S.Junken>
jjunken@nations.ucs.indiana.edu

Checking signatures...


Keyfile contains:
   1 new key(s)

One or more of the new keys are not fully certified.
Do you want to certify any of these keys yourself (y/N)? n
unix% pgp -ka Peter.asc temp.pgp
Pretty Good Privacy(tm) 2.6 - Public-key encryption for the masses.
(c) 1990-1994 Philip Zimmermann, Phil's Pretty Good Software. 23 May 94
Distributed by the Massachusetts Institute of Technology.  Uses RSAREF.
Export of this software may be restricted by the U.S. government.
Current time: 1994/07/12 23:43 GMT
```

```
Looking for new keys...
pub  1024/34D74DC1 1993/09/23  Peter Simons <simons@peti.GUN.de>

Checking signatures...


Keyfile contains:
   1 new key(s)

One or more of the new keys are not fully certified.
Do you want to certify any of these keys yourself (y/N)? n
unix%
```

Finally, I used the –kc (key check) option to check the signatures on these keys. The results were surprising:

```
unix% pgp -kc temp.pgp
Pretty Good Privacy(tm) 2.6 - Public-key encryption for the masses.
(c) 1990-1994 Philip Zimmermann, Phil's Pretty Good Software. 23 May 94
Distributed by the Massachusetts Institute of Technology.  Uses RSAREF.
Export of this software may be restricted by the U.S. government.
Current time: 1994/07/12 23:44 GMT


Key ring: 'temp.pgp'
Type bits/keyID    Date        User ID
pub  1024/34D74DC1 1993/09/23 Peter Simons <simons@peti.GUN.de>
     sig?   FA071DF9          (Unknown signator, can't be checked)
     sig?   F0841B11          (Unknown signator, can't be checked)
     sig?   FAC51B79          (Unknown signator, can't be checked)
     sig?   B2D6F0A5          (Unknown signator, can't be checked)
     sig?   DB3FCAC1          (Unknown signator, can't be checked)
     sig?   FA94CF7F          (Unknown signator, can't be checked)
     sig?   FF2B2B8F          (Unknown signator, can't be checked)
     sig?   6990EF5D          (Unknown signator, can't be checked)
     sig?   A88B3E19          (Unknown signator, can't be checked)
     sig?   921B7295          (Unknown signator, can't be checked)
     sig?   23D92BE3          (Unknown signator, can't be checked)
     sig?   A9D0A4C3          (Unknown signator, can't be checked)
     sig?   7BB75D89          (Unknown signator, can't be checked)
     sig?   027D0BD9          (Unknown signator, can't be checked)
     sig?   0DD19CC1          (Unknown signator, can't be checked)
     sig?   DDCD13C1          (Unknown signator, can't be checked)
     sig?   783C83F1          (Unknown signator, can't be checked)
     sig?   3ECF3225          (Unknown signator, can't be checked)
     sig?   B111A441          (Unknown signator, can't be checked)
     sig?   20555557          (Unknown signator, can't be checked)
     sig?   7FD36381          (Unknown signator, can't be checked)
     sig?   DA87C0C7          (Unknown signator, can't be checked)
     sig?   91ED69D5          (Unknown signator, can't be checked)
```

```
    sig?      217A3AB9                   (Unknown signator, can't be checked)
    pub  1024/50BCF5E9 1994/06/14 <Jeremiah S.Junken> jjunken@nations.ucs.indiana.edu

    KeyID     Trust       Validity  User ID
    34D74DC1  undefined   undefined Peter Simons <simons@peti.GUN.de>
              undefined             (KeyID: FA071DF9)
              undefined             (KeyID: F0841B11)
              undefined             (KeyID: FAC51B79)
              undefined             (KeyID: B2D6F0A5)
              undefined             (KeyID: DB3FCAC1)
              undefined             (KeyID: FA94CF7F)
              undefined             (KeyID: FF2B2B8F)
              undefined             (KeyID: 6990EF5D)
              undefined             (KeyID: A88B3E19)
              undefined             (KeyID: 921B7295)
              undefined             (KeyID: 23D92BE3)
              undefined             (KeyID: A9D0A4C3)
              undefined             (KeyID: 7BB75D89)
              undefined             (KeyID: 027D0BD9)
              undefined             (KeyID: 0DD19CC1)
              undefined             (KeyID: DDCD13C1)
              undefined             (KeyID: 783C83F1)
              undefined             (KeyID: 3ECF3225)
              undefined             (KeyID: B111A441)
              undefined             (KeyID: 20555557)
              undefined             (KeyID: 7FD36381)
              undefined             (KeyID: DA87C0C7)
              undefined             (KeyID: 91ED69D5)
              undefined             (KeyID: 217A3AB9)
      50BCF5E9  undefined undefined <Jeremiah S.Junken> jjunken@nations.ucs.indiana.edu
    unix%
```

Peter's PGP key, it turns out, is much longer than Jeremiah's because it contains 24 different signatures attesting to its veracity. Unfortunately, I don't know the names of any of the people who have signed Peter's key. Therefore, regrettably, I can't bring myself to trust them. So these 24 signatures are a waste for most people who receive this key. (The signatures belong to programmers in Germany that Peter knows.)

Peter's key, which is nearly two pages long, is just as valid and as trustworthy as Jeremiah's key; that is to say, it isn't. At least, they aren't valid and trustworthy to *me*. Indeed, all of the keys and signatures could have been created by a single person.[†]

What's the moral? It really doesn't matter how many people have signed a key. All that matters is that the signatures belong to people you already know and trust. If the key doesn't have any trusted signatures on it, it is as valid (or as suspect) as a key with no signatures at all.

---

† Much in the way that I have created many of the identities used in the examples throughout this book.

With that said, however, you can probably draw one conclusion: the keys allegedly belonging to Jeremiah and Peter were found at the bottom of the primer on PGP that I received directly from the email address *jjunken@nations.ucs.indiana.edu*. If I want to send encrypted mail to that email address using the PGP key belonging to Jeremiah, someone at the receiving end will probably be able to read it. That person is probably the same person who wrote the PGP primer. And that person might very well be Jeremiah S. Junken.

Then again, that person might be someone else. There might be no Jeremiah S. Junken; the name could be an alias.[†] Whether this possibility is important depends on you. I am more than willing to believe that *jjunken@nations.ucs.indiana.edu* is in fact Jeremiah S. Junken. If you are trying to track down the long-lost heir to a $100 million fortune, you may wish to make a more positive identification.

Certifying the Keys in keys.asc (Version 2.6.1)

You may remember in Chapter 9 when I added the keys in the file *keys.asc* to my public key ring but didn't certify them because I hadn't covered key certification yet.

Now you know how to certify keys; you do it by calling the registered key holder and asking her for the fingerprint of her key.

Unfortunately, it's not practical for everyone to call Phil Zimmermann, Jeff Schiller, Derek Atkins, Branko Lankester, and other PGP luminaries to check their keys. So I've decided to do the next best thing: print the key fingerprints for those keys in this book.

I added these keys to my public key ring. If you are adding them to yours, you may wish to add them to a different key ring, unless you plan to communicate frequently with these people. The following table provides the digital fingerprints for all of the people whose keys appear in the file *keys.asc*.

User ID	Key ID	Fingerprint
Jeffrey I. Schiller *<jis@mit.edu>*[†]	0DBF906D	DD DC 88 AA 92 DC DD D5 BA 0A 6B 59 C1 65 AD 01
Jeffrey I. Schiller *<jis@mit.edu>*	4D0C4EE1	BF 26 FA 39 50 04 5C BF 80 51 E3 52 4A 16 DF 96
Philip L. Dubois *<dubois@csn.org>*	0778338D	9C DC D8 1D 93 BA 1E CB 6C B4 01 A5 4E 1E AE 8F
Colin Plumb *<colin@nyx.cs.du.edu>*	FBBB8AB1	9F 08 ED 38 C4 FF 90 61 85 D9 E7 DD BF 37 2A 65

† For all you know, dear reader, "Simson L. Garfinkel" could also be an alias. A lot of people think it is.

User ID	Key ID	Fingerprint
Philip R. Zimmermann <prz@acm.org>	C7A966DD	9E 94 45 13 39 83 5F 70 7B E7 D8 ED C4 BE 5A A6
Derek Atkins <warlord@MIT.EDU>	C1B06AF1	A0 9A 7E 2F 97 31 63 83 C8 7B 9C 8E DE 0E 8D F9
Branko Lankester <branko@hacktic.nl>	8DE722D9	25 4D 9A 79 C7 A9 DC 48 67 13 24 F2 03 B7 D8 24
Peter Gutmann <pgut1@cs.aukuni.ac.nz>	9D997D47	7C 6D 81 DF F2 62 0F 4A 67 0E 86 50 99 7E A6 B1
Hal Abelson <hal@mit.edu>	7D63A5C5	52 F4 F3 11 16 5D A5 54 A2 79 62 9B E5 E6 0F 40

[†] Note that Jeffrey Schiller changed his PGP key between the release of PGP Version 2.6 and PGP Version 2.6.1. Originally, Schiller had a 512-bit key; in Version 2.6.1, he moved to a 1024-bit key. Both keys are included in the PGP Version 2.6.1 distribution: the 512-bit key is used to sign the 1024-bit one.

You can add these keys to your own key ring with the following command:

```
unix% pgp -ka keys.asc
```

Alternatively, you can place these keys in their own PGP key ring *keys.pgp* (this is what I do) with the following command:

```
unix% pgp -ka keys.asc keys.pgp
```

Since the output of this command is six pages long, I have not included it.

The following is what the public key ring looks like after the keys are added:

```
unix% pgp -kv keys.pgp
Pretty Good Privacy(tm) 2.6.1 - Public-key encryption for the masses.
(c) 1990-1994 Philip Zimmermann, Phil's Pretty Good Software. 23 May 94
Distributed by the Massachusetts Institute of Technology.  Uses RSAREF.
Export of this software may be restricted by the U.S. government.
Current time: 1994/09/17 20:09 GMT

Key ring: 'keys.pgp'
Type bits/keyID    Date       User ID
pub  1024/0DBF906D 1994/08/27 Jeffrey I. Schiller <jis@mit.edu>
pub   512/4D0C4EE1 1992/09/10 Jeffrey I. Schiller <jis@mit.edu>
pub  1024/0778338D 1993/09/17 Philip L. Dubois <dubois@csn.org>
pub  1024/FBBB8AB1 1994/05/07 Colin Plumb <colin@nyx.cs.du.edu>
pub  1024/C7A966DD 1993/05/21 Philip R. Zimmermann <prz@acm.org>
pub   709/C1B06AF1 1992/09/25 Derek Atkins <warlord@MIT.EDU>
pub  1024/8DE722D9 1992/07/22 Branko Lankester  <branko@hacktic.nl>
pub  1024/9D997D47 1992/08/02 Peter Gutmann <pgut1@cs.aukuni.ac.nz>
pub  1019/7D63A5C5 1994/07/04 Hal Abelson <hal@mit.edu>
unix%
```

13

Revoking, Disabling,
and Escrowing Keys

This chapter describes PGP key management functions that are somewhat off the beaten track. PGP allows you to perform these functions, but you're not likely to use them very often.

You use the –kd (key disable) option both to revoke and to disable keys. This chapter describes this option and the other procedures you need to follow to revoke or disable a key or if you use a manual key escrow system.

Revoking Your Public Key

Accidents happen. Consider the following scenarios.

You might be demonstrating PGP to a business associate. You unwittingly tell that seemingly honorable person your pass phrase. Next thing you know, you wake up on the floor with a sore head. On the computer's screen, you see the letters:

```
C:\PGP> copy secring.pgp a:
```

Then you check the Usenet and discover that your dirty rat-fink business partner has taken to posting obscene messages and signing them with *your PGP secret key.*

Or you might discover that the copy of PGP you have been using for the past three months, an "improved" version of PGP, called NPGP, is really a booby-trapped program that steals your secret key and your pass phrase and mails them to an anonymous remailer in Argentina; from there your key and pass phrase are forwarded to New Zealand, and from there, you know not where.

Or you might simply want to "retire" an old public key and delete your matching secret key without having to keep the secret key around just in case someone discovers your old key and tries to use it to send you electronic mail.

In any of these cases, what you probably want to do is create a PGP *key revocation certificate* and distribute it as widely as possible.

What is a Key Revocation Certificate?

A key revocation certificate is a special kind of public key certificate that says in effect, "this public key should not be used."

A PGP key revocation certificate:

*   Contains a copy of your public key

*   Is signed by your secret key

*   Is incorporated into a person's key ring

*   Prevents a person who receives it from using your public key

Making a Key Revocation Certificate (-kd Option)

To make a key revocation certificate, simply run PGP with the –kd (key disable) option. For example, suppose that Phil of Phil's Pretty Good Pizza discovers that his computer has been compromised by his arch rival, Frank's Franks. He fires up a copy of PGP:

```
phil@pgp.com--> pgp -kd phil
Pretty Good Privacy(tm) 2.6.1 - Public-key encryption for the masses.
 (c) 1990-1994 Philip Zimmermann, Phil's Pretty Good Software. 29 Aug 94
Distributed by the Massachusetts Institute of Technology.  Uses RSAREF.
Export of this software may be restricted by the U.S. government.
Current time: 1994/09/21 01:45 GMT

Key for user ID: Phil's Pretty Good Pizza <phil@pgp.com>
512-bit key, Key ID 43744F09, created 1994/07/07

Do you want to permanently revoke your public key
by issuing a secret key compromise certificate
for "Phil <Pretty Good Pizza>" (y/N)? y

You need a pass phrase to unlock your RSA secret key.
Key for user ID "Phil <Pretty Good Pizza>"
```

```
Enter pass phrase: Eye,Eye,PizzaPiePass phrase is good.  Just a moment....
Key compromise certificate created.
phil@pgp.com-->
```

Now when Phil runs PGP with the –kv (key view) option, PGP displays the following:

```
phil@pgp.com--> pgp -kv
Pretty Good Privacy(tm) 2.6.1 - Public-key encryption for the masses.
(c) 1990-1994 Philip Zimmermann, Phil's Pretty Good Software. 29 Aug 94
Distributed by the Massachusetts Institute of Technology.  Uses RSAREF.
Export of this software may be restricted by the U.S. government.
Current time: 1994/09/21 01:47 GMT

Key ring: '/u/phil/.pgp/pubring.pgp'
Type bits/keyID    Date         User ID
pub    510/8E5620D5 1992/11/15 Remailing Service <hfinney@shell.portal.com>
pub   1024/20BA80A9 1992/11/26 Remailer (remailer@rebma.mn.org)
pub   1024/63C0EA49 1993/08/30 Anonymous Remailer <catalyst@netcom.com>
pub    512/43744F09 1994/07/07 *** KEY REVOKED ***
                               Phil's Pretty Good Pizza <phil@pgp.com>
pub   1024/903C9265 1994/07/15 Simson L. Garfinkel <simsong@acm.org>
5 matching keys found.
phil@pgp.com-->
```

To use this key revocation certificate, Phil needs to extract it and mail it to his friends, to the PGP key servers, and probably hand it out at the pizza parlor. Here's the killer key:

```
phil@pgp.com--> pgp -kxfa phil
Pretty Good Privacy(tm) 2.6.1 - Public-key encryption for the masses.
(c) 1990-1994 Philip Zimmermann, Phil's Pretty Good Software. 29 Aug 94
Distributed by the Massachusetts Institute of Technology.  Uses RSAREF.
Export of this software may be restricted by the U.S. government.
Current time: 1994/09/21 01:53 GMT

Extracting from key ring: '/u/phil/.pgp/pubring.pgp', userid "phil".

Key for user ID: Phil's Pretty Good Pizza <phil@pgp.com>
512-bit key, Key ID 43744F09, created 1994/07/07
Key has been revoked.

Key extracted to file 'pgptemp.$00'.
-----BEGIN PGP PUBLIC KEY BLOCK-----
Version: 2.6.1

phil@pgp.com-->
```

```
mQBNAi4ci+IAAAECAJ+kloqjL0vHwkPkfSLyY1qMpXX8G6Jj9pp8EEBYw5YiLWAm
2koNER808aNxABk9aEedxVeuKL92J19DTkN0TwkABRGJAFUDBSAuf5AyJ19DTkN0
TwkBAUBoAf9+r1Ob+GivT+4csGb1okOuoc73Am+FyOuzYZdPGP04yjn69VjUp+5u
dUtptdOiG/eDcYw/iWeNJWUzAfm2u8PBtCdQaG1sJ3MgUHJ1dHR5IEdvb2QgUG16
emEgPHBoaWxAcGdwLmNvbT6JAJUCBRAuX3QPcPsJsJA8kmUBAdCbBADr1iWjmHA/
wuOE2JBd0DjPDKCu1jG4mXPz7dN55rMsil6fMsLbcxYgxPGeqfNHnMG03FMuDvYx
ucPaVnjMAg932O16xb+5YXV12eP2DTGxvsSPNTOjvOPvQus5xLk9ygEPJb8mnIMB
rTFvoVD1xNnXifnRt2PPaIE1oWSOU7B4vQ==
=nHbb
-----END PGP PUBLIC KEY BLOCK-----
phil@pgp.com-->
```

If I get a copy of Phil's key revocation certificate and add it to my public ring, this is what happens:

```
unix% pgp -ka phil-kill.asc
Pretty Good Privacy(tm) 2.6.1 - Public-key encryption for the masses.
 (c) 1990-1994 Philip Zimmermann, Phil's Pretty Good Software. 29 Aug 94
Distributed by the Massachusetts Institute of Technology.  Uses RSAREF.
Export of this software may be restricted by the U.S. government.
Current time: 1994/09/21 01:57 GMT

Looking for new keys...
Key revocation certificate from "Phil's Pretty Good Pizza <phil@pgp.com>".

Will be added to the following key:

Key for user ID: Phil <Pretty Good Pizza>
512-bit key, Key ID 43744F09, created 1994/07/07

Add this userid (y/N)? y

Checking signatures...
pub   512/43744F09 1994/07/07 *** KEY REVOKED ***
                              Phil's Pretty Good Pizza <phil@pgp.com>
sig!      903C9265 1994/08/27  Simson L. Garfinkel <simsong@acm.org>


Keyfile contains:
   1 new user ID(s)
   1 new revocation(s)
unix%
```

Be really careful with key revocation certificates! They are like poison. Once you incorporate one into your key ring, you've destroyed your copy of the public key. If you try to use a revoked key, PGP simply displays the following message:

```
This key has been revoked by its owner.
```

There is no way to unrevoke a key after the key revocation certificate has been added. If you try to use the –kr (key remove) option to get rid of it, PGP just removes the entire key.

Questions about Revoking Keys

Two questions commonly come up about revoking public keys:

Should I create a key revocation certificate if I just want to create a new public key?

No. You should use key revocation certificates only if your old key becomes *compromised*. If you just want to create a new key, make the key, and sign it with your old certificate.

If you create a key revocation certificate, how are you going to convince people that your new certificate is legitimate? Your only recourse will be to try to get all of the people who signed your first public key to sign your new one. What a pain!

Can I revoke my key if I forget my pass phrase, or if my secret key ring is deleted?

No, you can't.

You can't create a key revocation certificate if you forget your pass phrase or if your secret key ring is deleted because you need to use your secret key to sign your key revocation certificate. If you didn't, then anyone could create a key revocation certificate for your public key, and PGP would be worthless against this kind of attack.

This creates a serious problem, because one of the times that you might really want to send a key revocation certificate is when you don't have the secret key any more.

What to do?

According to the *PGP User's Guide*, "A future version of PGP will offer a more secure means of revoking keys in these circumstances, allowing trusted introducers to certify that a public key has been revoked. But for now, you will have to get the word out through whatever informal means you can, asking users to 'disable' your public key on their own individual public key rings."

One way around this problem is to create a key revocation certificate for your public key and save this revocation certificate in a special file for use in an emergency. On the other hand, if you can save your key revocation certificate, you could just as easily save a copy of your secret key in the first place! For hints on how to do this, see the section on "A Manual System for Escrowing Keys" later in this chapter.

Disabling a Public Key (–kd Option)

If you suspect that someone's public key isn't legitimate, you can disable it on your public key ring. Confusingly, you also do this with the –kd (key disable) option.

For example, if I want to disable Sam Spade's key, I would complete the following procedure:

```
unix% pgp -kd sam
Pretty Good Privacy(tm) 2.6.1 - Public-key encryption for the masses.
(c) 1990-1994 Philip Zimmermann, Phil's Pretty Good Software. 29 Aug 94
Distributed by the Massachusetts Institute of Technology.  Uses RSAREF.
Export of this software may be restricted by the U.S. government.
Current time: 1994/09/21 02:19 GMT


Key for user ID: Sam Spade <smokey@bureau.com>
768-bit key, Key ID 3F1DEA81, created 1994/08/27


Disable this key (y/N)? y
unix%
```

To reenable the key, I would simply run PGP with the –kd option a second time:

```
unix% pgp -kd sam
Pretty Good Privacy(tm) 2.6.1 - Public-key encryption for the masses.
(c) 1990-1994 Philip Zimmermann, Phil's Pretty Good Software. 29 Aug 94
Distributed by the Massachusetts Institute of Technology.  Uses RSAREF.
Export of this software may be restricted by the U.S. government.
Current time: 1994/09/21 02:22 GMT


Key for user ID: Sam Spade <smokey@bureau.com>
768-bit key, Key ID 3F1DEA81, created 1994/08/27
Key is disabled.


Key is already disabled.
Do you want to enable this key again (y/N)? y
unix%
```

According to the *PGP User's Guide*, "A disabled key may not be used to encrypt any messages, and may not be extracted from the key ring with the –kx command."

A Manual System for Escrowing Keys

The phrase *key escrow* refers to any system in which a cryptography key is stored in a special location from which it can be retrieved at a later point in time. Recently, the term *key escrow* has gotten a bad name, largely because of the U.S. government's efforts to standardize on the mandatory key escrow system. (See Chapter 4 for a discussion.) But, if you are storing encrypted files on a long-term basis or if your organization is using encryption for its day-to-day operations, you might want to set up a key escrow system of your own.

You might want to consider the following reasons for using a key escrow system for your own files:

- You might forget your key. If your key is escrowed, you can still read your files after you retrieve your key.

- You might get hit by a truck. While you are in the hospital, your friends or your spouse can use your escrowed key to access your files.

- You might get hit by a truck and be killed. Unless you want all of your secrets to die with you, you'll want to have some sort of key escrow system so that your heirs can get access to your files.

Organizations have even more reasons to consider key escrow:

- Most organizations want to be able to read an employee's files in the event that the employee unexpectedly leaves, is terminated, becomes incapacitated, or dies.

- Two people might be working on a project and need access to the same files. If one person is on vacation or otherwise inaccessible, the other needs a way to access the information.

- You might suspect that an employee is stealing trade secrets, acting illegally, or simply not acting in accordance with company policy. These are always difficult situations. When they arise, it may be important to be able to monitor the employee's files and communications.

PGP Version 2.0 makes no provisions for automated key escrow. (Version 3.0 may have some provisions, but these have yet to be finalized.) Until then, however, you can create your own manual key escrow system.

Simple Key Escrow

For a simple key escrow system, you need to create an envelope that contains all of the necessary information for people to decrypt your encrypted files. The following is one way to do this:

1. Make a copy of your secret ring file into a new file *secret.pgp*.

2. Use PGP's –ke (key edit) option to change the pass phrase on your secret key in the *secret.pgp* key ring.

3. Copy the new secret key ring *secret.pgp* onto a floppy disk.

4. Copy your public key ring file onto the same floppy disk.

5. Write your new pass phrase on a piece of paper. If you use PGP's conventional cryptography in addition to public key encryption, you can put those pass phrases on the paper as well.

6. Put the floppy disk and the piece of paper in an envelope.

7. Write your signature across the back flap of the envelope.

8. Put the envelope in a safe place.

The envelope is your escrowed key. Anyone who has access to the envelope can break the seal, recover the secret key ring, decrypt your secret key, and read files that have been encrypted with your public key.

Split-Key Escrow

The problem with the simple key escrow procedure described in the previous section is the single point of failure: the envelope with your secret key.

A better technique is to split your secret key into two parts and give each part to a different person. In order to decrypt your encrypted files, a legitimate authority (or an attacker) has to retrieve both parts. Presumably, retrieving the two parts is harder than getting a single envelope that has been locked in a safe.

PGP doesn't provide any direct support for split-key escrow. Fortunately, it is easy to improvise: simply treat the PGP secret key ring as one-half of the split and the piece of paper as the other. Put them in separate envelopes, seal each envelope, and give them to different people.

Remember: a key escrow won't do you any good if you forget where it is. And it won't do your heirs any good unless they have some way of finding it.

14

PGP Configuration File

You can use the PGP configuration file to change the way that PGP operates. A default configuration file comes with PGP. Although you don't need to make any changes to this configuration file to use PGP, you can make PGP easier to use by customizing it to your own system and security policies.

In this chapter, I take you through the PGP configuration file and all of its variables.

What is the PGP Configuration File?

When you start PGP, it reads a special configuration file called *config.txt*. This file contains the names of special PGP *configuration variables* and a value for each variable. The configuration file can also contain comments.

The following is an excerpt from the default PGP configuration file:

```
...
# BakRing is the path to a backup copy of your secret keyring, usually
# on floppy disk.  Your secret keys will be compared with the backup copy
# when doing a keyring check (pgp -kc)
# BakRing = "a:\secring.pgp"

# Number of completely trusted signatures needed to make a key valid.
Completes_Needed = 1
```

```
# Number of marginally trusted signatures needed to make a key valid.
Marginals_Needed = 2
...
```

As you can see, PGP uses the pound sign or hash mark (#) for comments. The example contains three variables. The variable COMPLETES_NEEDED is set to 1, and the variable MARGINALS_NEEDED is set to 2. The BAKRING variable is not set.

The variables set inside the PGP configuration file are internal PGP variables. They are not environment variables.

Where is the Configuration File?

The PGP configuration file, *config.txt*, normally resides in the directory pointed to by your PGPPATH environment variable. This is the same directory in which PGP keeps your public and secret key rings, *pubring.pgp* and *secring.pgp,* respectively.

If you have been using PGP, you've already got a configuration file.

Editing the Configuration File

To change the value of a configuration variable, simply edit the *config.txt* file with any standard editor. Do not delete any of the configuration variables because you may find it hard to reconstruct them later. Simply change the values as necessary. The "Configuration Variable Summary" section later in this chapter describes the variables and their default values.

Be careful when you edit your configuration file: if you screw it up, PGP may not work. Since there are no safeguards, it's a good idea to make a backup copy before starting your editor.

If you edit the PGP configuration file with a word processor such as Microsoft Word, be careful to save the file as ASCII; otherwise, PGP will be unable to read the file when you are finished with your edits.

Each item in the configuration file contains a configuration variable name, an equal sign, and a value, as follows:

```
ARMOR = ON
```

In this case, the configuration variable ARMOR is set to on.

PGP follows the following rules when it processes the configuration file:

* It ignores the case of the configuration variables. ARMOR=ON is equivalent to Armor=On or armor=on.

- The comment character is the hash mark or pound sign (#). Anything on a line following a # is ignored.

- If the same variable appears in the file more than once, only the *last* occurrence in the file has effect.

Specifying a Configuration Variable on the Command Line

Instead of editing the PGP configuration file, you can simply specify a temporary value for a PGP variable on the PGP command line. This technique is handy when you want to use PGP occasionally with a nonstandard configuration setting.

For example, if you normally send ASCII-armored files through a mail service that cannot handle messages longer than 64K, you probably have a line like the following in your *config.txt* file:

```
# ArmorLines is the maximum number of lines per packet when creating a
# transport armored file.  Set to 0 to disable splitting in parts.
Armorlines = 720
```

If at some point you want to encrypt a file using the ASCII armor option without having the message split into 720-line chunks (perhaps you are going to transfer the file using *kermit* or *Procomm* without sending it by electronic mail), you could encrypt it with the following command:

```
unix% pgp -eat bigfile Sam +ARMORLINES = 0
Pretty Good Privacy(tm) 2.6 - Public-key encryption for the masses.
(c) 1990-1994 Philip Zimmermann, Phil's Pretty Good Software. 23 May 94
Distributed by the Massachusetts Institute of Technology.  Uses RSAREF.
Export of this software may be restricted by the U.S. government.
Current time: 1994/08/28 21:13 GMT


Recipients' public key(s) will be used to encrypt.
Key for user ID: Sam Spade <smokey@bureau.com>
768-bit key, Key ID 3F1DEA81, created 1994/08/27

.
Transport armor file: bigfile.asc
unix%
```

Inside the PGP Configuration File

In this section, I have printed a copy of the default PGP configuration file from Version 2.6. (The same file is used by PGP Version 2.6.1.) As you look through it, you'll notice that most of the lines that define PGP's default values have actually been commented out. PGP can read (and ignore) a comment line faster than it can read a line from the configuration file, parse it, and set a variable to its default value.

```
# Sample config.txt file for PGP 2.6.
# Blank lines are ignored, as is anything following a '#'.
# Keywords are not case-sensitive.
# Whatever appears in here can be overridden on the command line,
# by specifying (for example) "+armor=on".

# MyName is substring of default user ID for secret key to make signatures.
# If not set, PGP will use the first key on your secret keyring (the last
# key you created) if you don't specify the user with -u
# MyName = "John Q. Public"

# The language we will be using for displaying messages to the user.
#
# Available languages:
#    en = English (default), es = Spanish, fr = French,
#    de = German, it = Italian, br = Brazilian portuguese
#
# Languages not yet available:
#    esp = Esperanto, lv = Latvian, lt3 = Lithuanian,
#    ru = Russian, nl = Dutch, #    fi = Finnish,
#    hu = Hungarian, no = Norwegian, pt = Portugese,
#    sv = Swedish, da = Danish, is = Icelandic,
#    zh = Chinese, ko = Korean, ar = Arabic, iw = Hebrew,
#    el = Greek, tr = Turkish, ja = Japanese
#
# Most of these codes are the ISO 639-1988 2-letter "Codes for
# Representation of Names of Languages"
#
Language = en

# Character set for displaying messages and for conversion of text files.
# If you set this variable to cp850, ascii or alt_codes, PGP will do
# character set conversions if TextMode = on or if you specify the -t
# option when encrypting or signing a file.
#
# Available character sets:
#    latin1, cp850, alt_codes, koi8, ascii
#
# For MSDOS with a standard character set you should use cp850 to get
# correct character translations.  Russian character sets for MSDOS are
```

```
# usually alt_codes.
#
# The default for CharSet is "noconv" which means no character conversion.
# Note that noconv, latin1, and koi8 are all treated as equivalent.
#
# CharSet = cp850

# TMP is the directory name for PGP scratch files, usually a RAM disk.
# TMP = "e:\"      # Can be overridden by environment variable TMP

# Pager is the file viewing program used for viewing messages with -m
# If not set or set to "pgp", a built-in pager will be used.  The pager set
# in config.txt will override the environment variable PAGER.
# Pager = "list"

# ArmorLines is the maximum number of lines per packet when creating a
# transport armored file.  Set to 0 to disable splitting in parts.
Armorlines = 720

# The following commented-out settings are *not* the defaults.
# Uncomment (remove the leading "#" character) them to get the
# non-default behaviour indicated.

# Armor = on           # Use -a flag for ASCII armor whenever applicable
# TextMode = on        # Attempt to use -t option where applicable
# KeepBinary = on      # Decrypt will not delete intermediate .pgp file
# verbose = on         # verbose diagnostic messages
# compress = off       # off means suppress compression to aid debugging
# showpass = on        # Echo password when user types it
# pkcs_compat = 0      # Use backwards-compatible formats


# BakRing is the path to a backup copy of your secret keyring, usually
# on floppy disk.  Your secret keys will be compared with the backup copy
# when doing a keyring check (pgp -kc)
# BakRing = "a:\secring.pgp"

# Number of completely trusted signatures needed to make a key valid.
Completes_Needed = 1

# Number of marginally trusted signatures needed to make a key valid.
Marginals_Needed = 2

# How many levels of introducers may introduce other introducers.
Cert_Depth = 4

# TZFix is hours to add to time() to get GMT, for GMT timestamps.
# Since MSDOS assumes local time is US Pacific time, and pre-corrects
```

```
# Pacific time to GMT, make TZFix=0 for California, -1 for Colorado,
# -2 for Chicago, -3 for NY, -8 for London, -9 for Amsterdam.
# However, if your MSDOS environmental variable TZ is properly defined
# for your timezone, you can leave TZFix=0.  Unix systems probably
# shouldn't need to worry about setting TZFix.
# TZFix = 0
```

Configuration Variable Summary

This section contains the meanings of the variables in the PGP configuration file. If the variable has a command line equivalent (other than simply its use on the command line with a plus sign), that equivalent is noted after the variable name in brackets [like this]. The defaults are listed in parentheses.

ARMOR [-a] (default OFF)

When turned on, this variable tells PGP to always use ASCII armor when encrypting, signing, or extracting keys into files.

ARMORLINES (default 720)

Some mailers do not forward electronic mail longer than a predefined limit. For this reason, PGP can automatically break a large file into several smaller chunks. The ARMORLINES variable specifies the maximum number of lines in a single chunk. Each line is 64 characters long. Setting ARMORLINES to 0 disables this feature.

If you are using Fidonet, set ARMORLINES to 450. (Note: if you are using Fidonet, you may discover that your encrypted email does not reach its destination. That's because some Fidonet system administrators think that *all* encryption is a cover for illegal activity and fear they will be held liable for the illegal activity of people who send mail through their systems. Since this implies that these same Fidonet administrators monitor the content of all messages that pass through their systems, perhaps their users should use encryption after all!)

BAKRING (no default)

This variable gives PGP the path of the backup copy of your secret key ring. If you define a BAKRING, the key ring check (-krc) option compares keys on your backup ring with those on your primary secret key ring.

The BAKRING variable is provided for the truly paranoid. Using it prevents someone from subverting your encryption system by changing your secret key stored in your secret key ring and then altering your copy of PGP so it allows your old pass phrase to decrypt the (new) secret key stored on the (altered) key ring. Having made these changes, your All Powerful Adversary would then distribute a subverted public key with your name on it, intercept your incoming email, and be able to read it without your knowledge.

The key check (–kc) option, used with a backup secret key ring, can prevent this nightmare scenario. Simply store a copy of your secret key on a floppy disk and, before using PGP, compare the two key rings using the key check option. (To do this, you need to set BAKRING to *a:\secring.pgp.*) If you're worried enough to set BAKRING, you'd probably better keep your backup floppy disk on your person at all times to avoid the possibility of covert action against it!

CERT_DEPTH (default 4)

The documentation for PGP states that the certificate depth variable specifies the number of levels of "introducers" that may introduce other introducers. In plain English, this variable controls how far you extend trust beyond your intimate circle of friends. If you always trust Tom to certify keys, and Tom always trusts Dick, and Dick always trusts Harry, you trust Harry when CERT_DEPTH is set to 3, but you won't trust Harry when it is set to 2. If CERT_DEPTH is set to 0, there are no introducers at all; you must certify each key on your public key ring yourself.

CHARSET (default noconv)

This variable specifies the character set you are using, so that PGP does not introduce nontext characters into text-only messages. This can be important when you are receiving messages from people who are using a different language or character set from your own. You can specify any of the following options:

noconv	No conversion
ascii	Minimal ASCII
alt_codes	IBM PC "alt codes" mapping for Cyrillic characters
latin1	ISO Latin-1
koi8	Cyrillic
cp850	IBM PC code page 850

CLEARSIG (default ON)

When turned on, this variable causes PGP to place a signature in a signed, unencrypted text file in the "clear" when text files are being signed with ASCII signatures. This allows you to read the contents of the file without using PGP (although you still need PGP and a copy of the person's public key to verify the signature). When CLEARSIG is turned off, signing a text file with an ASCII signature turns the entire file into Radix 64 gibberish, unreadable without PGP (or another suitable program).

Most people want to turn CLEARSIG on because they want to be able to read a file that has been signed without having to first run the file through PGP. On the other hand, some electronic mail systems make subtle changes to mail messages that pass through them. If your mail message ends up going through one of these mailers, the "clear" signature may not verify (and it shouldn't because the message has, in a very real sense, been changed).

COMMENT (no default)

When this variable is set to a value, the word *Comment:* followed by the contents of this option is printed at the beginning of every PGP ASCI armor file that you generate.

For example, suppose you set your COMMENT variable with the following line in your PGP *config.txt* file:

```
#
# Set a comment
Comment = Buy more O'Reilly Books.
```

Every message you encrypt begins with the following three lines:

```
-----BEGIN PGP MESSAGE-----
Version: 2.6
Comment: Buy more O'Reilly Books.
```

COMPRESS (default ON)

When turned on, this variable causes PGP to compress files before encrypting them. Compression usually compensates for the expansion you get when encoding a file in Radix 64; it also makes cryptanalysis harder. Under normal circumstances, there is no reason to turn this variable off.

COMPLETES_NEEDED (default 1)

This variable specifies the minimum number of completely trusted signatures needed to make a key valid.

ENCRYPTTOSELF (default OFF)

When turned on, this feature causes the user ID specified by MYNAME configuration variable to be automatically added to the list of recipients for any message that you encrypt with public key encryption. This allows you to read encrypted messages that you send. If you are using PGP for regular correspondence, you'll probably want to turn this feature on, because it allows you to recover the encrypted message in case the person you send it to loses her private key. On the other hand, if you are a human rights monitor in Central America, you'll probably want to leave this feature off; otherwise, the army could capture you and threaten to kill you unless you decrypt your messages. (Of course, they could still threaten you even if you have ENCRYTTOSELF turned off; you'll have to handle that situation yourself.)

LANGUAGE (default "en")

This variable enables PGP's automatic language translation feature. English is the default language. If you specify a different language in your configuration file and if that language is in the *language.txt* file, PGP uses that language for its program prompts. If the language that you specify isn't available, PGP continues to print prompts in English. If the particular prompt or message isn't in the *language.txt* file, PGP displays the English version of it.

The available languages are constantly changing. As of September 1994, the list of available languages includes those listed in the following table.[†] (Entries in the table followed by an asterisk (*) are available by anonymous FTP from the computer *ftp.informatik.uni-hamburg.de* in the directory *pub/virus/crypt/pgp/language.*)

Code	Language	Available for 2.6?
en	English	Yes, included *
es	Spanish	Yes, included[1]
fr	French	Yes, included
de	German	Yes*[2]
it	Italian	Yes*[3]
br	Brazilian Portugese	Yes, but not part of standard distribution
esp	Esperanto	Not yet
lv	Latvian	Yes*
lt3	Lithuanian	Yes*[4]
ru	Russian	Yes*
nl	Dutch	Not yet
fi	Finnish	Not yet
hu	Hungarian	Not yet
no	Norwegian	Yes*
pt	Portugese	Not yet
sv	Swedish	Yes*[5]
da	Danish	Not yet
is	Icelandic	Not yet
zh	Chinese	Not yet
ko	Korean	Not yet
ar	Arabic	Not yet

[†] Be aware that just because a language is present doesn't mean that all of PGP's strings have been translated. Phil Zimmermann is always looking for other people to put in some work on another PGP translation. Interested? Send Phil mail at *prz@acm.org*.

Code	Language	Available for 2.6?
ro	Romanian	Yes[5]
iw	Hebrew	Not yet
el	Greek	Not yet
tr	Turkish	Not yet
ja	Japanese	Yes*[6]

[1] Additional files are available on *ghost.dsi.unimi.it:/pub/crypt*.
[2] Additional files are available on *ftp.ox.ac.uk:/pub/crypto/pgp*.
[3] Additional files are available on *ghost.dsi.unimi.it:/pub/crypt*.
[4] Additional files are available on *ghost.dsi.unimi.it:/pub/crypt/pgp23ltk.zip*, *nic.funet.fi:/pub/crypt*, and *ghost.dsi.unimi.it/pgp23ltk.zip*.
[5] Additional files are available on *ftp.ox.ac.uk:/pub/crypto/pgp*.
[6] Additional files are available on *ftp.ox.ac.uk:/pub/crypto/pgp*.

INTERACTIVE (default OFF)

When turned on, this variable causes PGP to ask you for confirmation before adding a new key to your public key ring when you type **pgp –ka** filename. You might want to turn this feature on if you frequently receive key rings containing lots of people's keys and you want to add just one of them to your own key ring.

KEEPBINARY (default OFF)

When PGP creates an ASCII-armored file, it first creates a *.pgp* binary file, then converts the file to a *.asc* file, and finally deletes the *.pgp* file. When you turn the KEEPBINARY variable on, it prevents PGP from deleting the intermediate *.pgp* file. This is useful for debugging but probably not for much else.

MARGINALS_NEEDED (default 2)

This variable specifies the minimum number of marginally trusted signatures needed to make a key valid.

MYNAME [-u] (no default)

This variable specifies the default user ID for selecting the secret key for making signatures. If you do not set MYNAME, PGP uses the last secret key that you added to your secret key ring (via either the –ka or –kg options).

If you provide a name on the command line with the user (–u) option, PGP ignores the value of MYNAME.

NOMANUAL (default OFF)

When turned on, this variable allows PGP to generate a public key/secret key pair without requiring that the *PGP User's Guide* be on your hard disk. This feature is useful if you want to run PGP on a palmtop computer and don't have the space for the documentation files. (Normally, PGP won't allow you to use the key generate (–kg) option unless it can first find the documentation on your computer.)

The NOMANUAL variable is *dangerous* though, because it allows people to get working copies of PGP without also getting the manual. For this reason, *the NOMANUAL variable cannot be set in the config.txt configuration file.* You can set the NOMANUAL variable only from the command like, as follows:

```
unix% pgp -kg +NOMANUAL
```

PAGER (no default)

This variable specifies the program PGP should use when you specify the more (–m) option. If you do not set it, PGP uses its own built-in pager.

If you are using UNIX or DOS, you can specify "more" or "less" if you prefer those pagers to PGP's built-in pager.

PKCS_COMPAT (default 1)

This variable is ignored by PGP Versions 2.5 and 2.6. Previous versions of PGP used this option to allow nonstandard formats for encoding message digests and session keys. ("PKCS" stands for Public Key Cryptography Standards, a standard devised by RSA Data Security, Inc.)

PUBRING (default *$PGPPATH/pubring.pgp*)

This variable specifies the public key ring that PGP is to use by default for encrypting files with RSA and for verifying digital signatures.

RANDSEED (default *$PGPPATH/ranseed.bin*)

This variable specifies the location of the random number seed file that you created when you first created your public key.

SECRING (default *$PGPPATH/secring.pgp*)

This variable specifies the secret key ring that PGP should use for signing messages and decrypting RSA-coded files.)

SHOWPASS (default OFF)

When turned on, this variable tells PGP to echo the user's pass phrase as it is typed. Use this feature if you can't type your pass phrase without seeing it on the screen.

This option was added to PGP for people who have difficulty typing accurately on computer keyboards. Be aware, though, that other people might see your pass phrase as you type it! If you *can* type accurately without seeing the letters on the screen, you shouldn't be using this feature.

TEXTMODE [-t] (default OFF for UNIX, ON for VAX/VMS)

When turned on, this variable tells PGP that all plaintext files are text, not binary. If PGP thinks that your file is binary (by detecting 8-bit text or nonstandard control characters), it turns text mode off automatically. Even though the default is off, the PGP documentation states that it is safe to leave TEXTMODE on at all times. (If PGP determines that you are encrypting a binary file, it automatically turns TEXTMODE off.) Be sure to turn TEXTMODE on if you use PGP mostly to encrypt electronic mail.

TMP (no default)

This variable specifies the directory that PGP should use when it creates temporary files while decrypting messages. If this variable is not specified, PGP uses the environment variable TMP. If no TMP environment variable is specified, PGP uses your current directory. For optimal security, TMP should be a directory that is on your local computer (not a networked directory) and one that is protected so only you have read or write access to the files that it contains.

TZFIX (no default)

PGP needs to know how to calculate the Greenwich mean time from the local time. On UNIX systems, this calculation happens automatically (because UNIX systems know the time zone they are in). Computers running the DOS operating system must have the TZ environment variable set in their *autoexec.bat* files to tell them where they are. (See the section "TZ Environment Variable" in Appendix B for further information.)

If your DOS computer is set up badly and you are unwilling or unable to add the TZ variable to your environment, you can to some extent get around this problem by setting the TZFIX variable as follows:

    New York   −3
    Chicago   −2
    Colorado   −1
    California   0
    London   −8
    Prague   −9

Be sure to add 1 to this number, if appropriate, to accommodate daylight saving time.

TZFIX really isn't worth the effort; wouldn't you rather just set the TZ variable properly?

VEBOSE (default 1)

This variable controls the amount of information that PGP displays when it runs. The following table lists the possible settings and the information they cause to be displayed:

0   PGP displays only prompts and error messages.

1   Normal operation

2   PGP displays debugging information to tell you what it is doing.

In this chapter:
- *Communicating with a Key Server*
- *Key Server Commands*
- *Where are the Key Servers?*

15

PGP Internet Key Servers

If you have email and access to the Internet, you can easily obtain people's PGP public keys by using the PGP Internet key servers.

The PGP Internet key servers are an attempt to solve the fundamental problem of public key cryptography: how to get the public key of a person with whom you wish to communicate.

The key servers are basically copies of PGP that you can run by remote control. When you send your public key to a key server, it is added to the key ring on the key server. Anyone on the Internet can then look up your public key.

When you are using a key server, it's important to realize that there is really no way to verify whether a person's key is legitimate. It's also important to realize that most of the key servers are run by individuals; the key servers are not offered as officially supported services by the universities and businesses where they reside.

PGP and the World Wide Web

As this book went to press, an experimental PGP key interface was set up by Brian LaMacchia at the MIT Artificial Intelligence Laboratory, which lets you search for keys using World Wide Web (WWW) clients such as Mosaic. With access to the Internet and a Mosaic client, you can simply open the URL *http://www-swiss.ai.mit.edu/~bal/keyserver.html* and follow the directions.

Communicating with a Key Server

You communicate with a key server by sending and receiving electronic mail messages. To send the server a command, simply send a message to the server's email address. Include the actual text of the command you want to execute in the subject line of the message. Don't bother including any text in the message body; the key server ignores it.

A short time after you send a message to a key server, the server responds by sending you a message with the results of your command. The time it takes to receive the command output depends on the speed of the Internet connection between your computer and the server and on the number of people using the server.

For the examples in this chapter, I use the key server at MIT. The key MIT server's address is *pgp-public-keys@pgp.mit.edu*, and it is currently maintained by Derek Atkins.

Key Server Commands

The key servers support a set of commands that allow you to add your public key to the database, obtain someone else's public key, and do various related functions. The following are the main commands that the PGP public key server supports; in parentheses I've shown the corresponding PGP option, if appropriate:

help
> Sends you instructions.

add
> Adds a key to the database (–ka).

index
> Lists all PGP keys on the server (–kv).

verbose index
> Lists all of the PGP public keys with the verbose format (–kvv).

get
> Gets the whole public key database (–kxaf).

get userid
> Gets just one person's key (–kxaf *userid*).

mget regex
> Gets all the keys that match *regex*.

last days
> Gets all of the keys updated within the last *days*.

I explain these commands in the following sections of this chapter.

Getting Help

To obtain a list of commands that the key server currently supports, send a message to the key server with *help* in the subject line. The message you send might look as follows:

```
To: pgp-public-keys@pgp.mit.edu
From:your@some.company.com
Subject:help
```

The following are the first few lines of the lengthy message that the key server responds with:

```
Date: Wed, 27 Jul 94 15:30:05 EDT
To: simsong@next.cambridge.ma.us
From: PGP Key Service <pgp-public-keys@pgp.mit.edu>
Subject: Your command, HELP


Key server software written by Michael Graff <explorer@iastate.edu>

For questions or comments regarding this key server site,
contact warlord@MIT.EDU
Current version: $Revision: 2.2 $ $Date: 94/06/28 21:06:00 $


NOTE!

This service is NOT supported in any way whatsoever by MIT,
MIT/Athena, or any MIT organization.  It is here only to help transfer
keys between PGP users and is provided as a public service by myself.
```

Finding out Who is on the Server

You can use the *index* command to obtain a list of every person who has registered a key with the server. You have the following two choices:

index
Lists all the public keys.

verbose index
Lists all the public keys, along with the names of the signatures on each key.

Be advised that the public key list can be quite long! (In July 1994, it was more than half a megabyte.)

For example, to get the list of all keys, you might send the following email message to
the server:

```
To: PGP-PUBLIC-KEYS@PGP.MIT.EDU
Subject:Index
```

You can send the message with the following single UNIX command line:

```
unix% mail -s "index" pgp-public-keys@pgp.mit.edu < /dev/null
unix%
```

In response to your command, you receive a message that looks like the following:

```
Date: Wed, 27 Jul 94 15:30:28 EDT
To: simsong@next.cambridge.ma.us
From: PGP Key Service <pgp-public-keys@pgp.mit.edu>
Subject: Your command, INDEX

...


Pretty Good Privacy(tm) 2.6 - Public-key encryption for the masses.
 (c) 1990-1994 Philip Zimmermann, Phil's Pretty Good Software. 23 May 94
Distributed by the Massachusetts Institute of Technology.  Uses RSAREF.
Export of this software may be restricted by the U.S. government.
Current time: 1994/07/27 19:30 GMT

Key ring: '/site/pgp/keyring/pubring.pgp'
Type bits/keyID    Date        User ID
pub   512/0F0BBD29 1994/07/24 Robert Meier <robert@friendly.alt.za>
pub  1024/ED92A549 1994/07/27 Scott C. Best <sbest00@svpal.org>
pub  1024/FDD25D11 1994/07/27 Dennis L. Jones <dljones@powergrid.electriciti.com
pub   512/4ADCEDB5 1994/07/27 Aaron M. Huber <AaronH8025@aol.com>
pub  1024/9B17B0F9 1994/07/01 Michael J. Vargo <mvarg@ctp.com>
 ...
```

This message continues for another 300 pages.

Adding Your Key to the Server

To add your public key to the server, simply send it with ASCII armor and a subject
line of *add*. If you are using a UNIX computer, you can extract your public key from
your public key ring and send it to the server with the following single command line:

```
unix% pgp -kxfa simson | mail -s add pgp-public-keys@pgp.mit.edu
unix%
```

You only need to add your key to *one* of the PGP key servers: that server will automatically send your key to the others. Be sure to change the name "simson" to your
user ID!

Getting a Public Key from the Server

You can get public keys from the key server in two ways: all at the same time or one at a time.

Since the key server has thousands of keys (totaling several megabytes of data), I suggest that you get only the particular key that you are looking for. Simply specify in the subject line *get* followed by the user ID of the person whose key you want.

For example, to obtain my key, you could send the following message to the key server:

```
unix% mail -s "Get Simson" pgp-public-keys@pgp.mit.edu < /dev/null
Null message body; hope that's ok
unix%
```

Ignore the "Null message body" error message. Since the PGP key server looks only at the subject line, there is no message body.

Be sure that you specify a user ID! If you don't, you will get the entire key ring.

When you send an email to get my public key, the key server responds with a message similar to the following:

```
Date: Sun, 4 Sep 94 15:21:38 EDT
To: simsong@pleasant.cambridge.ma.us
From: PGP Key Service <pgp-public-keys@pgp.mit.edu>
Subject: Your command, GET Simson


Key server software written by Michael Graff <explorer@iastate.edu>

For questions or comments regarding this key server site,
contact warlord@MIT.EDU
Current version: $Revision: 2.2 $ $Date: 94/06/28 21:06:00 $


NOTE!

This service is here only to help transfer keys between PGP users and
is provided as a public service by myself.  It does NOT attempt to
guarantee that a key is a valid key; use the signators on a key for
that kind of security.  This service can be discontinued at any time
without prior notification.

Direct questions and comments to Derek Atkins <warlord@MIT.EDU>
```

```
Below is a Ascii Armored version of all or part of the master public
keyring.

To add this to your own keyring, save it to a file and "pgp -ka filename"

As a substitute to sending a ``get'' request, you may use FTP to get
        toxicwaste.mit.edu:/pub/keys/public-keys.pgp
This file is updated as new keys come in.


------8<------8<------8<------8<------8<------8<------8<------8<------8<----

-----BEGIN PGP PUBLIC KEY BLOCK-----
Version: 2.6

mQCNAi4mq/gAAAEEAPcbmtIyFTyqdpwU3HFP7XEIBGu1CXKZpzxDgDY21gKwy5uJ
nxsSbTaz//AxrHE6R1LXZXnZgEFJWp/AIr1PdwjKciRJFIvqdqooyZHSPFQ9r8oS
3Fq+0xPpOCEyPDb9+Ghv9HYcIepLwJJrcORinor5ZdzfWRyW13D7CbCQPJJ1AAUR
tCVTaW1zb24gTC4gR2FyZmlua2VsIDxzaW1zb25QGFjbS5vcmc+
=un1L
-----END PGP PUBLIC KEY BLOCK-----
```

You can save the above message to a file and use the –ka (key add) option to add my
key to your public key ring.

NOTE

Anyone can get PGP keys from the key servers: you do not need to have a
key of your own on file.

Getting a Set of Public Keys

You can get more than one key at a time by using the *mget* command. After the
command *mget,* you specify a pattern (known as a regular expression). The server
responds by sending you any key that has a user ID matching the pattern you specify.

To get all of the keys that have the letters *sim* in their user IDs, send the following
command:

```
To: PGP-PUBLIC-KEYS@PGP.MIT.EDU
Subject: MGET sim
```

To get all of the keys that have the letters *sim* or *jef* in their user IDs, send the
following command:

```
To: PGP-PUBLIC-KEYS@PGP.MIT.EDU
Subject: MGET sim|jef
```

Because the vertical bar (|) character is a special character for the UNIX shell, you need to specially quote it if you want to send this *mget* command from the command line:

```
unix% mail -s 'MGet sim|jef' pgp-public-keys@pgp.mit.edu < /dev/null
Null message body; hope that's ok
unix%
```

The regular expressions used by the *mget* command are the same as those used by the UNIX command *grep*. For example, to get all of the keys that begin with "sim", ask for "^sim". To get all of the keys that end with "edu>", ask for "edu>^".

If you have a lot of disk space, you can simply FTP the entire key ring with anonymous FTP. Look for the *public-keys.pgp* file in the directory */pub/keys*. On September 4, 1994, the key server file was 2,138,545 bytes and growing.

Getting Updated Keys

You can use the *last* command to get a list of all of the public keys added to the servers in recent days.

For example, to get a list of all the keys added in the last two days, send the following message to the key server:

```
To:PGP-PUBLIC-KEYS@PGP.MIT.EDU
Subject: LAST 2
```

I tried this command recently and received 26 keys and three key revocation messages; 3 of the keys belonged to the same person, 6 belonged to people with *.com* suffixes in their email addresses, 7 were from universities, and 5 came from outside the United States.

Where are the Key Servers?

The following is a list of PGP Internet key servers as of this printing. I have also included the names of the people who maintain the servers.

pgp-public-keys@pgp.mit.edu
Derek Atkins (*warlord@mit.edu*)
FTP: *toxicwaste.mit.edu:/pub/keys/public-keys.pgp*

pgp-public-keys@pgp.ai.mit.edu
Brian LaMacchia (*bal@zurich.ai.mit.edu*)

pgp-public-keys@pgp.ox.ac.uk
Paul Leyland (*pcl@sable.ox.ac.uk*)
FTP: ftp.ox.ac.uk:/pub/crypto/pgp

pgp-public-keys@cs.tamu.edu
Gary Ratterree (*garyr@cs.tamu.edu*)

pgp-public-keys@chao.sw.oz.au
Jeremy Fitzhardinge (*jeremy@sw.oz.au*)

pgp-public-keys@dsi.unimi.it
David Vincenzetti (*vince@dsi.unimi.it*)

pgp-public-keys@jpunix.com
John Perry (*perry@jpunix.com*)

pgp-public-keys@proxima.alt.za
Lucio de Re (*lucio@proxima.Alt.ZA*)

Appendices

This part of the book contains system-specific and summary material. It contains the following appendices:

- Appendix A, *Getting PGP*, explains how you can obtain your own copy of PGP.

- Appendix B, *Installing PGP on a PC*, explains how you can install and run PGP on a computer running DOS.

- Appendix C, *Installing PGP on a UNIX System*, explains how you can get PGP up and running on most computers running the UNIX operating system.

- Appendix D, *Installing PGP on a Macintosh*, explains how you can install and run PGP on a Macintosh computer.

- Appendix E, *Versions of PGP*, describes the different versions of PGP.

- Appendix F, *The Mathematics of Cryptography*, describes the underlying mathematics of the Diffie-Hellman algorithm that first defined public key cryptography, the mathematics of the RSA algorithm in PGP, and the mathematics of PGP itself.

In this appendix:
- *Getting PGP from MIT*
- *Other Ways of Getting PGP*

A

Getting PGP

Before you can use PGP, you must first get a copy and set it up.

Since PGP is freeware, you might be able to simply get a copy from a friend who happens to already have one. (Remember to get the documentation files and a copy of your friend's public key at the same time.) Remember, though, that you can't do this if you will be using PGP commercially and you can't get a copy in the U.S. to use overseas.

In some cases it's better not to acquire PGP in a casual way. You may not know anyone who has PGP, you may want to be sure that you get the most up-to-date version available, or, most importantly, you may want to get your copy of PGP directly from the source (to minimize the possibility of tampering or contamination by virus).

Getting a Commercial Version of PGP

To get a commercial version of PGP, contact:

ViaCrypt
9033 North 24th Avenue, Suite 7
Phoenix, AZ 85021
Voice: 602-944-0773
Fax: 602-943-2601

This appendix contains detailed instructions on how to get PGP Version 2.6.1 from its "official" source—the FTP server at MIT. It also explains how you can get additional online information about PGP, PGP shells for Windows and the Macintosh, other PGP-related products, and other security resources.

NOTE

You need to have full access to the Internet to follow the steps outlined in this appendix. If you have only electronic mail access to the Internet through an online service such as Prodigy, CompuServe, America Online, or Delphi, you might want to look at your service provider's library of downloadable files. PGP is probably available there, and getting it directly from your service will probably be easier than following the steps in this appendix.

Getting PGP from MIT

Since June 1994, the Massachusetts Institute of Technology has been the official home of PGP. That's great, because it means that you always know where to get the most up-to-date version of PGP—directly from the source in Cambridge, Massachusetts.

MIT has had to specially modify its FTP server to make it difficult and complicated to download the PGP program. MIT has done this not to make your life more complicated but to abide by the terms of the U.S. export laws, which forbid exporting cryptographic software without a license. MIT's convoluted FTP server is designed to prevent people outside the United States from getting a copy of PGP.

MIT's server attempts to enforce the U.S. export control laws and other requirements related to patents in three ways:

- The FTP server does not allow people outside the U.S. to download a copy of PGP. (The server determines whether you are inside or outside the United States from the address of the computer from which you are initiating your FTP request.)

- The FTP server makes you certify that you are a U.S. citizen (or a lawfully admitted alien), and it makes you promise that you won't export PGP in any way that is not lawful. It also makes you promise to abide by the terms of the RSAREF (RSA toolkit) license and not to use PGP for commercial purposes.

- The FTP server keeps its copy of PGP in a secret directory. After you answer "yes" to its questions, it puts a copy of PGP in a directory with a special name and tells you that name. You then have one minute to pick up the copy of PGP.

Notice that the only way that you can get the copy of PGP is by answering the server's questions. By doing this, MIT feels that it is discharging its responsibility under the law. If you break your word and export a copy of PGP, well, that's your business. Remember that doing so *is* illegal and the penalties are substantial (as much as a million dollars and ten years in jail *per offense*).

See Chapter 2 for more information about export and patent issues relating to PGP.

Getting PGP via the World Wide Web

If you have access to the World Wide Web (WWW) with Mosaic or some other Web browser, you can get PGP with a simple, graphical user interface rather than with the telnet and ftp approach described in this appendix. Simply open the URL *http://web.mit.edu/network/pgp-form.html* and follow the directions.

What to Type

Assume that you are sitting at the keyboard of a computer connected to the Internet. Your first step is to use the *ftp* command to connect to the appropriate FTP server. At the time I wrote this book, this server name was *net-dist.mit.edu*. Log in as **anonymous** and type your complete email address as the password. You should see something that looks like the following:

```
unix% ftp net-dist.mit.edu
Connected to BITSY.MIT.EDU.
220 bitsy FTP server (Version wu-2.4(1) Thu Apr 14 20:21:35 EDT 1994) ready.
Name (net-dist.mit.edu:simsong): anonymous
331 Guest login ok, send your complete e-mail address as password.
Password:simsong@acm.org
230-Welcome, archive user!  This is an experimental FTP server.  If have any
230-unusual problems, please report them via e-mail to ftp-bugs@bitsy
230-If you do have problems, please try using a dash (-) as the first character
230-of your password -- this will turn off the continuation messages that may
230-be confusing your ftp client.
230-
230-Please read the file README
230-  it was last modified on Sat May 28 19:19:36 1988 - 2247 days ago
230 Guest login ok, access restrictions apply.
ftp>
```

It is important that you follow the directions that the server gives you *to the letter*. If you do not, the FTP procedure may not work. The next step is to pick up a copy of the *README* file and look at it. (I read the file by typing Control-Z to suspend the *ftp* program and running the *cat* program to display the file on the terminal.)

```
ftp> get README
200 PORT command successful.
150 Opening ASCII mode data connection for README (597 bytes).
```

```
226 Transfer complete.
local: README remote: README
614 bytes received in 0.8 seconds (0.75 Kbytes/s)
ftp> ^Z
Stopped
unix% cat README
A description of the contents of public directories:

        /hosts          Contains various host tables, check the dates!
        /kerberos       Documents pertaining to the Kerberos Authentication
                        system.
        /netusers       Campus network users group info.  Archive file of
                        net-users@bitsy.mit.edu mailing list.
        /ols            Contains MIT Lab Supplies catalog, online form.
        /pub            Contains programs and documents.
        /unix           Network and mail configuration files for Unix systems.
        /vms            Network configration files for VAX/VMS systems.


Other directories are for maintenance purposes.

-Ron Hoffmann
 Telecommunications
 28 May, 1988
unix%>
```

Okay! Now we are getting somewhere! Apparently, Ron Hoffmann is telling us that the PGP program is in the */pub* directory. Let's restart the *ftp* program by typing a percent sign (%) and take a look:

```
unix% %
ftp net-dist.mit.edu

ftp> cd pub
250 CWD command successful.
ftp> ls -l
200 PORT command successful.
150 Opening ASCII mode data connection for /bin/ls.
total 17
drwxr-xr-x  3 435          512 Jul 18 16:50 PGP
drwxr-x---  3 435          512 Jul 18 16:50 TechMail-PEM
drwxrwxr-x  5 0            512 May 27  1993 anti-virus
drwxrwxr-x  2 0            512 Apr 30 14:05 assignments
drwxrwxr-x  4 0            512 Aug 12  1993 audit
drwxrwxr-x  2 17245        512 Jul 27  1992 cso
drwxrwxr-x 14 0            512 Jul 18 15:15 dos
drwxrwxr-x  2 0            512 Jul 27  1992 ethernet
drwxr-xr-x  3 0            512 Feb 22  1993 kerberos
drwxrwxr-x 20 15419        512 Jul 19 13:11 mac
drwxrwxr-x  3 0            512 Dec  4  1993 maps
```

```
drwxrwxr-x  2 0            512 Dec 16  1993 misc
drwxrwxr-x  2 0            512 Sep  4  1992 pop
drwxrwxr-x  2 0            512 Jun  8 16:37 resnet94-docs
drwxr-xr-x  3 435          512 Jul 27  1992 security
drwxrwxr-x  3 15806        512 Jul 18 16:50 telnet
drwxrwxr-x  2 425          512 Jul 27  1992 virus
226 Transfer complete.
remote: -l
918 bytes received in 0.78 seconds (1.15 Kbytes/s)
ftp>
```

Jackpot! At the top of the list is a directory called *PGP*. Change to that directory and take a look:

```
ftp> cd PGP
50-In order to get PGP, get the file labeled README and ***read*** it.
250-Note in particular that one of the steps involves ***telneting*** to
250-net-dist.mit.edu.
250-
250-In order for the procedure to work, you must be coming from an ftp
250-client whose IP address can be reversed resolved into a legal DNS
250-name.  Furthermore, the DNS name must either be "obviously" from the
250-U.S., or is on a special exception list.  If you have trouble getting
250-the files *AFTER* you have read and followed carefully the
250-instructions in the README file, AND your host is in the United States
250-or Canada, AND your host has an IP address which can be reversed
250-resolved into a legal DNS name, send mail to postmaster@bitsy.mit.edu.
250-Include the DNS name of your host, and the email address you entered
250-as a password when you started your anonymous FTP session.
250-
250-Please read the file README
250-  it was last modified on Tue Sep  6 14:17:53 1994 - 12 days ago
250 CWD command successful.
ftp>
```

We need to get another *README* file:

```
ftp> ls -l
200 PORT command successful.
150 Opening ASCII mode data connection for /bin/ls.
total 456
-rw-rw-r--  1 0             823 May 31 19:47 .message
-rw-rw-r--  1 0             819 May 31 19:45 .message~
-rw-rw-r--  1 0               0 Jul 18 16:50 .usa-only
-r--r--r--  1 435         15545 Jun  7 16:01 PGP_FAQ
-r--r--r--  1 435          3783 Sep  6 14:17 README
drwx--x---  4 1             512 Sep 18 15:30 dist
-r--r--r--  1 435          2539 May 24 11:56 mitlicen.txt
-r--r--r--  1 435         36518 May 21 18:10 pgformat.doc
-r--r--r--  1 435        163468 Sep  5 20:28 pgp261dc.zip
```

```
-r--r--r--  1 435           82964 Sep  3 00:28 pgpdoc1.txt
-r--r--r--  1 435          130164 Sep  4 21:46 pgpdoc2.txt
-r--r--r--  1 435            7483 May 23 22:39 rsalicen.txt
226 Transfer complete.
remote: -l
688 bytes received in 0.28 seconds (2.4 Kbytes/s)
ftp> get README
200 PORT command successful.
150 Opening ASCII mode data connection for README (3783 bytes).
226 Transfer complete.
local: README remote: README
3845 bytes received in 1.69 seconds (2.22 Kbytes/s)
ftp>
```

Now that we have the file, let's see what is inside it:

```
ftp> ^Z
Stopped
unix% cat README
This file contains  instructions on how  to obtain  PGP 2.6.1 from  MIT.
The PGP documentation is available  in this directory  either as the two
files  pgpdoc1.txt (Volume I of the  manual) and pgpdoc2.txt (Volume II)
or as the ZIP file pgp261dc.zip. This directory (/pub/PGP) also contains
the file  pgformat.doc which  describes  the  internal   format of PGP
messages.

In order get the PGP 2.6.1 software itself,  you need to first fetch and
read  the files  rsalicen.txt   and  mitlicen.txt. The   first  of these
contains the license agreement for the version of RSAREF that is used by
PGP 2.6.1.  The later  file contains a license  from MIT to you  (if you
choose to download PGP 2.6.1).

If you agree  with the licenses, you should  now "telnet" (remote login,
*not* FTP)  to net-dist.mit.edu and  login on  the "getpgp" account. You
will be required  to answer four questions after  which the location  of
the PGP software will  be provided to you. You  then again use anonymous
ftp (login  as anonymous giving  your e-mail  address as  your password,
note: do *not*  login as "getpgp") to  get the  actual  software. The
location of the software will be something of the form:

                    /pub/PGP/dist/U.S.-only-xxxx

where the -xxxx will be a randomly appearing set  of letters and digits.
Note:  you must change directly to  this directory  as the /pub/PGP/dist
directory itself is not listable.

There are two common reasons why  you may not  be able to change to this
directory. The first has to do with the fact that  the exact name of the
hidden directory is changed at the top and bottom of each hour. You must
```

be sure to attempt to change to the hidden directory within the same
half hour as you did the "telnet" command to obtain the filename.

The second reason you may have trouble is because our distribution FTP
server believes that your host is outside of the United States. If you
are in fact in the U.S. you should send mail to:

postmaster@net-dist.mit.edu. Please include the fully qualified domain
name of the system from which you attempted the FTP transaction.

Below is a copy of the questions you will be asked when you telnet to
net-dist.mit.edu and login as "getpgp":

This distribution of PGP 2.6.1 incorporates the RSAREF(tm) Cryptographic
Toolkit under license from RSA Data Security, Inc. A copy of that
license is in the file /pub/PGP/rsalicen.txt available via anonymous FTP
from net-dist.mit.edu (note: login as anonymous *not* getpgp). In
accordance with the terms of that license, PGP 2.6.1 may be used for
non-commercial purposes only.

PGP 2.6.1 and RSAREF may be subject to the export control laws of the
United States of America as implemented by the United States Department
of State Office of Defense Trade Controls.

Users who wish to obtain a copy of PGP 2.6.1 are require to answer the
following questions:

   Are you a citizen or national of the United States or a person who
   has been lawfully admitted for permanent residence in the United
   States under the Immigration and Naturalization Act?

<type "yes" or "no">

   Do you agree not to export PGP 2.6.1, or RSAREF to the extent
   incorporated therein, in violation of the export control laws of the
   United States of America as implemented by the United States
   Department of State Office of Defense Trade Controls?

<type "yes" or "no">

   Do you agree to the terms and conditions of the RSAREF license (in
   /pub/PGP/rsalicen.txt)?

<type "yes" or "no">

   Will you use PGP 2.6.1 solely for non-commercial purposes?

```
<type "yes" or "no">
-------------------------------------------------------------------------------
unix%
```

In case you're confused, I'll provide a brief explanation of what the *README* file is saying. MIT is unwilling to let people FTP a copy of the PGP program unless they answer "yes" to the following four questions:

- Are you a U.S. citizen?

- Do you promise not to export PGP or RSAREF outside the United States?

- Do you agree to abide by the terms of the RSAREF license?

- Will you use PGP solely for noncommercial purposes.

Unfortunately, there is no way to ask you these questions from within the *ftp* program. Therefore, MIT makes you use the *telnet* command to connect to a special program running on *net-dist.mit.edu* that can ask you these questions. After you answer these questions, the special program tells you how to get your own copy of PGP.

Let's do it! We'll look at the entire dialog and then follow it, step by step.

```
unix% telnet net-dist.mit.edu
Trying 18.72.0.3... Connected to BITSY.MIT.EDU.
Escape character is '^]'.


ULTRIX V4.2A (Rev. 47) (bitsy)

login: getpgp
Warning: no Kerberos tickets obtained.
Athena Server (DSMAXINE) Version 7.4G Mon Jul 27 10:22:03 1992


This distribution of PGP 2.6.1 incorporates the RSAREF(tm) Cryptographic
Toolkit under license  from RSA Data Security,  Inc. A copy  of  that
license is in the file /pub/PGP/rsalicen.txt available via anonymous FTP
from net-dist.mit.edu (note: login as  anonymous *not* getpgp).   In
accordance with  the terms of that license,  PGP 2.6.1  may be  used for
non-commercial purposes only.

PGP 2.6.1 and RSAREF may be subject to  the export  control  laws of the
United States of America as implemented  by the United States Department
of State Office of Defense Trade Controls.

Users who wish to obtain a copy of PGP 2.6.1 are required to  answer the
following questions:
```

```
    Are you a citizen or  national of the United States  or a person who
    has  been lawfully admitted   for permanent residence  in the United
    States under the Immigration and Naturalization Act?

<type "yes" or "no"> yes

    Do  you agree not to export  PGP 2.6.1,  or RSAREF  to the  extent
    incorporated therein, in violation of the export control laws of the
    United States   of  America as   implemented by the    United States
    Department of State Office of Defense Trade Controls?

<type "yes" or "no"> yes

    Do you agree  to the terms and  conditions of the RSAREF license (in
    /pub/PGP/rsalicen.txt)?

<type "yes" or "no"> yes

    Will you use PGP 2.6.1 solely for non-commercial purposes?

<type "yes" or "no"> yes

To get PGP 2.6.1  use anonymous FTP to net-dist.mit.edu and look  in the
directory:

                   /pub/PGP/dist/U.S.-only-91b3

Note:  Use anonymous FTP,  do  not attempt to login  to  on the "getpgp"
account.

Holding for 60 seconds ^C to quit sooner.
Connection closed by foreign host.
unix%
```

The *telnet* program allows us to log on to a workstation at MIT's Project Athena.
Specify the login **getpgp** to run the special PGP distribution program. The PGP distribution program first summarizes the licensing information we need to know and asks
us the four questions we discussed previously; we reply "yes" to each. Next the
program tells us where we can obtain our own copy of PGP. This time, the copy was
placed in the directory */pub/PGP/dist/U.S.-only-91b3*. Presumably, if you try to get
PGP from that directory, you are told that PGP is in a different directory. (The directory name changes every few minutes.)

Now that we know where PGP is hiding. Let's restart the FTP program by typing the
% sign and pick up our own copy:

```
unix% %
ftp net-dist.mit.edu
```

```
ftp> cd /pub/PGP/dist/U.S.-only-91b3
250 CWD command successful.
ftp> ls -l
200 PORT command successful.
150 Opening ASCII mode data connection for /bin/ls.
total 4281
-rw-rw-r--  1 0              0 Jul 18 16:50 .usa-only
-r--r--r--  1 435      504670 Jun 15 13:31 MacPGP2.6-68000.sea.hqx
-r--r--r--  1 0        504508 Jun  9 17:16 MacPGP2.6.sea.hqx
-r--r--r--  1 0        852665 Jun  9 17:08 MacPGP2.6.src.sea.hqx
-r--r--r--  1 435         560 Sep  5 20:31 files.md5
-r--r--r--  1 435      277952 Sep  5 20:28 pgp261.zip
-r--r--r--  1 435      163468 Sep  5 20:28 pgp261dc.zip
-r--r--r--  1 435      804754 Sep  5 20:26 pgp261s.tar.Z
-r--r--r--  1 435      532982 Sep  5 20:26 pgp261s.tar.gz
-r--r--r--  1 435      644653 Sep  5 20:27 pgp261s.zip
226 Transfer complete.
remote: -l
567 bytes received in 0.71 seconds (0.78 Kbytes/s)
ftp>
```

This directory contains several files that might be of interest to you. Note that these filenames were correct at the time of this writing, but they may change as new versions of PGP become available:

MacPGP2.6-68000.sea.hqx

MacPGP2.6.sea.hqx

MacPGP2.6.src.sea.hqx

These files are all versions of PGP for the Macintosh computer. The extension *.sea* means that the file in a self-extracting archive. The *.hqx* extension means that the file has been encoded in the special Macintosh binary ASCII file format. (This is similar to PGP's armor file format.) To read these files, you need BinHex or a similar Macintosh utility. See Appendix D for information about PGP for the Macintosh.

files.md5

This is a PGP-signed file containing the MD5 message digests for each of the PGP distribution files.

pgp261.zip

This is a version of PGP for DOS-based computers. This file is compressed with the ZIP format; it can be UNZIPped with a program called *unzip* or *pkunzip*. See Appendix B for information about installing PGP on a PC.

pgp261dc.zip

This is the documentation for PGP, and it's compressed with the *zip* program discussed previously.

pgp261s.tar.Z

This is the PGP source code, bundled together with the UNIX *tar* utility and compressed with the UNIX *compress* program See Appendix C for information about PGP for computers running UNIX.

pgp261s.tar.gz

This is the same PGP source code except this file is compressed with *gzip*, a more efficient file compression utility. (Notice that the file is smaller). Not everybody has *gzip*, so MIT includes versions of the source that are compressed with both *compress* and *gzip*.

pgp261s.zip

This is the same PGP source code except this file is compressed with the *zip* file format. This is probably the source code that you want to get if you need to compile PGP for a DOS-based computer.

Remember that the version numbers on these files may have changed from what you see in this appendix by the time you pick them up. The FTP server may also contain versions of PGP available for other computers.

MIT provides ready-to-run versions of PGP for Macintosh and DOS computers but not for UNIX. The folks at MIT do this for two reasons. First, they assume that most people who want to use PGP on a UNIX workstation already have a C compiler and they can probably compile their own versions. And second, they assume that most people who have a Mac or a PC probably *don't* have a C compiler, and they make things easier for them. Both of these assumptions are probably correct.

A third reason that MIT doesn't provide an executable version of PGP for UNIX work-stations is that there are *so many different kinds of UNIX workstations*, and it would be impractical to offer executables for every single one.

To transfer these files, first change the file type to binary. You don't need to set a binary file type if you are picking up the Macintosh **.hqx* files, but it won't hurt.

Let's pick up the Macintosh, DOS, and UNIX versions of PGP:

```
ftp> binary
200 Type set to I.
ftp> get MacPGP2.6.sea.hqx
200 PORT command successful.
150 Opening BINARY mode data connection for MacPGP2.6.sea.hqx (504508 bytes).
226 Transfer complete.
local: MacPGP2.6.sea.hqx remote: MacPGP2.6.sea.hqx
```

```
504508 bytes received in 2.5e+02 seconds (1.96 Kbytes/s)
ftp> get pgp261.zip
200 PORT command successful.
150 Opening BINARY mode data connection for pgp261.zip (277952 bytes).
226 Transfer complete.
local: pgp261.zip remote: pgp261.zip
277952 bytes received in 1.3e+02 seconds (2.08 Kbytes/s)
ftp> get pgp261s.tar.gz
200 PORT command successful.
150 Opening BINARY mode data connection for pgp261s.tar.gz (532982 bytes).
226 Transfer complete.
local: pgp261s.tar.gz remote: pgp261s.tar.gz
532982 bytes received in 2.6e+02 seconds (2.00 Kbytes/s)
ftp> quit
221 Goodbye.
unix%
```

Don't be confused by the scientific notation in which the UNIX *ftp* command prints the time required to transfer these files on some systems: just remember that "2.6+e02 seconds" really means "260 seconds," and you'll be just fine.

At this point, you have transferred all the files you need to install and run PGP. If you are running DOS, go to Appendix B; for UNIX, go to Appendix C; for the Macintosh, go to Appendix D.

Other Ways of Getting PGP

If you don't want to deal with the hassle of the MIT PGP server, you can pick up PGP from many other sites on the Internet. PGP 2.6 is available even on sites outside the United States (although most Europeans are using PGP Version 2.6ui, which does not include any code from RSA Data Security). The Internet contains many other PGP-related resources.

Remember that resources are always being added and filenames may change.

University of Hamburg: Lots of Crypto Resources

If you have Internet access, one European FTP site you may wish to check out is *ftp.informatik.uni-hamburg.de*. This site has many tools for encryption and computer security in general. It has translations for PGP in many languages other than English. It also contains a whole host of PGP and other security tools that are beyond the scope of this book.

The following is a sample from the University of Hamburg's *virus/crypt/pgp/tools* directory:

```
virus/crypt/pgp/shells:
total 1439
-rw-r--r--   1 bontchev       3391 Aug  7 15:45 X11pgp.zip
-rw-r--r--   1 bontchev     304556 Jul 18 16:15 jwps16.zip
-rw-r--r--   1 bontchev      62885 Jun  3 16:07 pgpfront.zip
-rw-r--r--   1 bontchev      13009 Jan 24  1994 pgpmenu.zip
-rw-r--r--   1 bontchev     135370 Jul 20 18:08 pgpsh32a.zip
-rw-r--r--   1 bontchev      65613 May 13  1993 pgpshel2.zip
-rw-r--r--   1 bontchev     233854 Jul 16 20:09 pgpw26.zip
-rw-r--r--   1 bontchev      13825 Jan 24  1994 pgpwin11.zip
-rw-r--r--   1 bontchev      67031 Jul 30 15:56 pgs099e.zip
-rw-r--r--   1 bontchev      62766 Jun  3 15:45 pwf20.zip
-rw-r--r--   1 bontchev     456860 Jun  3 15:08 winpgp10.zip

virus/crypt/pgp/tools:
total 1891
-rw-r--r--   1 bontchev       4362 Feb  9  1994 PGPTools.readme
-rw-r--r--   1 bontchev     127544 Feb  9  1994 PGPTools.tar.gz
-rw-r--r--   1 bontchev      58763 Jul  6 20:51 PGPsendmail-v1.2.tar.gz
-rw-r-----   1 bontchev     142422 Jul 26 16:11 apgp212.zip
-rw-r--r--   1 bontchev      26286 Jun 27 17:33 auto-pgp.tar.gz
-rw-r--r--   1 bontchev     119970 Jun  3 13:08 contrib.zip
-rw-r--r--   1 bontchev      17077 Jun 17 13:42 mess11.zip
-rw-r--r--   1 bontchev     888243 Jan 31  1994 pgp-elm.zip
-rw-r--r--   1 bontchev      40926 Jul 14 22:11 pgpblu25.zip
-rw-r--r--   1 bontchev       2940 Jun  9 12:54 pgpchat1.zip
-rw-r--r--   1 bontchev       4134 Nov 22  1993 pgpclient.zip
-rw-r--r--   1 bontchev      14222 Nov 20  1993 pgpd.tar.gz
-rw-------   1 bontchev      13924 Aug 18 19:12 pgpsort.zip
-rw-r--r--   1 bontchev     152755 Aug 24  1993 pgptalk.2.0.tar.gz
-rw-r--r--   1 bontchev     125130 Aug 23 04:35 phi-pgp.tar.gz
-rw-r--r--   1 bontchev      52767 Jul  5 14:54 privtool-0.80.tar.gz
-rw-------   1 bontchev      44052 Aug  7 14:28 rem200.zip
-rw-r--r--   1 bontchev       1411 Jul 27 11:38 remail.shar.gz
-rw-r--r--   1 bontchev      19172 Jun  7 19:02 stealth.zip
```

University of California at Berkeley: The Cypherpunks

The computer *ftp.csua.berkeley.edu* is the official Cypherpunk repository. In this computer's archives you can find copies of PGP, the source code for PGP key servers and remailers, polemics, the full text of the patents that affect public key cryptography, and much more.

Netcom: The PGP FAQ and Other Information

The user *qwerty@netcom.com* has amassed a large collection of cryptography-related files that are publicly available from the computer *ftp.netcom.com* in the directory */pub/qwerty*. A sampling of that computer's directory includes the following:

```
-rw-r--r--  1 13005        407 Aug  7 19:49 .message
-rw-r--r--  1 13005     121525 Feb 20  1994 Cryptography.FAQ
-rw-r--r--  1 13005      26491 Mar  3  1994 DOS.pgp.startup.guide
-rw-r--r--  1 13005     211470 Aug  7 19:46 Eudora.PGP.AppleScripts0.5.sea.hqx
-rw-r--r--  1 13005      34874 Mar 14 03:40 FBI.wants.to.tap.your.phone
-rw-r--r--  1 13005      15741 Aug 23 02:49 Greg.Eudora.PGP.scripts.hqx
-rw-r--r--  1 13005      21416 Apr 12 18:21 How.to.MacPGP2.3
-rw-r--r--  1 13005      21495 Jun 10 16:52 How.to.MacPGP2.3a
drwxr-xr-x  2 13005       4096 Aug  7 19:45 MCIP/
-rw-r--r--  1 13005      27862 Jul 16 23:30 MCIP.archive.July94
-rw-r--r--  1 13005     181571 Jul 29 01:53 MacPGP.Kit.1.1.Sources.hqx
-rw-r--r--  1 13005     940768 Aug 29 19:01 MacPGP.Kit.1.2.Installer.hqx
-rw-r--r--  1 13005         95 Aug 29 20:50 MacPGP.Kit.1.2.README
drwxr-xr-x  2 13005       4096 Jun 28 15:19 MacUtilities/
-rw-r--r--  1 13005      44509 Apr 18 01:23 PGP.FAQ.1
-rw-r--r--  1 13005      44345 Apr 18 01:23 PGP.FAQ.2
-rw-r--r--  1 13005      44382 Apr 18 01:23 PGP.FAQ.3
-rw-r--r--  1 13005      44627 Apr 18 01:23 PGP.FAQ.4
-rw-r--r--  1 13005      32938 Jun 15 04:59 PGP.FAQ.5
-rw-r--r--  1 13005      32892 Aug 12 04:41 PGP.FTP.Sites.FAQ
-rw-r--r--  1 13005      14497 Mar  8  1994 PGP.ftp.sites.plus.info
-rw-r--r--  1 13005       3512 May 13 06:45 PRZ.responds.to.Sternlight
-rw-r--r--  1 13005        447 Aug 23 02:49 Pete.Eudora.PGP.scripts.bin
-rw-r--r--  1 13005      16741 Apr 17 15:49 Remailer.list
drwxr-xr-x  2 13005       4096 May 15 17:49 Stealth.for.PGP/
drwxr-xr-x  2 13005       4096 Jul  4 06:41 Steganography/
-r--r--r--  1 13005      16331 Mar 12 21:47 TEMPEST.thwarting.info
-rw-r--r--  1 13005      50524 Feb 23  1994 USA.Crypto.policy.FAQ
drwxr-xr-x  2 13005       4096 May 15 04:39 Writings/
-rw-r--r--  1 13005        845 Feb 20  1994 Xenon.public.key.asc
-rw-------  1 13005        143 Aug 29 20:52 ed.hup
drwxr-xr-x  2 13005       4096 Aug  7 19:45 incoming/
```

Electronic Frontier Foundation

The Electronic Frontier Foundation (EFF) also distributes PGP. For information on how to get it, log in to *ftp.eff.org* (login: **ftp**) and go to the */pub/Net_info/Tools/Crypto* directory. Get the *README.Dist* file for instructions.

Other Sources

According to the PGP FAQ, PGP is also available from the following FTP sites. Since the list is always changing, you should check the FAQ for an up-to-date list.

ftp.csua.berkeley.edu/pub/cypherpunks/pgp (DOS, MAC)

ftp.informatik.tu-muenchen.de

ftp.funet.fi

ghost.dsi.unimi.it/pub/crypt

ftp.tu-clausthal.de (139.174.2.10)

wuarchive.wustl.edu/pub/aminet/util/crypt

src.doc.ic.ac.uk (Amiga)

   /aminet

   /amiga-boing

ftp.informatik.tu-muenchen.de/pub/comp/os/os2/crypt/pgp23os2A.zip (OS/2)

ftp.ox.ac.ok/pub/crypto/pgp

iswuarchive.wustl.edu/pub/aminet/util/crypt (Amiga)

csn.org/mpj

nic.funet.fi

van-bc.wimsey.bc.ca

ftp.uni-kl.de

qiclab.scn.rain.com

pc.usl.edu

leif.thep.lu.se

goya.dit.upm.es

tupac-amaru.informatik.rwth-aachen.de

ftp.etsu.edu

princeton.edu

pencil.cs.missouri.edu

In this appendix:
- *Choosing a Directory*
- *Unpacking PGP*
- *Verifying Your Copy of PGP*
- *Setting up the PGP Environment on a PC*
- *Creating Your Secret Key/Public Key Pair*

B

Installing PGP on a PC

After you pick up a copy of PGP from MIT or another source on the Internet (as described in Appendix A, *Getting PGP*), you need to install it. In this appendix, I show you how to install PGP Version 2.6.1 on a PC running DOS or Microsoft Windows.

If you are using Windows, you also need to obtain a Windows "shell" for PGP. See the documentation that comes with that shell for additional Windows setup information.

Choosing a Directory

Before you can use PGP on a PC, you need to pick a directory where you want to install the program and its associated files. Most people use a directory called *PGP* in the root directory of their C drive (*C:\PGP*). Other people put all of their applications in a special directory called *apps* or *usr* or something else, as I describe later in this appendix. For the examples in this appendix, I assume that you are installing the program in the directory *C:\PGP*.

Unpacking PGP

PGP Version 2.6.1 comes in an archive file called *pgp261.zip*. The file is compressed with a compression program called *pkzip*. To install PGP on a PC, get a copy of the *pkunzip* program. To unzip it, you will need to create a directory called *PGP* on your hard disk and put *pgp261.zip* in it. Then use *pkunzip* to expand the file:

```
C:\PGP> pkunzip pgp261.zip
PKUNZIP (R)    FAST!    Extract Utility    Version 2.04c  12-28-92
```

```
Copr. 1989-1992 PKWARE Inc. All Rights Reserved. Registered version
PKUNZIP Reg. U.S. Pat. and Tm. Off.

 80486 CPU detected.
 XMS version 3.00 detected.

Searching ZIP: PGP261.ZIP
  Exploding: setup.doc
 Extracting: pgp261i.asc
 Extracting: pgp261i.zip
C:\PGP>
```

The *pgp261.zip* file contains three files:

setup.doc
Detailed installation instructions

pgp261i.zip
DOS/Windows PGP and related files

pgp261Ii.asc
A PGP signature for the file *pgp261i.zip*. This signature is signed by Jeff Schiller's 1024-bit key. (See the section "Verifying Your Copy of PGP" later in this appendix.)

The signature file was created with PGP's –sb (sign by itself) option looks like this:

```
C:\PGP> type pgp261i.asc
-----BEGIN PGP MESSAGE-----
Version: 2.6.1

iQCVAwUALmu2psUtR20Nv5BtAQHgbAP/bNd5yKL6DRChU4AjYV1fm5fBJndGYfjm
8o166TEgTY/m3oBGfkrfXR5T8AalS0+4hMSUT06W556wmJ/pfY+Q2NvfS2Dn6Rhi
04DmIWfu/XuV4Roj3GvwV91zWCmGKDsvrt6q6pp8ioKq2TsTBgOsFFEXgoRzFgW7
Lk0IBVDz5Iw=
=GOnU
-----END PGP MESSAGE-----
C:\PGP>
```

The next step is to unpack the files in *pgp261i.zip*. You can unpack it with *pkunzip* again. (The –d (directory structure) option causes *pkunzip* to put the documentation files in a separate directory; I don't know why this isn't the default.)

```
C:\PGP> pkunzip -d pgp26i.zip

PKUNZIP (R)    FAST!    Extract Utility    Version 2.04c  12-28-92
Copr. 1989-1992 PKWARE Inc. All Rights Reserved. Registered version
PKUNZIP Reg. U.S. Pat. and Tm. Off.
```

```
 80486 CPU detected.
 XMS version 3.00 detected.

Searching ZIP: PGP261I.ZIP
  Exploding: config.txt
  Exploding: doc/pgformat.doc
  Exploding: doc/keyserv.doc
  Exploding: doc/pgpdoc1.txt
  Exploding: doc/pgpdoc2.txt
  Exploding: doc/setup.doc
  Exploding: doc/politic.doc
  Exploding: doc/changes.doc
  Exploding: doc/appnote.doc
  Exploding: doc/blurb.txt
  Exploding: es.hlp
  Exploding: fr.hlp
  Exploding: keys.asc
  Exploding: language.txt
  Exploding: mitlicen.txt
  Exploding: pgp.exe
  Exploding: pgp.hlp
  Exploding: readme.doc
  Exploding: rsalicen.txt
C:\PGP>
```

These files are generally the same as their counterparts in the UNIX PGP distribution described in Appendix C. (That's not surprising because the UNIX and PC versions of PGP are built from the same source code.) Let's look at the file sizes:

```
C:\PGP> dir

 Volume in drive C has no label
 Volume Serial Number is 12D9-1B44
 Directory of C:\PGP

 .            <DIR>           09-24-94   10:28a
 ..           <DIR>           09-24-94   10:28a
 PGP261   ZIP    277,952 09-24-94    5:34a
 SETUP    DOC     15,447 09-05-94    8:10p
 PGP261I  ASC        293 09-05-94    8:24p
 PGP261I  ZIP    270,610 09-05-94    8:22p
 CONFIG   TXT      3,986 05-21-94    6:06p
 DOC          <DIR>           09-24-94   10:31a
 ES       HLP      4,379 05-06-94    3:58p
 FR       HLP      4,467 05-06-94    3:58p
 KEYS     ASC      5,895 09-03-94   12:52a
 LANGUAGE TXT     70,744 05-23-94    6:40p
 MITLICEN TXT      2,589 05-24-94   11:56a
```

```
PGP        EXE      248,348 08-29-94  10:24p
PGP        HLP        3,983 06-19-94   5:15p
README     DOC        6,768 09-05-94   4:21p
RSALICEN   TXT        7,630 05-23-94  10:39p
        17 file(s)          923,091 bytes
                         21,831,680 bytes free

C:\PGP> dir doc

 Volume in drive C has no label
 Volume Serial Number is 12D9-1B44
 Directory of C:\PGP\DOC

 .                <DIR>         07-31-94    4:30p
 ..               <DIR>         07-31-94    4:30p
 PGFORMAT DOC        37,351 05-21-94    6:10p
 KEYSERV  DOC         4,295 05-23-94    6:21p
 PGPDOC1  TXT        84,757 09-03-94   12:28a
 PGPDOC2  TXT       132,963 09-04-94    9:46p
 SETUP    DOC        15,447 09-05-94    8:10p
 POLITIC  DOC        18,215 05-07-94    3:15p
 CHANGES  DOC        18,150 09-03-94   12:17a
 APPNOTE  DOC         6,368 05-20-94    3:47a
 BLURB    TXT           730 09-03-94   12:40a
        11 file(s)          318,276 bytes
 20,987,904 bytes free
C:\PGP>
```

At this point, PGP is decompressed and ready to run. The following are some of the more important files from the PC distribution:

CONFIG.TXT

The PGP configuration file

KEYS.ASC

PGP public keys of some important people involved in the development of PGP

MITLICEN.TXT

The PGP license from the Massachusetts Institute of Technology

RSALICEN.TXT

The RSA Data Security license for RSAREF

DOC\PGPDOC1.TXT

The first half of the PGP manual

DOC\PGPDOC2.TXT

The second half of the PGP manual

Verifying Your Copy of PGP

Probably the first thing you should do is to verify that your copy of PGP works—and works safely. One easy way that you can verify your copy of PGP is to use PGP itself to verify the PGP signature on the original PGP distribution file. Doing this will help you to determine if your copy of PGP has been compromised.

To verify the authenticity of the copy of PGP that you just built, first create your public key ring, and add the keys in the *keys.asc* file to it. Then check the *pgp261i.asc* signature against the archive file *pgp261i.zip*. (Throughout this procedure, I avoid having to set up the PGP environment variables simply by working inside the PGP directory. At the end of this appendix, I show you how to set up the environment variables so you can run PGP from any directory on your computer.)

First build the *keys.pgp* file from *keys.asc*:

```
C:\PGP> pgp -ka keys.asc keys.pgp
Pretty Good Privacy(tm) 2.6.1 - Public-key encryption for the masses.
(c) 1990-1994 Philip Zimmermann, Phil's Pretty Good Software. 23 May 94
Distributed by the Massachusetts Institute of Technology.  Uses RSAREF.
Export of this software may be restricted by the U.S. government.
Current time: 1994/09/29 14:03 GMT

Looking for new keys...
pub  1024/0DBF906D 1994/08/27  Jeffrey I. Schiller <jis@mit.edu>
pub   512/4D0C4EE1 1992/09/10  Jeffrey I. Schiller <jis@mit.edu>
pub  1024/0778338D 1993/09/17  Philip L. Dubois <dubois@csn.org>
pub  1024/FBBB8AB1 1994/05/07  Colin Plumb <colin@nyx.cs.du.edu>
pub  1024/C7A966DD 1993/05/21  Philip R. Zimmermann <prz@acm.org>
pub   709/C1B06AF1 1992/09/25  Derek Atkins <warlord@MIT.EDU>
pub  1024/8DE722D9 1992/07/22  Branko Lankester  <branko@hacktic.nl>
pub  1024/9D997D47 1992/08/02  Peter Gutmann <pgut1@cs.aukuni.ac.nz>
pub  1019/7D63A5C5 1994/07/04  Hal Abelson <hal@mit.edu>

Checking signatures...
pub  1024/0DBF906D 1994/08/27 Jeffrey I. Schiller <jis@mit.edu>
sig!      C7A966DD 1994/08/28  Philip R. Zimmermann <prz@acm.org>
sig!      C1B06AF1 1994/08/29  Derek Atkins <warlord@MIT.EDU>
sig!      4D0C4EE1 1994/08/27  Jeffrey I. Schiller <jis@mit.edu>
pub   512/4D0C4EE1 1992/09/10 Jeffrey I. Schiller <jis@mit.edu>
sig!      4D0C4EE1 1994/06/27  Jeffrey I. Schiller <jis@mit.edu>
sig!      C1B06AF1 1994/06/19  Derek Atkins <warlord@MIT.EDU>
sig!      C7A966DD 1994/05/07  Philip R. Zimmermann <prz@acm.org>
pub  1024/0778338D 1993/09/17 Philip L. Dubois <dubois@csn.org>
sig!      C7A966DD 1993/10/19  Philip R. Zimmermann <prz@acm.org>
pub  1024/FBBB8AB1 1994/05/07 Colin Plumb <colin@nyx.cs.du.edu>
sig!      C7A966DD 1994/05/07  Philip R. Zimmermann <prz@acm.org>
```

```
sig!      FBBB8AB1 1994/05/07  Colin Plumb <colin@nyx.cs.du.edu>
pub  1024/C7A966DD 1993/05/21  Philip R. Zimmermann <prz@acm.org>
sig!      0DBF906D 1994/08/30  Jeffrey I. Schiller <jis@mit.edu>
sig!      4D0C4EE1 1994/05/26  Jeffrey I. Schiller <jis@mit.edu>
sig!      C7A966DD 1994/05/07   Philip R. Zimmermann <prz@acm.org>
pub   709/C1B06AF1 1992/09/25  Derek Atkins <warlord@MIT.EDU>
sig!      0DBF906D 1994/08/30  Jeffrey I. Schiller <jis@mit.edu>
sig!      4D0C4EE1 1994/05/09  Jeffrey I. Schiller <jis@mit.edu>
sig!      C7A966DD 1994/05/07   Philip R. Zimmermann <prz@acm.org>
pub  1024/8DE722D9 1992/07/22  Branko Lankester  <branko@hacktic.nl>
sig!      C7A966DD 1994/05/07   Philip R. Zimmermann <prz@acm.org>
sig!      8DE722D9 1993/11/06   Branko Lankester  <branko@hacktic.nl>
pub  1024/9D997D47 1992/08/02  Peter Gutmann <pgut1@cs.aukuni.ac.nz>
sig!      C7A966DD 1994/02/06   Philip R. Zimmermann <prz@acm.org>
pub  1019/7D63A5C5 1994/07/04  Hal Abelson <hal@mit.edu>
sig!      0DBF906D 1994/09/03  Jeffrey I. Schiller <jis@mit.edu>
sig!      C7A966DD 1994/07/28   Philip R. Zimmermann <prz@acm.org>


Keyfile contains:
   9 new key(s)

One or more of the new keys are not fully certified.
Do you want to certify any of these keys yourself (y/N)? n
C:\PGP>
```

Now check the signature:

```
C:\PGP> pgp pgp261i.asc pgp261i.zip
Pretty Good Privacy(tm) 2.6.1 - Public-key encryption for the masses.
(c) 1990-1994 Philip Zimmermann, Phil's Pretty Good Software. 23 May 94
Distributed by the Massachusetts Institute of Technology.  Uses RSAREF.
Export of this software may be restricted by the U.S. government.
Current time: 1994/09/29 21:10 GMT


File has signature.  Public key is required to check signature.
Key matching expected Key ID 0DBF906D not found in file 'C:\PGP\pubring.pgp'.
Enter public key filename: keys.pgp
File 'pgp261i.$00' has signature, but with no text.
Please enter filename of material that signature applies to: pgp261i.zip

Good signature from user "Jeffrey I. Schiller <jis@mit.edu>".
Signature made 1994/09/06 00:24 GMT
```

```
WARNING:  Because this public key is not certified with a trusted
signature, it is not known with high confidence that this public key
actually belongs to: "Jeffrey I. Schiller <jis@mit.edu>".

Signature and text are separate.  No output file produced.

C:\PGP>
```

Ah! Jeffrey Schiller signed the PGP Version 2.6.1 distribution! Anyone who knows Jeff won't be surprised by this; *bitsy.mit.edu* (the real name of the computer *net-dist.mit.edu*) is Jeff's workstation at the MIT Network Services group. Jeff manages the entire MIT campus network. (He's also a really cool guy!)

Notice, however, that we have no real way of knowing if the key provided for Jeff with the PGP distribution is *really* Jeff's key. Some hacker extraordinaire could have broken into Jeff's machine and replaced the copy of PGP being sent out to the world with one that has a subtle security flaw (perhaps a flaw that put a copy of everyone's secret key in every electronic signature). The hacker could have then replaced the *keys.asc* file with another one, signed the compromised PGP with the bogus key, and left it for everyone to pick up. How do we know that this didn't happen?

We don't.

One way that you could tell, though, would be to call Jeff and ask him for the finger-print of his public PGP key. You could then compare that fingerprint with the fingerprint of the key in the file *keys.asc*: if the fingerprints match, you can rest assured that the two are in fact the same key. Or you could simply call Jeff and ask him to give you a copy of his public key. To save Jeff the hassle of thousands of people ringing his phone and asking him for the PGP fingerprint of his key, I've included it in this book. You can find the fingerprint in "Certifying the Keys in keys.asc (Version 2.6.1)" in Chapter 12.

Setting up the PGP Environment on a PC

DOS and MS Windows allow you to create *environment variables* to tell programs about the configuration of your system. Environment variables are set with the *set* command. They are usually set in the file *autoexec.bat* when your computer boots.

A Procedure from MIT for Testing PGP

In the PGP Version 2.6.1 documentation, MIT recommends the following six-step procedure for testing the newly compiled program:

1. Create a new public and secret key pair with the user ID *test*:

    ```
    C:\PGP> pgp -kg
    ```

2. Add the keys in the file *keys.asc* to your public key ring with the –ka option:

    ```
    C:\PGP> pgp -ka keys.asc
    ```

3. Do a key ring check:

    ```
    C:\PGP> pgp -kg
    ```

4. Encrypt the documentation file *pgpdoc1.txt* with your public key:

    ```
    C:\PGP> pgp -e pgpdoc1.txt test -o testfile.pgp
    ```

5. Decrypt the file with your secret key:

    ```
    C:\PGP> pgp testfile.pgp
    ```

6. Compare the decrypted file with the original *pgpdoc1.txt* to see if they match:

    ```
    C:\PGP> cmp pgpdoc1.txt testfile
    ```

By following this procedure, you can thoroughly test PGP.

Before you can use PGP on your PC, you must make sure that at least two environment variables are properly set up. The PGP environment variables (introduced in Chapter 1) are:

PATH

Specifies which directories are to be searched when you type the name of a program at the prompt. This environment variable must include the name of the directory that contains the *pgp.exe* program.

PGPPATH

Specifies the directory that contains your key rings, the PGP configuration file, and the random number seed file.

TMP

Specifies the directory in which PGP stores its temporary files (if this is not set in the TMP configuration variable).

TZ

Specifies the time zone you are in. If you do not set the TZ environment variable, you'll probably hear the bell ring and see the following output each time you run PGP:

```
WARNING: Environmental variable TZ is not defined, so GMT timestamps
may be wrong.  See the PGP User's Guide to properly define TZ
in AUTOEXEC.BAT file.
```

PGPPATH and TZ are described in greater detail in the sections that follow.

PGPPATH Environment Variable

PGP uses the PGPPATH environment variable to determine where the PGP files are located.

Most people who use PGP on a PC put these files in a directory called *PGP*. (I've done that in the examples in this appendix.) Usually, this directory goes in the root directory, giving it the name *C:\PGP*. You set the environment variable as follows:

```
SET PGPPATH=C:\PGP
```

A person using a large or complex computer might find that the root directory on their C drive is too crowded. She might create a directory called *apps* or *usr* in her root directory and make the *PGP* directory a subdirectory, as follows:

```
SET PGPPATH=C:\USR\PGP
```

or, using the *apps* directory:

```
SET PGPPATH=C:\APPS\PGP
```

TZ Environment Variable

The TZ environment variable is PGP's way of figuring out what time it really is. While most PCs know what the local time is, the TZ variable allows PGP to determine the time according to Greenwich mean time—that is, the current time at the Royal Naval Observatory in Greenwich, England.

It's important for PGP to know the real time because PGP inserts the time into keys and signature certificates. While it's usually not critical that your computer know the right time, it's important if you are exchanging encrypted electronic mail with people in other time zones. In any event, it's really not that hard to set your TZ variable: if you do so, every other program you have that needs to know the exact time will know it as well.

To set the TZ variable, you need to edit the *autoexec.bat* file in your root directory and add a line similar to the following:

```
SET TZ=EST5EDT
```

The first three letters, EST, are the abbreviation that you use for eastern standard time. The number 5 is the number of hours that the time in your time zone differs from the time at the Royal Naval Observatory. The second group of three letters, EDT, is the abbreviation that you use when daylight saving time is in effect. (If your community doesn't use daylight saving time, leave it out.)

The following are some sample TZ settings that you might use in your *autoexec.bat* file:

City	TZ Setting
Boston	SET TZ=EST5EDT
Chicago	SET TZ=CST6CDT
Denver	SET TZ=MST7MDT
San Francisco	SET TZ=PST8PDT
Indiana	SET TZ=CST6[1]
London	SET TZ=GMT0BST
Amsterdam	SET TZ=MET−1DST
Moscow	SET TZ=MSK−3MSD

[1] Indiana doesn't use daylight saving time. Some people in that state think that daylight saving time is a Communist plot, sort of like fluoride in the water.

As is the case with the other environment variables, it doesn't matter where you put the SET TZ statement in your *autoexec.bat* file.

You can make the changes to *autoexec.bat* with your PC's EDIT program or any other text editor. (If you use a word processor such as WordPerfect or Microsoft Word, you must be careful to save the file as ASCII TEXT, or DOS TEXT, or your system not work properly.)

A Sample autoexec.bat File

This section includes a sample *autoexec.bat* file, which contains the SET TZ statement for Los Angeles (the same time zone as San Francisco) and the PGPPATH environment variable pointing at the directory that contains the PGP files:

```
C:\> type autoexec.bat
@echo off
C:\DOS\SHARE.EXE /1:500 /f:5100
C:\DOS\SMARTDRV.EXE /X
C:\MOUSE\MOUSE.COM

SET PATH=C:\;C:\DOS;C:\WINDOWS;C:\MOUSE;C:\BIN;C:\PGP
SET PROMPT=$P$G
SET TZ=PST8PDT
SET PGPPATH=C:\PGP
C:\>
```

Notice that I've also added the directory *PGP* to the PATH environment variable. I've did that because I have put both the PGP program (*pgp.exe*) and the PGP files (*config.txt, pubring.pgp, secring.pgp, ranseed.bin,* and *language.txt*) into the same directory. Most people will probably want to use PGP this way.

Creating Your Secret Key/Public Key Pair

Before you can run PGP, you need to create your secret key/public key pair. This process is described in detail in Chapter 8, *Creating PGP Keys*. Briefly, all you need to do is to type **pgp –kg** and follow the directions.

C

Installing PGP on a UNIX System

In this appendix, I show you how to compile and install, on a UNIX system, the copy of PGP Version 2.6.1 that you picked up from MIT or another source, as described in Appendix A, *Getting PGP*.

Since versions of UNIX differ, the precise prompts and filenames shown in this appendix may be slightly different from those you see on your own UNIX workstation.

Unpacking PGP on UNIX

To begin, I'll assume that you've obtained a compressed copy of the PGP source code and have placed it in a directory by itself. Your first job is to decompress the source and extract it from the tar archive. I do this in a directory called *work* in my home directory:

```
unix% pwd
/Users/simsong/work
unix% ls
pgp261s.tar.gz
unix% gunzip < pgp261s.tar.gz | tar xfv -
x setup.doc, 15097 bytes, 30 tape blocks
x pgp261si.tar, 1679360 bytes, 3280 tape blocks
x pgp261si.tar.asc, 284 bytes, 1 tape blocks
x rsaref.tar, 286720 bytes, 560 tape blocks
x rsaref.tar.asc, 284 bytes, 1 tape blocks
unix% rm pgp261s.tar.gz
unix%
```

First I display my current directory. Then I use the UNIX *ls* command to show that the directory contains a single file *pgp261s.tar.gz*. The third command line uses the GNU

unzip utility to decompress this file and pipe the result into the *tar* utility with the
xfv – options. These options extract all of the files from the tar archive on standard
input and display their names and sizes on the console. (Note that you could have
run *gunzip* and *tar* in two separate steps.) Finally, I delete the compressed file; I don't
need it anymore.

The *pgp261src.tar.gz* file contains the following five files:

```
unix% ls -l
total 1953
-rw-r--r--  1 simsong  1679360 Sep  5 20:14 pgp261si.tar
-rw-------  1 simsong      284 Sep  5 20:24 pgp261si.tar.asc
-rw-r--r--  1 simsong   286720 Sep  5 20:15 rsaref.tar
-rw-------  1 simsong      284 Sep  5 20:25 rsaref.tar.asc
-r--r--r--  1 simsong    15097 Sep  5 20:10 setup.doc
unix%
```

pgp261si.tar

A tar file containing the PGP Version 2.6.1 source code

pgp261.si.tar.asc

A PGP signature for the file *pgp261si.tar*. This signature is signed by Jeff Schiller's
1024-bit key. (See the section "Verifying Your Copy of PGP" later in this chapter.)

rsaref.tar

A tar file containing the RSAREF distribution

rsaref.tar.asc

A PGP signature for the file *rsaref.tar*, also signed by Jeff Schiller

setup.doc

Detailed instructions on how to install PGP on DOS, UNIX, and VMS computers.

The signature files were created with PGP's –sb (sign by itself) option and looks like
this:

```
unix% cat pgp26srci.tar.asc
-----BEGIN PGP MESSAGE-----
Version: 2.6.1

iQCVAwUALmu2x8UtR20Nv5BtAQHt4gP/d7qARCzx3e9crmSjGlGd5TMjk42CpFxQ
M1Cu9tJTuDyxZbCwBwrMy/5Ny/ynhU/F0cFM11fVBORX0RLOic/j9RPWPDCLIMPK
UyyRrJsTv40rUhK1u3AW99hyXKqbMOMxzbwNU24R2T5fiyd0yU+ny3URrHrvxc2C
HBzbzyHhCy0=
=0N90
-----END PGP MESSAGE-----
unix%
```

In order to compile PGP, you must untar and compile the files *rsaref.tar* and *pgp261si.tar.* RSAREF and PGP are in two different tar files. (This is a way of stressing that RSA Data Security's RSAREF toolkit is not part of PGP; PGP simply uses RSAREF as an encryption engine.)

Getting a C Compiler

To compile RSAREF and PGP, you need a C compiler. Many versions of UNIX include a C compiler. If your version does not, I recommend that you get a copy of GCC, the C compiler developed by the Free Software Foundation. You can get a copy of GCC from the computer *prep.ai.mit.edu.* Alternatively, you can purchase a CD-ROM containing the GCC binaries quite inexpensively by contacting the Free Software Foundation in Cambridge at 617-876-3296. (Even if your computer has a C compiler, you might still want to get a copy of GCC, because GCC produces better compiled code than most other compilers on the market.)

Building the RSAREF Library

Before you can build your own copy of PGP, you first need to build a copy of RSAREF. That's because PGP Version 2.5 and later versions used RSAREF as the RSA encryption engine in order to avoid infringing upon the RSA patents.

To build RSAREF for UNIX, first untar the file with the *tar* command:

```
unix% tar xf rsaref.tar
unix%
```

This creates a *rsaref* directory. The following files are in this directory:

```
unix% cd rsaref
unix% ls -l
total 22
-r--r--r--  1 simsong     17247 Jan 18  1993 README
drwxr-xr-x  2 simsong      1024 Aug 22 23:15 doc/
drwxr-xr-x  6 simsong      1024 Aug 22 23:15 install/
drwxr-xr-x  2 simsong      1024 Aug 22 23:15 rdemo/
drwxr-xr-x  2 simsong      1024 Sep  3 00:31 source/
drwxr-xr-x  2 simsong      1024 Aug 22 23:15 test/
unix%
```

README
     A file containing the license and other information for RSAREF Version 1.0

doc
     A directory containing the RSAREF documentation

install

A directory containing directories for the DOS, Macintosh, UNIX, and VAX VMS RSAREF makefiles

rdemo

A directory containing the RSAREF demonstration program, which can perform basic cryptography functions

source

A directory containing the RSAREF C source files

test

A directory containing a variety of test programs

The RSAREF source is set up so that you only need to change directory to the appropriate *install* directory and type **make**. The program should then build itself.

Let's try it!

```
unix% cd install
unix% ls -l
total 4
drwxr-xr-x  2 simsong      1024 Aug 22 23:15 dos/
drwxr-xr-x  2 simsong      1024 Sep  5 16:25 mac/
drwxr-xr-x  2 simsong      1024 Sep  4 20:14 unix/
drwxr-xr-x  2 simsong      1024 Aug 22 23:15 vax/
unix% cd unix
unix% ls -l
total 4
-r--r--r--  1 simsong      1260 Jun 22 18:59 global.h
-rw-r--r--  1 simsong      1575 Sep  4 20:14 makefile
unix% make
gcc -I. -I../../source/ -I/usr/include -O -c -DPROTOTYPES=1 -DUSEMPILIB ../../
source/desc.c
sh: gcc: not found
*** Exit 1
Stop.
unix%
```

Oops! My C compiler is "cc", not "gcc". (It's the GNU C compiler installed under a different name.) The same may apply to your system. Fortunately, you can specify the name of your C compiler as a command line argument to *make*:

```
unix% make "CC=cc"
cc -I. -I../../source/ -I/usr/include -O -c -DPROTOTYPES=1 -DUSEMPILIB ../../
source/desc.c
cc -I. -I../../source/ -I/usr/include -O -c -DPROTOTYPES=1 -DUSEMPILIB ../../
source/digit.c

...
```

```
cc -I. -I../../source/ -I/usr/include -O -c -DPROTOTYPES=1 -DUSEMPILIB ../../
source/r_random.c
cc -I. -I../../source/ -I/usr/include -O -c -DPROTOTYPES=1 -DUSEMPILIB ../../
source/r_stdlib.c
ar r rsaref.a desc.o digit.o md2c.o md5c.o nn.o prime.o rsa.o r_encode.o
r_enhanc.o r_keygen.o r_random.o r_stdlib.o
ar: creating rsaref.a
ranlib rsaref.a
unix%
```

When you see `ranlib rsaref.a`, the RSAREF library is built. Now it's time to build PGP itself.

Building PGP

Change directory to PGP's source directory, and take a look at what's there:

```
unix% cd ../../..
unix% ls
pgp261si.tar      rsaref/        rsaref.tar.asc
pgp261si.tar.asc  rsaref.tar     setup.doc
unix%
```

Untar the PGP source code:

```
unix% tar xf pgp261si.tar
```

This creates numerous files in your work directory:

```
unix% ls -l
total 2069
-r--r--r--  1 simsong       3890 May 21 18:06 config.txt
drwxr-xr-x  4 simsong       1024 Sep  3 22:03 contrib/
drwxr-xr-x  2 simsong       1024 Sep  5 20:10 doc/
-r--r--r--  1 simsong       4256 May  6 15:58 es.hlp
-r--r--r--  1 simsong       4351 May  6 15:58 fr.hlp
-r--r--r--  1 simsong       5802 Sep  3 00:52 keys.asc
-r--r--r--  1 simsong      69031 May 23 18:40 language.txt
-r--r--r--  1 simsong       2539 May 24 11:56 mitlicen.txt
-r--r--r--  1 simsong       3867 Jun 19 17:15 pgp.hlp
-rw-r--r--  1 simsong    1679360 Sep  5 20:14 pgp261si.tar
-rw-------  1 simsong        284 Sep  5 20:24 pgp261si.tar.asc
-r--r--r--  1 simsong       6640 Sep  5 16:21 readme.doc
-r--r--r--  1 simsong       7483 May 23 22:39 rsalicen.txt
drwxr-xr-x  7 simsong       1024 Aug 22 23:15 rsaref/
-rw-r--r--  1 simsong     286720 Sep  5 20:15 rsaref.tar
-rw-------  1 simsong        284 Sep  5 20:25 rsaref.tar.asc
-r--r--r--  1 simsong      15097 Sep  5 20:10 setup.doc
```

```
drwxr-xr-x  2 simsong     2048 Sep  5 16:27 src/
drwxr-xr-x  2 simsong     1024 Sep  4 22:51 vmsbuild/
unix%
```

The following is a brief description of each file:

config.txt
> A PGP configuration file

contrib
> A directory of contributed programs that aren't part of PGP itself but are useful if you have PGP

doc
> A directory containing the PGP documentation. Phil Zimmermann's PGP documentation is in this directory, as well as political polemics, information on how to use the key servers, and notes on how to incorporate PGP into other applications.

es.hlp, fr.hlp
> PGP help files in Spanish and French

keys.asc
> An ASCII-armored key file containing public keys for many of the people involved in the development of PGP

language.txt
> PGP's automatic language translation file, with translations for French and English (Other languages are available on the Internet.)

mitlicen.txt
> The copyright license for PGP

pgp.hlp
> PGP's help file in English

pgp261si.tar
> This is the original tar file containing PGP. You can delete it later, but first you are going to use PGP to verify the signature.

pgp261si.tar.asc
> The PGP signature for the PGP 2.6.1 distribution

readme.doc
> More files to read

rsalicen.txt
> Another copy of the license for the RSAREF program

rsaref
> A directory containing the RSAREF source, documentation, license, and binary

rsaref.tar, rsaref.tar.asc

> The RSAREF distribution and signature

setup.doc

> Instructions for how to get going with PGP.

src

> A directory containing the PGP source

vmsbuild

> A directory that contains special provisions for building PGP under the VMS operating system

To compile the program, first change directory into the *src* directory:

```
unix% cd src
unix% ls
3b168000.s     genprime.c     md5.c          platform.h     zbits.c
68000.s        genprime.h     md5.h          r3000.c        zdeflate.c
68000_32.s     getopt.c       mdfile.c       r3000.s        zfile_io.c
80386.S        getopt.h       mdfile.h       r3kd.s         zglobals.c
8086.asm       global.h       memmove.c      random.c       zinflate.c
armor.c        idea.c         more.c         random.h       zip.c
armor.h        idea.h         more.h         randpool.c     zip.h
ccc            idea68k.s      mpiio.c        randpool.h     ziperr.h
ccc.x28        keyadd.c       mpiio.h        rsagen.c       zipup.c
cdefs.h        keyadd.h       mpilib.c       rsagen.h       zipup.h
charset.c      keymaint.c     mpilib.h       rsaglue.h      zmatch.S
charset.h      keymaint.h     noise.c        rsaglue2.c     zmatch.asm
config.c       keymgmt.c      noise.h        sleep.c        zrevisio.h
config.h       keymgmt.h      passwd.c       sparc.S        ztailor.h
crypto.c       language.c     pgp.c          stdlib.h       ztrees.c
crypto.h       language.h     pgp.def        system.c       zunzip.c
descrip.mms    lmul.h         pgp.h          system.h       zunzip.h
exitpgp.h      makefile       pgp.mak        usuals.h
fileio.c       makefile.msc   pgp.opt        vax.mar
fileio.h       mc68020.s      pgppwb.mak     vaxcrtl.opt
unix%
```

I won't describe all of the different source files in this directory. For our purposes, it's important to notice that there are two distinct makefiles: *makefile.msc* (for Microsoft C) and *makefile* (for UNIX).

For now, you might want to just type **make** without any arguments:

```
unix% make
type:
        make <system>
```

```
where <system> can be:
        sun4gcc, sun4cc(*), sun3gcc, sun3asm, sun3cc(*), sun386i, sunspc,
        sysv_386, sco-2.0, x286(*), linux, mips-ultrix, vax-ultrix,
        xenix386, mach_386, 386bsd, isc, isc_asm, 3b1, 3b1_asm, rs6000,
        bsd, bsdgcc, vax_bsd43, rt_aos4, osf, sgigcc_asm, sgigcc, irix,
        irix_asm, newsgcc, newsasm, aux(*), aux-gcc, os2, djgpp, sun4sunos5gcc,
        hpux-pa-ansi, hpux-pa-gcc, hpux-pa(*), hpux-68k-ansi, hpux-68k-gcc
        hpux-68k(*), next, next486, nextHP, netbsd, qnx4


for targets marked with (*) you must first get unproto, see
setup.doc for further details
unix%
```

As you can see, PGP provides a list of all of the different architectures it currently supports. This is the list for PGP Version 2.6.1; if you have a later version of PGP, you may be pleased to discover that it supports even more architectures. One of the benefits of free software is that your users port your program to new architectures for you when you distribute the source code!

To compile PGP, you need to know what kind of UNIX computer you are using. Is it a Sun SPARCstation? If so, type **make sun4gcc**, if you are compiling with the GNU C compiler; type **make sun4cc**, if you are compiling with Sun's C compiler. (If you are using Sun's C compiler, you need to read the file *setup.doc* for information on how to compile the program without function prototypes.)

My computer is a NeXTstation running NEXTSTEP Version 3.3. Fortunately, the NeXT is one of the computers supported by PGP, which means that all I need to do is to type **make next**:

```
unix% make next
make all  CFLAGS="-I../rsaref/source -I../rsaref/test -DUSEMPILIB -O -arch
m68k -DNEXT -DUNIX -DHIGHFIRST  -DMACH -DPORTABLE -DNOTERMIO"
cc -I../rsaref/source -I../rsaref/test -DUSEMPILIB -O -arch m68k -DNEXT -DUNIX
-DHIGHFIRST  -DMACH -DPORTABLE -DNOTERMIO -c pgp.c


...


cc -I../rsaref/source -I../rsaref/test -DUSEMPILIB -O -arch m68k -DNEXT -DUNIX
-DHIGHFIRST  -DMACH -DPORTABLE -DNOTERMIO -c rsaglue2.c
cc              -o pgp pgp.o crypto.o keymgmt.o fileio.o  mdfile.o more.o
armor.o mpilib.o mpiio.o  genprime.o rsagen.o random.o idea.o passwd.o  md5.o
system.o language.o getopt.o keyadd.o  config.o keymaint.o charset.o
randpool.o noise.o zbits.o zdeflate.o zfile_io.o zglobals.o  zinflate.o zip.o
zipup.o ztrees.o zunzip.o  rsaglue2.o    ../rsaref/install/unix/rsaref.a
unix%
```

Congratulations! If you've been following along at your workstation, you've now got a copy of PGP. Let's run it and see what happens:

```
unix% ./pgp
No configuration file found.
Pretty Good Privacy(tm) 2.6.1 - Public-key encryption for the masses.
 (c) 1990-1994 Philip Zimmermann, Phil's Pretty Good Software. 29 Aug 94
Distributed by the Massachusetts Institute of Technology.  Uses RSAREF.
Export of this software may be restricted by the U.S. government.
Current time: 1994/09/18 22:46 GMT

For details on licensing and distribution, see the PGP User's Guide.
For other cryptography products and custom development services, contact:
Philip Zimmermann, 3021 11th St, Boulder CO 80304 USA, phone +1 303 541-0140

For a usage summary, type:  pgp -h
unix%
```

Don't worry about the message No configuration file found. PGP is simply telling you that it hasn't yet been properly installed.

Verifying Your Copy of PGP

Probably the first thing you should do is verify that your copy of PGP works—and works safely. One easy way that you can verify your copy of PGP is to use PGP itself to verify the PGP signature on the original PGP distribution file. Doing this helps you to determine if your copy of PGP has been compromised.

How to be Really Secure

Although using your copy of PGP to check its own signature is clever, it isn't entirely secure. The reason is simple: if someone has taken the time to tamper with your copy of PGP, he probably has tampered with it so skillfully that it will say that it has not been tampered with when it attempts to check itself.

How do you get around this problem? One way is by examining your source code. If you carefully look through it (and you know the C programming language), you should be able to discover most acts of tampering.

A better way to discover tampering is by using a friend's copy of PGP to verify the digital signature on the copy that you just picked up off the Internet. (Obviously, this won't tell you anything if both you and your friend pick up the same versions of PGP from the same location.)

Your copy of PGP includes a *keys.asc* file. This file contains public keys for many people who have been involved in the creation of PGP. The first step to verifying the authenticity of the copy of PGP that you just built is to create your public key ring, and add these keys to it. Follow these steps:

1. Build a key ring from the keys provided in the file *keys.asc*. You can do this using PGP's –ka (key add) option:

```
unix% cd ..
unix% ls
config.txt        keys.asc         pgp261si.tar.asc  rsaref.tar.asc
contrib/          language.txt     readme.doc        setup.doc
doc/              mitlicen.txt     rsalicen.txt      src/
es.hlp            pgp.hlp          rsaref/           vmsbuild/
fr.hlp            pgp261si.tar     rsaref.tar
unix% src/pgp -ka keys.asc distkeys.pgp
No configuration file found.
Pretty Good Privacy(tm) 2.6.1 - Public-key encryption for the masses.
(c) 1990-1994 Philip Zimmermann, Phil's Pretty Good Software. 29 Aug 94
Distributed by the Massachusetts Institute of Technology.  Uses RSAREF.
Export of this software may be restricted by the U.S. government.
Current time: 1994/09/18 23:37 GMT

Looking for new keys...
pub  1024/0DBF906D 1994/08/27  Jeffrey I. Schiller <jis@mit.edu>
pub   512/4D0C4EE1 1992/09/10  Jeffrey I. Schiller <jis@mit.edu>
pub  1024/0778338D 1993/09/17  Philip L. Dubois <dubois@csn.org>
pub  1024/FBBB8AB1 1994/05/07  Colin Plumb <colin@nyx.cs.du.edu>
pub  1024/C7A966DD 1993/05/21  Philip R. Zimmermann <prz@acm.org>
pub   709/C1B06AF1 1992/09/25  Derek Atkins <warlord@MIT.EDU>
pub  1024/8DE722D9 1992/07/22  Branko Lankester  <branko@hacktic.nl>
pub  1024/9D997D47 1992/08/02  Peter Gutmann <pgut1@cs.aukuni.ac.nz>
pub  1019/7D63A5C5 1994/07/04  Hal Abelson <hal@mit.edu>

Checking signatures...
pub  1024/0DBF906D 1994/08/27 Jeffrey I. Schiller <jis@mit.edu>
sig!      C7A966DD 1994/08/28  Philip R. Zimmermann <prz@acm.org>
sig!      C1B06AF1 1994/08/29  Derek Atkins <warlord@MIT.EDU>
sig!      4D0C4EE1 1994/08/27  Jeffrey I. Schiller <jis@mit.edu>
pub   512/4D0C4EE1 1992/09/10 Jeffrey I. Schiller <jis@mit.edu>
sig!      4D0C4EE1 1994/06/27  Jeffrey I. Schiller <jis@mit.edu>
sig!      C1B06AF1 1994/06/19  Derek Atkins <warlord@MIT.EDU>
sig!      C7A966DD 1994/05/07  Philip R. Zimmermann <prz@acm.org>
pub  1024/0778338D 1993/09/17 Philip L. Dubois <dubois@csn.org>
sig!      C7A966DD 1993/10/19  Philip R. Zimmermann <prz@acm.org>
pub  1024/FBBB8AB1 1994/05/07 Colin Plumb <colin@nyx.cs.du.edu>
sig!      C7A966DD 1994/05/07  Philip R. Zimmermann <prz@acm.org>
sig!      FBBB8AB1 1994/05/07  Colin Plumb <colin@nyx.cs.du.edu>
```

```
pub  1024/C7A966DD 1993/05/21 Philip R. Zimmermann <prz@acm.org>
sig!      0DBF906D 1994/08/30  Jeffrey I. Schiller <jis@mit.edu>
sig!      4D0C4EE1 1994/05/26  Jeffrey I. Schiller <jis@mit.edu>
sig!      C7A966DD 1994/05/07  Philip R. Zimmermann <prz@acm.org>
pub   709/C1B06AF1 1992/09/25 Derek Atkins <warlord@MIT.EDU>
sig!      0DBF906D 1994/08/30  Jeffrey I. Schiller <jis@mit.edu>
sig!      4D0C4EE1 1994/05/09  Jeffrey I. Schiller <jis@mit.edu>
sig!      C7A966DD 1994/05/07  Philip R. Zimmermann <prz@acm.org>
pub  1024/8DE722D9 1992/07/22 Branko Lankester  <branko@hacktic.nl>
sig!      C7A966DD 1994/05/07  Philip R. Zimmermann <prz@acm.org>
sig!      8DE722D9 1993/11/06  Branko Lankester  <branko@hacktic.nl>
pub  1024/9D997D47 1992/08/02 Peter Gutmann <pgut1@cs.aukuni.ac.nz>
sig!      C7A966DD 1994/02/06  Philip R. Zimmermann <prz@acm.org>
pub  1019/7D63A5C5 1994/07/04 Hal Abelson <hal@mit.edu>
sig!      0DBF906D 1994/09/03  Jeffrey I. Schiller <jis@mit.edu>
sig!      C7A966DD 1994/07/28  Philip R. Zimmermann <prz@acm.org>


Keyfile contains:
   9 new key(s)


One or more of the new keys are not fully certified.
Do you want to certify any of these keys yourself (y/N)? n
unix%
```

2. Now you can use the key ring you just created to check the distribution's authenticity:

```
unix% src/pgp pgp261si.tar.asc
No configuration file found.
Pretty Good Privacy(tm) 2.6.1 - Public-key encryption for the masses.
(c) 1990-1994 Philip Zimmermann, Phil's Pretty Good Software. 29 Aug 94
Distributed by the Massachusetts Institute of Technology.  Uses RSAREF.
Export of this software may be restricted by the U.S. government.
Current time: 1994/09/18 23:41 GMT


File has signature.  Public key is required to check signature.
Keyring file '/Users/simsong/.pgp/pubring.pgp' does not exist. Enter public
key filename: distkeys.pgp


File 'pgp261si.t.$00' has signature, but with no text.
Please enter filename of material that signature applies to: pgp261si.tar


Good signature from user "Jeffrey I. Schiller <jis@mit.edu>".
Signature made 1994/09/06 00:25 GMT
```

```
WARNING:  Because this public key is not certified with a trusted
signature, it is not known with high confidence that this public key
actually belongs to: "Jeffrey I. Schiller <jis@mit.edu>".

Signature and text are separate.  No output file produced.
unix%
```

Ah! Jeffrey Schiller signed the PGP 2.6.1 distribution! Anyone who knows Jeff won't be surprised by this; *bitsy.mit.edu* (the real name of the computer *net-dist.mit.edu*) is Jeff's workstation at the MIT Network Services group. Jeff manages the entire MIT campus network. (He's also a really cool guy!)

Notice, however, that we have no real way of knowing if the key provided for Jeff with the PGP distribution is *really* Jeff's key. Some hacker extraordinaire could have broken into Jeff's machine and replaced the copy of PGP being sent out to the world with one that has a subtle security flaw (perhaps a flaw that put a copy of everyone's secret key in every electronic signature). The hacker could have then replaced *keys.asc* with another file, signed the compromised PGP with the bogus key, and left it for everyone to pick up. How do we know that this didn't happen?

We don't.

One way that you could tell, though, would be to call Jeff and ask him for the fingerprint of his public PGP key. You could then compare that fingerprint with the fingerprint of the key in the file *keys.asc*: if the fingerprints match, you can rest assured that the two are in fact the same key. Or you could simply call Jeff and ask him to give you a copy of his public key. To save Jeff the hassle of thousands of people ringing his phone and asking him for the PGP fingerprint of his key, I've included it in this book. You can find the fingerprint in the section "Certifying and Distributing Keys" in Chapter 12.

Finishing the PGP Installation Under UNIX

Now that I've verified that the PGP executable appears to be working, I'll finish installing PGP on my UNIX workstation. Basically, I've got four steps left to go:

1. Determine the directory where the PGP files will be kept. Make sure that the directory is referenced by the PGPPATH environment variable. To make it easy, I'll keep the PGP files in the default directory *~/.pgp* (the *.pgp* subdirectory in my home directory).

    ```
    unix% mkdir ~/.pgp
    unix% chmod 700 ~/.pgp
    ```

A Procedure from MIT for Testing PGP

In the PGP Version 2.6.1 documentation, MIT recommends the following six-step procedure for testing the newly compiled program:

1. Create a new public and secret key pair with the user ID *test*:

   ```
   unix% pgp -kg
   ```

2. Add the keys in the file *keys.asc* to your public key ring with the –ka option:

   ```
   unix% pgp -ka keys.asc
   ```

3. Do a key ring check:

   ```
   unix% pgp -kc
   ```

4. Encrypt the documentation file *pgpdoc1.txt* with your public key:

   ```
   unix% pgp -e pgpdoc1.txt test -o testfile.pgp
   ```

5. Decrypt the file with your secret key:

   ```
   unix% pgp testfile.pgp
   ```

6. Compare the decrypted file with the original *pgpdoc1.txt* to see if they match:

   ```
   unix% cmp pgpdoc1.txt testfile
   ```

By following this procedure, you can thoroughly test PGP.

---

2. Copy the PGP configuration and language files into this directory:

   ```
   unix% cp language.txt ~/.pgp
   unix% cp config.txt ~/.pgp
   unix%
   ```

3. Determine the directory where the PGP program will reside, and make sure that this directory is in your PATH environment variable. To make it easy, I'll also put the PGP executable in the directory *~/.pgp*:

   ```
   unix% cp src/pgp ~/.pgp
   unix%
   ```

4. Install the PGP documentation. (PGP Version 2.6.1 won't create public keys unless you have the documentation in a location where the program can find it; I'll use the same directory, *~/.pgp*, that I've used for everything else.)

   ```
   unix% cp doc/pgpdoc1.txt ~/.pgp
   unix% cp doc/pgpdoc2.txt ~/.pgp
   unix%
   ```

5. Now you need to edit your startup files to add the variable PGPPATH and the directory *~/.pgp* to your path. If you are using the C shell, you can do this by adding the following two lines to the end of the file *~/.cshrc*:

```
setenv PGPPATH ~/.pgp
setenv PATH $PATH:$PGPPATH
```

If you feel uncomfortable editing the *~/.cshrc* file, you can simply type the following two lines at the C shell prompt:

```
unix% echo 'setenv PGPPATH ~/.pgp' >> ~/.cshrc
unix% echo 'setenv PATH $PATH:$PGPPATH' >> ~/.cshrc
```

If you are using the Bourne (sh) or Korn (ksh) shell, you can add the following two lines to the *.profile* file in your home directory:

```
PGPPATH=$HOME/.pgp; export PGPPATH
PATH=$PATH:$PGPPATH; export PATH
```

As before, you can add these two lines to your *.profile* file by typing them at the prompt.

```
unix% echo 'PGPPATH=$HOME/.pgp; export PGPPATH' >> .profile
unix% echo 'PATH=$PATH:$PGPPATH; export PATH' >> .profile
unix%
```

6. Create a PGP public/secret key pair. This process is outlined in detail in Chapter 8, *Creating PGP Keys*. Briefly, all you need to do to create your public key is to type **pgp -kg** and follow the directions.

The Dangers of Using PGP in a Multi-User Environment

If you are using PGP on a multi-user computer (such as a UNIX workstation onto which several people can log at the same time), you might want to take precautions when using PGP:

• Basically, you cannot protect yourself against a user of the computer who has superuser (root) access. The UNIX superuser can read the memory of your copy of PGP as it runs, reading out of it your pass phrase, your unencrypted messages, and the names of the people with whom you are communicating.

• The superuser (or another user) can modify your copy of PGP. It is a simple homework exercise to modify PGP so that it records the user's pass phrase and secret key in a secret location on the system and retrieve this information at a later date. Another simple modification to PGP could cause it to send copies of every file it encrypts or decrypts to another computer on the network.

- If you use your copy of PGP over a network, each key press can be intercepted by a program called a "sniffer." Sniffers are rampant on the Internet today. In a recent incident, the passwords of more than 10,000 people were sniffed and automatically tabulated. (The sniffer was discovered only because it filled the disk on the computer that it was using.)

- If your system is backed up, then your secret key ring is on the backup tapes. (Of course, the secret key ring is still encrypted.) Perhaps more importantly, any files that you decrypted are on the backup tapes as well.

There is only one truly safe way around these problems: *don't use PGP on a networked UNIX workstation if you want maximum security*. Instead, encrypt your files at home on a personal computer or a non-networked UNIX workstation. Then upload the *encrypted* file to your networked computer.

D

Installing PGP on a Macintosh

The Macintosh version of PGP, MacPGP, is available from MIT and many other sources.[†] MacPGP is not a fundamentally different program from PGP; it is Phil Zimmermann's standard PGP program surrounded by a user-friendly Macintosh "shell." The shell relays commands to PGP and displays the results of those commands.

Getting MacPGP

In order to install MacPGP, you need a copy of the Macintosh PGP distribution. You can obtain this program from a computer such as *net-dist.mit.edu* using the procedure outlined in Appendix A, *Getting PGP*.

In preparation for this example, I picked up a copy of the file *MacPGP2.6.sea.hqx* (the most recent version of the program that was available when this book went to press) from the computer *net-dist.mit.edu* and placed it on a UNIX workstation. Here it is:

```
unix% ls -l MacPGP2.6.sea.hqx
-rw-r--r--  1 simsong   504508 Aug 29 15:59 MacPGP2.6.sea.hqx
unix%
```

Installing MacPGP

To install MacPGP, follow the steps described in the following sections.

---

† An "unauthorized international" edition is available from *ftp.informatik.uni-hamburg.de*.

Copying the File

First, you need to copy the MacPGP file to your Macintosh.

There are lots of ways to get a file from a UNIX computer to a Macintosh computer. The easiest ways are to copy the file to a floppy, send the file with electronic mail, or simply transfer the file directly to the Macintosh using *ftp*. If you don't know how to transfer the file, I recommend that you get help from someone who does.

Decoding the File

On the Macintosh, decode the PGP file with BinHex, Stuffit Expander, or another suitable Macintosh utility. This produces a file called *MacPGP2.6.sea,* which is a self-extracting archive, as shown in Figure D-1.

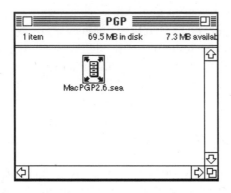

Figure D-1. MacPGP self-extracting archive

Creating a Setup Folder

Double-click on the self-extracting archive, and specify a folder to extract the MacPGP distribution. This creates a folder called *MacPGP2.6-setup*, as shown in Figure D-2.

The three files shown in Figure D-2 are *MacPGP2.6-Installer*, a self-extracting archive of the PGP program itself; *Macpgp2.6-installer.asc*, the PGP signature file for the self-extracting archive (signed with the public key of Jeff Schiller from MIT (the official source for PGP); and *Readme.asc*, a TeachText document describing the verification process.

Creating a PGP Folder

Double-click on the self-extracting archive, *MacPGP2.6-Installer*, and specify a folder in which to extract MacPGP itself. This step is shown in Figure D-3.

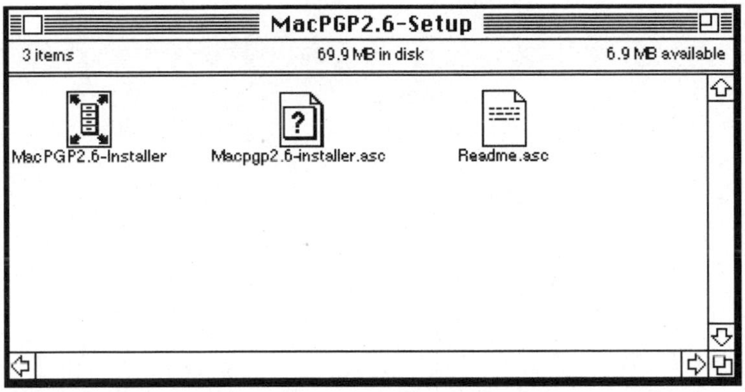

Figure D-2. MacPGP distribution folder

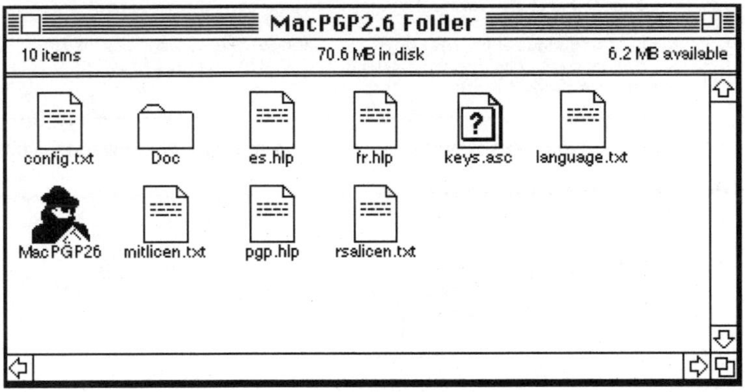

Figure D-3. Files in the MacPGP folder

Launching MacPGP

Double-click on the file *MacPGP2.6* to launch MacPGP, which creates a window titled "PGP Messages." This is the window where all the messages that PGP outputs are displayed, as shown in Figure D-4.

Creating Your Keys

The easiest way to create your public key/secret key pair with MacPGP is to chose the Generate key... option from the Key menu, as shown in Figure D-5.

Specify your key size and user ID, as shown in Figure D-6.

And type your pass phrase, as shown in Figure D-7.

Finally, type random text until PGP is satisfied.

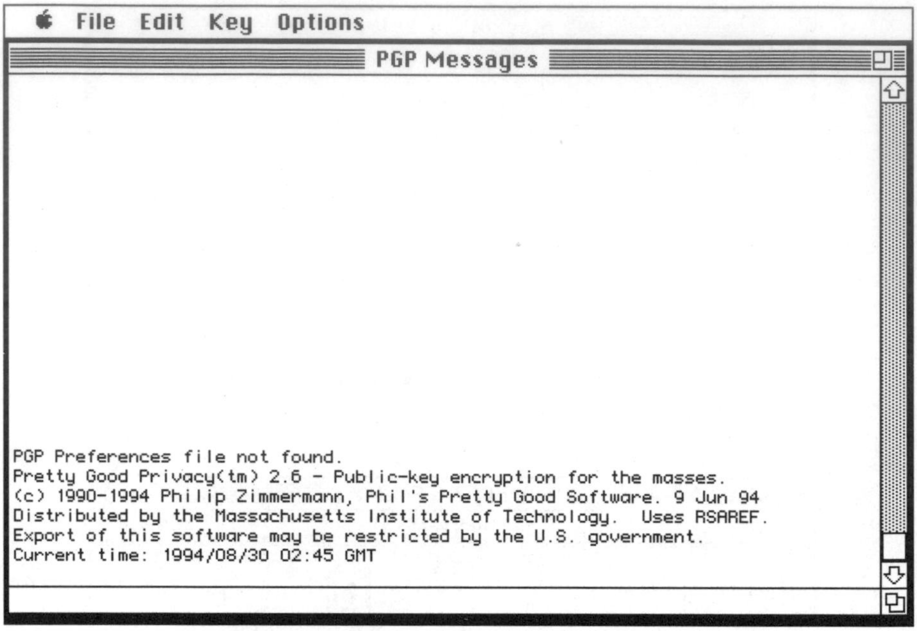

```
 ❖  File  Edit  Key  Options
╔══════════════════════════ PGP Messages ══════════════════════╗
║                                                              ⇧ ║
║                                                              ░ ║
║                                                              ░ ║
║                                                              ░ ║
║                                                              ░ ║
║                                                              ░ ║
║                                                              ░ ║
║                                                              ░ ║
║                                                              ░ ║
║                                                              ░ ║
║ PGP Preferences file not found.                              ░ ║
║ Pretty Good Privacy(tm) 2.6 - Public-key encryption for the masses. ░ ║
║ (c) 1990-1994 Philip Zimmermann, Phil's Pretty Good Software. 9 Jun 94 ░ ║
║ Distributed by the Massachusetts Institute of Technology.  Uses RSAREF. ░ ║
║ Export of this software may be restricted by the U.S. government. ░ ║
║ Current time: 1994/08/30 02:45 GMT                           ⇩ ║
╚══════════════════════════════════════════════════════════════╝
```

Figure D-4. PGP window used for messages

```
┌──────────────────────────┐
│ Key                      │
├──────────────────────────┤
│ Generate key...      ▷    │
│ Add keys...              │
│ View keyring...          │
│ Check signatures...      │
│ Extract keys...          │
│ Certify key...           │
│ Edit key...              │
│ Remove key...            │
│ Remove signatures...     │
│ Disable/Reenable key...  │
│ Fingerprint key...       │
└──────────────────────────┘
```

Figure D-5. Key menu (Generate key... option)

Adding Keys to Your Key Ring

Now you can add the distribution PGP public key ring to your public key ring. Select Add keys... from the Key menu, as shown in Figure D-8.

Specify the file *keys.asc* as the source of the keys, as shown in Figure D-9.

Specify the file *pubring.pgp* as the key ring where you want the keys added, as shown in Figure D-10.

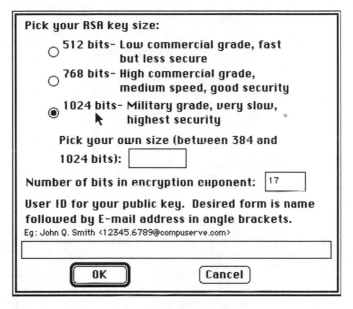

Figure D-6. Picking a key size

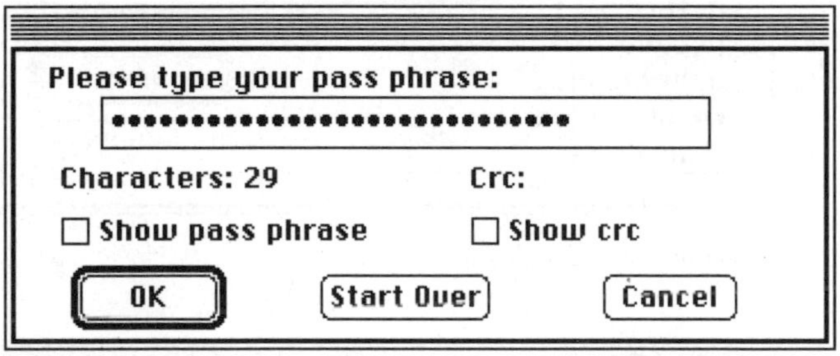

Figure D-7. Typing a pass phrase

You can certify the keys, if you wish, using the technique described in "Certifying the Keys in keys.asc" in Chapter 12, *Certifying and Distributing Keys.*

MacBinarizing the Distribution

You need to MacBinarize the PGP distribution before you can check the signature. Select MacBinarize... from the File menu, as shown in Figure D-11.

Select the input file *MacPGP2.6-installer*, as shown in Figure D-12.

Your original PGP distribution is now MacBinarized!

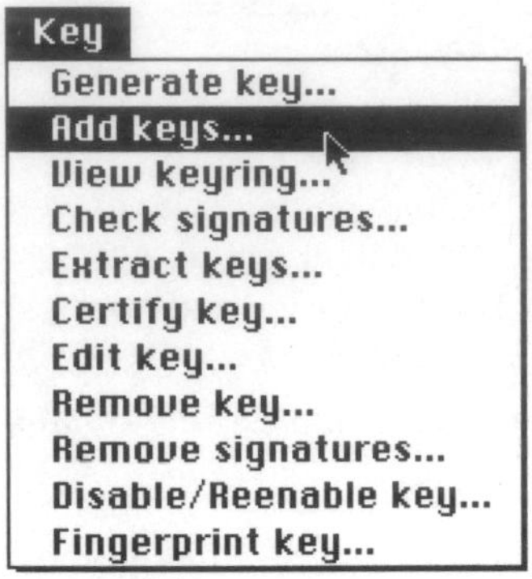

Key
- Generate key...
- Add keys...
- View keyring...
- Check signatures...
- Extract keys...
- Certify key...
- Edit key...
- Remove key...
- Remove signatures...
- Disable/Reenable key...
- Fingerprint key...

Figure D-8. Key menu (Add keys... option)

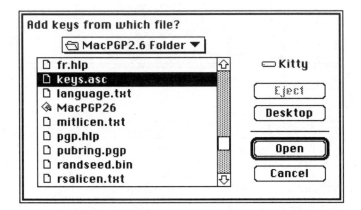

Figure D-9. Adding keys from the keys.asc file

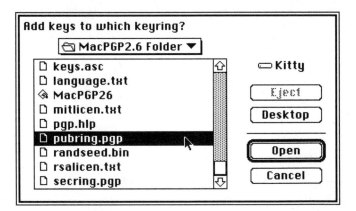

Figure D-10. Adding keys to the pubring.pgp file

Figure D-11. File menu (MacBinarize... option)

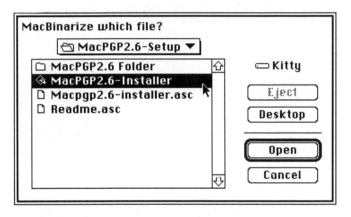

Figure D-12. MacBinarizing the MacPGP2.6-Installer file

Certifying the Keys

Select Open/Decrypt from the File menu, as shown in Figure D-13.

Select the PGP signature file for the self-extracting archive *MacPGP2.6-installer.asc*, as shown in Figure D-14.

Replace ".asc" with ".bin" in the Source cipherfile box, and click the Do It button, as shown in Figure D-15.

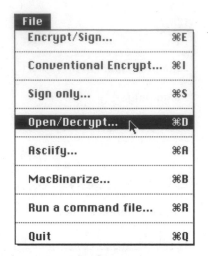

Figure D-13. File menu (Open/Decrypt... option)

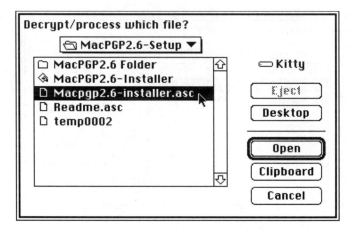

Figure D-14. Selecting a file for certification

Tell PGP once again that the file the signature applies to is the file *MacPGP2.6-installer.bin* (the fact that you have to tell MacPGP this twice appears to be a bug in the MacPGP interface), as shown in Figure D-16.

PGP should now report that you have a valid signature.

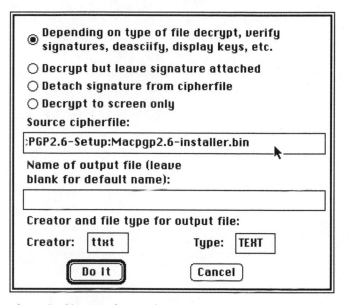

Figure D-15. Specifying the filename for certification

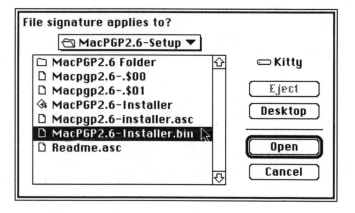

Figure D-16. Specifyng the filename again for certification

E

Versions of PGP

Since its initial release in 1991, PGP has gone through several versions. You need to know that some versions are not compatible with others to ensure that you are able to communicate with other people who are using PGP.

Version 1.0

PGP's initial release ran only on DOS-based computers. Although the RSA public key encryption was wonderful, problems with the private key encryption made this version patently insecure.

Version 2.0

PGP's second release. Version 2.0 was a massive rewrite of Version 1.0. The most important change was the replacement of the private key encryption system with IDEA, a new cipher developed in Switzerland.

Version 2.1

This version of PGP rewrote the key management routines in Version 2.0. (Under Version 2.0, key management was so slow that PGP was all but unusable for people who had more than a few dozen keys on their public key rings.)

Version 2.2

This version allowed you to encrypt a single email message for more than one recipient. It also improved the speed of the key management routines. The ASCII armor was fixed to work with Macintosh text files (which end each line with a carriage return instead of a line feed or a carriage return/line feed).

Version 2.3

Version 2.3 fixed many important bugs, including a memory allocation bug in the DOS version that sometimes trashed the content of messages. It also modified the ASCII armor to work properly with MIME mail systems.

Version 2.3a

This version fixed an important bug in PGP Version 2.3 that pertained to the ASCII armoring of files on DOS. (In so doing, PGP demonstrated once again the power of free software; when everyone has the source code, bugs tend to get fixed faster and programs tend to be ported to more platforms sooner.)

Version 2.4

This version limited RSA keys to 1024 bits in length, in preparation for the move to RSAREF and BSAFE (whose license agreements limit keys to this length). (The *PGP User's Guide* says "It used to be higher, but folks, if you think you need a key larger than that, do some research into the complexity of factoring.") Version 2.4 also fixed minor bugs in Version 2.3, which caused PGP to crash or behave unpredictably. Version 2.4 also decompressed faster.

Version 2.4 was never distributed as freeware; instead, it was the first version of PGP to be sold commercially by ViaCrypt.

Version 2.5

This was the first version of PGP to use RSAREF. This version of PGP used the RSAREF Version 2.0 released March 16, 1994. To comply with the RSAREF license, PGP was further modified to reject public or private keys longer than 1024 bits in length. Many contributed programs that had not been updated since PGP Version 2.3 were removed from the distribution. Key IDs increased from six hexadecimal characters to eight.

Because of a dispute with RSA Data Security, Version 2.5 was withdrawn shortly after it was released.

Version 2.6

This is the first "legal" version of PGP in the United States. After protracted negotiations between MIT and RSA, PGP was back-ported to RSAREF 1.0. More importantly, Version 2.6 was modified so that it would change its message format after September 1, 1994. Version 2.6 is able to read messages encrypted or signed after September 1, but previous versions of PGP can not. Version 2.6 contained an important bug in the routine that seeded the random number generator from keyboard input.

Version 2.6ui

This is the "unofficial international" version of PGP 2.6. Actually, Version 2.6ui is really PGP Version 2.3 with all of the Version 2.5 and Version 2.6 bug fixes and the format changes necessary to allow interoperation with Version 2.6 after September 1, 1994.

Version 2.6i

This is the international version of MIT's PGP 2.6. It is essentially MIT's Version 2.6.1 with the RSAREF RSA engine removed and replaced by an updated version of PGP's original RSA encryption engine.

Version 2.6.1

This is Version 2.6 with bug fixes, including an important bug fix in the random number seed routine.

Version 2.6.1ui

This is the "unofficial international" version updated to include the bug fixes from PGP Version 2.6.1.

Version 2.6.2

This version expands the maximum key size supported by PGP to 2048 bits, in preparation for moving to a maximum 2048-bit public key. The prime number-generating routines have been changed so that passed tests are printed as asterisks (*), rather than plus signs (+), because some kinds of modems change mode when they receive three plus signs in a row, followed by a long pause. Changes have been made to the *random.c* file so that the *randseed.bin* file is updated on each invocation of PGP; new randomness is generated from each key press. This version also fixes numerous bugs, most importantly a bug in the Clear Signature feature, which allowed an attacker to change the header of a PGP-signed message without altering the signature. Version 2.6.2 also works better under OS/2 than preceding versions did, and it can be compiled for HP-UX Version 9, Amiga UNIX, Encore UNIX, and MachTen (UNIX for the Macintosh). Finally, the PKCS_COMPAT configuration variable has been removed because PGP with RSAREF can operate only in PKCS-compatible mode

Version 2.7

This is ViaCrypt's version of PGP with modifications to read and write in the post-September 1 Version 2.6 format.

Version 3.0

What's coming in Version 3.0?

The most significant change is that all PGP 3.0 users will have not one, but *two* secret keys: one will be used exclusively for writing digital signatures; the other will be used exclusively for reading encrypted electronic mail.

The main reason for having two secret keys is not technical, but political. In the United States, it is believed that the government can subpoena encrypted files and force people to turn over the information necessary to decrypt those files (or risk being held in contempt of court). If you have separate signature and encryption keys, you can turn over your secret decryption key, yet keep your signature key secret. (There is no conceivable reason why the government would subpoena a person's signature key since its only use would be to forge people's digital signatures.)

An additional benefit to having separate signature and encryption keys is that you will be able to sign your own encryption key with your signature key; this makes it much easier to change your encryption key on a regular basis. In PGP Versions 1.x and 2.x, whenever you change your encryption key, you have to send it to all of your correspondents to get their signatures. In Version 3.0, you only have to send your signature key out for signatures once—when you create it. After that, you can simply sign your own encryption key and change it as often as you wish.

It is also likely that Version 3.0 will contain support for encryption standards other than RSA and IDEA. For example, the Diffie-Hellman key exchange algorithm can also be used as a public key algorithm; by using Diffie-Hellman, PGP encryption could become patent-free on August 19, 1997 (the day that the Hellman-Merkle patent expires), rather than on September 20, 2000 (the day that the RSA patent expires). PGP may also contain support for the DSS, the U.S. government's Digital Signature Standard. (The DSS may be a better signature algorithm than RSA with MD5 because the DSS uses a hash function that is 160 bits. On the other hand, some people wonder if the DSS may have certain vulnerabilities that its creators at the National Security Agency built into it. At this point, Zimmermann is reluctant to add support for the DSS to PGP, since doing so might be construed by some people as implicit support for the government's "Clipper" chip. The DSS may also be covered by another patent that has been exclusively licensed to Public Key Partners.) PGP may also support "Triple-DES," an encryption algrorithm that invoves using the Data Encryption Standard (DES) three times with diferent keys. The reason to use Triple-DES instead of IDEA is that the IDEA algrorithm is patented and must be licensed for some kinds of commercial use; Triple-DES has no similar restrictions. (I describe all of these algorithms, as well as the Clipper chip and the patent issues, in Part II of this book.)

PGP Version 3.0 may also contain support for "key escrow." If it does, it won't be the sort of back door, government-mandated key escrow that the Clinton administration is supporting. Instead, it will be a voluntary, individually controlled key escrow system. Using PGP's new key escrow system, it might be possible to give half of your secret key to one friend and half to another. If you forget your secret key, you could contact both of your friends, retrieve the two halves, and recreate your key. (I describe a simple key escrow system in Chapter 13, *Revoking, Disabling, and Escrowing Keys.*)

As this book is being written, two Internet IETF (Internet Engineering Task Force) standards for PGP are under development. Together, they describe the PGP file format. It is unlikely that PGP Version 3.0 will be completed in time to be described by these standards.

If all of this sounds confusing, well, it is. Figure E-1 may help you make sense of it all:

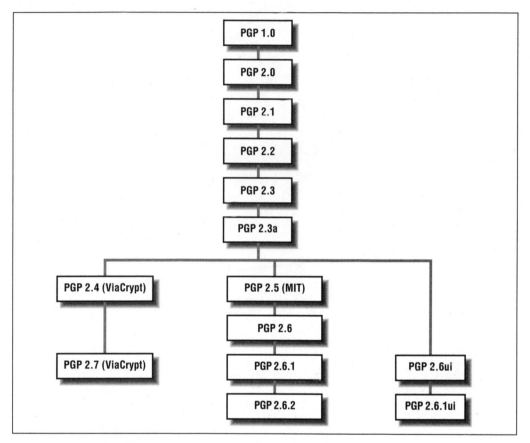

Figure E-1. Versions of PGP

F

The Mathematics of Cryptography

Cryptographers love mathematics, but most ordinary people don't. Rather than intimidate you with weird equations in the body of this book, I've thrown all of the interesting math into this appendix.

How Diffie-Hellman Works

Chapter 2 introduces the Diffie-Hellman algorithm (the first public key algorithm) and relates its history. In this appendix, I briefly describe the math behind the algorithm.

Before two people can communicate, they must agree on a large prime number q and a number α such that α is primitive mod q. Anyone can know the numbers α and q; they are not secret.

One person, Alice, chooses a random number X_a. She keeps this number secret but calculates a number Y_a with the following formula:

$$Y_a = \alpha^{X_a} \bmod q$$

Alice sends this number to her partner, Bob.

Bob, meanwhile, has chosen his own random number, X_b and sent his corresponding Y_b to Alice:

$$Y_b = \alpha^{X_b} \bmod q$$

Alice now computes the number K_{ab}, their shared key, with the following formula:

$$K_{ab} = Y_b{}^{X_a} \bmod q = \alpha^{X_b X_a} \bmod q$$

Bob, meanwhile, calculates the same number K_{ab} using the following formula:

$$K_{ab} = Y_a{}^X \bmod q = \alpha^{X_a Y_b} \bmod q$$

The number K_{ab} is secure because calculating it requires knowledge of either X_a or X_b. Alice knows X_a. Bob knows X_b. Someone who is eavesdropping on the line knows only Y_a and Y_b, and calculating X_a from Y_a or X_b from Y_b is a very difficult problem.

Let's work this example through with some real numbers:

Say we decide to use the numbers:

$\alpha = 5$

$q = 563$

Alice picks the number: 9

$X_a = 9$

She then sends the number 78 to Bob:

$5^9 \bmod 563 = 1953125 \bmod 563 = 78$

Bob picks the number: 14

$X_b = 14$

He then sends the number 534 to Alice:

$5^{14} \bmod 563 = 6103515625 \bmod 563 = 534$

Alice computes the number K: 117

$K = 534^9 \bmod 563 = 3530785328217308860798464 \bmod 563 = 117$

Bob computes the number K:

$K = 78^{14} \bmod 563 = 308549209196654470906527744 \bmod 563 = 117$

Alice and Bob can now communicate using the encryption key 117.

The security of this system rests on the difficulty of taking discrete logarithms *mod q*, which is effectively as difficult as factoring a number the size of *q*.

How RSA Works

The RSA public key algorithm on which PGP is based makes use of five numbers:

p   A very large prime number

q   Another very large prime number

n   Their product ($n = p \times q$)

e   The *encryption key*—this number can be any number that is *relatively prime* to the value $(p-1) \times (q-1)$. (*Relatively prime* means it has no common factors.)

d   The decryption key, which is derived from the values *p*, *q*, and *e* according to the following equation:

$$d = e^{-1} \;(\text{mod } (p-1) \times (q-1))$$

Notice that you need to know both *p* and *q* in order to derive the decryption key *d* from the encryption key *e*. The security of RSA depends on the numbers *p* and *q* never being revealed.

Once you have calculated the numbers *n*, *e*, and *d*, you can destroy the numbers *p* and *q*; they are no longer needed. (PGP actually keeps these numbers to use with the Chinese Remainder Theorem to speed decryption.)

Now we have the numbers, we need to perform public key encryption. The RSA algorithm can encrypt anything you want, as long as it is a number less than *n*. (In practice, this isn't a real limitation. Everything stored in a computer is stored as a number or a series of numbers; if you want to encrypt a number that is larger than *n*, simply encrypt the first half of it and then the second half.)

Take the number that you wish to encrypt. Call that number *m* (for *message*). You can encrypt your message *m* to produce the ciphertext *c* with the following formula:

$c = m^e \bmod n$

Likewise, you can decrypt your message with this formula:

$m = c^d \bmod n$

Thus, to encrypt a message you need the numbers (*n* and *e*).

To decrypt a message, you need the numbers (*n* and *d*).

In practice, programs such as PGP create a *public key* and a *secret key*. The *public key* consists of the numbers *n* and *e*. The *secret key* consists of just the number *d*. (This is why you need a copy of your public key to decrypt a message; you need to have a way of getting the number *n*).

The Security of RSA

The security of the RSA algorithm depends on the following factors:

- Making sure that the numbers p and q remain a secret.

  If you know p and q, it is a trivial matter to derive the decryption key d from the encryption key e.

- The difficulty of factoring the product n.

  If you could factor n, you would have p and q, and you could thus produce the decryption key d.

- The lack of other algebraic techniques for deriving the decryption key d from the encryption key e and the product n.

Someone interested in attacking the RSA algorithm has several obvious approaches to doing so. (*Successfully* attacking it is another matter entirely.)

Factoring attacks

Try to factor the number n.

Prime number attacks

Try to reverse-engineer the RSA prime number generator

Since most prime number generators are based on random numbers generators, the easy way to do this is by figuring out the initial state (called the *seed*) of the person's random number generator.

Math theory attacks

Discover a new principle of mathematics that reveals a fundamental flaw in RSA, or discover an ultra-high-speed way to factor large numbers.

Although none of these attacks are very practical, factoring attacks are the ones that get the most attention: they can be executed by anyone (or by any group of people) with a fast computer, provided that the factoring software has already been written.

Attacks on the prime number generator or the random number generator used to create the PGP session key can be much more rewarding—especially when many people are using the same widely available RSA implementation. Find a flaw in the random number generator or discover that the prime number algorithm tends to pick some kinds of prime numbers more than others, and you can simply search for all of these.

Finally, attacks on the mathematical theory of public key encryption are probably better left to serious mathematicians and cryptographers.

How Large is Very Large?

In recent years, factoring attacks on large numbers have become a popular sport. As I recount in Chapter 3, *Cryptography Before PGP*, the inventors of RSA proposed a challenge based on their algorithm—a message encrypted with RSA that was based on a 129-digit number. It was predicted that it would require 4,600 MIPS-years to factor this number. (This is the equivalent of 4,600 VAX 11/780 computers running for a year or a single Pentium computer running for 46 years.) The number was finally factored in April 1994 by an international collaboration of scientists and students who donated free time on their computers to the problem.

The RSA-129 number was the equivalent of a 429-bit key. According to a table distributed by Hal Abelson, Jeff Schiller, Brian LaMacchia, and Derek Atkins at MIT, the following factoring times are anticipated for the following PGP key lengths. (These times are based on the MPQS algorithm used by the RSA-129 team; better algorithms are now available.)[†]

RSA-129
(429-bit key)   4,600 MIPS-years

512-bit key   420,000 MIPS-years

700-bit key   4,200,000,000 MIPS-years

1024-bit key 2.8×10^{15} MIPS-years

An interesting aside to these numbers is that the most important aspect of a computer in determining its factoring speed is not the raw speed of the microprocessor but the speed with which the microprocessor can access its memory. This is because most factoring algorithms use working sets that are several megabytes in size—far too big to fit into the computer's cache. A computer that is optimized for high-speed CPU-to-memory data transfer factors far faster than a machine that is optimized to speed through industry benchmarks.

To put these numbers in perspective, realize that approximately 100 million personal computers will ship in 1995. If every one of those computers was a 100 MHz Intel Pentium computer (a 100-MIPS machine equipped with 8MB of RAM) and if all 100

[†] According to Atkins, the generalized number field sieve can factor a 512-bit number in one-third the time of MPQS. Factoring a 1024-bit key takes approximately 300,000 times longer.

million were working at cracking a single PGP key, it would take the following amount of time for the following key lengths:

Key length	Time required for 100 million 8MB Pentium computers to crack key
429-bit key	14.5 seconds
512-bit key	22 minutes
700-bit key	153 days
1024-bit key	280,000 years

In any case, anyone with enough political clout to force all 100 million computer buyers to devote their brand-new $2000 computers to breaking a PGP-encrypted message could probably afford the very latest up-to-date computer hardware, so the 1024-bit key would probably be factored in far fewer than the 280,000 years quoted above. (He could also employ a few mathematicians to develop improved factoring techniques. And they might even set up shop in Maryland.) On the other hand, someone with that much power could just as easily kidnap the code maker and her family and threaten them with torture until she revealed the secret key!

I have said that the primes used by RSA are "very large." How large are they? That's up to you. Generally speaking, the larger your key, the more secure your encrypted messages. The reason for this fact has to do with the way that the RSA algorithm encrypts information.

For a detailed discussion of RSA factoring, see "Dr. Ron Rivest on the Difficulty of Factoring" later in this appendix.

How Random is Random?

PGP uses random numbers for many different purposes:

- Random numbers determine your secret key.

- Random numbers determine the session key used to encrypt each message.

- Random numbers determine the key used in "conventional cryptography."

The best way to generate random numbers is by using a truly random natural process. Radioactive decay is the natural process that is most often cited by the literature.

Unfortunately, most computers aren't equipped with Geiger counters. Instead, computers typically use pseudo-random number functions, which generate an unpredictable sequence of numbers—a sequence that can be considered random if you don't know its internal state and what number it starts with.

PGP seeds its random number generator each time it is asked to generate a new public key. PGP seeds the generator by asking the user to type on the keyboard. PGP measures the time between successive keystrokes and slowly builds up a "random" number. PGP asks the user to stop typing when enough random bits have been accumulated.

Is keyboard typing really random? Beats me. A lot of people think it is.

One thing is certain, though. PGP Version 2.6 contained a flaw in its random number seed routine which made the random number generator significantly less random than it might otherwise have been. This flaw is fixed in PGP Version 2.6.1.

Dr. Ron Rivest on the Difficulty of Factoring

Reprinted, with permission and updates, from Ciphertext: The RSA Newsletter *Volume 1, Number 1, Fall 1993.*

(Since the difficulty of "cracking" a message encrypted with the RSA algorithm has long been believed to be roughly equivalent to the difficulty of factoring a given RSA modulus, I am reprinting one of Ron Rivest's classic papers on the difficulty of the factoring problem. At Dr. Rivest's request, I have updated the estimates originally published in the paper to take into account recent advances in factoring such as the generalized number field sieve.)[†]

Abstract

Here are the results of some simple estimates I have done on the projected difficulty of factoring various sizes of numbers for the next 25 years.

The basic question is:

"In the year YYYY, what size number will I be able to factor for an investment of $DDDD?"

To be specific, I've looked at:

YYYY = 1995, 2000, 2005, 2010, 2015, 2020

and

$DDDD = $25K, $25M, and $25G

[†] For detailed information about the number field sieve, see Lenstra, A.K., Lenstra Jr., H.W., Manasse, M.S., and J.M. Pollard, "The Number Field Sieve," *Proceedings of the 22nd ACM Symposium on the Theory of Computing*, ACM Press, Baltimore, Md., 1990, pp. 564–72. For detailed information about the generalized number field sieve, see Lenstra, A.K., Lenstra Jr., H.W., Manasse, M.S., and J.M. Pollard, "The Factorization of the Ninth Fermat Number," *Mathematics of Computation*, Volume 61, Number 203, July 1993, pp. 319–50.

(That is, $25,000, $25,000,000 and $25,000,000,000). These three levels might correspond to attacks mounted by an individual, by a corporation, and by a world government. All calculations are done in 1995 dollars.

Each of these estimates is also done for "high," "average," and "low" points of views. (That is, the high estimates are for the greatest number of digits possible to be factored, while the low estimates are for the least number possible.)

The estimates are done in terms of MIPS-years, a computational unit of power analogous to a "kilowatt-hour" of electricity. Specifically, a MIPS-year is the computational power of a one-MIPS machine running for one year. A MIPS is a "million-instruction per second" machine. Today's workstations run in the 10 to 100 MIPS range. One MIPS-year corresponds to 3.15×10^{13} operations.

Factoring Algorithms

To factor a number n with current technology using the best known algorithm (the Generalized Number Field Sieve), we need a number of operations roughly equal to the following formula (formula 1):

$$A(n) = exp\ (1.92(ln(n)^{1/3} ln(ln(n))^{2/3}))$$

We will use this number A(n) for both our low and average estimates. For the high estimates, we use the following formula (formula 2):

$$H(n) = exp\ (1.56(ln(n)^{1/3} ln(ln(n))^{2/3}))$$

which is the number of operations that NFS now uses for rarefied numbers. (Achieving this formula for general numbers would be quite a breakthrough.)

Costs of Computation

I estimate that today a MIPS-year costs about $4.00, as follows. You can buy (parts for) a 100-MIPS machine for about $2000. With a lifetime of five years, you get 500 MIPS-years out of the machine. (In 1990, I estimated that a MIPS-year cost about $10.)

As for rates of technological progress, for the "low" estimate I assume that technology only advances at 20%/year. For the "average" estimate I assume that technology advances at 33%/year, and for the "high" estimate I assume 45%/year. These are measured in terms of the drop in the cost of a MIP-year in constant 1995 dollars. Thus, under the high estimate, $2000 will buy 144 MIPS-years in 1996 and 210.25 MIPS-years in 1997, etc.

At this rate, we can estimate the number of MIPS-years that can be bought for $1000 as follows. (Here, *M* is the abbreviation for million.)

Table F-1. Number of MIPS-years that can be bought for $1000 for low, average, and high levels of technological growth

Year	Low	Average	High
1995	250	250	250
2000	622	1040	1602
2005	1548	4330	10271
2010	3852	18018	65835
2015	9584	74985	421988
2020	23849	312055	3M

NOTE: Cost per MIPS-year in 1995 is $4.00. Rate of technological growth is 20%/year for low, 33%/year for average, and 45%/year for high scenarios.

Combining the numbers in this table with our "low" ($25K), "average" ($25M) and "high" ($25G) estimates for dollars available, we arrive at the following chart for the number of MIPS-years available to an attacker to work on the factoring problem. (Here, T is the abbreviation for "tera," i.e., 10^{12}.

Table F-2. Number of MIPS-years that can be purchased by an attacker, combining money available and technological growth estimates

Year	Low	Average	High
1995	6250	6M	6250M
2000	15552	26M	40061M
2005	38698	108M	256779M
2010	96294	450M	2T
2015	239610	1875M	11T
2020	596226	7801M	68T

That is, in the year 2020, a determined opponent with $25G ($25,000,000,000) might be able to afford 68T MIPS-years to attack a number.

Results

We now give the number of operations required to factor numbers of various sizes under our low, average, and high estimates (formulas (1), (1) and (2)). These are given in MIPS-years:

Table F-3. Number of MIPS-years required to factor a number in low, average and high scenarios

Bits	Low	Average	High
512	5.1e+05	5.1e+05	59.23
768	3.1e+09	3.1e+09	6e+04
1024	3.8e+12	3.8e+12	1.6e+07
1536	3.7e+17	3.7e+17	1.5e+11
2048	4.2e+21	4.2e+21	2.6e+14
4096	3.4e+33	3.4e+33	7.6e+23
8192	1.4e+49	1.4e+49	2e+36

Combining the above charts with some additional calculations, we end up with our low, average, and high estimates for the size of a number (in bits) that an attacker would be able to factor at various points in time:

Table F-4. Size of a number (in bits) that an attacker would be able to factor at various points of time under various scenarios

Year	Low	Average	High
1995	405	579	1341
2000	425	619	1451
2005	447	661	1567
2010	469	705	1689
2015	493	751	1815
2020	515	799	1947

Conclusions

The estimates given here are admittedly extremely crude. They are intended merely to give a zero-th order approximation and simple intuitive guide to the difficulty of factoring. Algorithmic breakthroughs could cause dramatic changes in these estimates. If one wanted to proceed, nonetheless, and propose a "standard" key length for the next 25 years that would be likely to withstand an average attack (as defined above) over that time period, then a key length of 1024 bits seems justified based on these estimates. For "master keys," a key length two or three times longer might be well justified.

How PGP Picks Primes

In introductory programming classes, many people learn a very basic technique for picking prime numbers called the Sieve of Eratosthenes. The sieve simply makes a list of every prime number. It starts with the number *2*, sees if that number is divisible by any prime number that it has found. The number is not, so the sieve then tries the next number *3*, which is also prime. The sieve then tries the next number *4*, which is divisible by 2, and is therefore not prime. In this fashion, the sieve eventually finds every prime number.

The following example is a simple implementation of the sieve in C:

```
#define NUMPRIMES 1000

int     primes[NUMPRIMES];
int     totprimes = 0;

test(int x)
{
        int     i;
        int     top = sqrt((double)x);

        for(i=0;i<totprimes;i++){
                if(x % primes[i] == 0) return 0;
                if(primes[i] > top) return 1;
        }
        return 1;
}

main()
{
        int     i;

        for(i=2;totprimes < NUMPRIMES;i++){
                int j = test(i);
                if(j){
                        primes[totprimes++] = i;
                        printf("%d\n",i);
                }
        }

}
```

Although this technique works great for finding the first 1000 primes, it doesn't work well for finding primes that are hundreds of digits long: there are simply too many primes and not enough time in the universe.

Instead of using the sieve, PGP generates prime numbers by following this procedure:

1. To create a random prime of *n* bits, PGP first generates a random binary number consisting of two 1s followed by (*n*–2) random binary digits.

2. PGP checks to see if the random number is prime using a fast sieving algorithm, which PGP calls *fasttest*. The algorithm picks a random starting point in a table of the first 100 primes and calculates the remainder of dividing the random number by each of the primes, storing the result. By applying a number of heuristics on the remainders, PGP can throw away many composite numbers.

3. If *fasttest* decides that the number is not prime, PGP tries the next odd number.

4. If *fasttest* decides that the number might be prime, PGP prints a period (.) and checks for primality with Fermat's Little Theorem (which PGP calls *slowtest*).

5. Each pass through Fermat's algorithm rules out a minimum of 50 percent of all primes.

   PGP Version 2.6.1 runs Fermat's test four times. Each time this test succeeds, PGP prints an asterisk (*).

With this information, you can finally understand what PGP is printing when you generate a new key pair. For example, say we are trying to generate a 1024-bit prime and PGP prints the following:

```
........................**** ...............****
```

While generating the first prime number, PGP found 26 different prime number candidates that passed the sieve but were thrown out by Fermat's. The first number that passed the first Fermat test passed all four. (It looks as if Phil was right; Fermat's test is a lot better than 50 percent accurate.) For the second prime number, PGP found 16 different numbers that passed the sieve test. All of them were thrown out by Fermat's test except the last.

Once again, the first number that passed one round of Fermat's test passed all four.

Glossary

Adleman, Len

The *A* in RSA, Adleman is currently a professor at the University of Southern California

ASCII

The American Standard Code for Information Interchange. This is the coding that assigns numerical equivalents to printable letters and numbers. For example, the letter *A* is given the ASCII code of 65.

ASCII armor

A system used by PGP for encoding binary information in printable files

asymmetric key cryptography

See public key encryption

Austin Code Works

A company in Austin, Texas, that sells floppy disks of (mostly) freely redistributable software

Bidzos, Jim

President of RSA Data Security and Public Key Partners

Bass-O-Matic

A private key encryption algorithm developed by Phil Zimmermann before he realized that most people, including himself, do not have the expertise necessary to developed encryption algorithms. Bass-O-Matic was used in PGP Version 1.0 and was later shown to be insecure.

breaking a code

The process of examining a piece of encrypted text in order to determine the original plain text or the key that is needed to decrypt the message

brute force attack

  See key search attack

cipher

  A system for concealing the meaning of a message by rearranging the letters and/ or substituting some letters with others

ciphertext

  A message that has been encrypted so that it cannot be easily understood by anyone other than the intended recipient. *See also* plaintext.

Clipper chip

  A sophisticated, high-speed encryption chip designed by the National Security Agency. A Clipper chip encrypts data with the Skipjack algorithm. Clipper-encrypted communications can be decrypted by law enforcement agencies or others who possess the chip's secret key.

code

  A system for substituting letters or words in a message with a predefined set of symbols found in a *codebook*

codebook

  A book or table used for defining a *code*

composite

  A number that is evenly divisible by factors other than the numbers *1* and itself. The number *6* is composite because it is divisible by the numbers *2* and *3*. *See also* prime.

conventional cryptography

  See private key encryption

Cylink

  A Sunnyvale, California, company that specializes in making encryption and data communications hardware. Cylink has much less visibility than RSA Data Security but is approximately ten times the size.

cypherpunks

  An Internet mailing list for a group of people dedicated to the adoption and spread of strong cryptography. Send email to *cypherpunk-request@toad.com*.

Crypto

  An annual conference on cryptography held at the University of California at Santa Barbara

cryptography

  The science of using mathematics to hide the meaning of messages

DES

The Data Encryption Standard, developed in the 1970s by IBM, adopted as a standard by the National Bureau of Standards, and now used around the world. DES uses a 56-bit encryption key.

Diffie-Hellman key exchange

A secure public key exchange system, developed by Stanford professors Whitfield Diffie and Martin Hellman, which allows two parties to securely exchange cryptographic keys over insecure channels

Diffie, Whitfield

The co-inventor (with Martin Hellman) of public key cryptography, Diffie was formerly a professor at Stanford University and is currently a scientist at Sun Microsystems

digital signature

A block of data that is appended to the end of a message or that accompanies a binary file; the signature attests to the authenticity of the file. Digital signatures are created with a secret key and are verified with a public key. If any change is made to the signed file, the digital signature does not verify.

Digital Telephony

The title of an FBI proposal to force telecommunication providers and equipment manufacturers to design their systems to enable easy wiretapping by authorized law enforcement personnel

Double-DES

A technique for using DES that involves encrypting each message twice with the DES algorithm. Double DES has been shown to have nearly the same cryptographic strength as single DES. *See also* DES and Triple-DES.

Electronic Privacy Information Center (EPIC)

Formerly the Washington office of the Computer Professionals for Social Responsibility, an organization dedicated to assuring the right to privacy in cyberspace. Send email to *info@epic.org* for information.

Electronic Frontier Foundation (EFF)

A lobbying organization, located in Washington D.C., that fights for civil rights in cyberspace. Send email to *info@eff.org* for information.

Electronic Escrow Standard (EES)

A key escrow proposal by the U.S. government that requires that the encryption keys used by telecommunications equipment be split into two parts and stored at different escrow agencies. The keys would be given to law enforcement officials by the escrow agencies in order to facilitate a lawful wiretap.

encryption algorithm

The particular mathematical process used by a computer to encrypt or decrypt a message

encryption key

A word, number, or phrase that is used by an encryption algorithm to encrypt or decrypt a message. The same message encrypts different ways when it is encrypted with different keys.

exponential key exchange

Another name for Diffie-Hellman encryption

Federal Bureau of Investigation (FBI)

The top law enforcement agency in the United States. The agency has publicly led the charge against the widespread use of strong cryptography in the United States.

filter

A term borrowed from the UNIX operating system to denote any program that reads its input from *standard input* and writes its output to *standard output*

Hellman, Martin

The co-inventor (with Whitfield Diffie) of public key cryptography

ICAR

The International Cryptography research organization that organizes the Crypto and Eurocrypto conferences

IDEA

The International Data Encryption Algorithm, an encryption algorithm developed in Switzerland by James L. Massey and Xuijia Lai, which uses a 128-bit key

key

See encryption key

key certification

A process by which a public key is certified to belong to a particular individual or organization. Frequently, key certification is done with the *digital signature* of a trusted individual.

key escrow

Any system for making a copy of an encryption key so that it can be accessed at a later time by authorized individuals

key ID

A number that designates an RSA key pair. PGP uses a 64-bit key ID consisting of the lower 64 bits of the public key.

key length

The number of digits in a key, usually expressed as a number of binary bits. A key that can be expressed as eight printable characters and has a key length of 56 bits.

key ring

A file used by PGP to hold public and secret keys

key server

A program that operates a library for public keys, sending out copies of them on request

key search attack

A technique for forcibly decrypting an encrypted message by an attacker who does not possess the correct decryption key. A key search attack involves trying to decrypt the message with every possible key until the correct one is found. Also called *brute force attack*

knapsack

A public-key encryption technique developed by Ralph Merkle that was later shown by cryptographers to be not very secure

LEAF

The Law Enforcement Access Field. A block of data, generated by Clipper chips, which contains a copy of the current session key that has been encrypted with the chip's master encryption key.

Lucifer

A project at IBM aimed at developing a strong private key encryption algorithm. Also used for the name of the algorithm itself.

MD4

Message Digest #4, a message digest algorithm developed by MIT Professor Ron Rivest

MD5

Message Digest #5, another message digest algorithm developed by MIT Professor Ron Rivest. MD5 runs faster than MD4.

Merkle, Ralph

An early pioneer in public key cryptography, now at Xerox Palo Alto Research Center (PARC)

Merkle's puzzles

An early system for exchanging a cryptographic session key, which relied on the exchange of a million easy-to-solve puzzles

Merritt, Charlie

A computer programmer in Arkansas who specializes in writing public key cryptography implementations. Merritt wrote the first commercially successful implementation of RSA for a personal computer and taught Phil Zimmermann how to do arithmetic with hundred-digit numbers on a personal computer.

message

A block of information sent from a sender to a recipient. Encrypted messages are called *ciphertext*; unencrypted messages are called *plaintext*.

message digest

A number that is derived from a message. Change a single character in the message, and the message will have a different message digest.

Metamorphic Systems

A small startup company in Colorado in the mid-1980s that built a plug-in 8088 board for the Apple II microcomputer. Phil Zimmermann worked for Metamorphic Systems.

more

A UNIX program that displays a file on a screen one page at a time. PGP has a *more* function that causes decrypted files to be displayed on a screen but not stored in a file.

National Security Agency (NSA)

A branch of the U.S. Department of Defense, which is charged with making codes for the United States and breaking codes used by other countries

one-time pad

The only kind of encryption system that is absolutely secure, a one-time pad uses a different key for every character of the message. One-time pads thus eliminate the redundancies and mathematical hints that cryptanalysts can use to crack encrypted messages.

patent

A monopoly, granted by the government, that gives the patent holder the legal right to prevent other people from making, practicing, using, selling, or importing a particular invention.

PEM

See Privacy Enhanced Mail

PGP

See Pretty Good Privacy

plaintext

A message that can be easily read and understood without undergoing any special measures. *See also* ciphertext.

Pretty Good Privacy

A program written by Phil Zimmermann, which performs public key cryptography, private key cryptography, and key management

prime

A number that cannot be evenly divided by any numbers other than itself and the number *1*. For example, the number *7* is prime. *See* composite.

Privacy Enhanced Mail

An Internet standard for sending encrypted electronic mail using public key encryption

private key

A key that is used both for encryption and decryption

public key

A key that can be made widely available. With the RSA encryption system, public keys are used to encrypt messages and to verify digital signatures.

private key encryption

Also called *conventional encryption*, a technique for encrypting information such that the same key is used for encryption and decryption. Most encryption algorithms, including DES and IDEA, are private key algorithms.

public key encryption

A technique for encrypting information such that the key used to *decrypt* the message is different from the key used to *encrypt* the message. With a strong public key system, the encryption key can be made publicly available without compromising the security of encrypted messages. Diffie-Hellman and RSA are two popular public key encryption algorithms.

Public Key Partners

A partnership formed in 1991 by RSA Data Security and Cylink. PKP controls the licensing rights to many of the patents that are crucial to public key encryption.

random

Something that cannot be predicted

RC2

Rivest's Code #2, a proprietary block cipher developed by MIT Professor Ron Rivest and sold by RSA Data Security

RC4

Rivest's Code #4, a proprietary stream cipher developed by MIT Professor Ron Rivest and sold by RSA Data Security. In September 1994, an unauthorized but allegedly compatible implementation of RC4 was posted to the Internet in the Usenet news group *alt.security*.

RIPEM

An implementation of Privacy Enhanced Mail written by Mark Riordan that is based upon RSAREF

Rivest, Ron

The *R* in RSA, Rivest is currently a professor at the Massachusetts Institute of Technology

RSA

A popular public key encryption algorithm developed by MIT professors Ron Rivest, Adi Shamir, and Len Adelman

RSA-129

A 129-digit composite number that appeared as a challenge in the August 1977 issue of *Scientific American*. Thought to be unfactorable within the lifetime of the inventors of RSA, this number was finally factored by an international group of volunteers. The solution was announced in the spring of 1994.

RSA Data Security, Inc.

A company based in Redwood City, California, that sells encryption software

RSAREF

The RSA reference implementation, developed by RSA Data Security and made freely available over the Internet. RSAREF allows noncommercial programs to use RSA encryption without fear of patent infringement.

S.266

The U.S. Senate Omnibus Anti Crime Control Act of 1991 (which never passed). An amendment to S.266 introduced by Senator Joe Biden could have forbidden the use of cryptography on public communication networks.

Schiller, Jeff

Manager of network operations at MIT. Schiller's public key signs the PGP distribution from MIT.

secret key

A key that is kept secret. With RSA systems, the secret key is used to decrypt messages that are encrypted with the corresponding public key and to sign documents with digital signatures.

session key

A key, randomly generated, used by a private key algorithm to encrypt the contents of a message and/or the duration of a telecommunications session. Session keys themselves are usually encrypted with a public key system.

Skipjack

A secret, classified, encryption algorithm that is implemented in the NSA's Clipper chip. Skipjack uses an 80-bit key.

strong encryption

A cryptographic system that, when used properly, produces encrypted messages that cannot be read by people who are not in possession of the proper cryptographic key

substitution cipher

A system for enciphering text that relies on substituting one set of letters for another set of letters according to a substitution table. In order to be secure, a substitution cipher must change its substitution table on a regular basis.

symmetric key cryptography

See private key cryptography

Shamir, Adi

The *S* in RSA, Shamir is currently a professor at the Weizmann Institute of Science in Israel

transposition cipher

A system for enciphering text that relies on the rearranging of letters within the messages. Modern encryption systems use both transposition ciphers and substitution ciphers.

Triple-DES

A variant of the DES algorithm that involves encrypting every message three times with the DES algorithm. Triple-DES has been shown to be significantly stronger than single DES and has an effective key length of 112 bits (compared with the 56 bits used by single DES).

user ID

A character string that represents the owner of a public key

ViaCrypt

A division of the Phoenix-based company, Lemcom, that creates encryption programs. ViaCrypt sells a commercial version of PGP.

weak encryption

A cryptographic system that produces messages that can be read by people not in possession of the proper cryptographic key

Zimmermann, Phil

A computer programmer located in Boulder, Colorado. The lead author of PGP.

Bibliography

Books

Bamford, James. *The Puzzle Palace: A Report on America's Most Secret Agency*. Boston: Houghton Mifflin, 1982. The complete, inside story of the National Security Agency.

Denning, Dorothy E.R. *Cryptography and Data Security*. Reading: Addison Wesley, 1983.

Hinsley, F.H., and Alan Stripp. *Code Breakers: The Inside Story of Bletchley Park*. Oxford: Oxford University Press, 1993.

Hodges, Andrew. *Alan Turing: The Enigma*. New York: Simon & Schuster, Inc., 1983. The definitive biography of the brilliant scientist who broke "Enigma," Germany's deepest World War II secret, who pioneered the modern computer age, and who finally fell victim to the cold war world of military secrets and sex scandals.

Kahn, David. *The Codebreakers*. New York: Macmillan Company, 1972.

Kahn, David. *Seizing the Enigma: The Race to Break the German U-Boat Codes, 1939–1943*. Boston: Houghton Mifflin, 1991.

Merkle, Ralph. *Secrecy, Authentication and Public Key Systems*. Ann Arbor: UMI Research Press, 1982.

Schneier, Bruce. *Applied Cryptography: Ptrotocols, Algorithms, and Source Code in C*. New York: John Wiley & Sons, 1994. The most comprehensive book about computer encryption and data privacy techniques ever published.

RSA Data Security, Inc. *MailSafe: Public Key Encryption Software* (user's manual) Version 5.0. Redwood City, Calif.: 1994.

Smith, Laurence Dwight. *Cryptography: The Science of Secret Writing.* New York: Dover Publications, 1941.

Weber, Ralph Edward. *United States Diplomatic Codes and Ciphers, 1775–1938.* Chicago: Precedent Publishing Inc., 1979.

Papers and Other Publications

Association for Computing Machinery, "Codes, Keys, and Conflicts: Issues in U.S. Crypto Policy." *Report of a Special Panel of the ACM U.S. Public Policy Committee* (USACM) (June 1994). (URL: *http://info.acm.org/reports/acm_crypto_study.html*)

Coppersmith, Don. *IBM Journal of Research and Development* 38 (1994).

Diffie, Whitfield. "The First Ten Years of Public-Key Cryptography," *Proceedings of the IEEE* 76 (1988): 560–76. Whitfield Diffie's tour-de-force history of public key cryptography, with revealing commentaries.

Diffie, Whitfield, and M.E. Hellman. "New Directions in Cryptography." *IEEE Transactions on Information Theory* IT-22 (1976).

Hoffman, Lance J., Ali, Faraz A., Heckler, Steven L., and Ann Huybrechts. "Cryptography Policy." *Communications of the ACM* 37 (1994): 109–17.

Lai, Xuejia. "On the Design and Security of Block Ciphers." *ETH Series in Information Processing* 1 (1992). An article describing the IDEA cipher.

Lai, Xuejia, and James L. Massey. "A Proposal for a New Block Encryption Standard." *Advances in Cryptology—EUROCRYPT '90 Proceedings* (1992): 55–70. Another article describing the IDEA cipher.

Lenstra, A.K., Lenstra, Jr., H.W., Manasse, M.S., and J.M. Pollard. "The Number Field Sieve." *Proceedings of the 22nd ACM Symposium on the Theory of Computing.* Baltimore: ACM Press, 1990, pp. 564–72.

Lenstra, A.K., Lenstra, Jr., H.W., Manasse, M.S., and J.M. Pollard. "The Factorization of the Ninth Fermat Number." *Mathematics of Computation* 61 (1993): 319–50.

Merkle, Ralph. "Secure Communication Over Insecure Channels." *Communications of the ACM* 21 (1978): 294–99 (submitted in 1975).

Merkle, Ralph, and Martin E. Hellman. "On the Security of Multiple Encryption." *Communications of the ACM* 24 (1981): 465–67.

Merkle, Ralph, and Martin E. Hellman. "Hiding Information and Signatures in Trap Door Knapsacks." *IEEE Transactions on Information Theory* 24 (1978): 525–30.

National Bureau of Standards. *Data Encryption Standard* FIPS PUB 46-1 (1987).

Rivest, Ron. *Ciphertext: The RSA Newsletter* 1 (1993).

Rivest, Ron, Shamir, A., and L. Adleman. "A Method for Obtaining Digital Signatures and Public Key Cryptosystems." *Communications of the ACM* 21 (1978).

Simmons, G. J. "How to Insure that Data Acquired to Verify Treaty Complicance are Trustworthy," in "Authentication without secrecy: A secure communications problem uniquely solvable by asymmetric encryption techniques." *IEEE EASCON '79,* Washington, D.C. 1979, pp. 661–62.

Thompson, Ken. "Reflections on Trusting Trust." *Communications of the ACM* 27 (1984). This is a "must read" for anyone seeking to understand the limits of computer security and trust.

Electronic Resources

Cypherpunk Internet mailing list. To obtain information from the Cypherpunk mailing list, send email to *cypherpunk-request@toad.com.*

Edstrom, Gary B. "Frequently Asked Questions" (PGP FAQ). Available electronically in the Usenet group *alt.security.pgp,* with occasional updates.

Electronic Privacy Information Center (EPIC). Send email to *info@epic.org.*

Electronic Frontier Foundation (EFF). Send email to *info@eff.org.*

Hastur, Henry. "Stealth," a program that strips PGP messages so that they cannot be readily identified. Available by anonymous FTP from *wuarchive.wustl.edu:/pub/aminet/util/crypt/StealthPGP1_0.lha.*

Meeks, Brock N. *Cyberwire Dispatch.* This is a mailing list that follows electronic privacy issues. You can subscribe by sending the message, "subscribe cwd-1" to *majordomo@cyberwerks.com.*

Xenon (anonymous pseudonym). "Here's How to MacPGP!" Available by sending email to *qwerty@netcom.com* with a subject of "Bomb me!" Also available in *ftp://ftp.netcom.com/pub/qwerty.*

Zimmermann, Phil. *PGP User's Guide.* Boulder, Colo., 1994. Included with PGP software.

You might find these Usenet newsgroups of interest: *alt.security.pgp, alt.privacy, comp.security.misc, sci.crypt.*

Although there are many sources of PGP and related files (see Appendix A), *ftp.ox.ac.uk* has an especially complete set of PGP resources, including up-to-date language files.

Index

About the Author

Simson Garfinkel is a computer consultant, a science writer, Contributing Writer at *WIRED* magazine, and Senior Editor at *SunExpert Magazine*. He is the developer of a Polaroid physician's workstation and the NeXT CD-ROM file system. He has also been Principal Scientist at N/Hance Systems, a company that sold optical file systems, and Senior Editor at *NeXTWorld Magazine*. He is the coauthor of *Practical UNIX Security* (O'Reilly & Associates), *NeXTStep Programming* (Springer-Verlag), and *The UNIX-Haters Handbook* (IDG). Mr. Garfinkel writes frequently about science and technology for *Technology Review Magazine*, the *Christian Science Monitor*, the *Boston Globe*, and many other publications.

Colophon

The image on the cover of *PGP: Pretty Good Privacy* is of a padlock. Although the remains of simple key locks have been found dating back to ancient Assyria, the basic form of the modern padlock was invented by Linus Yale in about 1860. In the Yale lock, or pin-tumbler cylinder lock, a cylindrical core, rotated by a key, moves the bolt of the lock, releasing it. The ridges on the key raise pins of different sizes in the cylindrical core. If these pins are not raised to the proper height, the core will not move.

The keys in PGP serve a similar purpose to a padlock key. Once you have used a PGP key to "lock" a file or an electronic mail message, you, or the recipient of your message, must use a corresponding key to "unlock" it.

Edie Freedman designed the cover of this book. The padlock image is adapted from *Scan This Book*, a copyright-free collection of old engravings compiled by John Mendenhall and published by Art Direction Book Company. The cover layout was produced with Adobe Photoshop 2.5 and QuarkXPress 3.3 for the Macintosh, using the Adobe ITC Garamond fonts.

The interior format was designed by Edie Freedman and Jennifer Niederst, using Adobe ITC Garamond fonts and implemented in FrameMaker by Mike Sierra. The figures were created in Aldus Freehand 4.0 by Chris Reilley and Hanna Dyer. This colophon was written by Clairemarie Fisher O'Leary.

SYSTEM ADMINISTRATION

Books from O'Reilly & Associates, Inc.

Fall/Winter 1994-95

"Good reference books make a system administrator's job much easier. However, finding useful books about system administration is a challenge, and I'm constantly on the lookout. In general, I have found that almost anything published by O'Reilly & Associates is worth having if you are interested in the topic."

—*Dinah McNutt*, UNIX Review

TCP/IP Network Administration

By Craig Hunt
1st Edition August 1992
502 pages, ISBN 0-937175-82-X

A complete guide to setting up and running a TCP/IP network for administrators of networks of systems or lone home systems that access the Internet. It starts with the fundamentals: what the protocols do and how they work, how to request a network address and a name (the forms needed are included in an appendix), and how to set up your network. Beyond basic setup, the book discusses how to configure important network applications, including sendmail, the r* commands, and some simple setups for NIS and NFS. There are also chapters on troubleshooting and security. In addition, this book covers several important packages that are available from the Net (such as *gated*). Covers BSD and System V TCP/IP implementations.

"Whether you're putting a network together, trying to figure out why an existing one doesn't work, or wanting to understand the one you've got a little better, *TCP/IP Network Administration* is the definitive volume on the subject."
—Tom Yager, *Byte*

Managing Internet Information Services

By Cricket Liu, Jerry Peek, Russ Jones,
Bryan Buus & Adrian Nye
1st Edition December 1994 (est.)
668 pages, ISBN 1-56592-062-7

This comprehensive guide describes how to set up information services to make them available over the Internet. It discusses why a company would want to offer Internet services, provides complete coverage of all popular services, and tells how to select which ones to provide. Most of the book describes how to set up email services and FTP, Gopher, and World Wide Web servers.

"*Managing Internet Information Services* has long been needed in the Internet community, as well as in many organizations with IP-based networks. Although many on the Internet are quite savvy when it comes to administering these types of tools, *MIIS* will allow a much larger community to join in and perhaps provide more diverse information. This book will be a welcome addition to my Internet shelf."
—Robert H'obbes' Zakon, MITRE Corporation

Linux Network Administrator's Guide

By Olaf Kirch
1st Edition Winter 1994-95 (est.)
400 pages (est.), ISBN 1-56592-087-2

A UNIX-compatible operating system that runs on personal computers, Linux is a pinnacle within the free software movement. It is based on a kernel developed by Finnish student Linus Torvalds and is distributed on the Net or on low-cost disks, along with a complete set of UNIX libraries, popular free software utilities, and traditional layered products like NFS and the X Window System.

Networking is a fundamental part of Linux. Whether you want a simple UUCP connection or a full LAN with NFS and NIS, you are going to have to build a network.

Linux Network Administrator's Guide by Olaf Kirch is one of the most successful books to come from the Linux Documentation Project. It touches on all the essential networking software included with Linux, plus some hardware considerations. Topics include serial connections, UUCP, routing and DNS, mail and News, SLIP and PPP, NFS, and NIS.

DNS and BIND

By Paul Albitz & Cricket Liu
1st Edition October 1992
418 pages, ISBN 1-56592-010-4

DNS and BIND contains all you need to know about the Internet's Domain Name System (DNS) and the Berkeley Internet Name Domain (BIND), its UNIX implementation. The Domain Name System is the Internet's "phone book"; it's a database that tracks important information (in particular, names and addresses) for every computer on the Internet.
If you're a system administrator, this book will show you how to set up and maintain the DNS software on your network.

"*DNS and BIND* contains a lot of useful information that you'll never find written down anywhere else. And since it's written in a crisp style, you can pretty much use the book as your primary BIND reference."
—Marshall Rose, *ConneXions*

---

sendmail

By Bryan Costales, with Eric Allman & Neil Rickert
1st Edition November 1993
830 pages, ISBN 1-56592-056-2

This Nutshell Handbook® is far and away the most comprehensive book ever written on sendmail, the program that acts like a traffic cop in routing and delivering mail on UNIX-based networks. Although sendmail is used on almost every UNIX system, it's one of the last great uncharted territories—and most difficult utilities to learn—in UNIX system administration. This book provides a complete sendmail tutorial, plus extensive reference material on every aspect of the program. It covers IDA sendmail, the latest version (V8) from Berkeley, and the standard versions available on most systems.

"The program and its rule description file, sendmail.cf, have long been regarded as the pit of coals that separated the mild UNIX system administrators from the real fire walkers. Now, sendmail syntax, testing, hidden rules, and other mysteries are revealed. Costales, Allman, and Rickert are the indisputable authorities to do the text."
—Ben Smith, *Byte Magazine*

Essential System Administration

By Æleen Frisch
1st Edition October 1991
466 pages, ISBN 0-937175-80-3

Like any other multi-user system, UNIX requires some care and feeding. *Essential System Administration* tells you how. This book strips away the myth and confusion surrounding this important topic and provides a compact, manageable introduction to the tasks faced by anyone responsible for a UNIX system.

If you use a stand-alone UNIX system, whether it's a PC or a workstation, you know how much you need this book: on these systems the fine line between a user and an administrator has vanished. Either you're both or you're in trouble. If you routinely provide administrative support for a larger shared system or a network of workstations, you will find this book indispensable. Even if you aren't directly responsible for system administration, you will find that understanding basic administrative functions greatly increases your ability to use UNIX effectively.

Computer Security Basics

By Deborah Russell & G.T. Gangemi Sr.
1st Edition July 1991
464 pages, ISBN 0-937175-71-4

There's a lot more consciousness of security today, but not a lot of understanding of what it means and how far it should go. This handbook describes complicated concepts, such as trusted systems, encryption, and mandatory access control, in simple terms. For example, most U.S. government equipment acquisitions now require Orange Book (Trusted Computer System Evaluation Criteria) certification. A lot of people have a vague feeling that they ought to know about the Orange Book, but few make the effort to track it down and read it. *Computer Security Basics* contains a more readable introduction to the Orange Book—why it exists, what it contains, and what the different security levels are all about—than any other book or government publication.

"A very well-rounded book, filled with concise, authoritative information...written with the user in mind, but still at a level to be an excellent professional reference."
—Mitch Wright, System Administrator, I-NET, Inc.

Practical UNIX Security

By Simson Garfinkel & Gene Spafford
1st Edition June 1991
512 pages, ISBN 0-937175-72-2

Tells system administrators how to make their UNIX system—either System V or BSD—as secure as it possibly can be without going to trusted system technology. The book describes UNIX concepts and how they enforce security, tells how to defend against and handle security breaches, and explains network security (including UUCP, NFS, Kerberos, and firewall machines) in detail. If you are a UNIX system administrator or user who deals with security, you need this book.

"The book could easily become a standard desktop reference for anyone involved in system administration. In general, its comprehensive treatment of UNIX security issues will enlighten anyone with an interest in the topic."
—Paul Clark, Trusted Information Systems

PGP: Pretty Good Privacy

By Simson Garfinkel
1st Edition December 1994 (est.)
430 pages (est.), ISBN 1-56592-098-8

PGP, which stands for Pretty Good Privacy, is a free and widely available program that lets you protect files and electronic mail. Written by Phil Zimmermann and released in 1991, PGP works on virtually every platform and has become very popular both in the U.S. and abroad. Because it uses state-of-the-art public key cryptography, PGP can be used to authenticate messages, as well as keep them secret. With PGP, you can digitally "sign"a message when you send it. By checking the digital signature at the other end, the recipient can be sure that the message was not changed during transmission and that the message actually came from you. The ability to protect the secrecy and authenticity of messages in this way is a vital part of being able to conduct business on the Internet.

PGP: Pretty Good Privacy is both a readable technical users guide and a fascinating behind-the-scenes look at cryptography and privacy. Part I of the book describes how to use PGP: protecting files and email, creating and using keys, signing messages, certifying and distributing keys, and using key servers. Part II provides background on cryptography, battles against public key patents and U.S. government export restrictions, and other aspects of the ongoing public debates about privacy and free speech.

System Performance Tuning

By Mike Loukides
1st Edition November 1990
336 pages, ISBN 0-937175-60-9

System Performance Tuning answers the fundamental question: How can I get my computer to do more work without buying more hardware? Some performance problems do require you to buy a bigger or faster computer, but many can be solved simply by making better use of the resources you already have.

"This book is a 'must' for anyone who has an interest in making their UNIX system run faster and more efficiently. It deals effectively with a complex subject that could require a multi-volume series."
—Stephan M. Chan, *ComUNIXation*

Managing UUCP and Usenet

By Grace Todino & Tim O'Reilly
10th Edition January 1992
368 pages, ISBN 0-937175-93-5

For all its widespread use, UUCP is one of the most difficult UNIX utilities to master. This book is for system administrators who want to install and manage UUCP and Usenet software.

"Don't even TRY to install UUCP without it!"—Usenet message 456@nitrex.UUCP

"If you are contemplating or struggling with connecting your system to the Internet via UUCP or planning even a passing contact with Usenet News Groups, this book should be on your shelf. Our highest recommendation."
—Boardwatch Magazine

Managing NFS and NIS

By Hal Stern
1st Edition June 1991
436 pages, ISBN 0-937175-75-7

Managing NFS and NIS is for system administrators who need to set up or manage a network filesystem installation. NFS (Network Filesystem) is probably running at any site that has two or more UNIX systems. NIS (Network Information System) is a distributed database used to manage a network of computers. The only practical book devoted entirely to these subjects, this guide is a "must-have" for anyone interested in UNIX networking.

termcap & terminfo

By John Strang, Linda Mui & Tim O'Reilly
3rd Edition April 1988
270 pages, ISBN 0-937175-22-6

For UNIX system administrators and programmers. This handbook provides information on writing and debugging terminal descriptions, as well as terminal initialization, for the two UNIX terminal databases.

"I've been working with both termcap and terminfo for years now, and I was confident that I had a handle on them, but reading this remarkable little book gave me some valuable new insights into terminal setting in UNIX."
—Root Journal

X Window System Administrator's Guide: Volume 8

By Linda Mui & Eric Pearce
1st Edition October 1992
372, pages, ISBN 0-937175-83-8

As X moves out of the hacker's domain and into the real world, users can't be expected to master all the ins and outs of setting up and administering their own X software. That will increasingly become the domain of system administrators. Even for experienced system administrators X raises many issues, both because of subtle changes in the standard UNIX way of doing things and because X blurs the boundaries between different platforms. Under X, users can run applications across the network on systems with different resources (including fonts, colors, and screen size). Many of these issues are poorly understood, and the technology for dealing with them is in rapid flux.

This book is the first and only book devoted to the issues of system administration for X and X-based networks, written not just for UNIX system administrators, but for anyone faced with the job of administering X (including those running X on stand-alone workstations).

Note: The CD that used to be offered with this book is now sold separately, allowing system administrators to purchase the book and the CD-ROM in quantities they choose. *The X Companion CD for R6*, estimated release November 1994.

The X Companion CD for R6

By O'Reilly & Associates
1st Edition Winter 1994-95 (est.)
(Includes CD-ROM plus 80-page guide)
ISBN 1-56592-084-8

The X CD-ROM contains precompiled binaries for X11, Release 6 (X11R6) for Sun4, Solaris, HP-UX on the HP700, DEC Alpha, and IBM RS6000. It includes X11R6 source code from the "core" and "contrib" directories and X11R5 source code from the "core"and "contrib" directories. The CD also provides examples from the O'Reilly *X Window System* series and *The X Resource* journal.

The package includes an 80-page booklet describing the contents of the CD-ROM, how to install the R6 binaries, and how to build X11 for other platforms. O'Reilly and Associates used to offer this CD-ROM with Volume 8, *X Window System Administator's Guide*) of the *X Window System* series. Offering it separately allows system administrators to purchase the book and the CD-ROM in any quantities they choose.

AUDIOTAPES

O'Reilly now offers audiotapes based on interviews with people who are making a profound impact in the world of the Internet. Here we give you a quick overview of what's available. For details on our audiotape collection, send email to **audio@ora.com**.

"Ever listen to one of those five-minute-long news pieces being broadcast on National Public Radio's 'All Things Considered' and wish they were doing an in-depth story on new technology? Well, your wishes are answered." —Byte

---

Global Network Operations

Carl Malamud interviews Brian Carpenter, Bernhard Stockman, Mike O'Dell & Geoff Huston
Released Spring 1994
Duration: 2 hours, ISBN 1-56592-993-4

What does it take to actually run a network? In these four interviews, Carl Malamud explores some of the technical and operational issues faced by Internet service providers around the world.

Brian Carpenter is the director for networking at CERN, the high-energy physics laboratory in Geneva, Switzerland. Physicists are some of the world's most active Internet users, and its global user base makes CERN one of the world's most network-intensive sites. Carpenter discusses how he deals with issues such as the OSI and DECnet Phase V protocols and his views on the future of the Internet.

Bernhard Stockman is one of the founders and the technical manager of the European Backbone (EBONE). EBONE has proven to be the first effective transit backbone for Europe and has been a leader in the deployment of CIDR, BGP-4, and other key technologies.

Mike O'Dell is vice president of research at UUNET Technologies. O'Dell has a long record of involvement in data communications, ranging from his service as a telco lab employee, an engineer on several key projects, and a member of the USENIX board to now helping define new services for one of the largest commercial IP service providers.

Geoff Huston is the director of the Australian Academic Research Network (AARNET). AARNET is known as one of the most progressive regional networks, rapidly adopting new services for its users. Huston talks about how networking in Australia has flourished despite astronomically high rates for long-distance lines.

The Future of the Internet Protocol

Carl Malamud interviews Steve Deering, Bob Braden, Christian Huitema, Bob Hinden, Peter Ford, Steve Casner, Bernhard Stockman & Noel Chiappa
Released Spring 1994
Duration: 4 hours, ISBN 1-56592-996-9

The explosion of interest in the Internet is stressing what was originally designed as a research and education network. The sheer number of users is requiring new strategies for Internet address allocation; multimedia applications are requiring greater bandwidth and strategies such as "resource reservation" to provide synchronous end-to-end service.

In this series of eight interviews, Carl Malamud talks to some of the researchers who are working to define how the underlying technology of the Internet will need to evolve in order to meet the demands of the next five to ten years.

Give these tapes a try if you're intrigued by such topics as Internet "multicasting" of audio and video, or think your job might one day depend on understanding some of the following buzzwords:

- IPNG (Internet Protocol Next Generation)
- SIP (Simple Internet Protocol)
- TUBA (TCP and UDP with Big Addresses)
- CLNP (Connectionless Network Protocol)
- CIDR (Classless Inter-Domain Routing)

or if you are just interested in getting to know more about the people who are shaping the future.

Mobile IP Networking

Carl Malamud interviews Phil Karn & Jun Murai
Released Spring 1994
Duration: 1 hour, ISBN 1-56592-994-2

Phil Karn is the father of the KA9Q publicly available implementation of TCP/IP for DOS (which has also been used as the basis for the software in many commercial Internet routers). KA9Q was originally developed to allow "packet radio," that is, TCP/IP over ham radio bands. Phil's current research focus is on commercial applications of wireless data communications.

Jun Murai is one of the most distinguished researchers in the Internet community. Murai is a professor at Keio University and the founder of the Japanese WIDE Internet. Murai talks about his research projects, which range from satellite-based IP multicasting to a massive testbed for mobile computing at the Fujisawa campus of Keio University.

Networked Information and Online Libraries

Carl Malamud interviews Peter Deutsch & Cliff Lynch
Released September 1993
Duration: 1 hour, ISBN 1-56592-998-5

Peter Deutsch, president of Bunyip Information Services, was one of the co-developers of Archie. In this interview Peter talks about his philosophy for services and compares Archie to X.500. He also talks about what kind of standards we need for networked information retrieval.

Cliff Lynch is currently the director of library automation for the University of California. He discusses issues behind online publishing, such as SGML and the democratization of publishing on the Internet.

European Networking

Carl Malamud interviews Glenn Kowack & Rob Blokzijl
Released September 1993
Duration: 1 hour, ISBN 1-56592-999-3

Glenn Kowack is chief executive of EUnet, the network that's bringing the Internet to the people of Europe. Glenn talks about EUnet's populist business model and the politics of European networking.

Rob Blokzijl is the network manager for NIKHEF, the Dutch Institute of High Energy Physics. Rob talks about RIPE, the IP user's group for Europe, and the nuts and bolts of European network coordination.

Security and Networks

Carl Malamud interviews Jeff Schiller & John Romkey
Released September 1993
Duration: 1 hour, ISBN 1-56592-997-7

Jeff Schiller is the manager of MIT's campus network and is one of the Internet's leading security experts. Here, he talks about Privacy Enhanced Mail (PEM), the difficulty of policing the Internet, and whether horses or computers are more useful to criminals.

John Romkey has been a long-time TCP/IP developer and was recently named to the Internet Architecture Board. In this wide-ranging interview, John talks about the famous "ToasterNet" demo at InterOp, what kind of Internet security he'd like to see put in place, and what Internet applications of the future might look like.

John Perry Barlow
Notable Speeches of the Information Age

USENIX Conference Keynote Address
San Francisco, CA; January 17, 1994
Duration: 1.5 hours, ISBN 1-56592-992-6

John Perry Barlow—retired Wyoming cattle rancher, a lyricist for the Grateful Dead since 1971— holds a degree in comparative religion from Wesleyan University. He also happens to be a recognized authority on computer security, virtual reality, digitized intellectual property, and the social and legal conditions arising in the global network of computers.

In 1990 Barlow co-founded the Electronic Frontier Foundation with Mitch Kapor and currently serves as chair of its executive committee. He writes and lectures on subjects relating to digital technology and society and is a contributing editor to *Communications of the ACM*, *NeXTWorld*, *Microtimes*, *Mondo 2000*, *Wired*, and other publications.

In his keynote address to the Winter 1994 USENIX Conference, Barlow talks of recent developments in the national information infrastructure, telecommunications regulation, cryptography, globalization of the Internet, intellectual property, and the settlement of Cyberspace. The talk explores the premise that "architecture is politics": that the technology adopted for the coming "information superhighway" will help to determine what is carried on it, and that if the electronic frontier of the Internet is not to be replaced by electronic strip malls, we need to make sure that our technological choices favor bi-directional communication and open platforms.

Side A contains the keynote;
Side B contains a question and answer period.

O'Reilly & Associates—
GLOBAL NETWORK NAVIGATOR™

The Global Network Navigator (GNN)™ is a unique kind of information service that makes the Internet easy and enjoyable to use. We organize access to the vast information resources of the Internet so that you can find what you want. We also help you understand the Internet and the many ways you can explore it.

In GNN you'll find:

Navigating the Net with GNN

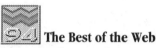 The *Whole Internet Catalog* contains a descriptive listing of the most useful Net resources and services with live links to those resources.

The *GNN Business Pages* are where you'll learn about companies who have established a presence on the Internet and use its worldwide reach to help educate consumers.

The *Internet Help Desk* helps folks who are new to the Net orient themselves and gets them started on the road to Internet exploration.

News

NetNews is a weekly publication that reports on the news of the Internet, with weekly feature articles that focus on Internet trends and special events. The Sports, Weather, and Comix Pages round out the news.

Special Interest Publications

Whether you're planning a trip or are just interested in reading about the journeys of others, you'll find that the *Travelers' Center* contains a rich collection of feature articles and ongoing columns about travel. In the *Travelers' Center*, you can link to many helpful and informative travel-related Internet resources.

The *Personal Finance Center* is the place to go for information about money management and investment on the Internet. Whether you're an old pro at playing the market or are thinking about investing for the first time, you'll read articles and discover Internet resources that will help you to think of the Internet as a personal finance information tool.

All in all, GNN helps you get more value for the time you spend on the Internet.

The Best of the Web

GNN received "Honorable Mention" for **"Best Overall Site," "Best Entertainment Service,"** and **"Most Important Service Concept."**

The *GNN NetNews* received "Honorable Mention" for **"Best Document Design."**

Subscribe Today

GNN is available over the Internet as a subscription service. To get complete information about subscribing to GNN, send email to **info@gnn.com**. If you have access to a World Wide Web browser such as Mosaic or Lynx, you can use the following URL to register online: http://gnn.com/

If you use a browser that does not support online forms, you can retrieve an email version of the registration form automatically by sending email to **form@gnn.com**. Fill this form out and send it back to us by email, and we will confirm your registration.

O'Reilly on the Net—
ONLINE PROGRAM GUIDE

O'Reilly & Associates offers extensive information through our online resources. If you've got Internet access, we invite you to come and explore our little neck-of-the-woods.

Online Resource Center

Most comprehensive among our online offerings is the O'Reilly Resource Center. Here, you'll find detailed information and descriptions on all O'Reilly products: titles, prices, tables of contents, indexes, author bios, software contents, reviews... you can even view images of the products themselves. We also supply helpful ordering information: how to contact us, how to order online, distributors and bookstores world wide, discounts, upgrades, etc. In addition, we provide informative literature in the field: articles, interviews, and bibliographies that help you stay informed and abreast.

 The Best of the Web

The *O'Reilly Resource Center* was voted "**Best Commercial Site**" by users participating in "Best of the Web '94."

To access ORA's Online Resource Center:

Point your Web browser (e.g., `mosaic` or `lynx`) to:

`http://gnn.com/ora/`

For the plaintext version, `telnet` or `gopher` to:

`gopher.ora.com`

(telnet login: `gopher`)

FTP

The example files and programs in many of our books are available electronically via FTP.

To obtain example files and programs from O'Reilly texts:

`ftp` to:

`ftp.ora.com`

or

`ftp.uu.net`

`cd published/oreilly`

Ora-news

An easy way to stay informed of the latest projects and products from O'Reilly & Associates is to subscribe to "ora-news," our electronic news service. Subscribers receive email as soon as the information breaks.

To subscribe to "ora-news":

Send email to:
listproc@online.ora.com

and put the following information on the first line of your message (not in "Subject"):
subscribe ora-news "your name" **of** "your company"

For example:
subscribe ora-news Jim Dandy of Mighty Fine Enterprises

Email

Many customer services are provided via email. Here's a few of the most popular and useful.

nuts@ora.com
    For general questions and information.
bookquestions@ora.com
    For technical questions, or corrections, concerning book contents.
order@ora.com
    To order books online and for ordering questions.
catalog@ora.com
    To receive a free copy of our magazine/catalog, "ora.com" (please include a postal address).

Snailmail and phones

O'Reilly & Associates, Inc.
103A Morris Street, Sebastopol, CA 95472
Inquiries: **707-829-0515, 800-998-9938**
Credit card orders: **800-889-8969** (Weekdays 6a.m.- 6p.m. PST)
FAX: **707-829-0104**

O'Reilly & Associates—
LISTING OF TITLES

INTERNET

!%@:: A Directory of Electronic Mail
    Addressing & Networks
Connecting to the Internet: An O'Reilly Buyer's Guide
Internet In A Box
The Mosaic Handbook for Microsoft Windows
The Mosaic Handbook for the Macintosh
The Mosaic Handbook for the X Window System
Smileys
The Whole Internet User's Guide & Catalog

SYSTEM ADMINISTRATION

Computer Security Basics
DNS and BIND
Essential System Administration
Linux Network Administrator's Guide (Winter '94/95 est.)
Managing Internet Information Services
Managing NFS and NIS
Managing UUCP and Usenet
sendmail
Practical UNIX Security
PGP: Pretty Good Privacy (Winter '94/95 est.)
System Performance Tuning
TCP/IP Network Administration
termcap & terminfo
X Window System Administrator's Guide: Volume 8
The X Companion CD for R6 (Winter '94/95 est.)

USING UNIX AND X

BASICS

Learning GNU Emacs
Learning the Korn Shell
Learning the UNIX Operating System
Learning the vi Editor
MH & xmh: Email for Users & Programmers
SCO UNIX in a Nutshell
The USENET Handbook (Winter '94/95 est.)
Using UUCP and Usenet
UNIX in a Nutshell: System V Edition
The X Window System in a Nutshell
X Window System User's Guide: Volume 3
X Window System User's Guide, Motif Ed.: Vol. 3M
X User Tools (with CD-ROM)

ADVANCED

Exploring Expect (Winter 94/95 est.)
The Frame Handbook
Learning Perl
Making TeX Work
Programming perl
sed & awk
UNIX Power Tools (with CD-ROM)

PROGRAMMING UNIX, C, AND MULTI-PLATFORM

FORTRAN/SCIENTIFIC COMPUTING

High Performance Computing
Migrating to Fortran 90
UNIX for FORTRAN Programmers

C PROGRAMMING LIBRARIES

Practical C Programming
POSIX Programmer's Guide
POSIX.4: Programming for the Real World
    (Winter '94/95 est.)
Programming with curses
Understanding and Using COFF
Using C on the UNIX System

C PROGRAMMING TOOLS

Checking C Programs with lint
lex & yacc
Managing Projects with make
Power Programming with RPC
Software Portability with imake

MULTI-PLATFORM PROGRAMMING

Encyclopedia of Graphics File Formats
Distributing Applications Across DCE and
    Windows NT
Guide to Writing DCE Applications
Multi-Platform Code Management
ORACLE Performance Tuning
Understanding DCE
Understanding Japanese Information Processing

BERKELEY 4.4 SOFTWARE DISTRIBUTION

4.4BSD System Manager's Manual
4.4BSD User's Reference Manual
4.4BSD User's Supplementary Documents
4.4BSD Programmer's Reference Manual
4.4BSD Programmer's Supplementary Documents
4.4BSD-Lite CD Companion
4.4BSD-Lite CD Companion: International Version

X PROGRAMMING

Motif Programming Manual: Volume 6A
Motif Reference Manual: Volume 6B
Motif Tools
PEXlib Programming Manual
PEXlib Reference Manual
PHIGS Programming Manual (soft or hard cover)
PHIGS Reference Manual
Programmer's Supplement for Release 6 (Winter '94/95 est.)
Xlib Programming Manual: Volume 1
Xlib Reference Manual: Volume 2
X Protocol Reference Manual, R5: Volume 0
X Protocol Reference Manual, R6: Volume 0
    (Winter '94/95 est.)
X Toolkit Intrinsics Programming Manual: Vol. 4
X Toolkit Intrinsics Programming Manual,
    Motif Edition: Volume 4M
X Toolkit Intrinsics Reference Manual: Volume 5
XView Programming Manual: Volume 7A
XView Reference Manual: Volume 7B

THE X RESOURCE

A QUARTERLY WORKING JOURNAL FOR X PROGRAMMERS

The X Resource: Issues 0 through 13
    (Issue 13 available 1/95)

BUSINESS/CAREER

Building a Successful Software Business
Love Your Job!

TRAVEL

Travelers' Tales Thailand
Travelers' Tales Mexico
Travelers' Tales India (Winter '94/95 est.)

AUDIOTAPES

INTERNET TALK RADIO'S "GEEK OF THE WEEK" INTERVIEWS

The Future of the Internet Protocol, 4 hours
Global Network Operations, 2 hours
Mobile IP Networking, 1 hour
Networked Information and
    Online Libraries, 1 hour
Security and Networks, 1 hour
European Networking, 1 hour

NOTABLE SPEECHES OF THE INFORMATION AGE

John Perry Barlow, 1.5 hours

O'Reilly & Associates—
INTERNATIONAL DISTRIBUTORS

Customers outside North America can now order O'Reilly & Associates books through the following distributors. They offer our international customers faster order processing, more bookstores, increased representation at tradeshows worldwide, and the high-quality, responsive service our customers have come to expect.

EUROPE, MIDDLE EAST, AND AFRICA
(except Germany, Switzerland, and Austria)

INQUIRIES
International Thomson Publishing Europe
Berkshire House
168-173 High Holborn
London WC1V 7AA
United Kingdom
Telephone: 44-71-497-1422
Fax: 44-71-497-1426
Email: ora.orders@itpuk.co.uk

ORDERS
International Thomson Publishing Services, Ltd.
Cheriton House, North Way
Andover, Hampshire SP10 5BE
United Kingdom
Telephone: 44-264-342-832 (UK orders)
Telephone: 44-264-342-806 (outside UK)
Fax: 44-264-364418 (UK orders)
Fax: 44-264-342761 (outside UK)

GERMANY, SWITZERLAND, AND AUSTRIA

International Thomson Publishing GmbH
O'Reilly-International Thomson Verlag
Attn: Mr. G. Miske
Königswinterer Strasse 418
53227 Bonn
Germany
Telephone: 49-228-970240
Fax: 49-228-441342
Email: anfragen@orade.ora.com

THE AMERICAS, JAPAN, AND OCEANIA

O'Reilly & Associates, Inc.
103A Morris Street
Sebastopol, CA 95472 U.S.A.
Telephone: 707-829-0515
Telephone: 800-998-9938 (U.S. & Canada)
Fax: 707-829-0104
Email: order@ora.com

ASIA
(except Japan)

INQUIRIES
International Thomson Publishing Asia
221 Henderson Road
#05 10 Henderson Building
Singapore 0315
Telephone: 65-272-6496
Fax: 65-272-6498

ORDERS
Telephone: 65-268-7867
Fax: 65-268-6727

AUSTRALIA

WoodsLane Pty. Ltd.
Unit 8, 101 Darley Street (P.O. Box 935)
Mona Vale NSW 2103
Australia
Telephone: 61-2-979-5944
Fax: 61-2-997-3348
Email: woods@tmx.mhs.oz.au

NEW ZEALAND

WoodsLane New Zealand Ltd.
21 Cooks Street (P.O. Box 575)
Wanganui, New Zealand
Telephone: 64-6-347-6543
Fax: 64-6-345-4840
Email: woods@tmx.mhs.oz.au